CONSTITUTIONAL FREE SPEECH
DEFINED AND DEFENDED

A Da Capo Press Reprint Series

CIVIL LIBERTIES IN AMERICAN HISTORY

GENERAL EDITOR: LEONARD W. LEVY

Brandeis University

CONSTITUTIONAL FREE SPEECH

DEFINED AND DEFENDED

IN AN UNFINISHED ARGUMENT IN A
CASE OF BLASPHEMY

BY THEODORE SCHROEDER

DA CAPO PRESS • NEW YORK • 1970

A Da Capo Press Reprint Edition

Library of Congress Catalog Card Number 72-106497

SBN 306-71872-3

Published by Da Capo Press
A Division of Plenum Publishing Corporation
227 West 17th Street, New York, N. Y. 10011
All Rights Reserved

Manufactured in the United States of America

CONSTITUTIONAL FREE SPEECH

DEFINED AND DEFENDED

IN AN UNFINISHED ARGUMENT IN A

CASE OF BLASPHEMY

THEODORE SCHROEDER
OF THE N. Y. BAR
14 W. 12 ST.

FREE SPEECH LEAGUE
56 EAST 59TH STREET
NEW YORK CITY
1919

EXPLANATORY INTRODUCTION.

By some the character of the following argument may be considered uncommon. The unusual content is due to two circumstances. The first of these is the belief that our courts are too strongly predisposed to follow the letter of precedent, even though none of these precedents came into being under modern conditions. This fact created a very strong necessity and urge toward impairing the influence of such authorities as could serve to justify a desire to uphold blasphemy statutes. The second source of novelty is in the viewpoints, which are predominantly historical and psychological. As to these latter something in further explanation will be helpful.

There never has been a case involving freedom of speech in which the historical interpretation of our constitutional guarantees has received serious consideration. I desired to make such a presentation, and the task became enormous. The historic issues of free speech upon the subject of religion, present the controversy which finally resulted in our constitutional guarantees. These issues were made in England by means of long-forgotten sermons, only a small part of which are preserved in rare and obscure books and pamphlets. Even these inadequate records are not accessible except to a very few American readers, and then only by great effort. Many important libraries were carefully searched. Some very rare pamphlets had to be photographed in the Library of the British Museum and elsewhere in order to make their contents available for this discussion. Under such circumstances it was obviously useless to state their substance and cite the books wherein this could be verified. · Such considerations seemed to necessitate the exact reproduction of large masses of material, so that every one can easily check up the interpretation that I put upon it. This requirement also resulted in making the quotations of considerable length, so that a fair impression could be obtained of the import of the more salient passages. Thus has been produced what is almost a small cyclopedia of source-material on this question.

The psychologic approach to social problems is lately being impressed upon all the social sciences. It belongs inevitably to intellectual evolution that legal problems, like all other social phenomena, will yield new meanings when we view them as expressions of human desires becoming effective through thinking expressed in laws, political institutions, etc.

From the viewpoint of a deterministic and evolutionary psychology every human action, including judicial decisions, is conditioned upon the past experiences and the present development of individual desires and of mental processes. So then, at some level of understanding, "reasons" can be found to justify any desire that is dominant. Reasons alone never determine judicial or human action. On the contrary, judicial and human predispositions (desires) quite as certainly determine the choice of "reasons" and the relative weight to be given them, as well as the use to which they will be put in formulating judicial action. That our past is ever at work in the present is an established psychologic truth. If its operation is by subconscious processes, then even our judges may be tempted to deny its existence. For the genetic psychologist such denial is to be often expected and proves only that those who make it do not possess the psychologic intelligence necessary for an adequate self-understanding. Many parts of the following discussion are very consciously formulated with the desire to impress this psychologic viewpoint into the service of juridicial evolution.

Furthermore, in some respects, this presentation is less partisan than is usual in legal arguments. Many times materials and authorities have been presented which can be used against the main contention of this book.

9

Nothing has been concealed or omitted merely because of its adverse tendency. All opposing theories and authorities have been frankly and exhaustively criticized. All unpopular implications have been fully accepted. The effort has been to enlarge the understanding and to be understood. These desires have extended even to the mental processes which are involved in the judicial consideration of such problems.

Those who look merely for a conventional legal argument will be as much disappointed as those who expect an entertaining agitator's passionate appeal. The ensuing discussion is as far from each of these types as possible. Perhaps now I have almost said that this argument is in a class by itself, both as to the material woven into the discussion, and the viewpoints that dominated their choice and use. Perhaps even the mental processes employed will seem a bit out of the ordinary. All this means that the following pages will interest only those who are dominated by the same purpose that inspired and determined the character of the book. Then only those will care to read who are very much in earnest in their desire to understand the past and present human forces involved in our human attitudes toward freedom of speech.

Consequently, this is perhaps more than a lawyer's argument. There is presented much of the psychology and philosophy of the law, and more or less of discussion as to the intellectual methods involved in the formation of legal opinions. Perhaps for most minds this will seem irrelevant and remote. Those who are best informed about the factors involved in the intellectual evolution of the race will perhaps be most pleased to find here a discussion of intellectual method and of the psychologic and philosophic aspects of juridical action. Here as everywhere, whatever of interest the reader sees in the following pages will depend largely upon what kind of eyes and of intellect he brings to the task of reading. Of course, the material was prepared for a wider audience than that which is found in the court room. I expect sometime to complete this argument. If the conditions require it, I will add a review of any adverse judicial action thereon and publish the whole in a new edition of this book. The pressure of a time limit for the preparation of this discussion is my excuse for many literary defects. THEODORE SCHROEDER.

CONTENTS.

11

State of Connecticut

DISTRICT COURT OF WATERBURY.

STATE OF CONNECTICUT

against

MICHAEL X. MOCKUS

ARGUMENT ON BEHALF OF THE ACCUSED IN SUPPORT OF A DEMURRER TO THE INFORMATION CHARGING HIM WITH THE CRIME OF BLASPHEMY.

HISTORY OF THE CASE.

The Defendant, Michael X. Mockus, is a Free Thought lecturer of Detroit, Michigan. He came to Waterbury, Conn., pursuant to an engagement to deliver a series of lectures in the Lithuanian language to an incorporated Lithuanian Free Thought Association. In his third lecture some phrases were used which, dissociated from their context, are alleged to be blasphemous, under a statute passed in 1642. He was arrested, tried in the City Court of Waterbury, and found guilty. A penalty of ten days in jail was inflicted. An appeal was taken to the District Court. There a trial resulted in a disagreement of the jury. A re-trial was set for December 6, 1916. At that time permission was given to re-argue a demurrer. At the conclusion of a lengthy argument, by general consent, further proceedings in the case were continued for the term, during which time the argument in support of the demurrer was to be extended in writing, and submitted to the Court. The following pages present the oral argument, corrected and revised.

I.
STATEMENT OF THE CASE.

The Defendant is charged in the language of the Connecticut statute with having blasphemed against God, the Christian religion and the Holy Scriptures. The demurrer is general, and raises the question of the sufficiency of the complaint to state facts constituting a crime. Under this head the contention which is of most general and of the greatest importance is that the Connecticut statute against blasphemy is unconstitutional under several provisions of both State and National constitutions.

STATUTES INVOLVED.

Sec. 1323, General Statutes of Connecticut: "Every person who shall blaspheme against God, either of the persons of the Holy Trinity, the Christian religion, or the Holy Scriptures, shall be fined not more than one hundred dollars, and imprisoned in a jail not more than one year, and may also be bound to his good behavior."—A. D. 1642-1821, Rev. 1888, Sec. 1535.

CONNECTICUT CONSTITUTION, DECLARATION OF RIGHTS, 1818.

Sec. 1. "That all men when they form a social compact, are equal in rights; and that no man or set of men are entitled to exclusive public emoluments or privileges from the community."

Sec. 3. "The exercise and enjoyment of religious profession and worship without discrimination, shall forever be free to all persons in this state, provided that the right hereby declared and established, shall not be so construed as to excuse acts of licentiousness, or to justify practices inconsistent with the peace and safety of the state."

Sec. 4. "No preference shall be given by law to any Christian sect or mode of worship."

Sec. 5. "Every citizen may freely speak, write and publish his sentiments on all subjects, being responsible for the abuse of that liberty."

14

Sec. 6. "No law shall ever be passed to curtail or restrain the liberty of speech or of the press."

Sec. 9. "In all criminal prosecutions the accused shall have the right * * * to demand the nature and cause of the accusation; * * * He shall not * * * be deprived of life, liberty or property but by due course of law."

Sec. 12. "All courts shall be open, and every person, for an injury done to him in his person, property, or reputation, shall have remedy by due course of law and right and justice, administered without sale, denial or delay."

Sec. 16. "The citizens have a right, in a peaceable manner, to assemble for their common good, and to apply to those invested with the powers of government, for redress of grievances or other proper purposes, by petition, address or remonstrance."

U. S. CONSTITUTION.

Amend. Art. 1. "Congress shall make no law respecting an establishment of religion, or prohibiting the free exercise thereof; or abridging the freedom of speech or of the press; or the right of the people peaceably to assemble, and to petition the government for a redress of grievances."

Article 5. * * * "Nor shall any person * * * be deprived of life, liberty or property, without due process of law." * * *

Article 6. * * * "In all criminal prosecutions, the accused shall enjoy the right * * * to be informed of the nature and cause of the accusation."

Article 14. * * * "No state shall make or enforce any law which shall abridge the privileges or immunities of citizens of the United States, nor shall any State deprive any person of life, liberty or property, without due process of law, nor deny to any person within its jurisdiction the equal protection of the laws."

The constitutional problems arrange themselves quite naturally into three groups:

The first group arises from the abridgment of freedom

of speech and religious liberty, thus violating several constitutional provisions.

The second group arises from the inequalities created by this law, and makes it a violation of "due process of law," and other guarantees of equal liberty, under both State and Federal Constitutions.

The third group arises from the uncertainty of the criteria of guilt under the blasphemy statute, which makes it a violation of the right to "due process of law" and of the right to know the nature of the accusation against the accused, under both State and Federal Constitutions.

GENERAL SUGGESTIONS.

There can be no religious liberty, in the sense of a complete separation of church and state, which does not include freedom of speech for religious subjects. Likewise, there cannot be general freedom of speech without including the whole of religious mental freedom. Of course, religious freedom includes more than religious free speech as, for example, exemption from taxation for religious purposes. Likewise, free speech includes intellectual liberty upon other subjects besides religion. However, so far as the blasphemy statutes are concerned, it makes no difference whether, considered under one or the other of these constitutional provisions, the line of demarcation between liberty and its unconstitutional abridgment is the same. This aspect of the question will be presented from the viewpoint that, so far as concerns the blasphemy statute, three different constitutional phrases are but different ways of expressing the same idea, and accomplishing the same end.

It is, of course, known that judicial decisions sanction the view that the earlier amendments to the Federal Constitution are limitations only upon the powers of the Federal Government and not limitations upon State action. This conclusion undoubtedly presents the whole truth, under the conditions existing prior to the adoption of the fourteenth amendment. Even after that amendment, if we consider the prior amendments as dissociated from it, the same result will be asserted. A different situation is presented if we undertake a synthetic construction of the first and fourteenth amendments.

Then we are compelled to ask ourselves: what "liberties" and "equal protection of the laws" are the states prohibited from invading by the fourteenth amendment. Obviously one cannot determine what is that equal religious and intellectual freedom, guaranteed by the fourteenth amendment of the Federal Constitution, without at the same time construing the first amendment. In other words the fourteenth amendment protects against State infringement all that "liberty" which was of sufficient importance to have been previously protected against congressional encroachments. Upon such reasoning it will be claimed that the Federal amendments are a limitation upon State powers. Thus the "liberty" which by the fourteenth amendment is protected against State action, necessarily includes all those liberties theretofore inadequately protected, and now more fully protected even against State action. This is accomplished by at least a limited incorporation of the liberties of the first amendment within the "liberty" of the fourteenth amendment It is believed that this point has never yet been decided by any court. In consequence of this it is now claimed that the Connecticut blasphemy statute violates also the first and sixth amendments as well as the fourteenth amendment to the Federal Constitution.

Hereinafter it will be also contended that the constitutional guarantees for equality, for religious liberty, and for freedom of speech were not limited in their operation to those who possess any particular degree of culture, or a polite and approved vocabulary, or an alluring oratorical and literary style, or for the protection of persons expressing only "safe and sane" popular opinions. On the contrary, it will be asserted that these constitutional liberties were designed to limit the powers of government, and to protect *human* rights, not merely the rights of those possessed of a clever technique for insinuating heresy or agnosticism with a minimum of offence. Equality, religious liberty, and free speech being *human* rights, in the most fundamental sense of a democracy, the defendant and every one else, discussing religious subjects, must be allowed to express themselves with impunity in such vocabulary as they possess, within the limits of doing actual and material injury. In this matter of constitutional law we are dealing with the powers of government rather than with the opinions or education of any particular person.

II.

THE IMPORTANCE OF THIS CONTROVERSY.

May it please your honor to give me patient indulgence, while I urge upon your attention those considerations which I believe will induce you to annul the blasphemy statutes under which this prosecution is brought.

I believe the future historian will say that this case is the most important prosecution that has come before a court of this State for a century. I know that if this case is not terminated in accord with the sentiments of the more enlightened portion of the community, your decision will necessarily place a club in the hands of the intolerant and bigoted, whereby the intelligent ones can be cowed and silenced in matters of religious controversy. Therefore, unless this cause is decided in accord with the Constitution, as interpreted in the light of the best understanding of the preceding historical controversy that can be brought to bear upon it, your decision, instead of terminating a controversy, may but kindle the flames of a most bitter future contest.

Fanaticism is not the characteristic monopoly of any party or sect. It is an accompaniment of those immature modes of feeling and thinking where the primitive impulses dominate, unchecked by any adequate understanding of self or the related environment. Such waves of fanaticism come and go. They manifest themselves in support of all creeds. Now, to help the catholic party; then to help one, and again another, protestant sect; likewise it has given support to Mohammedans, to Mormons and even to avowed atheists. The decision in the present case will determine how the machinery of our democratic constitutions is to be used when the next revival of fanaticism shall possess some considerable portion of our community.

This precedent will determine measurably whether in
our Intermountain States, Mormons may make it a crime
to speak disparagingly of the utterances of their "living
oracles of God"; whether in Maryland they can re-enact
a law protecting the Virgin Mary against criticism permitted against all other women; and the penalizing of
Protestantism; whether in Georgia Catholicism may be
penalized, etc., etc.   If the courts have any power to punish blasphemy, then the legislatures have the power to
penalize as blasphemy almost anything at least within the
range of· the common law, which they choose to believe is
of a dangerous tendency, and so include it in their definitions of blasphemy.   Then Massachusetts and Connecticut
are free to re-enact the barbarous codes of their colonial
regime.   If that shall be so, then our constitutional guarantee of equality, of freedom of speech, and for a separation of church and state, have accomplished nothing
whatever toward the enlargement of intellectual liberty.
All is left a matter of legislative discretion, just as it was
from the beginning of government, down to the American
Revolution.

Defendant Unimportant.

In the City Court this defendant was found guilty and
sentenced to ten days in jail, and required to give a bond
to keep the peace.   If this were simply a matter of one
more person inhabiting our jails for ten days, this argument would never have been made.

At the former trial in the District Court it was suggested to the defendant that he might get off with a suspended sentence, if he would plead guilty.   If he had seen
in this case nothing more important than his personal
safety, this case would have been terminated.

The defendant Mockus himself realizes that he is of very
little importance here, relative to a precedent which may
be established in his case.   Such a precedent will probably
be followed in other states, and so, for generations to
come, it will fix the limits of religious liberty for many
millions of people.   There can be no constitutional question of more importance than this one.   "A point that

is carried for the sake of punishing a worthless fellow, may be cited hereafter as a precedent for the most dangerous prosecution and oppression of an excellent patriot."[1] Precedents which are favorable to the official's lust for power are easiest secured and most readily followed. Precedents favorable to intellectual liberty are few and far between because we all have too little democracy and too much of the tyrant in us.

In this case there will be presented a class of argument, much of which has never before been considered in a case of this character. The inevitable consequence is that the decision in this case will be the beginning of a new line of precedent on the most important of all subjects; namely, the powers of government in dealing with the subject of religion.

In this great world probably no one man, or the opinion of any one man, is of very great importance; but the legal authority and power to suppress any man's opinions is of the utmost importance, because it implies the authority and power to suppress all expression of opinion on a given subject, or all opinions of a disapproved character. Thus, to confirm judicially the power to punish this man for merely expressing an opinion is to place the destiny of intellectual progress in the hands of legislators, judges and jurors, instead of allowing it to rest in the unhampered intellectual activity of the people at large, where it rightfully belongs in a democracy. This defendant's liberty is of importance primarily to him, but to confirm the power to imprison him for a mere psychologic offense imperils the liberty of many generations to come. In that consists the importance of this case.

For the purpose of upholding the defendant's constitutional right of free speech, it is not at all necessary to approve either his opinions or his mode of expressing them. Here, we are concerned with a conflict between human rights, and the powers of government, not with irreligion or oratorical style. In this argument, we may and should ignore the man, his message, his style or the

---

[1] A letter concerning Libels, etc. Lond. 1764, p. 22.

psychologic tendency of any or all of these. The importance of the case does not arise from any of these things,
but from the fact that the issue is one of the constitutional
power of the State authorities to meddle with a religious
subject.

PRIESTLY ON IMPORTANCE OF AUTHORITY.

Upon this subject the following observations by the
Rev. Dr. Joseph Priestly are worth quoting. In his "View
of the Principles and Conduct of the Protestant Dissenters," (p. 58), he makes these sensible remarks: "It
should be considered that a power of decreeing rites and
ceremonies, is a power absolutely indefinite, and of the
very same kind with those claims, which, in things of a
civil nature, always give the greatest alarm. A tax of a
penny is a trifle; but a power of imposing that tax is never
considered as a trifle, because it may imply absolute
servitude in all who submit to it. In like manner, the
enjoining of the posture of kneeling at the Lord's Supper
is not a thing worth disputing about in itself, but the
authority of enjoining it is; because it is, in fact, a power
of making the Christian religion as burdensome as the
Jewish, and a power that hath actually been carried to
that length in the church of Rome. Nor do we see any
consistence in the church of England rejecting the authority of Rome in these things, and imposing her own upon
us." * * Again (p. 66): "Our ancestors, the old Puritans, had the same merit in opposing the imposition of
the surplice, that Hampden had in opposing the levying
of ship-money. In neither case was it the thing itself
they objected to, so much as the authority that enjoined
it, and the danger of precedent. And it appears to us,
that the man who is as tenacious of his religious as he is
of his civil liberty, will oppose them both with equal firmness.

"All the difference then, in the conduct of men who
equally value their liberty, will be in the time and manner
of opposing these incroachments upon it. The man of a
strong and enlarged mind will always oppose these things

in the beginning, when only the resistance can have any effect; but the weak, the timid, and the short-sighted, will attempt nothing till the chains are rivetted, and resistance is too late. In civil matters, the former will make his stand at the levying of the first penny by improper authority; and in matters of religion, at the first, though the most trifling ceremony, that is, without reason, made necessary; whereas the latter will wait till the load, in both cases, is become too heavy to be either supported or thrown off."[2]

It has been generally believed that here in America we had permanently barred the door against a recurrance of religious persecution. Practically it now comes to this: shall we reopen that door, and thereby invite the next onslaught of fanaticism to rekindle the fires of persecution? There can be no assurance that a frenzied revival of religion will not again bring on a persecution mania to which in times of excitement, vote-seeking legislators and even courts will give heed. Four years ago none of us could have believed possible the present riot of blood that is now devastating Europe.

---

[2] Requoted from Furneaux's Letters on Toleration, Footnote to Letter V. pp. 158-160.

III.

REASON *versus* PRECEDENT.

I should be ignoring such intelligence as I have, if I did not take cognizance of the fact that, too frequently, judicial controversies are ill determined, because of an undue valuation of precedents as a whole, or because of the relative over-valuation of some precedents and the ignoring of others, which may be supported by the better understanding. We all know very well of the existence of a great multiplicity of rules to guide us toward the solution of every legal problem, including those of statutory and constitutional construction. These rules are very useful, if our conscious desire to administer justice, according to the most enlightened standards, is not inhibited by subconscious impulses to justify a particular predisposition in a pending controversy. In this latter event we may be tempted "to have our way" and justify it by immature arguments not exhibiting the use of an understanding so superior as to compel conviction among the more enlightened.

Our "rules of construction," though expressed in general terms, present only highly concrete and dissociated aspects of the problems of construction. If any urge is strong enough, it will impel a choice of those rules which satisfy its demands, and to ignore those which interfere with the dominant impulse. Thus come erroneous precedents, and better precedents. So also come the abuse and misuse of precedents, through their selection according to immature preconceptions, often determined from subconscious sources. From such considerations I am led to the conviction that there is need for a revaluation of precedents.

QUESTIONING PRECEDENTS.

It may be you will think that the defendant is inviting you to over-rule such precedents as Com. vs. Kneeland,

24

37 Mass. (20 Pick.) 206, and People vs. Ruggles, 8 John (N. Y.) 290; 5 Am. Dec. 335, and in this you are perfectly correct. However, in doing this we will appeal only to perfectly orthodox modes of reasoning and to other well-established principles. It will presently be made to appear that in those decisions the judges ignored the most essential factor for reaching a correct conclusion.

It may be impossible to combine all rules for construing statutes and constitutions into one comprehensive generalization, adequate for all cases. There is a better way of acquiring a synthetic grasp of the legitimate aims which these rules promote. To this end we need to minimize the importance of the rules themselves, and correspondingly intensify our desire to understand the facts which the rules formulate, and the legitimate ends which they may promote. In other words, we will aid the progressive enlightenment of our concepts of justice and liberty, just to the extent to which we cease quarreling about the dictionary meaning and the wording of precedents, and acquire an understanding of that behavior and those relations among humans, which express themselves in ever-changing social institutions. So long as we view social institutions and constitutions as static things, we will never adequately understand them. Correctly to interpret the process of their change and growth is the best way to promote an understanding of "the reason of the law" and to insure the highest efficiency in a harmonious adjustment between governments and the people.

RELATIVE UNIMPORTANCE OF PRECEDENTS.

This, then, is our conception of promoting the larger peace, always founded upon an ever growing enlargement and perfection of human understanding. The promotion of general intellectual hospitality, by the judicial action in this case, is the important end sought. The defendant, Mockus, and his case now before the court, are but the humble instrument of the court in furthering that end.

"I remind you that it has been judicially said that it would be of ill consequence, to authenticate a body of

laws that have lain dormant for two hundred years."[1]
The blasphemy statutes of Connecticut have lain
dormant perhaps for more than 200 years. Lest
you have too much reverence for some judicial precedents,
I recall to your memory that Blackstone in his Commentaries (v. p. 71) informs us that "the law and the opinion
of the judge are not always convertible terms, or one and
the same thing; since it sometimes may happen that the
judge may mistake the law." I believe with the late
Chief Justice Eyre, when he said that "the sooner a bad
precedent was gotten rid of, the better." This sentiment
was later approved by Lord Chief Justice Kenyon.[2]

"Precedent indeed may serve to fix principles, which
for certainty's sake are not suffered to be shaken, whatever might be the weight of the principle, independent of
precedent. But precedent, though it be the evidence of
law is not law in itself; much less the whole of the law." [3]

I therefore make bold to invite your endorsement of
the sentiment of another English judge, who said this:
"It was said that there is an authority which binds this
court, and that I am not to exercise my reason and common sense, because I am so bound. I cannot bear to be
told when an argument has been addressed to me by which
I am not convinced, that there is a case decided which I
am bound to follow."[4]

This, then, is going to be an appeal to the understanding, rather than to the blind following of precedents. To
improve the law, we must sometimes get behind the letter
of judicial opinions to understand the reasons which may
or may not justify them. Thus pinning our faith to the
reason of the law rather than to its verbal expression, we
need to emphasize the importance of the former. This
will now be done by re-stating some of those aphorisms
which we learned at the law-school.

[1] Foster, J. in The King vs. Bishop of Ely, 1750, 1 Blackstone Rep. 59.
[2] See King vs. Stone, 1801, 1 East. 648.
[3] Lord Mansfield, in Jones vs. Randall, 1774, Lofft 386.
[4] Kay, J. in re Holmes, 1890, Law Jour. Rep. n. s., 60 Chan. Div. 269.

IMPORTANCE OF KNOWING THE REASON.

"We know anything [only] when we know the parts of it, and have conned and seen them through and through."[5] In a case such as that now before the court, where religious and moral sentimentalism so easily and stealthily creeps in, it is too true that, "What reason weaves, by passion is undone."[6]

I therefore invite your honor, in the language of Sir John Powell[7]: "Let us consider the reason of the case. For nothing is law that is not reason."

If my memory serves me, it was Lord Coke who said something like this: "Reason is the life of the law; nay, the common law itself is nothing else but reason. * * Law is the perfection of reason. * * How long so ever it hath continued, if it be against reason it is of no force in law. * * * *He that knows not the reason of the law knows not the law.*"

"The law is the perfection of reason, that it always intends to conform thereto and that what is not reason is not law. * * * Much more if it be clearly contrary to the divine law."[8]

Another has put it: "Law is nothing else than right reason drawn from the will of the gods, commanding what is right and prohibiting the contrary."[9]

Let us prove the correctness of Lord Mansfield when he said that "very happily the more the law is looked into the more it appears founded in equity, reason, and good sense."[10]

I am going to invite this Court to a searching inquiry as to the reasons which once made courts and legislators deem laws against blasphemy vital to the very existence of the State, and then I will show you that these conditions

[5] Coke's Tracts, 226.
[6] Pope, "Essay on Man."
[7] See: Coggs v. Bernard, 2 L'd Raymond Rep. p. 911.
[8] V. 1 Black. Com. 70.
[9] Footnote to, 3 Lewis' Blackstone 1019, and evidently quoted from Cicero.
[10] James v. Price, 1773, Lofft's Rep. K. B. 221.

have been designedly abrogated by the constitutions of the
United States and of the State of Connecticut. By thus
understanding the reason of both the statute law and
constitutional law, I believe the consequence will be a
complete annulment of these blasphemy laws here involved.

This does not mean that I am going to ask you to ignore
any of the fundamental principles of the law. Rather is
it my purpose to invite you to enforce the more fundamental and important principles of our constitutions, and
emphasize these at the expense of some lesser theories
which I will show you are misconceived principles, and
have been outgrown.

EVOLUTION BY NEW PRECEDENT.

Perfectly understood, the principles of the law are
eternal, but our understanding of them and of the conditions of their application is subject to change with the
changing circumstances of the times.[11]

In that sense "law grows" with the growth of our understanding, and the old formulas of our legal principles are
"only broken down slowly by legislation and decisions of
the courts."[12]

It is then nothing revolutionary that I am inviting you
to do. I simply ask the recognition and recording of a
development that has long been achieved.

Presently I will invite you to look into the immediate
constitutional problems more thoroughly than has been
done heretofore. We will seek a solution to them by
understanding very thoroughly the historic controversies
that embody the essence of the reasons which led to the
adoption of these constitutional provisions,

All through the argument which follows there will be
a conscious effort to get behind the letter of the law in
order to understand its reasons. To do this efficiently it
will often be advantageous to ask ourselves why some

---

[11] See Lord Coleridge, in Reg. vs. Ramsey, 1883 blasphemy case, 1 Cababe & Ellis, Q. B. D. 135.
[12] Kay, J. in Whitby v. Mitchell 1889, L. R. 4 C Ch. Div. 500.

Courts sometimes have failed to see the larger considerations which should have influenced them. This unavoidably requires some inquiry into the mental operations involved.

It is possible that at first blush these psychologic and evolutionary concepts which have been suggested will be thought somewhat foreign to the law. To those to whom it seems so, I can now say only that the best correction of their error can be found in a genetic and evolutionary study and understanding of their own impulses, especially the unconscious ones. Even in the absence of that I hope to make the importance of this at least partly evident. I venture to persist in pressing this viewpoint, because I am confident that it will be the dominant basis of our future criticism of judicial action.[13]

---

[19] See my essay, "The Psychology of Judicial Opinions," soon to be published.

IV.

CONSTITUTIONAL CONSTRUCTION AND INTELLECTUAL METHOD.

It is frankly admitted that there exists no judicial precedent directly supporting the contention that blasphemy laws are unconstitutional. It is also admitted that there are two precedents directly in point and against the main contention of this argument. Beyond these there is much of dictum that can be easily used by way of analogy to support either side of this controversy. This situation makes it important to have a conscious and intelligent attitude toward precedents as a whole, and of the legitimate use to be made of them. Beyond these we need an understanding of the intellectual methods by which the over-valuation and misuse of precedents may be prevented.

Precedents are valuable for the discovery of what has been achieved, but the uncritical following of precedent can contribute little to progress in refining our sense of justice or of the limits of liberty. To evolve beyond existing precedents it becomes necessary to give them a sympathetic understanding without reverential parroting. In its best aspect precedents are studied with the object of promoting a still more clarified and comprehensive view of social problems and in the hope of finding their solution upon a higher intellectual level, than that offered by existing precedents, or that on which the problem arises.

From this viewpoint it follows that the chief value of precedents does not consist in the fact that a formula has been worked out, but in such understanding as is imparted concerning the reasons which make both for and against the formula as a guide to future conduct. Through the stimulation of a new situation, sometimes we may be led to take the next step in our intellectual and juridical evolution. It is believed that this present controversy affords such an opportunity. Precedents will be cited, but much more time and space will be devoted to achieving a critical understanding of the underlying behavior of social forces than the meaning of judicial formula.

With this in mind we will begin with quoting some judicial decisions prescribing some of the rules of constitutonal construction. This will be followed by some general discussion of the use to be made of them and the intellectual methods involved. The following rules are copied from the Encyclopedia of U. S. Supreme Court Reports (1909), vol. 4, where references can be found to the justifying decisions. In rare instances the footnotes will contain references to similar statements from the decisions of state courts.

RULES OF CONSTRUCTION.

When there is no ambiguity in words used, taken separately or in connection, as a term or phrase, they require no other interpretation than is to be found in the known and universally received standard by which they are defined, nor can they be taken in any other sense or by any other reference, unless there appears from the context or other parts of the same instrument an obvious intention to use and apply them differently from their ordinary or legal acceptation.[1]

This rule requiring adherence to the literal meaning of the constitutional words should settle all questions of intellectual freedom. It would have done so long ago had it not been that some judges have had a strong emotional aversion to the inevitable results of following the letter of the constitutions. In consequence these have read

---

[1] Briscoe v. Bank, 11 Pet. 257; 9 L. Ed. 709.
Gibbons v. Ogden, 9 Wheat. 524; 9 L. Ed. 519.
Hodge v. U. S., 203 U. S. 1-11; 51 L. Ed. 65.
Denn v. Reid, 10 Pet. 524; 9 L. Ed. 519.
Kidd v. Pearson, 128 U. S. 1-20; 32; L. Ed. 346.
Lake Co. v. Rollins, 130 U. S. 662-670; 32 L. Ed. 1060.
R. I. v. Mass., 12 Pet. 657-721; 9 L. Ed. 1233.
McPherson v. Blacker, 146 U. S. 1-27; 36 L. Ed. 869.
Hill v. City of Chicago, 60 Ill. 90.
Green v. Weller, 32 Miss. 652.
Chesapeake & O. R. Co. v. Miller, 19 W. Va. 408.
Lee Bros. Furniture Co. v. Cram; 63 Conn. 438.

meanings and exceptions into the constitutions by annexing Blackstone or themselves to it. Whatever doubt exists about the meaning of religious liberty, intellectual equality and freedom, does not arise out of the constitutions, but out of the judicial amendments that have been made thereto.

"The constitution is a written instrument. As such its meaning does not alter. That which it meant when adopted it means now."[2]

"It is not only the same in words, but the same in meaning, and delegates the same powers to the government, and reserves and secures the same rights and privileges to the citizens; and as long as it continues to exist in its present form, it speaks not only in the same words, but with the same meaning and intent with which it spoke when it came from the hands of its framers, and was voted on and adopted by the people of the United States. Any other rule of construction would abrogate the judicial character of this court, and make it a mere reflex of the popular opinion or passion of the day."[3]

"We cannot recognize the doctrine that because the constitution has been found in the march of time sufficiently comprehensive to be applied to conditions, not within the minds of its framers, and not arising in their time, it may, therefore, be wrenched from the subjects expressly embraced within it, and amended by judicial decision without action by the designated organs in the mode by which alone amendments can be made."[4]

In all instances where construction becomes necessary, therefore, we must place ourselves in the position of the men who framed and adopted the constitution, and inquire what they must have understood to be the meaning and scope of the language used. To this end the courts must look to the history of the times and examine the state

---

[2] Scott v. Sandford, 19 How. 393-426; 15 L. Ed. 691.
McPherson v. Blacker, 146 U. S. 1-36; 36 L. Ed. 869.
Pollock v. Farmers' Loan, Etc., Co., 158 U. S. 601-621; 39 L. Ed. 1108.
South Carolina v. U. S., 199 U. S. 437-448; 50 L. Ed. 261.
[3] South Carolina v. U. S., 199 U. S. 437-449; 50 L. Ed. 261.
[4] McPherson v. Blacker, 146 U. S. 1-36; 36 L. Ed. 869.

of things existing when it was framed and adopted, in order to correctly interpret its meaning.[5]

"When called upon to construe and apply a provision of the constitution of the United States, we must look not merely to its language, but *to its historical origin*, and to those decisions of this court in which its meaning and the scope of its operation have received deliberate consideration."[6]

"The necessities which gave birth to the constitution, the controversies which preceded its formation, and the conflicts of opinion which were settled by its adoption, may properly be taken into view for the purpose of tracing to its source any particular provision of the constitution, in order thereby to be enabled to correctly interpret its meaning."[7]

"In construing any act of legislation whether a statute enacted by the legislature, or a constitution established by the people as the supreme law of the land, *regard is to be had, not only to all parts of the act itself, and of any former act of the same lawmaking power, of which the act is an amendment; but also to the condition, and to the history of the law as previously existing, and in the light of which the new act must be read and interpreted."*[8]

In construing a constitutional provision the courts inquire as to *the provision superseded* by the one to be construed, the *evils and defects for which it did not provide, the remedy adopted, and the reason for it,* and will adopt

---

[5] R. I. v. Mass., 12 Pet. 657-723; 9 L. Ed. 1233.
Passenger Cases, 7 How. 283-428, 429; 12 L. Ed. 702.
Ex Parte Bain, 121 U. S. 1-12; 30 L. Ed. 849.
Pollock v. Farmers L. & T. Co., 157 U. S. 429-558; 39 L. Ed. 759.
Pollock v. Farmers L. & T. Co., 158 U. S. 601-621; 39 L. Ed. 1108.
In re Debs, 158 U. S. 564-591; 39 L. Ed. 1092.
U. S. v. Wong Kim Ark, 169 U. S. 649-653; 42 L. Ed. 890.
Maxwell v. Dow, 176 U. S. 581-602; 44 L. Ed. 597.
Knowlton v. Moore, 178 U. S. 41-95; 44 L. Ed. 969.
Missouri v. Ill., 180 U. S. 208-219; 45 L. Ed. 497.
South Car. v. U. S., 199 U. S. 437-450; 50 L. Ed. 261.
[6] Missouri v. Ill., 180 U. S. 208-219; 45 L. Ed. 497.
Reynolds v. U. S., 98 U. S. 145-163.
[7] Pollock v. Farmers L. & T. Co., 157 U. S. 429-558; 39 L. Ed. 759.
Knowlton v. Moore, 178 U. S. 41-95; 44 L. Ed. 969 (requoting above).
[8] U. S. v. Wong Kim Ark, 169 U. S. 649-653; 42 L. Ed. 890.

that construction which will suppress the mischief and advance the remedy.[9]

"Just so is it with the grant to the national government of power over interstate commerce. The constitution has not changed. The power is the same. But it operates today upon modes of interstate commerce unknown to the fathers, and it will operate with equal force upon any new modes of such commerce which the future may develop."[10]

But while the meaning of the language employed does not change, it applies from generation to generation to all things to which it is, in its nature, applicable, embracing within its operation all new conditions which are within the scope of the powers in terms conferred.[11]

It is only in cases of doubtful construction that resort is to be had to the practical construction placed upon the constitution by the legislative and executive departments. The plain language or historic meaning of the constitution cannot be altered by the practice prevailing in any department of the government nor by the interpretation placed upon any particular provision by legislative enactment.[12]

"It is a maxim, not to be disregarded, that general expressions, in every opinion, are to be taken in connection with the case in which those expressions are used. If they go beyond the case, they may be respected, but ought not to control the judgment in a subsequent suit, when the very point is presented for decision. The reason of this maxim is obvious. The question actually before the court is investigated with care, and considered in its full extent. Other principles which may serve to illustrate it are considered in their relation to the case decided, but their

---

[9] Town of McGregor v. Baylies, 19 La. 43.
Fox v. McDonald, 101 Ala. 51-13 South. R. 416.
Bandel v. Isaac, 13 Md. 202.
People v. State Treas., 23 Mich. 499.
Minn. & P. R. Co. v. Sibley, 2 Minn. 13.
Wisc. Cent. R. Co. v. Taylor, 52 Wisc. 37-8 N. W. 833.
[10] In re Debs 158 U. S. 564-591 ; 39 L. Ed. 1092.
[11] In re Debs, 158 U. S. 564-591 ; 39 L. Ed. 1092.
South Carolina v. U. S., 199 U. S. 437-448 ; 50 L. Ed. 261.
De Lima v. Bidwell, 182 U. S. 1-197 ; 45 L. Ed. 1041.
[12] Fairbank v. U. S., 181 U. S. 283-307 ; 45 L. Ed. 862.
U. S. v. Wong Kim Ark, 169 U. S. 649-699 ; 42 L. Ed. 890.

possible bearing on all other cases is seldom completely investigated."[13]

In the construction of all laws and constitutions we look to the old law, the mischief and the remedy, and so expound the law as to suppress the mischief and advance the remedy.[14]

In the absence of a saving clause the adoption of a new constitution, or the amendment of an old, operates to supersede and revoke all previous inconsistent and irreconcilable constitutional and statutory provisions and rights exercisable thereunder at least so far as their future operation is concerned.[15]

"The safe way is to read its language in connection with the known condition of affairs out of which the occasion for its adoption may have arisen, and then to construe it, if there be therein any doubtful expressions, in a way, so far as is reasonably possible, to forward the known purpose or object for which the amendment was adopted. This rule could not, of course, be so used as to limit the force and effect of an amendment in a manner which the plain and unambiguous language used therein would not justify or permit."[16]

RULES VERSUS DESIRES.

These are some of the rules of construction which seem most directly applicable to our present problem. Probably all other rules of construction are also more or less remotely applicable.

A moment's reflection will make it plain that it is not rules of constitutional construction which will decide this

[13] Cohen v. Virginia, 6 Wheat. 264-399; L. Ed. 257.
[14] Briscoe v. Bank, 11 Pet. 257-328 n.; 9 L. Ed. 709.
Jarrolt v. Moberly, 103 U. S. 580-586; 26 L. Ed. 492.
[15] Republica v. Chapman, 1 Dall. 53-56; L. Ed. 33.
Neal v. Delaware, 103 U. S. 370-389; 26 L. Ed. 567.
Commissioners v. Loague, 129 U. S. 493; 32 L. Ed. 589.
Shreveport v. Cole, 129 U. S. 36-42; 32 L. Ed. 589.
Kankauna Water Power Co. v. Green Bay, 142 U. S. 252-269; 35 L. Ed. 1004.
U. S. v. Villato, 2 Dall. 370-373; 1 L. Ed. 419.
Ex parte Yarbrough, 110 U. S. 651-665; 28 L. Ed. 274.
Norton v. Board of Com., 129 U. S. 479-493; 32 L. Ed. 774.
[16] Maxwell v. Dow, 176 U. S. 581-602; 44 L. Ed. 597.

case. The result will be determined by a choice among the rules that can be made applicable, and the use which will be made of them. We may go still farther back and say that the very choice of rules to be applied and the manner of using them, will be (at least in part) determined by a previous desire operating in the mind and emotions of the judge. From this psychologic viewpoint the ultimate decision will be determined according to the relative maturity of the desires and intellectual processes of those judges, who shall deal with this case. The rules of construction merely become the tools by which they justify their desires and incidentally and unconsciously exhibit their relative stations in an evolutionary scale of emotional maturity and of intellectual development. This is a general truth, applicable to all cases but seldom acknowledged.

Let me state this same truth in another form. It is obvious that in the consideration of problems of religious liberty there are great differences of opinion, each view being advocated with more or less intensity of feeling. Since the objective factors of the problem are substantially the same for all of us, it seems to follow that the immediate cause of our differences must be sought within ourselves. That is to say, our differences are due to differences of temperament (predisposition), and differences in mental processes, and in the materials which are thus excluded from consideration or co-ordinated by one or another of us. Because of these considerations, it becomes important that we should consider our mental methods as a conscious part of the process of reaching a more satisfactory conclusion upon this perplexing problem, which has cost so much blood and life.

THE SCIENTIFIC METHOD.

If our mental processes were uniformly those of the trained scientist dealing with the material universe, there would be quite as great uniformity of result in the field of religion as in the realm of mathematics. While there are those who know nothing about mathematics, yet among its devotees there is no serious disagreement about results.

If we are to promote growth toward a more uniform solution of this problem of religious liberty, it must be done by finding a solution on a higher intellectual level—that is, a closer adherence to the scientific method—than that which is customary. Only thus can we attain a more perfect co-ordination of larger ranges of the related factors of this problem. Only thus can we hope for a more satisfactory and more lasting solution of the problem of intellectual freedom.

When considering problems of liberty of conscience it is easy to find very many judicial opinions and dicta, which lend themselves to justifying the practical annulment of our constitutional guarantees. There also exist some few which could be used by way of analogy to justify the result herein contended for. Upon this subject, an argument by analogy from precedent upon either side can do little more than furnish a misleading justification for whatever predisposition one may entertain. This is believed to be so, because none of these dicta appear to be the result of such intellectual processes as are best calculated to produce the more permanent solution.

CHECKING PREDISPOSITIONS.

If we are bringing to our problem a desire and a capacity to understand *the reason* of things, by the use of mature intellectual methods, then our effort must be to submit all our predispositions to the check and justification of the realties of our problem. These realities consist of the impulses and ideals which the makers of our constitutions sought to record and perpetuate in those instruments, and the evils which they sought to end. We can not acquire this understanding by merely seeing if the words they used can possibly be construed in harmony with our desires. Neither will it do to see one part of our guarantees of liberty dissociated from the rest. Nor should we be content to see our constitutions dissociated from the trend of the previous human progress. The better understanding can be achieved only by an inquiry into the minutiae of the historic issues in the making, a decision upon which issues was recorded in our constitutions. This knowledge must then be used as a check upon our predisposition.

Here again,' these historic issues and debates must be studied, not with the view of reading our predispositions into them, but rather with the view to understanding the ideals of principle behind the rhetoric of polemics. We must not be content to ask how many of the controversialists defended predispositions like our own, but rather should we ask what purpose was sought to be accomplished. What was the line of cleavage between that purpose which prevailed in the constitutional conventions, and that older view which was then and there overcome?

MATURE AND IMMATURE METHODS.

If we approach the discussion with the dominant desire to understand our problem in its larger evolutionary relations, and allow our predispositions to be checked and subordinated to such an understanding as we may read out of our constitutions, then there can hardly be much difference of opinion.[17]

This is only another way of saying that if, in the first instance, our legal problems are decided by the inductive and synthetic methods, applied to *all* the objective factors of the problem, the result will be as acceptable to all persons capable of mature methods of reasoning, as is the multiplication table to mathematicians. If, however, we are content to read our own prior impulses into the problem, the inductive checks and synthetic process will be ignored, and the proof of it will be evident in the resultant special plea, and all that it distorts, perverts or ignores. Such a decision will satisfy all those, and only those, who are possessed by similar and equally unreasoned impulses which need intellectualization; it cannot enlighten, much less convince, those of contrary predisposition, who find their contrary special pleas evaded, instead of answered or co-ordinated; neither can it command the respect of those who are conscious of the difference between mature and immature intellectual processes.

---

[17] For an elaboration of this thought see "Intellectual Evolution and Pragmatism" in *The Monist,* Jan., 1915.

DOGMA AND SENTIMENT.

We need constantly to remind ourselves of the difference between mere dogma and conventional moral sentimentalism, on the one hand, and mature intellectual method on the other hand. In the latter no factor of the problem is ignored, and all are co-ordinated and used as inductive checks upon our preconceptions. This is deemed important because my reading has persuaded me that, in dealing with questions of religious liberty, these intellectual methods are the most neglected. It is always upon the subject of religion that we most need an efficient check upon our unconscious urge to act as though we ourselves were gods, engaged in the task of avenging a personal insult.

If we no longer use the fagot or branding iron to punish for mere psychologic offences, but punish them in more humane fashion, this speaks well for our sentiments, but in itself is no recommendation for our intellect. So long as we punish any mere psychologic offence, there must prevail the old method of dogmatising in defense of mere blind, automatic, emotional reactions. This is manifestly so because we do not punish upon the basis of an inductively determined relation between the penalized idea and any consequent actual and material injury.

MAKING BAD PRECEDENTS.

The immature method applied to social sciences and the law, means little more than the intellectualization of our impulses into a formula. At its best this method only utilizes a special plea to justify an emotional predisposition. In the process, old precedents are often misapplied and distorted, and pernicious new precedents are created. It is by such processes that we arrive at most of our fine moral sentimentalizings which so enthral the multitude, whose enthusiasm for them often becomes so amazing to the intelligence of future generations. *Thus it comes that we know because we feel, and are firmly convinced because strongly agitated.* Thus it comes that we enshrine our unenlightened impulses into solemn decree and sacred dogma, and denounce all dissent as dangerous to morality, church and state. If our impulses are sufficiently morbid, our "morality" may achieve such a compelling importance that, under the pretence of the love of God or country, we become willing to incarcerate, maim, hang, or, with a red-hot iron bore a hole in the tongue of the heretic, or burn him to ashes, even though he has done no actual or material injury to anyone. Has the time arrived when a Court has been founded with sufficiently strong desire and intelligence, to decide such a controversy according to the requirements of mature mental methods?

EVOLUTION BEYOND RELIGIOUS FEELINGS.

Religion is always largely a matter of feelings, and the emotions are predominant just in proportion as our mental processes in relation to religion are relatively primitive. It follows that when we are dealing with a problem of constitutional law and intellectual liberty in relation to religion, we always need to exercise special precaution. It is precisely because religious feelings are stimulated that we are prone to regress to more immature methods of reasoning. It is the consciousness of this which induces me to persist still further in my exposition of the meaning of mature mental processes, to be applied to constitutional construction.

This intellectual evolution which I seek to bring to consciousness, involves the use of a progressively more inclusive understanding of the relation and behavior of human forces as expressed in human institutions. This is a means to the end that this understanding may operate as a check upon immature intellectual methods for satisfying an immature urge, toward the consciousness of power arbitrarily to impose our will upon others. All blasphemy laws are conceived as of this character. I will endeavor to make this general statement as to method more concrete by exhibiting its significance as applied to the problem of constitutional construction.

THE SYNTHETIC VIEW.

If a judge's dominant desire is to get behind the

acquired meaning of the constitutional words, in order to understand better the human desires and ideas of which those words are symbols, and if he seeks thus to acquire a more precise and yet more comprehensive concept of intellectual liberty, he will pursue a different mode of thinking than that of Blackstone, or the courts in the Ruggles and Kneeland cases, to be presently reviewed. Then he will not be content to use his astute intellect, even in the most precise kind of word-jugglery. If we bring to such a problem the larger understanding, we cannot be content with even a very critical analysis of separate constitutional phrases, treating each as something wholly dissociated from everyhing else. The facts of human intelligence and growth, even as expressed in human institutions and constitutions, never exist in such isolation. If we see them thus, and treat them thus, it must be that our intellectual vision is unfortunately limited, at least as to this particular problem. It will be shown that where religion is concerned, eminent judges felt too intensely to make it easy for them to see, or to co-ordinate, all the factors of such a problem, with the same impersonal attitude and the same acumen that is usually brought to bear upon other juridical problems.

PREVIOUS HISTORIC TREND.

The true purposes of our constitutional guarantees of liberty can only be determined by studying the trend and tendencies of the historic controversies which culminated in the Bill of Rights as a whole. From this viewpoint, each part of the Bill of Rights is but a separate and distinct means, to the end of protecting a larger concept of liberty—a concept much more inclusive than is indicated by the mere words of any of the fragmentary barriers erected for its protection. Probably we have not yet reached that stage of intellectual development where liberty and tyranny can be differentiated by a single phrase, or defined with precision in a single generalization, which is broad enough to cover accurately every issue between them. But we can see clearly some concrete means by which our liberties have been destroyed, and we can and do erect equally concrete barriers against the repetition of those particular methods of the tyrant. Probably that is all the Constitutions really recorded, leaving the Courts to interpret these acts, declare the principle and apply it to any concrete situation which might thereafter arise, even though it had not previously entered the imagination of man.

DISCOVERING THE REASON AND PRINCIPLE.

If, then, we desire to achieve an accurate understanding of the meaning of our constitutional rights, in relation to a concrete problem, the mode of procedure is fairly obvious. First we should acquire a clear view of the relation of the present problem to those historic controversies which eventuated in our constitutional guarantees The details of separate problems so remote from one another in point of time will doubtless be very unlike. However, the older controversies always involved, more or less consciously, some definite and ascertainable general principles applicable to the present situation. Undoubtedly, at first, these were imperfectly conceived, and, even in the end, perhaps, crudely stated; but they were always there, implicit, and more or less clearly expressed. Our object must be to discover with growing accuracy those principles which the Constitution makers were striving to protect against future invasion, and then to ask ourselves whether any such principle is in danger of being violated in the present instance.

Our constitutional guarantees, like our concepts of liberty, are the product of previous development. As we seek gradually to correct the evil, it is by first generalizing separate aspects of it. As fast as our vision clarifies, we negative one barrier after the other, and finally we may achieve a fairly comprehensive prevention of tyranny and a synthetic concept of freedom. A history of the English Constitution perfectly illustrates this point. Beginning with the Charter of Henry the first, followed by the Great Charter of King John, we have a series of charter amendments, each necessitated to inhibit a new aspect of tyranny, brought about by the official attempt to evade the true meaning and purposes of the former concessions of liberty. If kings and judges had honestly and intelligently attempted to understand and to live up to the purposes of Magna Charta, instead of exercising great ingenuity in interpreting its words so as to evade its object, much suffering and bloodshed would have been spared. Let us be warned not to follow so immature a method of dealing with our own social problems.

CONTINUOUS EVOLUTION.

Our Constitutions are the expressions of a slow intellectual growth. Our Constitution-makers had the benefit of much of England's experience, and were seeking as best they could to generalize that experience according to their understanding of it. Not being near to omniscience, the vision was incomplete. Notwithstanding this, a study of those past conflicts is quite indispensible for the clarification of our present understanding. In fact, our concepts of justice and liberty are always in the making and are always in conflict with the new invasion resorted to by individuals and governments, sometimes sanctioned by Courts. Accordingly, amendments or new applications of our guarantees of liberty are made necessary.

If, then, we would get the true meaning of our Constitutions, we must view the provisions both historically and synthetically. We must see each of the guarantees as a fragmentary means of accomplishing a unified purpose, which in this case is the protection of an ever-perfecting concept of enlarging intellectual freedom. These constitutional objectives must be seen as the expression of a living, changing, growing, human intelligence, which at any moment can be adequately understood only if seen in true perspective and evolving relations to what has gone before.

READING INTO AND OUT OF THE CONSTITUTION.

Here let me say that this view of constitutional interpretation, though progressive, is something very different from that "elastic constitution" of which certain reformers spoke so loudly a few years ago. The difference is one between reading new meanings out of the Constitution by a more thorough studying of its antecedent history and genesis, and on the other hand, reading a meaning into it, solely by a study of subsequent extraneous developments. It is the former that I propose, and the historic, synthetic, and psychologic method as the means. From this retrospective evolution, if seen in process of change, conforming to a general law of development, we secure also a concept of prospective evolution. When we acquire an intellectual grasp adequate for such a task, our decisions will always be abreast of the best thought of our time. If judges lack this development, their decisions will retard the progressive clarification of concepts of liberty and justice. So our Courts, by attempting to block the natural forces that make for social evolution, may become the undesigning promotors of riot and revolution. The larger understanding of natural law in the social organism impels toward a ready and cheerful conformity to its evolutionary process.

DETECTING MERE PLAUSIBLE PRETENCES.

Where desire is strong, sophistry comes easy. Whether consciously or unconsciously, if judges are impelled to the doing of that which in the larger view is to be regarded as mischievous, an abundance of righteous and plausible pretenses can always be found, for the justification of any desired means or ends. Yet herein lies some public safety, that it is just as impossible to conceal ignorance and prejudice as it is impossible to justify error, without ignoring or misusing some essental factors of the problem. Whether on or off the judicial bench, the ignorance and prejudices of men are accurately measurable, by the quantity of material factors which are overlooked, or misused, in the special plea that is offered for self-justification. If all our energies are unified upon the task of looking all the facts of our problem square in the face, with the single purpose of trying to understand the human behavior and relations involved therein, then that fact will also be apparent upon the face of the justification supporting the decision. When we develop the objective method in judicial problems, to the same extent that we have done in the material sciences, then there will be no more disagreement among judges than now obtains among mathematicians. Then also will the public discontent over courts be no greater than it is with the multiplication table. It is hoped that the method here outlined, by its application to the problem now before the court, may do a little something toward this desirable end.

The excuse for this elaborate discussion of principles and methods is not to be found in an assumption that judges are ignorant of them, but in the belief that in a case such as this one, they are most likely to be overlooked and ignored. By refreshing our memory, and holding these matters firmly in consciousness, we will see all that follows as part of a coherent process.

V.

RUGGLES DECISION CRITICISED.

Every attempt to uphold the constitutionality of blasphemy laws will necessarily depend in some measure upon the New York decision of 1811, in the case of People vs. Ruggles.[1] In order to secure a more open-minded attitude, it becomes necessary to question the reasoning and the authority of that decision. To that end we will proceed to a critical review of it. This is done in the confidence that it will appear that the Ruggles decision expressed a misconception of the law at the time of its rendition, and that since then it has been over-ruled, both as to its essential foundations and its conclusions.

A careful and critical review of the English decisions in blasphemy cases shows that they were essentially based on the English conception of the State and the Church as being but different aspects of the same human institution. Many times, in giving their reasons for the blasphemy laws, the English courts have repeated Lord Hale's statement that "The Christian religion is part of the law itself." Of course, recent decisions say this is no longer true in any such sense as was then implied. Blackstone,[2] declaring the law as it was understood at his time, said that: "Law is the perfection of reason, that it always intends to conform thereto, and that what is not reason is not law; * * * much more if it be clearly contrary to the divine law." Thus divine law is as fundamental as are our constitutions in relation to mere statutes. Coke reports that "Words against an archbishop are words against the Government" and punishable as treason.[3]

KENT ON CHURCH AND STATE.

In contradiction to much more of this, Justice Kent in the Ruggles case declared of blasphemy that "such of-

---

[1] 8 Johnson 290; 5 Am. Dec. 335. [2] v. 1, p. 70.
[3] See Mencle on Libel, p. 288, A. D. 1823.

fences have always been considered independent of any religious establishment or the right of the church." The falsehood of this will be demonstrated in our later study of the blasphemy decisions. That he should thus ignore what would seem to be patent facts to most lawyers of our time suggests that this statement was the result of an overwhelming impulse in Judge Kent to explain away the natural effect of the New York Constitutional provisions against a union of church and state and for tolerance.

If by the above statement Justice Kent had meant only to convey the idea that the essential motive for blasphemy laws was a protection for royalty and aristocracy in the continued enjoyment of privileges and prerogatives, then the statement has some truth in it, but loses its importance. Even though in this light the protection of the church was not an end in itself, it became an essential objective means for the accomplishment of the royalists' political desire. An inseparable part of the program was the protection of the "rights" of the Church as embodied in the temporal privileges of the "spiritual" aristocracy, such as "benefit of clergy," state support, etc., etc. In return, the established clergy always supported the King and the temporal aristocrats. The consequence of so using the church and its ecclesiastical machinery has been to create the substance of a legally established church organization and an official theology. The mode of its verbal acknowledgment is unimportant. In the light of this, Justice Kent's statement must be regarded as untrue, or a mere verbalism, void of significance.

In the same opinion, Justice Kent practically admits the error of the statement already quoted, when he says: "The very idea of jurisprudence with the ancient law-givers and philosophers embraced the religion of the country." There we have it in a nutshell. There never has been a government which had a *complete* separation from religion. Even in America, the present separation is complete only in theory, not in practice. In most countries the word "church" symbolizes one aspect, the word "state" another aspect, of the same thing. The distinction is rhetorical only, and blasphemy laws are but one manifestation of a religion which is in fact more or less completely and legally established. It would seem to follow that where the constitution prohibits a union of church and state, that thereby it prohibits the punishment of blasphemy.

TOLERATION FOR DUTCH CHURCH.

Let us now examine into the growth of intellectual hospitality during New York's Colonial period. It is highly probable that this will shed some light on the correctness of the constitutional interpretation which was undertaken by Justice Kent, in the Ruggles case. It is a little singular that he should have ignored the developments which led up to the adoption of the constitutional provisions separating church and state, because a consideration of contemporary and antecedent historical events have always been considered an essential factor to statutory and constitutional construction.

The first mention of toleration that I have found is contained in the Articles of Capitulation by the Dutch to the English, dated August 27, 1664. Article 8 declares that: "The Dutch here shall enjoy the liberty of conscience in Divine worship and Church Discipline."[4] To be sure, this is a very narrow limit of toleration, both as to persons and subject matter. Subsequent references in the laws lead me to believe that "liberty of conscience in Divine Worship and Church Discipline" were meant to include the use of the taxing power for the support of the Dutch clergy and the perpetuation of such privileges as had been enjoyed by them as the official Dutch Church. The seed of tolerance being once planted, subsequent agitation and the blood of martyrs would compel its growth.

The second official recognition of any toleration is to be found in "The Charter of Liberties and Privileges Granted by His Royal Highness [Charles II.] to the Inhabitants of New York and its Dependencies," passed October 30, 1683, by the Governor, Councill, and the Representatives in General Assembly. This Bill of Rights is quite comprehensive, and was passed "thatt Justice and Right may

---

[4] Laws of New York. Revision of 1813, vol. 2, p. 1, of Appendix.

be *equally* done to all persons." Among other important matters, it contains this:

TOLERATION FOR ALL CHRISTIAN PROTESTANTS.

"No person or persons *which professe ffaith in God by Jesus Christ,* shall at any time, be any ways molested, punished, disquieted, or called in question for any difference in opinion or matter of religious concernment, *who do not actually disturbe the civil peace* of the province, but that all and every person or persons may, from time, and at all times, freely have, and fully enjoy, his or their judgments, or consciences, in matters of religion throughout all the province, they behaving themselves peaceably and quietly, and *not using the liberty to licentiousnesse nor to the civil injury or outward disturbance* of others. Provided always, Thatt this liberty or anything conteyned therein to the contrary shall never be construed or improved to make void *the settlement of any public minister on Long Island.* * * *

"And whereas all the respective Christian Churches now in practice within the Citty of New Yorke and the other places of this province do appear to be privileged, and have been so established and confirmed by the former authority of this government, be it hereby enacted by this present General Assembly, and by the authority thereof, That all the said respective Christian churches be hereby confirmed therein, and that they and every one of them shall from henceforth for ever be held and reputed as priviledged churches, and enjoy all their former freedoms of their religion in divine worship and church discipline, and *that all former contracts made and agreed on for the maintenances of the several ministers* of the said churches [be upheld]. * * * Provided also that all other Christian churches that shall hereafter come and settle within this province, shall have the same privileges."[5]

If we view this language in the light of the preceding Treaty, its purpose is plain. The Treaty with Holland had evidently continued undisturbed the privileges of the

[5] Laws of N. Y., Revision of 1813, vol. 2, Appendix, p. v-vi.

established Dutch Church and its clergy and lay members. This Act of the Assembly was manifestly an effort to destroy the relative privilege of the Dutch religionists without violating the Articles of Capitulation. This was done by the simple expedient of elevating all other churches to the same degree of privilege. That is to say, the same degree of toleration and state recognition and support, which by Treaty had been insured to the Dutch, were now made the heritage of all Christians.

It is important to note here that this is the first official concession of English royalty, to the New York Colonists, by amending the common law as to blasphemy so as to make the limit of religious toleration, as between varying groups of Christians, to consist of *an actual breach of the civil peace*, instead of a speculative *tendency* founded upon a breach of the spiritual, or religious, peace. Now there could not be punishment of a Christian for a mere heretical misinterpretation of the Bible. While narrowing the scope, the language follows the essential part of the Rhode Island Act of Toleration of 1664. This presented the first experiment in toleration. In the phraseology of our time, it is the difference between an *actual* breach of the peace, and a *constructive* breach of the peace, which latter is always based upon a mere speculation as to a psychologic tendency. Insofar as the common law based criminality for intellectual offences upon psychologic tendency only speculatively ascertained, this enactment was a beneficial modification thereof.

TOLERATION AS RIGHT NOT PRIVILEGE.

The third enactment affecting religious freedom was passed by the General Assembly of the Colony of New York, May 13, 1691. It is entitled: "An Act Declaring What Are the Rights and Privileges of Their Majesties' Subjects Inhabiting Within Their Province of New York." On the subject of religion we find this declaration:

"No person or persons *which profess faith in God by Jesus Christ His Only Son* shall at any time be any ways molested, punished, disturbed, disquieted, or called in question for *any Difference in Opinion on matters of conscience* in Religious Concernment, who do not, under that pretence, disturb the civil peace of the Province. And that all and every such person and persons may from time to time and at all times hereafter freely and fully enjoy his or their opinion, Perswasion, Judgement, in matters of conscience and religion thro-out all this Province, and freely meet at convenient places within this Province, and there worship according to their respective Perswasions without being hindered or molested, they behaving themselves peaceably, quietly, modestly and religiously, and not using this liberty to licentiousness nor to the civil injury or outward disturbance of others. Always Provided, that nothing herein mentioned nor contained shall extend to give liberty to any persons of the Romish Religion to exercise their manner of worship contrary to the laws and statutes of Their Majesties' Kingdom of England."[6]

William Smith[7] informs us that this enactment was designed as a declaration that the Colonists repudiated the idea that they held their rights of representation in the Assembly as a liberty by permission of the Crown. By their act they meant to affirm that this right and others were inherent in them as men. In 1697, King William made his contrary claim, by repealing the Declaration of Rights of 1691.

ACTUAL V. CONSTRUCTIVE INJURY.

Waiving the questions involved as to any change of rights affected hereby, we may concern ourselves again with the important fact that here the Colonists a second time registered their aversion to constructive or psychologic breaches of the peace. More clearly than in the previous charter, they insisted upon liberty, and not mere toleration, up to the point of an actual resultant breach of the peace. This officially expressed opinion should be of importance as registering in New York the acceptance of a progressive change of opinion as to tolerance that was taking place among all English-speaking peoples. This

---

[6] Acts of Assembly Passed in the Province of New York from 1691-1725, p. 5. Bradford, printer, 1726.
[7] History of N. Y., p. 127, A. D. 1814.

conception had its first effective advocate in John Milton.
Briefly expressed, that change was a growth *toward* a tolerance of all intellectual differences, short of their actually
having produced material injury. Those wishing to attain
an intelligent opinion as to the meaning of our constitutional guarantees of freedom will not exclude from their
consideration or understanding those previous changes
and expressions of public sentiment which finally were
recorded in our written constitutional guarantees of liberty. We best understand their meaning by knowing the
trend of thought of which they were the culmination and
that against which they were aimed. In this view we
will see also a growth from mere tolerance to a conceded
claim of irrevocable right. Justice Kent entirely ignored
this historic controversy and development.

JEWS STILL EXCLUDED.

Under the influence of the conflict with the Crown, there
came another important decision about tolerance in connection with an election contest about 1736. Here the
General Assembly decided that Jews could not vote for
Representatives, nor be permitted as witnesses touching
any contested elections.[8] Jews and Catholics still suffered disadvantages, which the subsequent Constitution
removed, not to produce a return to common law conditions, but to liberalize the common law, by bringing all
up to the level of equality of tolerance with the formerly
favored Protestant sects, who were punishable only for
an actual breach of the peace. Thus tolerance was to
evolve to religious liberty.

ZENGER'S SEDITIOUS LIBEL.

Concurrent with the growing dissentions between the
Colonists and the representatives of the Crown, there came
into being John Peter Zenger's *New York Weekly Journal*. Zenger was soon arrested for seditious libel. A
stormy contest ensued, during which Zenger's two attorneys were disbarred, and he found it necessary to bring

---

[8] Smith's Hist. of N. Y., p. 423, A. D. 1814.

Andrew Hamilton from Philadelphia to conduct his defence. The judges clung to all those old rules designed to bring about a conviction, but the jury acquitted. This trial, in 1735, "was far-reaching in its consequences, and was of such importance that it is doubtful if any case in American had a more thoroughly interested and attentive audience. * * * This event has been called 'the Morning Star of that Liberty which subsequently revolutionized America'."[9] From such events and in fragmentary form came the clarification of people's thinking about the meaning of free speech. The Court had instructed the jury to find only on the fact of publication, which had been admitted, leaving it to the Court to determine the character of the paper. The argument of Hamilton was a frank appeal to the jury to disregard the instruction of the Judge and find upon their own knowledge such questions as criminal intent and the truth of the publication, which they did.[10]

Soon after the organization of the State Government and the divided court in People v. Croswell,[11] a bill was passed affecting libels. The preamble read: "Whereas, doubt exists whether on a trial of an indictment or information for a libel, the jury have a right to give their verdict on the whole matter in issue," therefore it was enacted that the jury had such right, and the truth, good motives, and justifiable ends should be a defense. It also prohibited the prosecution of libel on information. All this was manifestly the legislative confirmation of the issues vainly contended for in the Zenger case, which were designed to promote freedom of the press. The Zenger case almost found a reversal in the famous Croswell case[12] and the principle involved in both was firmly fixed, for the further enlargement of intellectual liberty, in the New York Constitutional Convention of 1821.

---

[9] XIII Nat. Ency. of Amer. Biography, 298-9.
[10] Several editions of this trial have been published. It is also reported in 17 Howell's State Trials, p. 675-764.
[11] 3 John. 393.
[12] 3 John. Cases 337; 1805.

THE ENGLISH TEST OATH.

Between 1743 and 1745 a bill was introduced, requiring persons in the Colony to take the Test Oaths, appointed by Parliament for the security of Government and Protestantism. The bill passed the Assembly by a vote of 14 to 7. In the meantime, the war between England and France was progressing. Manifestly, fear of Catholic France, pressure from England, and a desire for the greater liberty of Protestantism were the inspiring motives for this anti-Catholic legislation.

ISSUES THE SAME EVERYWHERE.

A review of this Colonial record exhibits the same conflict of ideals as to the limits of toleration as that which is found everywhere. Those who stood for tyranny, usually stood for the repression of heretical opinions about human institutions, whether in their religious or political aspects. These persons fell back on the reasonings of the English courts about seditious libels, whether concerned with religious or political doctrines. The legislative and judicial tests for penalization, both in England and in most American Colonies where the common law prevailed, were dependent upon a problematical and speculative theory about a prospective psychologic tendency of the incriminated utterance to produce a constructive or real breach of the peace, through some hypothetical future hearer or reader.

The friends of freedom always complained of this, because of the certainty that tyranny would result from such unreal and uncertain tests for determining the limits of intellectual liberty. Hence, the opponents of the official theory of religious liberty always tend toward an insistence that the limit thereof shall be an actually ascertained and resultant material injury, or real disturbance. This tendency is portrayed in all discussion for the promotion of religious liberty, and shows itself in the utterances of the Colonists of New York, just as it did in Rhode Island, and among the dissentors of England. As the opposition to the English judicial conception grew in clarity of understanding, the issues became more definite.

These issues, as to the growth of religious liberty, were decided by the Constitutions. The growth through enlarging tolerance to true liberty has been a progressive elimination of unrealized psychologic tendency as an excuse for penalization.

THE N. Y. CONSTITUTION OF 1777.

The New York Constitution of 1777 begins with a recital of grievances, which, among many, includes these: "He [the King] refused his assent to laws the most wholesome and necessary to the public good. * * * For depriving us in many cases of the benefits of trial by jury." Here we have substantially a reaffirmance of that declaration of rights which the King had annulled, and from which was quoted hereinabove the provision for mutual toleration among Christian sects, up to the point of an actual disturbance of the peace. We also see the influence of the trial of Zenger, and Judge DeLancy's effort to deprive the jury of the right to declare upon the whole issue.

The New York Constitution of 1777, in Article 7, provides that Quakers shall be allowed to declare their allegiance to the government by affirmation instead of by oath. The common law and colonial statutes in force April 19, 1775, are continued in force; but it is provided "that all such parts of the said common law, and all such of the said statutes and acts aforesaid, or parts thereof, as may be construed to establish or maintain any particular denomination of Christians or their ministers, or concern the allegiance heretofore yielded to [the English sovereign, etc.] or are repugnant to this Constitution, be and hereby are abrogated and rejected." The real question in the Ruggles case was whether or not the common law crime of blasphemy was repugnant to the Constitution, interpreted, of course, in the light of these past controversies of which its provisions for the separation of church and state were a culmination. These provisions, which supplement the foregoing act of disestablishment, will now be discussed.

DISABILITIES OF THE CLERGY.

Section 38 [N. Y. Constitution, 1777]: "Whereas, we

are required by the benevolent principles of rational liberty, not only to expel civil tyranny, but also to guard *against that spiritual oppression and intolerance wherewith the bigotry and ambition of weak and wicked priests and princes* have scourged mankind: This Convention doth further and in the name and by the authority of the good people of this State, ordain, determine and declare, that the free exercise and enjoyment of religious profession and worship, without discrimination or preference, shall for ever hereafter be allowed within this State to all mankind. Provided that the liberty of conscience hereby granted shall not be so construed as to excuse acts of licentiousness, or justify practices inconsistent with the peace or safety of the State."

Section 39 provides: "And whereas the ministers of the Gospel are by their profession dedicated to the service of God and the cure of souls, and ought not to be diverted from the great duties of their function; therefore, no minister of the gospel, or priest of any denomination whatsoever, shall at any time hereafter under any pretence or description whatever be eligible to or capable of holding any civil or military office or place within this State."

The proviso in Section 38 against licentiousness may be interpreted in the light of the past colonial controversies as to the limit of tolerance. Thus construed, in connection with the declaration of rights above quoted, there can be no doubt but that "licentiousness" meant actual, and not merely a constructive, licentiousness. The line had been plainly drawn by the Colonial General Assembly. To make their meaning plain beyond reasonable chance of controversy they expressed it in the alternative, thus: "To excuse *acts* of licentiousness *or* justify practices inconsistent with the peace [actual peace] and safety [actual safety] of the State."

That my interpolations express the true purpose and spirit of those who adopted this provision is plain, not only from the prior colonial declarations, but also from the disestablishment of the church, which removed the reason for blasphemy as a part of constructive treason. Especially is this apparent from the preamble, which again

draws the lines between civil tyranny and actual breach
on the one hand, as against spiritual oppression and mere
tolerance on the other, together with their attendant tendency to fall back upon a constructive civil disturbance.
If Justice Kent had looked his problem squarely in the
face with a dominant desire to meet every issue fairly,
he would have answered this question: How can I "guard
against that spiritual oppression and intolerance" sought
to be abrogated by the constitution, and yet enforce blasphemy laws?

THE RUGGLES DECISION AGAIN.

It was charged in the Ruggles case that the defendant
did "wickedly, maliciously and blasphemously utter," etc.
The question was whether or not the common law crime
of blasphemy had been abrogated by the constitutional
provisions above quoted. *It is noteworthy. that the New
York Constitution at that time did not yet expressly guarantee, in any form, freedom of speech and press.*

A careful reading of Justice Kent's decision in the Ruggles case suggests that, when not engaged in the mere
logmatic assertion of his ultimate conclusion, his acute
intellect is devoted to reading a meaning into the Constitution, not to an endeavor to read a meaning out of it.
Through the entire length of his opinion, the argument is
obviously directed to justify what he thought the Constitution ought to be, rather than to discovering the
opinion upon that subject entertained by those who framed
that Constitution, and the people who adopted it.   In
other words, under the influence of his Christian zeal, Mr.
Justice Kent neglected the distinction between construction and interpolation.   We shall presently see that his
Christian zeal was coupled with a strong aversion to that
conception of religious liberty in which Roger Williams
and Thomas Jefferson believed, and which our constitutions adopted.

LICENTIOUSNESS OF THE PRESS.

Mr. Justice Kent is equally careless in his intellectual
processes, when he holds that the common law crime of

blasphemy may be enforced under the saving clause
against "acts of licentiousness or [to] justify practices
inconsistent with the peace or safety of the State." His
conception of "licentiousness" was that of the English
courts, after the repeal of the licensing laws and when
therefore the word had lost its former certain meaning of
"unlicensed." Now English Courts began to punish men
for constructive breaches of the peace, and justified themselves by theories about the problematical and speculative
psychologic tendencies of an idea to influence some hypothetical hearer or reader of the future. By their Declaration of Rights in 1691 the Colonists of New York had
already made it plain that they repudiated Justice Kent's
conception of constructive "licentiousness" and constructive breaches of "peace and safety of the state." Both by
that, and by the Charter of August 27, 1683, with royal
approval, they had enjoyed freedom "for any difference in
opinion or matter of religious concernment" for all those
"who do not *actually* disturb civil peace * * * nor
to the civil injury or outward disturbance of others."

In view of the strong constitutional language against
"the bigotry and ambition of weak and wicked priests"
and the disabilities declared against all priests and ministers, it is simply preposterous to say that by this Constitution it was intended to perpetuate the common law as
to blasphemy, which, insofar as penalization was justified
by speculations upon psychologic "tendency," they, in
their charter and Declaration of Rights, had long ago
repudiated. Justice Kent evidently had difficulty in seeing the bearings of those constitutional provisions, which
reflected so strongly on the clergy, because that class included his revered grandfather.

KENT'S EMOTIONAL DISABILITY.

Like himself, his father and grandfather had been educated at Yale University, in a colony which was ruled by
a spiritual aristocracy, where none could hold office without church membership; and a property aristocracy, where
none could vote without taxpaying qualification; and a
church-state in which the spiritual aristocrats were sup-

ported by the taxing power exercised by the political aristocrats. Reared and educated under such influences, it
was quite natural that he should have an emotional aversion to those provisions of the New York constitution
which cast odium upon the system of his human idols, by
reference to the "spiritual oppression and intolerance
wherewith the bigotry and ambition of weak and wicked
priests and princes have scourged mankind." Ruggles,
the blasphemer before the court, was one of the party for
whose benefit the constitution had inveighed against the
judge's clerical ancestor, and declared all like him to be
ineligible for public office. The analytic psychologist
knows best how to value the potency of that paternal influence upon the aristocratic feelings of Justice Kent, and
can see in it the genesis of those tory predispositions
which he carried through life. The psychologist under-
stands perfectly how these feeling attitudes, these emotional predispositions, precluded Justice Kent from seeing the hated constitutional provisions, as being important factors in the interpretation of that other provison,
which he was impelled to explain away. Through Ruggles
Justice Kent retaliated upon those who had done violence
to his spiritual aristocracy.

The influence of his aristocratic ancestors was still at
work upon Justice Kent while in the constitutional convention of 1821. In addition to his opposition to the free
speech amendment we find him "opposing without success
the extension of the electoral franchise and other democratic innovations."[13]

When all the related facts are taken into account which
Justice Kent ignored, then intellectual self-respect will
preclude our acceptance of his opinion in People v. Ruggles as an authority upon the meaning of a separation of
church and state and its implied intellectual freedom.

[13] Appleton's Cyclop of Amer. Biography, v. 3, p. 521..

VI.
RUGGLES CASE OVERRULED.

In July, 1894, the Grand Jury of Lexington, Ky., indicted C. C. Moore on a charge of blasphemy, at the instigation of Rev. E. L. Southgate, a Methodist clergyman. The Ruggles case was the chief reliance of the Prosecutor. The Court sustained a demurrer to the complaint, and overruled the decision of Justice Kent in the Ruggles case. The following is the opinion, never officially printed, but now reproduced from the *Truthseeker Annual* for 1895:

DECISION OF JUDGE PARKER OVERRULING JUDGE KENT.

"The defendant, C. C. Moore, is charged with having committed the offense of blasphemy. It is alleged in the indictment that the defendant, intending to treat with offensive levity and ridicule the scriptural account of the divine conception and birth and to bring contempt against Almighty God and his divine purpose in causing the birth of Christ, did maliciously and blasphemously publish in a newspaper known as the 'Blue Grass Blade' the following words:

" 'When I say that Jesus Christ was a man exactly like I am, and had a human father and mother exactly like I had, some of the pious call it blasphemy. When they say that Jesus Christ was born as the result of a sort of Breckinridge-Pollard hyphenation between God and a Jew woman, I call it blasphemy, so you see there is a stand-off.'

"It is further charged that, by this language, the defendant meant that pious and religious persons stated and believed that the birth of Jesus Christ was the result of an unholy and illicit connection between Almighty God and Mary, the mother of Christ.

"To this indictment the defendant has filed a demurrer, and thereby made the claim that no offense against the

60

laws of Kentucky had been charged against him. This demurrer having been argued with singular earnestness and ability by counsel both for the prosecution and the defense, and the question presented being a new one in this state, the court has given the case unusual consideration.

"We have no statute against blasphemy, and our Court of Appeals, so far as we know, has never passed upon this or any similar question. We must, therefore, in our investigations have recourse to the common law and to the judicial decisions of other states and countries.

"Blackstone, in treating of offenses against God and religion, speaks of this offense as 'blasphemy against the Almighty by denying his being or providence or by contumelious reproaches of our Savior Christ.' The punishment, he says, is by fine and imprisonment or other infamous corporal punishment. The ground upon which blasphemy is treated as an offense is that 'Christianity is part of the laws of England.' The leading case in this country in which the crime of blasphemy was discussed was that of the People vs. Ruggles [8 John. 290; s. c. 5 Am. Dec. 335], decided by the Supreme Court of New York in 1810, Chief Justice Kent delivering the opinion. In that case it was decided that the common law against blasphemy was still in force, and a judgment to pay a fine of $500 and be imprisoned three months was affirmed. The court in this opinion cited with approval a number of English cases, in which the right to punish blasphemy had been vigorously upheld, and quoted the words of Lord Bacon, 'profane scoffing doth by little and little deface the reverence for religion' and 'two principal causes I have and know of Atheism—curious controversies and profane scoffing.' Whilst this opinion did not declare that Christianity was part of the law of the state of New York, but expressly disclaimed that there was an established religion in that state; yet the closeness with which it adhered to the definition of blasphemy as laid down by Blackstone, and the great reliance placed upon the English decisions, make us hesitate to walk in the path trod by Chief Justice Kent himself. For in England there was an established church. The church was part of the state. Apostasy and heresy were punished; the first commission of either offense disqualifying the offender for holding office, and the second being punished by three years' imprisonment without bail. Even witchcraft was claimed by Blackstone to be an offense against God and religion, and to deny the existence of such a crime, as he said, was "at once to flatly contradict the revealed word of God," though he appeared to think it well that the punishment of this crime had fallen into disuse, as there had been no well authenticated modern instance of its commission.

"In this country, where the divorce between church and state is complete and final, we should examine with care and accept with caution any law framed and intended for a country where church and state are one. The difficulties in reconciling religious freedom with the right to punish for an offense against any given religion are manifest. From the opinion given in the People vs. Ruggles, we may deduce as conclusions of the court that the people generally in this country are Christians; that Christianity is engrafted upon the morality of the country; that all religions are tolerated, but that this toleration, as to false religions, means immunity from test oaths, disabilities, and the burdens of church establishments; that to revile the Christian religion is an offense, but that to revile other religions is not an offense punishable by law.

"In the bill of rights in the Kentucky Constitution it is declared that all persons have 'the right to worship Almighty God according to the dictates of their consciences;' that 'no preference shall be given by law to any religious sect, society, or denomination, nor to any particular system of ecclesiastical polity,' and that 'the civil rights, privileges, or capacities of no person shall be taken away or in anywise diminished or enlarged on account of his belief or disbelief of any religious tenet, dogma, or teaching.'

"It is difficult to conceive how language could be made plainer. If the framers of the constitution intended to place all religions on an exact equality before the law, they appear to have employed language well calculated to express their purpose. They recognized the fact that men were religious, that they held different religious views, that some had no religious faith, and, granting the fullest religious freedom, they declared that the rights of none should be 'diminished or enlarged on account of his belief or disbelief of any religious tenet, dogma or teaching.'

"Under this Constitution no form of religion can claim to be under the special guardianship of the law. The common law of England, whence our law of blasphemy is derived, did have a certain religion under its guardianship, and this religion was part of the law. The greatest concession made to religious liberty was the right of learned persons to decently debate upon controverted points. The essence of the law against blasphemy was that the offense, like apostasy and heresy, was against religion, and it was to uphold the established church, and not in any sense to maintain good order, that there was a law against blasphemy. The most superficial examination of the chapter in Blackstone treating of offenses against God and religion, must convince any mind that the sole aim and object of these laws was to preserve the Christian faith, as it was then understood and accepted by the established church. It may seem to us that the punishments for these offenses were severe in the time of Blackstone, but they had then been greatly mitigated, as the stake and fagot had been of but too frequent use in propagating what was deemed to be the true religion. Even Blackstone complains that the definition of heresy had been too uncertain, and that the subject had been liable to be burnt for what he had not understood to be heresy until it was decided to be so by the ecclesiastical judge who interpreted the canonical scriptures. To deny any one of the persons of the trinity, or to allege that there were more gods than one, was a heresy and was punished in the same manner as apostasy.

"Blasphemy is a crime grown from the same parent stem as apostasy and heresy. It is one of a class of offenses designed for the same general purpose, the fostering and protecting of a religion accepted by the state as the true religion, whose precepts and tenets it was thought all good subjects should observe. In the code of laws of a country enjoying absolute religious freedom there is no place for the common law crime of blasphemy. Unsuited to the spirit of the age, its enforcement would be in contravention of the constitution of this state, and this crime must be considered a stranger to the laws of Kentucky.

"Wherefore it is adjudged that the demurrer be and it is hereby sustained, the indictment is dismissed, the defendant's bail bond is quashed, and the defendant is dismissed hence without delay. To this ruling of the Court the Commonwealth of Kentucky excepts, and prays an appeal to the Court of Appeals, which is granted."

A careful examination of the Kentucky reports has failed to show that this appeal was ever perfected. Evidently the Attorney General became satisfied with the law as laid down by Judge Parker.

THE IMPLICATION OF RUGGLES DECISION.

To say that the common law as to blasphemy was, by the framers of the New York Constitution, designed to be continued in force, is to assume without evidence, that the colonists, without cause, deliberately repudiated those two enactments of the General Assembly which had declared that, as between contending Christians, the test of psychologic tendency should no longer determine guilt, and that only *actual* disturbance of the realm should be foundation for a criminal prosecution against religionists, who theretofore had been penalized as "blasphemers." Justice Kent's ruling was a retrogression, in conflict with the evidence that the Constitution was designed to be progressive. That is to say, the Constitution, construed as a whole, was evidently designed to make applicable *to all* as a matter of right, what had been previously a privilege and a modification of the common law, for the benefit of only those who believed in God by Christ.

OTHER REASONS FOR OVERRULING RUGGLES CASE.

Let us now endeavor to study the Constitutional provisions above quoted, in connection with a brief recapitulation of colonial history as to toleration. And let us proceed with that study with a view to understanding the impulses and ideas which inspired the choice of constitutional language rather than to be content with the mere words themselves.

We know of the Established Church in England. We have seen the Treaty of Capitulation confirm certain privileges for the Dutch Colonial Church. We have seen how the same rights were subsequently extended so as to make them the equal property of all denominations in the colony. In the light of these prior events the language of the Constitution first above quoted becomes plain. *"No* denomination of Christians, *or their ministers,* are to be established or maintained." In other words, all privileges heretofore extended to Christians, as such, are now withdrawn, whether arising from the common law or colonial enactment.

The colonial Declaration of Rights and the Royal Charter had provided toleration for all those "which professed faith in God by Jesus Christ." A very contrary. spirit is breathed in the Constitution which declares its purpose to protect the citizen "against that spiritual oppression .and intolerance wherewith the bigotry and ambition of weak and wicked priests and princes have scourged mankind." To make this changed sentiment effective they also provide that "no minister of the gospel or priest of any denomination whatsoever shall at any time hereafter under any pretence or description whatever be eligible to or capable of holding any civil or military office or place within this State."

To my mind it seems impossible for a man of unprejudiced intelligence to read these provisions in the light of the antecedent controversy and Declaration of Rights, and the preamble to the constitutional provision above quoted, and then draw the conclusion that the framers of the Constitution intended to leave in force the common law as to blasphemy, which restricted religions much more than the colonial charters under which they had been living. Indeed, Mr. Justice Kent does not claim to do any such thing. He did not even consider the colonial controversies which the Constitution was designed to settle. He made no comparison between conditions under the colonial charter, and those which his interpretation of the constitution re-established. He did not attempt to co-ordinate Section 39, or the preamble to Section 38, with the Declaration of Right contained in Section 38. If he had undertaken to construe these together, in the light of the antecedent colonial conditions, with the desire to discover the purpose of the Constitutional Convention, he could scarcely have said in 1810, that the common law offense of blasphemy was a part of the law of New York State.

INDUCEMENTS TO CONSTITUTIONAL CHANGES IN 1821.

It has been pointed out that, in 1810, when Justice Kent decided the Ruggles case, the Constitution of New York contained no guarantee of freedom of speech and press. That provision was first adopted in the Constitutional Convention of 1821. It may help us toward an understanding of the Ruggles case in its relation to constitutional intellectual liberty to ascertain a little more in detail the attitude of Justice Kent toward the general issue.

The very celebrated case of the People vs. Croswell[14] makes clear one aspect of the free speech issue. It will be remembered and shown hereafter that Milton, Luther, Roger Williams, Thomas Jefferson and their adherents demanded in the interests of free speech that the test of the psychologic tendency to promote disorder should be abolished, and that only actual disorder should be punished. This of course was in opposition to the view promulgated by the English courts generally and summarized by Blackstone. It will be interesting to understand Justice Kent's attitude upon that issue, because we can then know best how to value his opinion in the Ruggles case, as an authority on constitutional interpretation.

The issue in the Croswell case was the right in certain libels to publish with impunity truth, with good motives and for justifiable ends, and, as inseparably associated

14 3 Johnson's Cases, 337.

with this the right of the jury to pass upon the intent
and psychologic tendency. These rights were upheld by
Justice Kent in an opinion which took a wide range. Let
us study his words upon freedom of utterance.

KENT FOR SEDITIOUS LIBEL LAWS.

He first quotes Lord Camden as saying: "A paper that
tended to excite sedition was libelous." And a discussion,
with that thesis, Justice Kent called "a vigorous and
eloquent defense of the freedom of the press." I should
rather call it a vigorous and eloquent misapplication of
the words "freedom of the press" to justify the English
system of censorship of the press.

Further on, Justice Kent comments on the Virginia
Resolution on tolerance, and he uses this language:
"I am far from intending that these authorities mean, by
the freedom of the press, a press wholly beyond the
reach of the law, for this would be emphatically Pan-
dora's box, the source of every evil. *And yet* the house
of delegates, in Virginia, by their resolution of the 7th
January, 1800, and which appears to have been intended
for benefit and instruction of the Union, came forward
as the advocates of a press totally unshackled, and declare,
in so many words, that 'the baneful tendency of the sedition act was but little diminished by the privilege of giving
in evidence the truth of the matter contained in political
writings.' They seem also to consider it as the exercise
of a pernicious influence, and as striking at the root of
free discussion, to punish, even for a false and malicious
writing, published with intent to defame those who administer the government. If this doctrine was to prevail,
the press would become a pest, and destroy the public
morals. Against such a commentary upon the freedom
of the American press, I beg leave to enter my protest.
The founders of our governments were too wise and too
just, ever to have intended, by the freedom of the press,
a right to circulate falsehood as well as truth, or that the
press should be the lawful vehicle of malicious defamation, or an engine for evil and designing men, to cherish,
for mischievous purposes sedition, irreligion and im-

purity. Such an abuse of the press would be incompatible with the existence and good order of civil society. The true rule of law is, that the *intent and tendency* of the publication is, in every instance, to be the substantial inquiry on the trial, and that the *truth is admissible in evidence, to explain that intent,* and not in every instance to justify it."

JEFFERSON AND NEW YORK AGAINST KENT.

Here, then, we have a clean-cut issue between the views of Jefferson and Kent on the rightful limits of toleration. We have by common consent disapproved of Justice Kent's opinion about seditious libel and none of the calamities which he prophesied have come to pass. Before that the people of New York, in the Convention of 1788 had, according to Kent,[15] "declared unanimously that the freedom of the press was a right which could not be abridged or violated." This convention was considering matters of Federal concern, and, while it expressed the sentiments of the people of New York, it had no authority to bind the N. Y. Court. Therefore Justice Kent even went so far as to ignore it entirely in the Ruggles case, where it would still have shed some light on the probable meaning of the constitutional provisions for a separation of church and state which he had under consideration. The same might be said of the election of Jefferson on the issue of his opposition to the Alien and Sedition Law.

Since the Croswell decision, the United States Supreme Court[16] upheld Jefferson, and by that act disavowed Justice Kent as an authority on the limits of religious liberty. In the Reynolds case the Court approvingly quotes Jefferson's conception, of which Justice Kent had disapproved.

Furthermore, the people of New York also overruled Mr. Justice Kent in their Constitutional Convention of 1821. Justice Kent was a distinguished member of that Convention, and opposed the free speech clause when it came up for adoption. The vote was 97 for such a provision; Jus-

---

[15] p. 391.
[16] In U. S. v. Reynolds, 98 U. S. 163.

tice Kent and eight others voted against it.[17] This constitutional guarantee was necessary to annul the restrictive
effect of Justice Kent's decisions in the Ruggles case, and
the inconclusive result of the decision in the Croswell
case. If Justice Kent had expressed a different view about
existing constitutional provisions in relation to religious
liberty, there would have been one less need for the free
speech clause adopted in the Constitution of 1821.

AFTER THE CONSTITUTION OF 1821.

The following is the opinion of Judge William Jay, as
delivered to the Grand Jury in Westchester County, New
York, after the addition of the free speech amendment to
the New York Constitution. This shows clearly a contemporary view of the meaning of free speech and of the
abuse of it as held by a friend of this constitutional provision. Justice Jay was one of the conspicuous ornaments of the judicial bench of his time. His brother,
Peter Jay, was a member of the Constitutional Convention
of 1821 which adopted the free speech amendment, and
one of those who voted for it and against Justice Kent.
Both were sons of John Jay.[18] Our libraries still contain
evidences of William Jay's efficiency as a libertarian
pamphleteer.

It is especially desired to point out that, in effect, Justice Jay limits "the abuse of that right" (of freedom of
the press) to personal libels when actual injury results,
and then only in those cases where there is not truth, good
motives, and justifiable ends. I say that it is the effect of
the language of the following opinion, because manifestly
truth cannot be made an issue of fact in those impersonal
discussions which deal with problematical, speculative
and abstract theories about government. Still more con-
spicuously is this true when we are dealing with the
metaphysical issues of religion. In such matters we do
not have such objective standards of judgment as form
proper evidence in courts of law. Therefore, in such impersonal matters the issue of truth must be irrelevant.

[17] Journal of the Convention, pp. 275-6.
[18] Appleton's Cyclo. Amer. Biog., v. 3, p. 411.

JUDGE JAY ON FREE SPEECH.

Justice Jay's charge to the jury was as follows:
"The preamble of our State Constitution declares: 'We
The People of the State of New York, do establish this
Constitution.' The Constitution thus established, ordains
that 'every citizen may freely speak, write and publish his
sentiments on all subjects, being responsible for the abuse
of that right; and *no law shall be passed to restrain or
abridge the liberty of speech or of the press.' The Constitution explains what it means by the citizens being responsible for the abuse* of this most inestimable right, by
providing that no man shall be convicted by a jury for a
libel in thus speaking, writing and publishing his sentiments on any subject, provided the jury shall be satisfied
that the matter charged as libelous *is true, and was published with good motives, and for justifiable ends.* It is
therefore evident that a citizen of New York is responsible
for speaking, writing and publishing his sentiments only
to a jury of this country, and to no other men under
heaven. This guaranty of freedom of discussion which the
people of this state have given to every citizen, extends
equally to religious and political topics. And *it is impossible to conceive any subject which we may not constitutionally discuss.* The right is sacred, and no individuals whether magistrates or others can interfere, to
prevent its exercise. *Hence, infidels and Christians, and
politicians of every name and character, have an equal
and undoubted right to publish their sentiments, and to
endeavor to make converts to them.* Of the abuse of this
right, Grand Juries are in the first instance the only judges,
and courts and juries are the only persons to whom the
people have delegated the power of punishing it. Even the
legislature cannot meddle with this right, and any law that
might be passed to *abridge in the slightest degree* the freedom of speech or of the press, *or to shield any one subject
from discussion,* would be utterly null and void: and it
would be the duty of every genuine republican, to resist,
with energy and decision, so palpable a violation of the
constitution, so audacious an outrage on the declared will
of the people."

This statement rested at first upon a mere newspaper report. Abner Kneeland, in 1835, used this charge in his own defence. So he wrote to Judge Jay and received a letter confirming the accuracy of this report, as expressive of his sentiments.[19]

RUGGLES DECISION OBSOLETE ERROR.

All the circumstances herein narrated combine to show that the Ruggles decision was error at the time of its rendition, and therefore has been overruled in Kentucky and authoritatively repudiated in New York, by the constitutional convention, and the contemporaneous interpretation of the courts; and its fundamental hostility to the conception of Thomas Jefferson on this subject, has been decisively repudiated by the Supreme Court of the United States. In consequence of all this, and of the defective intellectual processes which entered into the reasoning, and induced the judge to ignore the most essential factors of his problem, it is believed that the decision in People v. Ruggles is not deserving of any influence in any case involving a problem of our constitutional religious liberty.

Kent himself seemed to recognize in later years that he was not in harmony with the prevailing American idea of intellectual liberty. In his Commentaries he laments that "the tendency of measures in this country has been to relax too far the vigilance with which the common law surrounded and guarded character, while we are animated with a generous anxiety to maintain freedom of discussion." Furthermore, in the entire four volumes of his Commentaries (6th Edit.) he never once refers to the decision in People v. Ruggles.

---

[19] Kneeland's Speeches, Preface to Speech of Abner Kneeland, Delivered before The Full Bench of Judges of The SUPREME COURT In His Own Defense, for the alleged crime of BLASPHEMY. Law Term, March 8, 1836. pp. vi-vii.

VII.
KNEELAND DECISION CRITICISED.

In upholding the old Colonial statute the Prosecutor relies largely upon the case Com. v. Kneeland.[1] Hence the present and future importance of a critical review of that decision. Perhaps we are now far enough removed from the theocratic regime of early Massachusetts to be able to estimate that opinion at its true worth.

CASE INADEQUATELY ARGUED.

In the opinion of the majority it is said: "It is perhaps a subject of regret that the cause was argued by the defendant himself, without the aid of counsel competent to assist him, since it may leave some reason to apprehend that the questions really intended to be submitted to the consideration of the Court may not have been presented in the manner adapted to a clear and satisfactory statement and discussion of them."[2]

In the dissenting opinion occurs this similar complaint: "I have also some apprehension that all the grounds which might have been relied upon in defence, have not been raised and presented so clearly and fully as they might have been. The defendant, availing himself of his constitutional right to manage his own cause, and being not only unused to technical forms, and the mode of conducting trials, but unversed in some of the principles and distinctions of criminal law, and the authorities by which they are supported, has been unable to render us all the aid in raising and discussing the points essential to his defence, which might have been derived from the learning and experience of a professonal advocate."[3]

---

[1] 37 Mass. (20 Pick) R. p. 206, 1833-1836.
[2] p. 212.
[3] p. 225-226.

These quotations indicate a distrust which should warn us against a too hasty acceptance of the result. Inadequate argument is a poor corrective for emotional predispositions, if such existed, which is always quite probable where questions of religion were involved in Boston in 1833 to 1836. When our analysis of the decision shall have been completed, perhaps even Mr. Justice Shaw may be presumed to desire a reconsideration.

RUGGLES DECISION FOLLOWED.

The only judicial precedent approximately in point upon the constitutional questions involved was the decision in People v. Ruggles.[4] It has already been shown that the Ruggles decision ignored those factors that were most essential to a correct conclusion. The Ruggles case is not analagous to the Massachusetts case, because at that time the New York Constitution had not guaranteed freedom of the press; and, furthermore, its basic theories have been over-ruled by subsequent decisions and by constitutional amendment. In the light of the critical review of the Ruggles case that has been made, it ceases to be of any value, either as an authority, or even as an illuminating precedent. Thus the Kneeland case must stand or fall upon the merits of its own reasoning.

BLACKSTONE ERRONEOUSLY FOLLOWED.

Kneeland's claim, that he was protected by the free press clause of the Massachusetts Constitution, was met in several ways. The first answer of the Court expresses the sentiment of Blackstone, without citing him as an authority. The Court says: "The obvious intent of this provision was to prevent the enactment of license laws, or other direct restraints upon publication, leaving individuals at liberty to print, without the previous permission of any officer of government, subject to responsibility for the matter printed."[5]

Upon critical examination, the similar sentiment of

---

[4] 8 John. (N. Y.) R. 225.
[5] p. 219.　See: Blackstone as hereinafter reviewed.

Blackstone will be seen to have no application to the construction of American constitutional guarantees. Blackstone, in the language referred to, only recorded the fact of English juridical history as related to prosecutions for libels, and without intending to declare a general principle for differentiatng between an ideal liberty of the press and its opposite. Indeed, Blackstone never dreamed of attempting such a thing, for he heartily approved of the existing restrictive measures, as any other good Tory of his time would do. He complained only of the uncertainty of the criteria of guilt in some crimes against religion. Manifestly, our American constitutions were neither designed nor needed, if the purpose had been to perpetuate crimes against religion, and their *ex post facto* punishment.

OBJECTS OF OUR CONSTITUTIONS.

Anyone, honestly endeavoring to give to our constitutional guarantees of liberty a sympathetic understanding, must see that a dominant object of them was to get away from the then existing English system, and the previous Colonial methods, of penalizing mere psychologic offenses: that is to say, our forebears were seeking to overturn the English practice, as reported by Blackstone, in favor of that larger intellectual freedom advocated by his opponents. The Massachusetts Court did not consider this historical method of interpreting the Constitution and is therefore undecisive and of little importance as a precedent. Furthermore, the Kneeland decision entirely ignores the opposition that had existed to having a mere speculation about psychologic tendency used as the criteria of guilt, instead of making guilt depend upon actually ascertained material injury.

KNEELAND ON LIBERTY OF PRESS.

Chief Justice Shaw states Kneeland's contention as to the meaning of freedom of the press in these words: "Every act, however injurious or criminal, which can be committed by the use of language, may be committed with impunity if such language is printed. Not only, therefore, would the [constitutional] article in question become a general license for scandal, calumny and falsehood against indivduals, institutions and governments, in the form of publication, a form in which it would be the most injurous, and most speedily, certainly and extensively diffused; but all incitation to treason, assassination, and all other crimes, however atrocious, if conveyed in printed language, would be dispunishable. A mere statement of the direct and obvious consequences of the doctrine contended for, shows that it cannot be sound."[6]

It is fair to assume that this little explosion of "righteous indignation" would not have occurred if an adequate and discriminating theory of liberty of the press had been presented, such as an historical research would have suggested. The remarks of the Chief Justice convey an impression of considerable feeling, and a corresponding and consequent confusion of ideas.

ANOTHER VIEW OF FREEDOM OF PRESS.

If it had been suggested to the Court that freedom of speech and the press were primarily designed to protect the public in its right to hear and read everything that concerns it, and which any one is willing to offer, then a line might perhaps have been drawn between a personal libel upon a purely private citizen, and a defamatory statement against a candidate for public office, which defamation related only to matters directly and immediately affecting his fitness as a public servant.[7] Such a discriminating view would have suggested a like difference between the personal libel upon a mere private citizen, and every abstract discussion of religious, ethical and governmental problems, including seditious utterances. The English Courts characterized this distinction by the words "private libels" and "public libels." From this viewpoint the Judge might have avoided all the imaginary horrors which seem to have frightened him, and yet he might have upheld Kneeland's contention, so far as to hold the blasphemy statute unconstitutional.

[6] p. 219.
[7] See: 151 Mass. R. 54.

Again, if a discriminating argument had been made, pointing out the difference between an utterance which had resulted in an ascertained actual and material injury, thus affecting property rights or bodily personal injury, and a speech wholly void of resultant material harm, then, no matter upon what subject, or in what vocabulary or literary style it was expressed, the Court could have reached a different conclusion, without converting all of its imaginary fears into actual experiences. Certainly, it would not have put all personal libel, blasphemous and seditious utterances in the same category of public concern, and that wholly irrespective of differences in consequences.

IGNORED HISTORIC FACTORS.

Furthermore, if the Judges had been enlightened as to the controversy between the Puritan theocrats of the early witch-burning Massachusetts type, and the Puritan libertarians of the Rhode Island type, they might not have been so much horrified at the thought of opening the flood-gates of blasphemy, but would have considered that the public had a right to know, not only what scholars were thinking about religion, but also what the less enlightened were thinking and feeling about it. The Constitution guaranteed human rights to all, not merely free speech for the learned and the polite.

Then again, if the Court's attention had been called to the historic controversy for free speech as to government, and to the opinion upon that subject by the Continental Congress; and if the judges had read some of the speeches of the Massachusetts patriots before the American Revolution, and Jefferson's attitude toward rebellion and sedition[8]; if these matters, and Jefferson's opinion on toleration had been given their due weight as authoritative on the meaning of free speech[9], then it is hardly likely that the Judges could have been so shocked at the thought of a possible unpunished seditious speech. Even a study of the

[8] See: Methods of Constitutional Construction.
[9] Reynolds v. U. S., 98 U. S. 163.

Alien and Sedition Law and its fruits would have given a cooling light.[10]

SYNTHETIC METHOD IGNORED.

If, in addition to this historical data, used as a means of constitutional interpretation, the Court had viewed the Constitution as a whole, and, by a synthetic view of the several related parts, had endeavored to make each provision contribute something toward a better understanding of the meaning behind the words of every other part of the Bill of Rights, then again a different result might have been attained. These are commonplaces in statutory and constitutional construction, and yet this method was not used. We may wonder why. Mr. Justice Shaw has a deservedly high reputation for possessing an acute intellect. What precluded him from using it in the manner indicated? Is it possible that he was dominated by unconscious religious prejudices? Let us examine a little further.

TIME LIMIT FOR OPEN-MINDEDNESS.

Mr. Justice Shaw says: "It seems now somewhat late to call in question the constitutionality of a law, which has been enacted more than half a century, which has been *repeatedly enforced,* and the validity of which, it is believed, until this prosecution, has never been doubted, *though there have been many prosecutions and convictions under it.*"[11]

It was not altogether in harmony with legal reasoning for the Court even to suggest that Kneeland might be "somewhat too late" to urge the claim of a constitutional personal liberty, merely because *other* blasphemers were too ignorant to make the claim, or too poor to have it properly defended. He points to no Massachusetts statute of limitation which prohibits a judge from bringing an open mind to the discussion of problems of personal liberty, that have never before been adjudicated in a court of last resort; neither is there a statute of limitations against

---

[10] See: Methods of Constitutional Construction.

[11] p. 217.

78 BLASPHEMY.

the open-minded consideration of *new* reasoning upon questions already determined in other cases, especially if no property rights are involved through long acquiescence. A judge who, in face of such a problem, invokes the argument of time limitation, arouses the suspicion that he is only intellectualizing an impatience which is the product of passion and not of understanding. I have already hinted a distinction between a problem of purely personal freedom, and one where a long acquiescence in a particular construction of law, had determined great property rights, which would be disturbed by a new interpretation. Even then there would be no conclusiveness resulting from habit.

THE KNEELAND DECISION IGNORED.

Kneeland republished his "blasphemous" articles after his trial. Others publicly posted the blasphemous phrase for which the conviction was sustained. Still others published similar "blasphemies" in defiance of Justice Shaw's decision.[12] All this occurred right in Boston, and no prosecution followed. If we were to follow Justice Shaw's process of reasoning, it might be said that in Massachusetts, for nearly a century since the Kneeland prosecution, blasphemy has been published in open defiance of the statute and Justice Shaw's decision without judicial action, which proved that the community generally, and the courts, all acquiesced in the belief that Justice Shaw's decision was not the law, and that the blasphemy statutes are unconstitutional. It is now therefore too late to enforce the statute on the claims that it is valid.

RELIGIOUS LIBERTY IN MASSACHUSETTS.

If the "many prosecutions and convictions" referred to by Justice Shaw really existed, they may have aided the people to see that they still had too much union of church and state, to insure a proper interpretation of guarantees for intellectual freedom. The Massachusetts Constitution of 1780 made provision for the "support and maintenance

---

[12] See: A Review of Trial, etc., of Abner Kneeland. Also: An Introduction to the Defence of Abner Kneeland.

of public *Protestant* teachers of piety, religion, and morality." It also provided that "every denomination *of Christians* demeaning themselves peaceably * * * shall be equally under the protection of the law, and no subordination of any one sect or denomination to another shall ever be established by law."[13] It will be observed that this Constitution did not prohibit privileges to a group of Protestants as against the Catholics or against such Protestants as they chose to designate as unchristian. Some experimentation, and the active agitation of the Baptists, Unitarians, Universalists and Quakers, evidently convinced the people of Massachusetts that the separation of church and state needed to be more complete, if intellectual freedom were to be actually achieved. The sixth and eleventh amendments of the Massachusetts Constitution were obviously the product of a desire to eliminate discriminations, at least against Quakers, Catholics and non-Christian religionists. Article 11 became effective on November 11, 1833. Kneeland's "crime" was committed the next month. If there really had been any such numerous convictions as Justice Shaw asserts, it may have been that Kneeland felt that this last more complete separation of church and state was the people's way of overruling the former (hypothetical) decisions. The prior existent union of the State and Protestantism may formerly have induced an acquiescence in blasphemy prosecutions, which would naturally disappear with the coming of the constitutional amendments just referred to. *At best,* it was an unfortunate oversight that Justice Shaw should not have taken these changes into account. *At worst,* it looks like the product of his religious prejudice.

SHAW'S ERROR OF FACT.

Justice Shaw, in the passage already quoted, says that this blasphemy statute "has been repeatedly enforced," and that there "have been many prosecutions and convictions under it." My suspicions were aroused by the total absence of detailed information. I have just read: "Re-

---

[13] Mass. Declaration of Rights, Art. 3.

port of the Argument of the Attorney of the Commonwealth at the Trial of Abner Kneeland," to see upon what
facts Judge Shaw's statement might be justified. On page
48 the Prosecutor tells of one known prosecution, and
rumors of only one other of which any particulars were
given, and then only the name of the locality. The statement of the one known case is justified by a reference to
vol. VI, Dane's Abridgement and Digest of American Law,
p. 667. This publication is dated 1823. Turning to the
page indicated, we find only this brief reference: "Prosecutions under these laws [creating crimes against re-
ligion] have been very rare. One Avery was indicted in
the Supreme Judicial Court for this crime of blasphemy,
on the last mentioned statutes [in 1795], and sentenced to
be set on the gallows one hour, and to be whipped twenty
stripes. *No other prosecution on this statute has been
found.*" This covers from 1782 to 1823, a period of 41
years.

In the face of this record, what shall we think of Justice Shaw's statement that this statute "has been repeatedly enforced," and that "there have been *many* prosecutions and convictions under it"? We may at least suspect that upon the subject of religion the learned justice
was moved by some very intense feelings which obscured
the usual clarity of his vision. If this suspicion was warranted by the fact, then we see in it that which made Justice Shaw desire that Kneeland be estopped from requiring the Court to be open-minded about a question of constitutional and personal liberty, which had never before
been presented. The learned justice convinces us that he
is quite human, like the rest of us, and therefore when
zeal speaks, a rumor becomes a multitude.

COLONIAL BLASPHEMY LAWS.

The Massachusetts colonists at first legally established
a strictly sectarian theology. In harmony therewith, the
first blasphemy statute (1646) protected the reputation of
"the true God," only. For attempting to impair that reputation, no matter how futile the attempt might be, or for
any other blasphemy, those loving followers of a loving

God decreed that the recreant "shall be put to death," and the statute cited Levit. xxiv, 15, 16.

By the year 1697 these good people had been so far led astray, by the satanic influence of such as Roger Williams, that they were willing to turn their backs on Leviticus, and spare the life, even of a blasphemer. So, from the mercy of their heretical souls, came an amendment to the statute, changing the punishment to imprisonment not exceeding six months, by pillory, whipping, *by boring through the tongue with a red hot iron,* or setting on the gallows, etc.; provided that *no more than two of said punishments should be inflicted* for one and the same fact. Thus amended and humanized, according to the dictates of Puritanic love, the statute appears to have remained until 1782.[14] Under the latter amendment Kneeland was prosecuted.

THE INFLUENCE OF DISSENTERS.

The Colonial theocracy was frankly sectarian. Under the contaminating and depraving influence of Roger Williams, the Quakers, Universalists, Baptists and Unitarians, the orthodox Puritan mind became polluted. By the time of the adoption of the Constitution of 1780 it had become a "Protestant" Commonwealth, thus broadening out far enough to recognize at least some rights of some of those who were formerly regarded as dangerous heretics deserving the death penalty. (Was it by hanging, stoning or burning?)

The polluting influence of the Baptists and Unitarians grew rapidly under this recognition extended to them in an unguarded moment. Consequently, the Constitutional Amendments of 1820 and 1833 entirely eliminated the substance of the theocratic recognition of Christianity. Probably as a sop to the wounds of a few remaining faithful ones, the Constitution retained a harmless old homily about Christian duty, although everything was done that was possible to preclude the enforcement of those "duties" by law. Of course, a "duty" without a corresponding en-

---

[14] See Dane's Abridgement, vol. VI, p. 666.

forceable right is mere meaningless and idle rhetoric. As a judicial problem, this issue seems to resolve itself into a question whether duties to God shall be legally treated as mere empty rhetoric, or whether our constitutional guarantees for a separation of church and state and for intellectual freedom and equality, shall be treated as meaningless and idle rhetoric. Judges will choose according to their intelligence. Justice Shaw chose the latter, as is plain, and it is believed that in his decision he quite unconsciously exhibited the motive therefor.

INFLUENCE OF ROGER WILLIAMS.

In 1636 Roger Williams was banished from Massachusetts by a Court which had already decided "that any one was worthy of banishment who should obstinately assert that the civil magistrate might not intermeddle, even to stop a church from apostasy and heresay."[15] In spite of laws against everything unorthodox, the ideas of Roger Williams were dominant in the Massachusetts Constitution as amended in 1833. Notwithstanding this tremendous overturning of public opinion, Mr. Justice Shaw, in 1834-1836, sees in it nothing which suggests to his mind that the Constitution guaranteed freedom of utterance to the ex-clergyman and Pantheist, Kneeland. In all this record of extraordinary intellectual growth, he sees no sign that the framers of the Constitution desired to make impossible a return to the days of burning witches and hanging heretics, or to the days of boring a blasphemer's tongue with a red hot iron. He does not persuade us that the Constitution fails to record a growth from barbarous intolerance, through moderation, to complete religious liberty. He only convinces us that his own mind had escaped very much of the polluting influence of the religious libertarians. He evidently could not turn his back on the lessons of his childhood, derived from a father and grandfather both of whom were ministers in the orthodox persecuting church of colonial Massachusetts.[16]

---

[15] Bloody Tenet of Persecution, p. xv.
[16] See: Appleton's Cyclopedia of Amer. Biog. v. 5, p. 487; also: A Sermon Preached in Barnstable at the Ordination of Mr. Oakes Shaw. . . by John Shaw. Bost. 1761.

Let us look still closer into the performances of the Massachusetts Colonial legislature. This may help us to understand what possibilities Justice Shaw's opinion protected, and what it was that some people thought they had made impossible by constitutional provisions.

EVILS THAT WERE REMEDIED BY RELIGIOUS LIBERTY.

In 1646 the Colonial legislature of Massachusetts enacted: "that if any Christian within this jurisdiction shall go about to subvert and destroy the Christian faith and religion, by preaching and maintaining *any* damnable heresies, as denying the immortality of the soul, or resurrection of the body, or any sin to be repented of in the regenerate, or any evil done by the outward man, to be accounted sins; or shall affirm that we are not justified by His death and righteousness, but by the perfection of our own works; or shall deny the morality of the fourth commandment; or shall openly condemn and oppose the baptising of infants; or shall purposely depart the congregation at the administration of that ordinance; or shall deny the order of the magistracy, or their lawful authority to make war, or to punish the outward breaches of the first table; or shall endeavor to seduce others to any of the errors or heresies above mentioned; every such person, continuing obstinate therein, after due means of conviction, shall be sentenced to banishment." A second offence was punished with death or banishment.

The next year, 1647, it was enacted: "That no Jesuit or spiritual or ecclesiastical person," ordained by the Pope or See of Rome, at any time shall come into this Colony; and that if any one was justly suspected of being a Jesuit, he should be brought before the magistrates, and if he could not clear himself of suspicion [could not prove himself innocent?] he was to be committed to prison, or bound to the next court of assistants, to be tried and proceeded with by banishment or otherwise, as the Court might order. And if such Jesuit was banished, and returned, his punishment was death."[17]

[17] Dane's Abridgement, vol. VI, p. 667-668.

RECORDS OF PERSECUTION.

One can never secure an adequate picture of the evils and barbarity of these laws merely from reading the statutes. To this must be added a reading of such books as, George Bishop's "New England Judged," published in London in 1661. Therein he tells what happened to the Quakers within the four years after their arrival in Massachusetts. This included "cruel whippings and scourgings, bonds and imprisonment, beatings and chainings, starvings and huntings, fines and confiscations of estates, burning in the hand and cutting of ears, orders of sale for bondmen and bondwomen, banishment upon pain of death, and putting to death of some." Yet, according to Blackstone and Justice Shaw, proper liberty of speech obtained here because there was no "previous restraint," against Quakers expressing themselves.

According to the same author, a man was fined ten pounds for merely having in his possession a copy of John Lilburn's Resurrection, and of W. Dusberrie's, Mighty Day of the Lord. Yet religious and intellectual liberty existed because the publishers of these books were not restrained previous to publication.

Peter Folger, father in law to Benjamin Franklin[18] tells of a man who was put to death in Massachusetts before 1675 for saying that God's wrath would be spent upon the Colonists if they did not repeal their persecuting laws. There was no law imposing a previous restraint to this utterance. The man was only killed according to law because his dangerous and offensive speech was of pernicious tendency, and all this was "necessary for the preservation of peace and good order of government and religion, the only solid foundation of civil liberty." These cases, the banishment of Roger Williams, the burning by order of the House of Commons of his plea for toleration, are perfect illustrations of what is meant by constitutional liberty of speech and press, but only according to such Tories as Mansfield, Kenyon, Ellenborough, Blackstone, and Justice Shaw.

---

[18] See: Looking-glass for the Times, p. 5.

SHAW'S VIEW OF INTELLECTUAL LIBERTY.

All these Colonial laws our own learned Justice Shaw evidently considered to be in entire harmony with constitutional liberty of speech and of the press, for he has told us in this same Kneeland opinion that "the obvious intent of this provision was to prevent licensing laws, or other direct restraints upon publication." Not to prevent *ex post facto* punishment! Not to make impossible a repetition of Colonial barbarities! Of course not! The teachings of his clerical father, perhaps made the thought unbearable.

In a community which had conducted burning, hanging, branding and maiming as part of the "current amenities of theological parting," Justice Shaw saw no other motives for constitutional guarantees of intellectual freedom, except to prevent previous restraint. If burning a man to death, or boring his tongue with a red hot iron, comes as an *ex post facto* punishment of expressed heretical opinions, then perfect intellectual liberty is maintained. If, however, the life and the tongue are saved whole, by a previous restraint upon offensive utterance, then only is constitutional freedom of utterance destroyed. The corollary and natural effect of Justice Shaw's criteria of free speech is that the Constitution was really meant to keep alive and protect the possibility of re-enacting the above laws of Colonial Massachusetts. Is such an interpretation to be followed in 1917?

Some will refuse to follow Justice Shaw in his conclusions, because he shows no sign of understanding, or of willingness to examine, previous controversies and the resultant intellectual development which had expressed itself in the Constitution of 1833. Likewise to some who, upon such subjects of religious liberty are more enlightened than himself, he may perhaps appear to be merely making a special plea in justification of seventeenth century preconceptions. For all of these reasons Justice Shaw's opinion in the Kneeland case cannot be recognized as of any authoritative value. Its chief usefulness lies in its exhibition of a weak spot in an otherwise great man. Thus it may remind us of the folly of hero-worship.

SOURCES OF SHAW'S PREDISPOSITIONS.

For two or more generations Mr. Justice Shaw's ancestors had enjoyed the special privileges of ecclesiastical aristocrats, in an established state-church. For a time he and his aristocratic relatives were efficient bulwarks against the rising tide of democracy. His cousin William Smith Shaw was prominently identified with the "Monthly Anthology" wherein democratic conceptions of free speech received vigorous, tory criticisms, not help.[19] Such matter was but an echo from that aversion to democratic free speech, which found expression in the Alien and Sedition Law. This reminds me to say that he was the private secretary to his uncle President John Adams, the father of that law.[20]

Justice Lemuel Shaw has left another record suggesting his fear or aversion of complete democracy. His conception of government appears to have been something which governed the people from above, not as something arising out of the people. This I think is shown by a phrase in "A charge delivered to the Grand Jury for the County of Essex, at the Supreme Judicial Court held at Ipswich, May term 1832." There he said that government guards against "wild and licentious democracy." Those who feel and believe in a government from out of the people will never fear any democracy, by limiting the intellectual liberty of any part of it. Those judges who are truly republican in feeling and thought will hesitate to follow Mr. Justice Shaw's opinion in this Kneeland case.

THE RECURRENCE OF TYRANNY.

The battle for intellectual liberty is never finished, because tyrannous tendencies will never be entirely outgrown by all of the human family. With each suspension of aggressive libertarian work there necessarily comes into

---

[19] See: the review of Tunis Wortman's, Treatise on Liberty of the Press, vol. 3, p. 544, Oct., 1806, when the book was six years old.
[20] Appleton's Cyclopedia of Amer. Biog. v. 5, p. 487.

being a regression toward tyrannous modes of dealing with social problems. The signing of Magna Charta remedied nothing. Successive kings and courts ignored its manifest purpose. In consequence of this it became necessary, with the aid of more or less of coercion, to secure over thirty reaffirmations and supplements to it.

The same thing has occurred in New York and Massachusetts concerning intellectual liberty. Guaranteeing such freedom in paper constitutions did not eliminate the tyrannous tendencies of an efficient minority of spiritual aristocrats. Those men who in the early days of our Republic became judges, as in New York and Massachusetts, were very apt to approach these problems of intellectual freedom with the characteristic timidity of the English Tories. Thus have come the judicial annulments of our charters of liberty, through the pretense of interpretation. This is illustrated in the Kneeland and the Ruggles cases. In consequence of this, additional amendments to the constitutions became necessary, just as in England repeated affirmations of the Great Charter became necessary. The practical question is whether now we have got far enough away from the anti-Republican states of mind, of men like Justice Kent and Justice Shaw to make possible a synthetic and historical interpretation of our guarantees of liberty and thus achieve an over-ruling of the precedent created by these judges.

KNEELAND CASE BIBLIOGRAPHY.

Appeal to common sense in behalf of the freedom of public discussion on the late trial of Abner Kneeland, Boston, 1834.

An introduction to the defense of Abner Kneeland, charged with blasphemy before the Municipal Court, in Boston, Mass., at the January term in 1834, by Abner Kneeland, the defendant. Boston: Printed for the publisher 1834, 43 p.

Report of the argument of the attorney of the commonwealth at the trials of Abner Kneeland, for blasphemy, in the Municipal and Supreme Courts, in Boston, January and May, 1834. (Collected and published at the request of some Christians of various denominations.) Printed by Beals, Horner & Co., 1834.

A review of the prosecution against Abner Kneeland for blasphemy. By a Cosmopolite, Boston, 1835. 32 p.

Speech of Abner Kneeland delivered before the full bench of judges of the Supreme Court in his own defense for the alleged crime of blasphemy. Law term March 8, 1836. Boston: Published by J. Q. Adams, 44 p.

A speech delivered before the Municipal Court of the City of Boston in defense of Abner Kneeland on an indictment for blasphemy. January term, 1834, by Andrew Dunlap. Boston. Printed for the publisher 1834. 132 p.

Speech of Abner Kneeland delivered before the Supreme Court of the City of Boston in his own defense on an indictment for blasphmy. November term, 1834. Boston: Printed and published by J. Q. Adams, 1834. 32 p.

VIII.

BLACKSTONE NO AUTHORITY ON FREE SPEECH.

Judges are the evolutionary successors of the priest and of those who ordered the affairs of men for the rulers by divine right. Yet judges are human, quite human. This means that sometimes they are overworked, and, quite as often perhaps, are just a little bit indolent. These human qualities imply that sometimes they may be content to solve a large problem by misusing a phrase which has associations giving the atmosphere of "authority." The process is to dissociate it from its original setting, and so misapply it to inappropriate facts. This is made easily possible because the chosen sentence or paragraph expresses to the uncritical mind something which seems so obviously true as to preclude inquiry as to how small a part of the truth is really expressed, or how doubtful is its legitimate application to the new conditions.

I suspect that it has been by such process that several of our courts have come to accept Blackstone as an authority on the meaning of freedom of speech and of the press, as that is guaranteed in our American Constitutions. The present purpose is to point out the error of. such a procedure in the hope of correcting it.

BLACKSTONE AN EXPOSITOR, NOT A PHILOSOPHER.

To this end we need to remind ourselves that Blackstone's legitimâte rôle was that of an expositor and juridicial historian. He did not attempt to make any original contribution to the philosophy of law, nor pretend to point out the road of progress. He was never guilty of attempting a reform. This was especially true as to his comments upon freedom of speech and press. He reported all the current and some of the past abridgments of intellectual freedom, and expressed his satisfaction with things as they

89

were. This task and this attitude of mind gave him no capacity for speaking with authority on the meaning of that larger mental liberty contended for by those whose claims were subsequently conceded and guaranteed by the American constitutions.

Even in 1804 an English Lord Chancellor protested against the misuse of the great commentator: "I am always sorry to hear Mr. Justice Blackstone's Commentaries cited as an authority. He would have been sorry himself to hear the book so cited. He did not consider it such."[1] The proof of this is to be found in a footnote by Blackstone, placed at the end of his introduction to the fourth edition. Others have also questioned Blackstone's accuracy as a commentator.

For the purpose of this argument, we may agree that, as a mere reporter of juridical events, Blackstone possesses a high order of accuracy and utility. It does not follow that, if he leaves the task of a historian or an expositor, to express an opinion upon controversial matters of policy, his opinion upon the latter is entitled to any weight beyond that which his assigned reasons can supply. To illustrate, we may accept as true what Blackstone says about the law concerning witchcraft without giving any of the weight of authority to his personal endorsement of the witchcraft delusion.[2] Likewise, we may agree that he has accurately reported the abridgements of intellectual freedom which existed under English law, without accepting his personal endorsement of the current practice as expressing the whole end and aim of those agitators for a larger intellectual liberty who succeeded in having their views about free speech written into our constitutions. We may agree that Blackstone accurately reported the law as it was, without acting as though his opinions, which were so sympathetic with and expressive of those of the English Tories, are any authority as interpretive of our more democratic constitutions.

---

[1] Shanon v. Shanon, 1 Schoales & Lefroy's Ch. R. 324-327.
[2] Book 4, p. 60.

BLACKSTONE ANTI-REPUBLICAN.

In the beginnings of our country, Blackstone was almost the only law book read. It is said that there were more sets of his Commentaries in America than in England. Jefferson laments that "Blackstone is to us what the Alcoran is to the Mahometans."[3]   Again Jefferson says: "The exclusion from the courts of the malign influence of all authorities after the *Georgium sidus* became ascendant, would uncanonize Blackstone."[4]   And a reason why this might not be regrettable is that "Blackstone and Hume have made Tories of all England, and are making Tories of those young Americans whose native feelings of independence do not place them above the wily sophistries of a Hume or a Blackstone."[5]

After quoting Blackstone's doctrine of the absolute sovereignty of the king, the Supreme Court of the United States makes this comment: "This last position is only a branch of a much more extensive principle on which a plan of systematic despotism has been lately formed in England, and prosecuted with unwearied assiduity and care. Of this plan the author of the Commentaries was, if not the introducer, at least the great supporter. He has been followed in it by writers later and less known; and his doctrines have, both on the other and this side of the Atlantic, been implicitly and generally received by those who examine neither their principles nor their consequences. That principle is, that all human law must be prescribed by a superior. This principle I mean not now to examine. Suffice it at present to say, that another principle, very different in its nature and operations, forms, in my judgment, the basis of sound and genuine jurisprudence; laws derived from the pure source of equality and justice must be founded on the *consent* of those whose obedience they require. The *sovereign* when traced to his source must be found in the *man*."[6]

[3] Vol. xii, Writings of Thomas Jefferson, p. 392, Library Edition.
[4] Vol. xiii, Writings of Thomas Jefferson, p. 166, Library Edition.
[5] Vol. xiv, Writings of Thomas Jefferson, p. 120, Library Edition.
[6] Chisholm v. Georgia, 1 U. S. 419-458.

Even an English Court as early as 1784 has told us that "Mr. Justice Blackstone, we all know, was an anti-republican lawyer."[7] And yet some Americans are impelled to forget that when Blackstone was describing liberty of the press under a system of what he conceived as an absolute monarchy, he was describing only a limited intellectual liberty by permission. They forget also that Blackstone's opponents demanded an unabridged intellectual liberty as a conceded and constitutionally guaranteed right. These latter views, not those of Blackstone, were written into our constitutions. When our courts forget this they use Blackstone's views as interpretive of our constitutions instead of absolute monarchy.

TEXT WRITERS VS. BLACKSTONE.

Those authors not on the judicial bench are less restrained in their utterances of condemnation than are the judges. In order that Blackstone may be duly uncanonized, it becomes necessary to quote also a few professional critics who are not constrained by judicial etiquette. One of the most influential libertarians who took issue with Blackstone was Jeremy Bentham. He intimates in Blackstone the existence of "a resolution to justify everything at any rate, and to disapprove of nothing. * * * [He] stands forth as the professed champion of religious intolerance; or openly sets his face against all civil reformation."[8]

Mr. John Austin, one of the founders of the analytic school of jurists, in addition to voluminous concrete criticism, makes this general indictment against Blackstone: "He owed the popularity of his book to a paltry but effectual artifice, and to a poor, superficial merit. *He truckled to the sinister interests and to the mischievous prejudices of power;* and he flattered the overweening conceit of their national or peculiar institutions which then was devoutly entertained by the body of the English people, though now it is happily vanishing before the ad-

---

[7] King v. Shipley, Dean of Asaph, 4 Douglas 73-172-3.
[8] Fragments of Government, p. xxvii, Edit. 1823.

vancement of reason. And to his paltry but effectual artifice he added the allurements of a style which is fitted to tickle the ear."[9]

Mr. Rice, author of a book on "The Law of Evidence," has written a searching criticism under the title, "The Blackstone Craze." In it he says: "Especially is it in order * * * to refer to the vigorous protest of two distinguished former occupants of the New York Appellate Bench, who based their aversion to Blackstone, first, on account of its utter uselessness as a repository of existing law; and second, *because of its direct inculcation of vicious doctrines that have been wholly repudiated,* and yet leave upon the impressionable mind of the student the contour of a false theory that is apt to infest and hamper much of his subsequent research.

"It is a rank and driveling insult to the common intelligence of our profession even to refer to the major portion of Blackstone's Commentaries as affording even a feeble exposition of the modern law. Whole chapters devoted to *the ecclesiastical and governmental policy of Great Britain have not even a nebulous bearing upon any rule whatever in vogue in this country;* and in fact they have long been superseded by elaborate works on the British constitution that have been out of print for half a century. What species of mental leprosy will still insist upon feeding legal minds upon such Blackstonian draff as is found in his chapters on Benefit of Clergy * * * and particularly the chapters on English Criminal Law?

"Summarizing the contention * * * we may be allowed to say that a course of study that aims at the laborious exposition of principles of law that have lost their efficacy or application * * * of *criminal laws that are a smear alike upon our civilization, our humanity and our common sense, is* * * * an imposition upon practical methods, a prostitution of practical energy."[10]

"It has become quite the fashion to depreciate the study

[9] Albany Law Journal, vol. viii, p. 290, quoting Austin's Lectures on Jurisprudence, 3d ed., vol. i, p. 71; or vol. i, p. 69, ed. of 1911.
[10] Frank S. Rice, "The Blackstone Craze," Columbia Law Times, vol. vi, p. 1.

of Blackstone's Commentaries, on the ground that they are 'the charnel-house of dead law.' "[11]

Another critic, Mr. Reuben E. Sears, adds this: "It is this adoration of his for the then dominant feeling of society that makes him (in his fourth book) the servile apologizer of Charles I * * * that makes him brand the judges * * * as 'military hypocrites and enthusiasts'; *that leads him to say that the penalties for speaking in derogation of the Established Church are 'not too severe and intolerant'; that prompts him to exhibit his ideas of a merciful Providence when he tells us that these penalties 'proved a principal means, under Providence, of preserving the purity as well as decency of the national worship.'*

"*He tramples on the right of private judgment.* He insults our understanding. He tells us that those who act in opposition to the Established Church 'cannot be prompted by any laudable motive,' not even 'by a mistaken zeal for reformation'; that their arguments are 'the virulent declamations of peevish and opinionated men,' and 'calculated for no other purpose than merely to disturb the consciences and poison the minds of the people.'

"Thus, in an age when the great principles of civil and religious liberty were being so strongly agitated which are now so well established, he stands forth *the professional champion of religious intolerance,* the determined opponent of civil reformation. He records the abominable laws against Dissenters and Papists, by which they are, in effect, deprived of nearly all civil rights, and then adds: 'Everything is as it should be.'

"Thus, he treats with scorn those glorious, all-enduring principles for which Huss and Jerome went to the stake; for which honest-hearted Luther waged his long warfare against the Romish church; for which Zwingle, fired with the spirit of Swiss liberty, poured out his life-blood on the heights of Cappel; the same principles which were sanctified by the suffering zeal of Hooper and Latimer; the same principles for which glorious Pym and valiant Hampden

[11] Albany Law Journal, vol. viii, p. 290.

offered their heroic resistance to the tyrannic encroachments of Charles I, and whose independent sentiments
were made to be respected and triumphant by the invin-
cible Ironsides, of lion-hearted Cromwell at Marston Moor,
Naseby and Worcester; the same principles which lost to
James II his throne, and placed thereon the courageous
Prince of Orange; *the same principles for which our Revolutionary sires fought* so nobly and won so gloriously;
which in our own country again, and in our own times,
have been so honorably vindicated—the eternal and im-
mutable principles of civil and religious liberty."[12]

"It is true Blackstone in the later editions of his works
somewhat modified his expressions in regard to the Toleration Act and the offenses against the Established Church.
Yet by a subtle use of rhetorical expletives, he has left the
meaning the same as at first, or else left no meaning at all.
This led Bentham to say that our author had been made 'to
sophisticate, even expunge, but all the doctors in the world
would not bring him to confession.' "

My researches have failed to uncover one single writer
who has combined both the inclination and the courage to
say that Blackstone was even in the least degree qualified
to interpret our American democratic constitutions. Not
even those judges who read into our constitutions Blackstone's conception of liberty of the press have considered
his fitness to be accepted for such an authority.

BLACKSTONE AND GENERAL LIBERTY.

Of course Blackstone had to justify blasphemy laws because his assumed task was to defend the absolute sovereignty of the ruling caste. Literary talent alone could
never have given him distinguished political preferment.
But his great literary ability, devoted to the unflinching
defence of every existing tyranny, contributed mightily
toward his development from a pauper orphan to a celebrated public functionary, whose official acts contributed
absolutely nothing to his fame.[13]

---

[12] William Blackstone, in Western Jurist, vol. v, p. 529, 1871.

[13] But for an interesting and sympathetic account of Blackstone's career
see Charles B. Wheeler, "Blackstone the Lawyer and the Man,"
University of Cal. Publications, vol. xii; Univ. Chronicle, pp. 323-349.

We can best understand the value of Blackstone's conception of toleration if we see it in relation to his more general philosophy of government. He says: "This law of nature being coeval with mankind, and dictated by God himself, is of course superior in obligation to any other. It is binding over all the globe and in all countries, and at all times; no human laws are of any validity if contrary to this; * * * Upon these two foundations, the law of nature and the law of revelation, depend all human laws."[14]

From such a theory of government he must of course believe in laws against blasphemy, and, like our own Puritans, he could no doubt quote the revealed will of God in support. However, some American judges, in harmony with our American conception of a secular state, have said that "reason and the nature of things will impose laws even on the Deity."[15] Austin calls the most probable interpretation of the foregoing quotations from Blackstone "sheer nonsense."[16] Having such a medieval conception of the nature and origin of civil law, it was inevitable that Blackstone should also have a similar view of personal liberty.

To make it plain just how true all these criticisms are, if we view Blackstone from a democratic and libertarian viewpoint, it would be necessary to present a volume in critical review of his commentaries. Manifestly, this cannot be done here. The authors quoted above have performed that task in part, and yet not thoroughly from the viewpoints of which I am speaking.

ENDORSING TYRANNY AS PERFECT LIBERTY.

Those who are familiar with English history during the period just preceding our American revolution will know how to gauge the import of the following brief quotations from the Commentaries. Space limits forbid the reproduction of more. Blackstone exhibits his great devotion to

---

[14] Vol. i, p. 42.
[15] Fletcher v. Peck, 6 Cranch 8-143.
[16] Austin's Lectures on Jurisprudence, sec. 174.

tyranny by his extravagant praise of it under the name of liberty. He says that the "idea and practice of political and religious liberty flourish in their highest vigor in these kingdoms, *where it falls little short of perfection.*"[17]

"All these rights and liberties it is our birthright to enjoy entire; unless where the laws of our country have laid them under necessary restraints—*restraints in themselves so gentle and moderate as will appear upon further inquiry that no man of sense or probity would wish to see them slackened.* For all of us have it in our choice to do everything that a good man would desire to do; and are restrained from nothing but what would be pernicious either to ourselves or our fellow citizens."[18]

No man is an authoritative interpreter of our democratic and constitutional rights who cannot give them a more sympathetic understanding than is possible to a man capable of penning the foregoing paragraphs. Blackstone did not, nor did he attempt it, because the constitutions had not come into existence when he wrote, and he was incapable of sympathy with the spirit and ideals which called them into being.

BLACKSTONE ON FREE SPEECH.

The one paragraph on freedom of the press which our Courts have cited, and the sentiment of which has been appropriated by others of them without credit to Blackstone is the following, which is quite in accord with his general defense and love of tyranny.

"In this, and in other instances which we have lately considered, where blasphemous, immoral, treasonable, schismatical, seditious or scandalous libels are punished bv the Engish law, some with greater, others with less degrees of severity, the liberty of the press, *properly understood, is by no means infringed or violated.*

"The liberty of the press is indeed essential to the nature of a free state; but this consists in laying *no previous restraint upon publication,* and not in freedom of censure

---

[17] Vol. i, p. 126.
[18] Vol. i, p. 140.

for criminal matter when published. Every free man has an undoubted right to lay what sentiments he pleases before the public; to forbid this is to destroy the freedom of the press; but if he publishes what is improper, mischievous or illegal, he must take the consequences of his own temerity. To subject the press to the restrictive power of a licenser, as was formerly done both before and since the revolution, is to subject all freedom of sentiment to the prejudices of one man and make him the arbitrary and infallible judge of all controverted points in learning, religion and government. But to punish, as the law does at present, *any dangerous or offensive writings* which, when published, shall on a fair and impartial trial, be *adjudged of a pernicious tendency,* is necessary for the preservation of peace and good order of government and religion, the only solid foundations of civil liberty."[19]

Constitutions Overruled Blackstone.

As far as it can be done by a mere abstract statement of the law, Blackstone has given us a good portrayal of the various modes of restraining free speech for the protection of the prerogatives of royalty and the privileges of aristocracy. Usually this was the real object of censorship, even when the pretense was to protect religion, morality, God and peace. When our judges accept Blackstone as an authority on the meaning and limits of constitutional free speech, they overlook one very important fact, namely: *the only occasion for our constitutional phrases upon the subject was the desire to make it impossible for our legislators to re-enact those English laws against free speech which Blackstone approved.*

In other words our constitutions were never intended to endorse Mansfield, Kenyon, Ellenborough, Blackstone or any other Tory-Royalist conception of free speech. On the contrary, our constitutional guarantees were meant to register the fact that these English judicial conceptions of free speech had been overruled by the American people. If Blackstone's paragraph above quoted is an authority

---

[19] Com. vol. iv, p. 151.

upon the meaning of unabridged liberty, then he is equally an authority on the meaning of our constitutional guarantees for a separation of church and state. Thus, by the easy device of a Blackstonian interpretation of our constitutional guarantees of freedom, we may revive, not only the laws against Catholics, impostors, Nonconformists and heretics, but also those legally establishing a favored church. Here also Blackstone gave his endorsement. To show this I am going to quote Blackstone again. This time I will quote the first edition:

"Everything is now as it should be[20] unless perhaps that heresy ought to be more strictly defined, and no prosecution permitted, even in the ecclesiastical courts, till the tenets in question are by proper authority previously declared to be heretical. Under these restrictions, it seems necessary, for the support of the National Religion, that the officers of the Church should have power to censure heretics, but not to exterminate or destroy them."

To punish seditious utterances by boring a hole through the tongue with a red hot iron, as was lawful in Maryland, or to inflict the same punishment for denying the resurrection of the body, as was lawful in Massachusetts, does not involve either previous restraint or complete extermination. These, therefore, are in complete harmony with religious liberty and unabridged freedom of speech, "properly understood," as by Blackstone and by those American courts which accept him as an authority on constitutional liberty of speech and press.

Shall we now believe that a separation of church and state and religious equality mean only that heretics ought no longer to be destroyed or burnt? Is that not just as sensible as to accept Blackstone as an authority on the meaning of free speech or the existence of witches?

It is hoped that the foregoing considerations have much impaired Blackstone's toryism as an authority on the meaning of our religious liberty and free speech guarantees. Later will be exhibited the contrary views of Blackstone's critics. Then it will be claimed that it was the

---

[20] Book IV, ch. iv, p. 49, ed. of 1769.

opinions of the friends of intellectual liberty and not Blackstone's that were meant to be expressed in our constitutional guarantees of free speech. Likewise it will be contended that their opinions shall be used as an authoritative interpretation of the constitutional language, and that Blackstone's definition shall be disregarded.

IX.

BLACKSTONE'S CRITICS.

Having disposed of Blackstone as an "authority" on the meaning of our American constitutional religious and intellectual liberty, we may proceed to use him as a means of clarifying the issues that were fought out between those who were content with the conditions approved by Blackstone, and those who sought intellectual liberty, as that was afterwards assured by our constitutions. If we can get a clear view of the essence of the controversy between them, we shall have an exact understanding of that which our constitutions were meant to prevent in future. This may or may not give us the whole of the meaning of mental liberty, but it will surely give us one aspect, or one indispensable factor of our guaranteed liberty of conscience, of speech and of the press. It may be that absence of previous restraint is another such factor, or was but one of several different methods by which the more fundamental principle was denied. So, then, for the purpose of making clear the pre-revolutionary historic issues over intellectual freedom, and for the purpose of showing what intellectual freedom meant to those whose views were incorporated into our American constitutions, we will state a little more at length the defences for censorship as that was regarded at about Blackstone's time, and then contrast that with the opinions of Blackstone's critics.

THE DEFENSE OF CENSORSHIP.

Then, as now, the advocates for the suppression of unpopular opinions refused to see that, to admit the existence of the power to suppress any opinion, is, in the long run, more destructive to human well-being than the ideas against which they would have the powers exercised. Then, as now, the alleged immediate public welfare was the justification for every form of censorship, and some dangerous "tendency," only speculatively ascertained, and usually discovered in a feverishly apprehensive imagina-

101

tion, was always the test of guilt. "The most tyrannical
and the most absolute governments speak a kind of par-
ental language to the abject wretches who groan under
their crushing and humiliating weight."[1]

To make this clear it is necessary only to quote a few
passages from a publication dated A. D. 1680, written in
defense of the abridgements of freedom of speech and
press. Sir Roger L'Estrange,[2] quotes Calvin as saying:
"There are two sorts of seditious men, and against both
these must the sword be drawn; for they oppose the King
and God himself." He then exhibits the evolution of dangerous tendencies by these words: "First, they find out
corruptions in the Government, as a matter of grievance,
which they expose to the people. Secondly, they petition
for Redress of those Grievances, still asking more and
more, till something is denied them. And then, Thirdly,
they take the power into their own hands of Relieving
themselves, but with oaths and protestations that they act
only for the Common Good of King and Kingdom. From
the pretense of defending the Government, they proceed
to the Reforming of it; which Reformation proves in the
end to be a final dissolution of the order both of Church
and State. * * * Their consciences widened with their
interest. * * * First, they fell upon the King's Reputation; they invaded his authority in the next place; after
that they assaulted his Person, seized his Revenue; and
in the conclusion, most *impiously* took away his *Sacred
Life.* * * * *The Transition is so natural from Popular
Petition to Tumult that the one is but a Hot Fit of the
other; and little more than a more earnest way of peti-
tioning.* * * * They Preach the People into murther,
sacrilege, and Rebellion; they pursue a most gracious
Prince to the scaffold; they animate the Regicides, calling
that execrable villany an act of Public Justice, and entitling the Holy Ghost to Treason."[3]

---

[1] Erskine in defense of Carnan.

[2] A Seasonable Memorial in Some Historical Notes upon the Liberties
of the Press and Pulpit.

[3] In addition to "A Seasonable Memorial," see for similar argument
"A Discourse of Ecclesiastical Politic, wherein the Mischiefs and
Inconveniences of Toleration are Represented." London, 1670.

PREFERING LIBERTY WITH ITS DANGERS.

This argument, backed by the historical fact, is unanswerable to the point that to permit freedom of criticism of religion or of government and its priests or officials, and to allow the presentation of petitions for the redress of grievances, is to permit that which *tends* to promote actual treason or rebellion. It follows that those who were demanding the opportunity to express their sentiments in criticism of official conduct and petitions for redress, were in effect demanding the right verbally to promote treason with impunity, because that was the demonstrated tendency, more or less remote, of all reformatory effort. That freedom, with its attendant dangerous tendency, is exactly what unabridged freedom of speech and of the press meant to its advocates, and our constitutional guarantee for religious liberty and an *unabridged* freedom of utterance was a final decision in favor of that view and against all mere psychologic crimes, including even verbal "treason." In other words, the friends of free speech contended with Salust, that: "Liberty with danger is to be preferred to servitude with security."

Heretofore we have seen the views of those who believed in the absolutism of government, and *all* liberty as a revocable, limited liberty by permission. Our constitutional guarantees of liberty of speech and press were manifestly desired to secure some other conception of liberty, some irrevocable and "inalienable" right. What were the practical, essential and fundamental differences between these two conceptions of freedom?

Every censorship so far has made its defense behind question-begging epithets of undefinable meaning. In the language of Blackstone, already quoted, by means of subsequent punishment everything should be suppressed which can be characterized as "dangerous and offensive writings," adjudged to be so because of a "pernicious tendency." This also was the excuse for laws creating restraint previous to publication. The friends of free speech always denied that a mere "pernicious tendency" was a sufficient excuse for suppressing or punishing the expression of any unpopular idea.

THE DANGER OF MORALITY IN HERETICS.

Of course the determination of the existence of such a psychologic tendency before its fruition in actual or material injury, or in an overt act which is capable of inflicting it according to the known laws of the physical universe, is to make the law a mere matter of guess-work. Just so soon as we get away from scientifically established fact into the infinite sea of metaphysical speculation, every semblance of "law" disappears. Many have reasoned about atheism and agnosticism as Bishop Horsley did about Unitarians. He said: "Unitarianism being heresy, even the moral good of the Unitarians is sin."[4] Of course it must be so, because their every moral virtue made the major sin of their heresy more alluring, and so more effective for evil.

The processes of balancing the psychologic tendencies of an opinion in the minds and the emotions of an undefined hypothetical reader or hearer of the future is a task which the most skilled psychologist probably would not have the courage to undertake. Those who know the least about mental and emotional mechanisms are the most certain about their ability to decide such questions, and those who are the most intense in their moralistic vociferations upon this subject are, of course, the least capable of making a dispassionate study of that which they understand so little. Such a task requires the highest of specialized scientists, not moral sentimentalists.

A review of the opinions of the defenders of unabridged free speech will show that, aside from arguments for its morality and expediency, the essence of their contention was an opposition to making excuse for suppression, or the test of criminality, to depend upon an uncertain guess about the problematical, speculative, and prospective, psychologic influence of an idea upon a mere undescribed hypothetical hearer or reader of the future. The demand was that the jurisdiction of the magistrate should be withheld until that assumed psychologic tendency had ceased to be a mere matter of imagination, by having been ex-

---

[4] See: Dunlap's Defense of Abner Kneeland, p. 125.

pressed in an overt act of disorder doing actual and material injury.

FURNEAUX ON LIMITS OF TOLERATION.

Now we come to an exposition of the views of those who rejected Blackstone's defense of absolutism in the tyrant, —those who stood for religious liberty and free speech, and whose agitation crystalized into our constitutional guarantees upon that subject.

First and chief among the critics of Blackstone's conception of toleration was the Rev. Philip Furneaux (1726-1783). This learned dissenting divine not only induced Blackstone to modify his views somewhat, in the later edition of his Commentaries, but was also a principal factor in securing a more liberal attitude of the English government toward dissenters.[5] His pamphlets in favor of unabridged free speech grew into a book and appeared in several editions.

Here, then, is the statement of the Rev. Philip Furneaux. He says: "For if the magistrate be possessed of a power to restrain and punish any principles relating to religion, because of their tendency, and he be the judge of that tendency; as he must be, if he be vested with authority to punish on that account; religious liberty is entirely at an end; or, which is the same thing, is under the control, and at the mercy of the magistrate, according as he shall think the tenets in question affect the foundation of moral obligation, or are favorable or unfavorable to religion and morality. But, if the line be drawn between mere religious principle and the tendency of it, on the one hand; and those *overt acts* which affect the publick peace and order on the other; and if the latter alone be assigned to the jurisdiction of the magistrate, as being guardian of the peace of society in this world, and the former, as interfering only with a future world, be reserved to a man's own conscience, and to God, the only sovereign Lord of conscience; the boundaries between civil power and liberty, in religious matters, are clearly marked

---

[5] Vol. XX, Dict. of Nat. Biog., p. 331.

and determined; and the latter will not be wider or nar-
rower, or just nothing at all, according to the magistrate's
opinion of the good or bad tendency of principles.

"If it be objected, that when the tendency of principles
is unfavorable to the peace and good order of society, as it
may be, it is the magistrate's duty then, and for that reason, to restrain them by penal laws; I reply, that the tendency of principles, though it be *unfavorable,* is not
prejudicial to society, till it issues in some overt acts
against the publick peace and order; and when it does,
then the magistrate's authority to punish commences;
that is, he may punish the *overt acts,* but not the *tendency,*
which is not *actually* hurtful; and, therefore, his penal
laws should be directed against *overt acts only,* which are
detrimental to the peace and good order of society, let
them spring from what principles they will; and not
against *principles* or the *tendency* of principles.

"The distinction between the tendency of principles, and
the overt acts arising from them, is, and cannot but be,
observed in many cases of a *civil* nature; in order to determine the bounds of the magistrate's power, or at least
to limit the exercise of it, in such cases. It would not be
difficult to mention customs and manners, as well as principles, which have a tendency unfavorable to society; and
which, nevertheless, cannot be restrained by penal laws,
except with the total destruction of civil liberty. And
here, the magistrate must be content with pointing his
penal law against the evil overt acts resulting from them.
* * * * Punishing a man for the *tendency* of his principles, is punishing him *before* he is guilty, for fear he
should be guilty."[6]

These sentiments of Furneaux, and even the very language in which they are expressed, are so in conformity
with the Virginia Religious Liberty Statute as to leave
little doubt that the latter was taken from the former.
Jefferson himself said there is not an original thought or
word in the Virginia Religious Liberty Statute.[7] I continue to quote from Furneaux:

---

[6] pp. 52-55, ed. of 1770.
[7] V. IX, Publications Amer. Sociol. Soc., p. 78.

"For, though calumny and slander, when affecting our fellow men, are punishable by law; for this plain reason, *because an injury is done, and a damage sustained,* and a reparation therefore due to the injured party; yet, this reason cannot hold where God and the Redeemer are concerned; who can sustain *no injury from low malice and scurrilous invective;* nor can any reparation be made to them by temporal penalties; for these can work no conviction or repentence in the mind of the offender; and if he continue impenitent and incorrigible, he will receive his condign punishment in the day of final retribution. Affronting Christianity, therefore, does not come under the magistrate's cognizance, in this particular view, as it implies an offence against God and Christ."[8]

Let me continue to quote from Furneaux' Letters to Blackstone even at some length, so as to give a more accurate view of the attitude of those opposed to Blackstone's views. After this longer sample, we will content ourselves with more brief extracts from other writers of similar views.

"So that the particular reason on which you ground the 'indecency of reviling the liturgy,' namely, that it is 'setting up private judgment in opposition to publick,' appears to me to be very inadequate and unsatisfactory."[9]

"The next article in the composition of this crime, namely, reviling the common prayer, is, you say, "arrogance.' It is 'arrogant to treat with rudeness and contempt what hath a better chance to be right, than the singular notions of any particular man.' [Blackstone.]

"In using the phrase, 'the singular notions of a particular man,' you [Blackstone] put the case very favorably for drawing your own conclusions. To be sure, if a man adopts sentiments which never entered into anybody's head but his own, or which no one will embrace when proposed, the odds are against him. But this is not often the case; and is not so, in particular, with regard to the debate between the church and the Dissenters, the point

---

[8] pp. 61-62.
[9] p. 79.

here in question. However, he who treats the notions of
others with a rude contempt, does, I think, in most cases,
appear to affect a sort of superiority (call it arrogance, or
insolence, if you please), which usually ill becomes him
who assumes it, and is never very agreeable to those who
are the objects of it.

"But with relation to the query, Who have the fairest
chance of being in the right? those who follow the lead
of a publick establishment? or those who are, or profess
to be, impartial enquirers after truth? that, I think, is
not so clear, at least on one side of the question, as you
seem to imagine.

"Most establishments, even those which have been settled by authority of the civil power, have originated from
the clergy; at least, with respect to their formularies of
doctrine and worship; and the magistrate hath had little
more to do in the affair, than to establish what hath been
already prepared to his hands. Let us, then, look into
ecclesiastical history, and see what the councils, synods,
convocations, and other general, national, or provincial
assemblies of the clergy, have, for the most part, been,
from the first famous and revered Council of Nice, down to
the last session of our own convocation in England. When
I reflect on the policy and artifice used in the management
of such assemblies; on their obsequiousness to the caprices
of princes, and ministers of state, or of potent ecclesiastics,
and even of some of their own ambitious and turbulent
members; on their prejudices and passions, their private
and party views, their scandalous animosities and contentions; on the small majorities by which questions of
importance, intended to bind not only the men of that age
but their posterity, have been determined: on the respectable characters which have often appeared in the minor
number: and above all, on their self-contradictions, and
their mutual censures and anathemas; I say, when I consider these things, I own, they somewhat abate my reverence for the determinations of such bodies. * * *10

"The third article which you [Blackstone] exhibit

---

10 pp. 79-83.

against *reviling* the liturgy, is, that it involves in it 'ingratitude, by denying indulgence and liberty of conscience to the members of the national church.' There would be little room, surely, sir, to complain of violations of liberty of conscience, if, in contending for their respective dogmas, men never went beyond *contemning and ridiculing* one another; for, however censurable this may be, it certainly is not denying them liberty of conscience; that always implies restraint or compulsion, ideas very different from contempt and ridicule.

"But perhaps, reviling the liturgy may be censured, as ungrateful, on account of the toleration indulged to Dissenters. It is not, however, to the Church the Dissenters are peculiarly indebted for this blessing. For though her governors promised them every mark of Christian temper and brotherly affection, when her fears of Popery ran high in the reign of James the Second; yet, as soon as the storm subsided, these promises were, in great measure, forgotten. It is to that great prince, King William, to whom the British constitution and liberties owe their preservation and security; and to those renowned patriots who first engaged, and then supported him, in the glorious enterprise; it is to these, and such as these, the Dissenters are, under God, alone obliged for their deliverance from unjust violence and oppression; and for being restored, in part, to their natural rights by the toleration. I say, to their natural rights; for religious liberty- is one of those rights to which men are entitled by nature; as much so, as to their lives and properties; and it should be remembered, therefore, that the Dissenters cannot be justly reckoned to be any more obliged to those who *kindly* do not again deprive them of it, than they are to those who *as kindly* do not seize on their estates, or take away their lives; an obligation which, I suppose, hath never been esteemed a reason for any *peculiar gratitude.*

"And now, sir, notwithstanding the exceptions which I have taken to your premises, I will leave you in full possession of your conclusion; I will suppose, that the crime of *reviling* the liturgy is a complication of '*indencency, arrogance, and ingratitude;*' and I will add, moreover, that it may possibly imply (and, I think, it is the principal thing that can be implied in it, though you have not at all mentioned it), *great malignity and inveterancy* against the church. But, surely, to confiscate a man's goods, and imprison him for life, *for any degree of any of these evil dispositions towards the church, when discovered only by words (though it be frequently, and they be ever so open and explicit) and not by any injurious and dangerous overt acts;* must be considered, one would think, by persons of humanity, and doubtless, therefore, by you, sir, upon further reflection to be somewhat too severe and intolerant. Notwithstanding all the *bitterness* with which the puritans inveighed against the offices of the church (and which they did not do, till by oppression they were provoked almost to madness), the passing this act, in my opinion, discovered a very intolerant spirit in those who, at that time, had the conduct of publick affairs.

"But perhaps it may be said, that this measure was adopted only out of prudence, for the *security* of the national establishment. You inform us, that 'the terror of these laws (for, you say, they seldom or never were fully executed) proved a principal means, under Providence, of preserving the purity as well as decency of our national worship.' Which, give me leave to say, sir, is passing no great compliment upon the national worship.

"But however that may be: what had the church to fear from the *revilings* of the puritans, that she must fence herself around with human terrors? We are to suppose, she had all the truth and argument, as well as the encouragement of the civil magistrate, on her side. In this case, having recourse to human terrors was bringing disgrace on a good cause, and doing credit to a bad one. For the presumption, in most men's minds, is always in favor of the cause which is oppressed and persecuted; and that this is the case, is owing, partly, to a certain generosity in mankind, which inclines them to side with the weakest, and those who are ill-treated; and partly to a persuasion, which appears not wholly unreasonable, that while argument can be maintained, terror will not be employed. And for my own part, I am persuaded, that the church, instead

of insuring its safety by these methods, greatly increased
the number of its enemies, and inflamed their animosity
and inveteracy. Had the governors of the church or state,
at that time, made a few concessions, such as not only the
puritans, but many wise and great men in the church,
desired; or, in case * * * they had indulged and tolerated those puritans, who could not in conscience conform, it is my opinion, the church would have been in no
more danger from the puritans of that age, that it is now
in from the Dissenters of this. Such severe *laws occas-
sioned the very crime they were intended to prevent;* for
they imbittered men's spirits, and inflamed their passions;
and when the mind is greatly irritated, it is hardly in
human nature to speak with temper and moderation,
either of those by whom, or of that for which, men feel
themselves ill-treated and oppressed.

"I would further observe (and it is an observation I
would submit to a gentleman of your profession, in particular) that, on supposition this act was levelled only,
as you seem to imagine, against the *bitter reproaches and
insults* of the puritans, it seems to have been drawn with
too great latitude of expression. I believe you will admit,
and, I think, you have somewhere said something like it,
that it is the excellence of any law *to define offences and
punishments with the utmost precision, that the subject
may know distinctly what is lawful and what is forbidden.*
But is this the case with the act before us, supposing it to
be designed merely against reviling and outraging the
offices of the church? For, what is the precise idea of one
who speaks, in open words, in derogation of the common
prayer? Surely, under an expression of such latitude
may be included every man, who openly declares his dis-
approbation of any part of it; that is, any one who gives
his reasons for not joining in the offices of the church;
and he may, by a willing judge and jury, nay, ought, according to the literal sense of the words, to be convicted
upon this statute. Now, supposing this law was intended
only, as you seem to think, against *insulting and reviling
the liturgy; can so good a lawyer as Dr. Blackstone ap-*

*prove of a statute, which is so worded as to comprehend
persons who are entirely innocent of the crime intended?*

"But in truth, I cannot help thinking, that it was the
actual intention of those who promoted this act, to put
an effectual stop, if possible, to the puritans' *arguments* as
well as their *revilings;* and that, on this account, the act
was so expressed, as to include every man who finds fault
with the common prayer, though only in a way of argument. For certainly, that is, 'in open words speaking in
derogation of it.' The intent of the act at that time, I
am afraid, was, to prevent the questioning any part of the
service of the church, either in a way of reasoning or
reviling.

"Before Dr. Blackstone, therefore, had declared his
approbation of this statute, and much more of the continuance of it to the present time, he should have considered, what persons and what cases, according to its
literal and just construction, and perhaps according to
its original intention, may be affected by it; and whether
he would chuse to vindicate it in its full extent. In every
view it appears to me very surprising, that you, sir, who
have expressed yourself, on various occasions, with so
much liberality of sentiment, should think 'the continuance of this act not too severe and intolerant.' "[11]

This ends the quotations from Furneaux. It is believed
that enough has been shown to make it very plain that
this friend of free speech repudiated all the arguments of
moral sentimentalism, which either the past or present
friends of blasphemy laws put forth in justification.
Neither he nor any other friend of complete mental freedom ever dreamed of contenting themselves with arguing
against previous restraint, or censorship of literary style.
The censorship laws which had provided for previous restraint had been repealed for nearly four score years when
Furneaux wrote his criticism of Blackstone's endorsement
of then existing intolerance. The demand was not for
relief from previous restraint, but from subsequent pun-

---

[11] Furneaux, Letters on Toleration, Letter IV, pp. 89-100. Different
editions of these "Letters" vary a little.

ishment, and from being penalized upon uncertain speculations about psychologic tendencies. The demand was for a resort only to overt acts to produce actual and material injury. It will be observed that there is also a repudiation of the idea that punishmenc may properly be based upon the style or temper of the utterance.

BENTHAM ON FREE SPEECH.

Furneaux had his mind focussed on religious toleration, but by insisting on an overt act as the only proper basis of suppression or test of crime, and in opposing a mere guess about a psychologic tendency as criteria of guilt, he furnished a general standard of judgment, applicable to all problems of free speech that can arise under our constitutions. Jeremy Bentham, another of the distinguished critics of Blackstone, approached the problem of tolerance more from the point of view of a political and parliamentary reformer. The interesting and important thing about it is that Bentham reaches the same concluson as Furneaux, namely, that if intellectual liberty is to be maintained we must abolish speculations about psychologic tendencies as the criteria of guilt, and substitute therefor overt acts, actually constituting real disturbance and real injury. Jeremy Bentham, in his criticism of Blackstone's views on free speech says:

"In regard to a government that is free and one that is despotic, wherein is it then that the difference consists? * * * * On the liberty of the press; or the security with which every man, be he of the one class or the other, may make known his complaints and remonstrances to the whole community; on the liberty of public association; on the security with which malcontents may communicate their sentiments, concert their plans, *and practice every mode of opposition short of actual revolt,* before the executive power can be legally justified in disturbing them."[12]

REV. JOSEPH FOWNES.

The next person whom I will quote is the Rev. Joseph Fownes, as to whom little seems to be known. His book

---

[12] Bentham's, Fragment on Government, p. 153-154, Edit. 1776.

"An Enquiry Into the Principles of Toleration," was published in the second edition in England in 1773. The first
edition was published anonymously. In the catalogue of
the library of the British Museum, it appears that he also
published several items under the pseudonym of "Phile-
leutheros." Notwithstanding such literary prominence
his name does not appear among collections of English
biographies which I have examined. I suspect the explanation for this absence of information is to be found
in his coming to America. Some time about 1810 there
appeared in Boston a pamphlet entitled "A Blow at the
Root of Aristocracy, or an Appeal to Matters of Fact, in
Support of Religious Freedom," and signed "Phileleu-
theros." Insofar as this speculation identifies Joseph
Fownes with agitation for intellectual freedom in America,
his opinions acquire an added force as a factor in construing our constitutional guarantees. This first book
was in part inspired by Blackstone, and definitely took
issue with his conception of intellectual liberty. In the
second edition, 1773,[13] he answers an objection such as
doubtless had been made often, and must have been in the
minds of those who framed the Constitution of Connecticut. He says:

"Religion, it will be urged, may be made a plea for
anything; and, if governors must never interpose to restrain it, there is no enormity but what will pass unpunished."

Then he goes on to explain away the fear by calling
attention to the same old line between actual injury and
constructive injury, though I think he uses less precision
therein than some others. The Supreme Court of the
United States answers the same contention as to Mormon
polygamists in U. S. v. Reynold, 98 U. S. 163. That
Court, by following Jefferson and the Virginia Act of
Toleration, in fixing the limits of intellectual liberty,
reaches the same conclusion as Furneaux, Fownes, Milton,
Bentham, and the rest. The makers of the Connecticut
Constitution were unwilling to leave it to future construc-

---

[13] Page 18, of "An Enquiry Into the Principles of Toleration."

tion, such as was made in the Reynold case, and so sought to compel the same construction by appropriate words, answering to the fears of the people.

Fownes[14] says: "The instances, in which this inconvenience may be supposed to arise from liberty of conscience, may, I presume, be generally reduced to one of these cases. The case of persons who think themselves bound to use force for the propagation of what they apprehend to be truth. The case of those, whose principles lead them to judge, what are commonly thought vices hurtful to society, to be innocent, and what may be indulged without scruple. Or, lastly, the case of those, who are so unhappily misled as to incorporate things hurtful to society into their religion, and account it their duty to practice them." He shows that the principles of toleration and religious freedom neither lead to these evils nor take away the power of the magistrate to restrain them, insofar as they are real and not imaginary or merely psychologic.

To the first he answers: "Every attack which he makes upon their person, liberty or estate, for this purpose, is an injury, which comes within the limits of the civil power.[15] To the second he answers that: "Fraud, robbery, perjury, and other crimes of the like nature, are directly repugnant to all the essential and acquired rights of men."[16] Manifestly, he is writing of property rights. To the third he answers thus: "If his judgment should unhappily lead him to make anything a part of his religion, *which is injurious to others,* and contrary to the fundamental laws of society; he so far still falls under the animadversion of the magistrate. * * * He acts *not as the dictator to his subjects in spirituals, but as the guardian of their temporalities.* * * * By attending to this obvious distinction, the rights of conscience and the real rights of government will both be preserved, and the pernicious extremes of calling either in question will be avoided.

[14] In an Appendix, p. 114.
[15] p. 115.
[16] p. 116.

Religious liberty will be kept from running into licentousness; civil authority be preserved from degenerating into tyranny."[17]

AN ANONYMOUS CRITIC.

Next I quote from an interesting essay entitled: "Areopagitica, an essay on the Liberty of the Press, dedicated to the Rt. Hon. Charles James Fox, the friend of Truth and Liberty, London, 1791" (Not by Milton and anonymous). About the criminality of publishing truth he says: "To punish the effects of virtue, is to punish virtue itself. It surely can never be admitted as a reason for such an attack upon the moral obligations of society, 'That every libel has a *tendency* to a breach of the peace, by provoking the person libelled to break it.' If such argument is to prevent us from the publication of Truth, there is an end of all active morality, and there is no distinction, in the eye of the law, betwixt crimes and virtues."[18]

"What reason can be given for the punishment of moral duty? Is it a satisfactory answer, that the provocation to others to commit crimes is a reason why men should not be virtuous? Laws which punish Truth cannot be made for the protection of good men, and surely laws for the protection of villiany are inconsistant with public happiness."[19]

"Thus in the eye of the law [as quoted from Blackstone], it is not a previous restraint to be restrained from publishing the Truth, or to be certain of fine, imprisonment and pillary, for the publication of what can be proved to be true, and intended for public good or private vindication, or any other general or individual advantage."[20]

"To say that the press is free when the punishment of publication is certain, is to place a trap for virtue, honor, and good conduct. The Author is indeed in a much worse condition than he was in the times before mentioned, for he might then be secure by procuring a license."[21]

[17] pp. 116-117.
[18] p. 12.
[19] p. 15.
[20] p. 18.
[21] p. 19.

"The case of (a) trial for a breach of the peace [committed] by the publication of truth, is surely a mockery of common sense and common justice."[22]

"We have seen from the law laid down by Blackstone, and the present practice of the courts in cases of libel, that the boasted Liberty of the Press, consists in being able to publish, with a probable certainty of punishment, and without a possibility of vindication, in a prosecution by indictment. The business of the jury is very short and the proceedings summary."[23]

WORTMAN ON BLACKSTONE.

Unfortunately no biographical data as to Tunis Wortman was found beyond two books and two pamphlets of his authorship. From these it appears that he was a strong advocate of the election of Jefferson. After his election he delivered an oration on the occasion of celebrating his inauguration. One of Wortman's books is entitled "A Treatise Concerning Political Inquiry and Liberty of the Press," New York, 1800. Wortman was a member of the New York Bar and in this volume wrote an eloquent and impassioned defence for unabridged liberty of political inquiry. On the whole, it is a defence of Jefferson's conception of intellectual liberty. In the course of this treatise, he makes the following comment on Blackstone:

"It is essential to examine the prominent principles of the present doctrine of Libels, in order that we may accurately appreciate the ground upon which it is usually vindicated. Its first proposition is, that in criminal prosecutions *the tendency which all Libels have to foment animosities, and to disturb the public peace, is the sole consideration of the law;* and that it is, therefore, perfectly immaterial, with respect to the essence of a Libel, whether the matter of it be true or false—since the *provocation*, and not the *falsity*, is the thing to be punished criminally. * * *

---

[22] pp. 38-39.
[23] p. 40.

"Truth can never be a Libel. The system which maintains so odious a proposition, is founded in the most palpable injustice. * * *

"Criminal prosecutions for Libels can never be necessary to preserve the public tranquility: the coercion of Violence is abundantly sufficient for that purpose. * * *

"It perpetually implies a want of confidence in the energy of the law, and conveys an impolitic acknowledgment of the imbecility or the insincerity of Government. It tells us that the Civil Magistrate is too impotent to suppress the ebullitions of Wrath, and must therefore act the tyrant over Truth. * * *

"The public peace must be preserved. Our laws are so disgracefully imbecile and imperfect, that we cannot maintain tranquility without the sacrifice of Truth. * * *

"Another prominent principle of the present doctrine concerning Libels, is, that 'the Liberty of the Press entirely consists in laying no previous restraints upon publications, and not in freedom from Censure for Criminal matter when published.' This definition, of which the principal force consists in its excluding the idea of a prevous *imprimatur*, is true as far as it extends; but it is extremely imperfect. Of what use is the liberty of doing that for which I am punishable afterwards? In the same sense it may be said that I have the liberty to perpetrate felony or murder, if I think proper to expose myself to the penalties annexed to those crimes. In ascertaining the rights I possess, it is not to be enquired what I may do, and be punished; but what I am entitled to perform without being subjected to punishment."[24]

PRIESTLY ON BLACKSTONE.

The Rev. Joseph Priestly did not believe in the total immediate disestablishment of all churches. On page 197 of "Essay on First Principles of Government," he endorses the levying of taxes to support all religions, everyone being obliged to support some church. He says: "It would not indeed be perfect and unbounded liberty in

---

[24] Wortman's Treatise on Liberty of the Press, Chap. XVI., pp. 251-256

matters of religion, but it would be pretty near it, and might make way for it" (p. 202). Later on Dr. Priestly came to America, and this together with his conservatism makes his comments on Blackstone doubly important.

Dr. Priestly criticised Blackstone, in a pamphlet: "Remarks on Some Paragraphs in the Fourth Volume of Dr. Blackstone's Commentaries." Priestly, however, attempted mainly to criticise Blackstone's historical accuracy in dealing with dissenters, rather than his generalization about the meaning of free speech. He begins with criticising the laws against speaking derogatively of the prayer books. "Why may I not speak in derogation of the book of common prayer, or even in contempt of it, if I really think it a defective and contemptible performance? Where is the great crime if, insulted as Dissenters have always been, with the malice, and nonsense of high churchmen, they should now and then speak or even write in their own vindication? * * * How is it possible to vindicate our conduct as Dissenters, that is our not using the common prayer book, without speaking in derogation of it? (p. 8.) * * * The paragraph [from Blackstone] I am animadverting upon, is calculated to do as much mischief as most things I have ever read, tending to inflame the animosity of a party and to increase our unhappy division (p. 10) * * * and propose that instead of 'virulent declamations of peevish and opinionated men' he [Blackstone] would write the calm reasonings of sober and consciencious men." So Priestly really makes a plea for equality of liberty for excited speech.

He does not demand Blackstone's suppression for excitement against dissenters, but demands that Blackstone and the law should give Dissenters the same freedom exercised against them.

"Besides, there is something in the nature of religion that makes it more than out of the proper sphere, or province of the civil magistrate, to intermeddle with it" (p. 139).

"The sanctions of the church of Christ in this world are, like itself, and like the weapons of the Christian warfare, not carnal and temporal, but of a spiritual nature;

and do not affect a man's person, life, liberty or estate
(p. 153). * * * All that the New Testament author-
izes a Christian church or its officers to do, is to exclude
from their society those persons whom they do not deem
worthy of it. * * * All that can be done to those who
are guilty of contempt against church power, is to leave
them to the judgment of God * * * who is *a better judge
of its real danger* than man can be (p. 155). * * * Let
them not only predict, but if their zeal prompt them to it
let them impricate divine judgment. Let them pray that
God *would speedily plead his own cause,* taking it for
granted to be their own. Were I the obnoxious person, I
should be very easy upon the occasion, provided their own
cruel and merciless hands were not upon me" (p. 156).
This then is free speech and religious liberty as conceived
by Blackstone's critics. This is the conception written
into our constitutions.

FURNEAUX AND PRIESTLY TO JEFFERSON.

What interests us now is the fact that Priestly and
Furneaux's criticism of Blackstone were re-published in
Philadelphia in 1773,[25] and so became a part of the American agitation for freedom of the press and strengthens
the arguments that their views and not Blackstone's were
meant to be incorporated in your Constitution.

It is hoped that this makes clear the issue between
Blackstone and his critics. Governments that abridge intellectual liberty always make the same justification as
Blackstone did. That is, the dominant class wishes to
relieve itself of the annoyance and the disturbance inci-
dent to having the wisdom or the justice of its dominance
questioned. That and not a longing for general justice
or truth is the real motive for wishing to prohibit "dangerous and offensive writings." When the danger has

---

[25] The *palladium* of conscience, or the foundation of religious liberty
displayed, asserted and established, agreeable to its true and genuine
principles, above the reach of all petty tyrants who attempt to lord
it over the human mind. Containing Furneaux's letters to Blackstone, Priestly's remarks on Blackstone, Blackstone's reply to Priestly
and Blackstone's Case of the Middlesex Section * * * Philadelphia,
P. Bell, 1773.

become realized in overt acts, which are injurious to persons or property, the purveyor of dangerous ideas becomes liable as an accessory before the fact, of some other crime, or more directly liable, as in personal libel. In such cases there is no need to resort to speculation about psychologic tendency because the actual and material injury are evident and can be easily proven if they exist.

The foregoing quotations make it plain that the critics of Blackstone demanded that the state have no jurisdiction until the "dangerous and pernicious tendency" eventuates in an overt act, which is actually dangerous to person or property according to the known laws of the physical universe, and not merely dangerous according to a metaphysical speculation about the unrealized psychologic tendency of an idea or of literary or oratorical style, upon some hypothetical hearer or reader of the future. From the standpoint of Blackstone's critics this was the essence of mental freedom, as to religion.

X.
U. S. A. *versus* BLACKSTONE.

In the year 1803, at Philadelphia, there was published an American edition of Blackstone's Commentaries. It was edited by St. George Tucker. To each volume is attached an appendix containing short tracts upon such subjects as seemed to the editor to be necessary to an understanding of the changes wrought by our Constitutions and the laws of Virginia. Under Blackstone's definition of liberty of the press is a reference to an "Appendix to volume first part second.... Note G.." That note reveals so much of the past and contemporaneous attitude toward religious and intellectual liberty and contains so much of exact and close reasoning that it will be reproduced in its entirety.

Prof. St. George Tucker, who edited this American edition of Blackstone's Commentaries, and so wrote the accompanying declaration and justification of the American constitutional concept of intellectual liberty was one of a family of distinguished statesmen of the revolutionary period. At the time of writing the following discussion he was a professor of law in the College of William and Mary, and Judge of the General Court of Virginia. In 1804 he was appointed a judge of the Virginia Court of Appeals, and in 1813 Judge of the United States District Court of Virginia. The italics are not Prof. Tucker's.

"This right of personal opinion, comprehends first, liberty of conscience in all matters relative to religion; and, secondly, liberty of speech and of discussion in all speculative matters, whether religious, philosophical, or political.

"1. Liberty of conscience in matters of religion consists in the absolute and unrestrained exercise of our religious opinions, and duties, in that mode which our own reason and conviction dictate, without the control or intervention of any human power or authority whatsoever. This lib-

erty though made a part of our constitution, and interwoven in the nature of man by his Creator, so far as the
arts of fraud and terrors of violence have been capable of
abridging it, hath been the subject of coercion by human
laws in all ages and in all countries as far as the annals
of mankind extend. The infallibility of the rulers of nations, in matters of religion, hath been a doctrine practically enforced from the earliest periods of history to the
present moment among jews, pagans, mahommetans, and
christians, alike. The altars of Moloch and of Jehovah
have been equally stained with the blood of victims, whose
conscience did not receive conviction from the polluted
doctrines of blood thirsty priests and tyrants. Even in
countries where the crucifix, the rack, and the flames have
ceased to be the engines of proselitism, civil incapacities
have been invariably attached to a dissent from the national religion: the ceasing to persecute by more violent
means, has in such nations obtained the name of toleration.[1] In liberty of conscience says the elegant Dr. Price,

---

[1] There is something so truly original in the following observations
of the celebrated author of Common Sense, on the subject of toleration, that I shall give it at full length....."Toleration is not the opposite of intolerance, but is the counterfeit of it. Both are despot-
isms. The one assumes to itself the right of withholding liberty of
conscience, and the other of granting it. The one is the pope armed
with fire and faggot, and the other is the pope selling, or granting
indulgences. The former is church and state; and the latter is
church and traffic.
   "But toleration may be viewed in a much stronger light. Man
worships not himself, but his Maker; and the liberty of conscience
which he claims, is not for the service of himself, but of his God.
In this case, therefore, we must necessarily have the associated idea
of two beings; the mortal who renders the worship, and the immortal being who is worshipped.... Toleration, therefore, places
itself, not between man and man, nor between church and church,
nor between one denomination of religion and another, but between
God and man; between the being who worships, and the being who
is worshipped; and by the same act of assumed authority by which
it tolerates man to pay his worship, it presumptuously and blasphemously sets itself up to tolerate the Almighty to receive it.
   "Were a bill brought into any parliament, entitled, "An act to
tolerate or grant liberty to the Almighty to receive the worship of a
Jew or a Turk," or "to prohibit the Almighty from receiving it:"
all men would startle, and call it blasphemy. There would be an
uproar. The presumption of toleration in religious matters would
then present itself unmasked: but the presumption is not the less because the name of "man" only appears to those laws, for the associated idea of the worshipper and worshipped cannot be separated:
Who, then, art thou, vain dust and ashes! by whatever name thou

I include much more than toleration. Jesus Christ has established a perfect equality among his followers. His command is, that they shall assume no jurisdiction over one another, and acknowledge no master besides himself. It is, therefore, presumption in any of them to claim a right to any superiority or pre-eminence over their bretheren. Such a claim is implied, whenever any of them pretend to tolerate the rest. Not only all christians, but all men of all religions, ought to be considered by a state as equally entitled to it's protection, as far as they demean themselves honestly and peaceably. Toleration can take place only where there is a civil establishment of a particular mode of religion; that is, where a predominant sect enjoys exclusive advantages, and makes the encouragement of it's own mode of faith and worship a part of the constitution of the state; but at the same time thinks fit to suffer the exercise of other modes of faith and worship. Thanks be

art called, whether a king, a bishop, a church or a state, a parliament or any thing else, that obtrudest thine insignificance between the soul of man and it's Maker? Mind thine own concerns. If he believes not as thou believest, it is a proof that thou believest not as he believeth, and there is no earthly power can determine between you.

"With respect to what are called denominations of religion, if every one is left to judge of it's own religion, there is no such thing as a religion that is wrong; but if they are to judge of each other's religion, there is no such thing as a religion that is right; and, therefore, all the world is right, or all the world is wrong. But with respect to religion itself, without regard to names, and as directing itself from the universal family of mankind to the divine object of all adoration, it is man bringing to his Maker the fruits of his heart; and though those fruits may differ from each other like the fruits of the earth, the grateful tribute of every one is accepted.

"A bishop of Durham or a bishop of Winchester, or the archbishop who leads the dukes, will not refuse a tythe-sheaf of wheat, because it is not a cock of hay; nor a cock of hay, because it is not a sheaf of wheat; nor a pig because it is neither one nor the other; but these same persons, under the figure of an established church, will not permit their maker to receive the varied tythes of man's devotion.

"One of the continual chorusses of Mr. Burke's book is "church and state": he does not mean some one particular church, or someone particular state, but any church and state; and he uses the term as a general figure, to hold forth the political doctrine of always uniting the church with the state in every country; and he censures the national assembly for not having done this in France. Let us bestow a few thoughts on this subject.

"All religions are in their nature, kind and benign, and united with principles of morality. They could not have made proselytes at first, by professing any thing that was vicious, cruel, persecuting, or immoral. Like every thing else they had their beginning; and to God, the new American states are at present strangers to such establishments. In this respect, as well as many others, they have shewn in framing their constitutions, a degree of wisdom and liberality which is above all praise.

"Civil establishments of formularies of faith and worship, are inconsistent with the rights of private judgment. They engender strife....they turn religion into a trade....they shore up error....they produce hypocrisy and prevarication....they lay an undue bias on the human mind in its inquiries, and obstruct the progress of truth....genuine religion is a concern that lies entirely between God and our own souls. It is incapable of receiving any aid from human laws. It is contaminated as soon as worldly motives and sanctions mix their influence with it. Statesmen should countenance it only by exhibiting, in their own example, a conscientious regard to it in those

they proceeded by persuasion, exhortation, and example. How is it then that they lose their native mildness, and become morose and intolerant?

"It proceeds from the connection which Mr. Burke recommends. By engendering the church with the state, a sort of mule animal, capable only of destroying, and not of breeding up, is produced, called the church established by law. It is a stranger, even from it's birth, to any parent mother on which it is begotten, and whom in time it kicks out and destroys.

"The inquisition in Spain does not proceed from the religion originally professed, but from this mule animal, engendered between the church and state. The burnings in Smithfield proceeded from the same heterogeneous production; and it was the regeneration of this strange animal in England afterwards, that renewed the rancour and irreligion among the inhabitants; and that drove the people called quakers and dissenters to America. Persecution is not an original feature in any religion; but it is always the strongly marked feature of all law religions, or religions established by law. Take away the law-establishment, and every religion re-assumes its original benignity. In America, a catholic priest is a good citizen, a good character, and a good neighbour; an episcopalian minister is of the same description: and this proceeds independently of the men, from there being no law-establishment in America.

"If also we view this matter in a temporal sense, we shall see the ill effects it has had on the prosperity of nations. The union of church and state has impoverished Spain. The revoking the edict of Nantz drove the silk manufacture from France into England; and church and state are now driving the cotton manufacture from England to America and France. It was by observing the ill effects of it in England, that America has been warned against it; and it is by experiencing them in France, that the national assembly have abolished it; and, like America, have established universal right of conscience, and universal right of citizenship.

Paine's Rights of Man, part 1, p. 58, &c. Albany, 1794.

forms which are most agreeable to their own judgments, and by encouraging their fellow citizens in doing the same. They cannot, as public men, give it any other assistance. All, besides, that has been called a public leading in religion, has done it an essential injury, and produced some of the worst consequences.

"The church establishment in England is one of the mildest sort. But even there what a snare has it been to integrity? And what a check to free inquiry? What dispositions favourable to despotism has it fostered? What a turn to pride and narrowness and domination has it given the clerical character? What struggles has it produced in its members to accommodate their opinions to the subscriptions and tests which it imposes? What a perversion of learning has it occasioned to defend obsolete creeds and absurdities? What a burthen is it on the consciences of some of its best clergy, who, in consequence of being bound down to a system they do not approve, and having no support except that which they derive from conforming to it, find themselves under the hard necessity of either prevaricating or starving? No one doubts but that the English clergy in general could with more truth declare that they do not, than that they do give their unfeigned assent to all and every thing contained in the thirty-nine articles, and the book of common prayer: and, yet, with a solemn declaration to this purpose, are they obliged to enter upon an office which above all offices requires those who exercise it to be examples of simplicity and sincerity....Who can help execrating the cause of such an evil?

"But what I wish most to urge is the tendency of religious establishments to impede the improvement of the world. They are boundaries prescribed by human folly to human investigation; and enclosure, which intercept the light, and confine the exertions of reason. Let any one imagine to himself what effects similar establishments would have in philosophy, navigation, metaphisics, medicine, or mathematics. Something like this, took place in logic and philosophy, while the *ipse dixit* of Aristotle, and the nonsense of the school, maintained, an authority like that of the creeds of churchmen; and the effect was a longer continuance of the world in the ignorance and barbarity of the dark ages. But civil establishments of religion are more pernicious. So apt are mankind to misrepresent the character of the Deity, and to connect his favour with particular modes of faith, that it must be expected that a religion so settled will be what it has hitherto been .... a gloomy and cruel superstition, bearing the name of religion.

"It has been long a subject of dispute, which is worse in it's effects on society, such a religion or speculative atheism. For my own part, I could almost give the preference to the latter....Atheism is so repugnant to every principle of common sense, that it is not possible it should ever gain much ground, or become very prevalent. On the contrary, there is a particular proneness in the human mind to superstition, and nothing is more likely to become prevalent....Atheism leaves us to the full influence of most of our natural feelings and social principles; and these are so strong in their operation, that, in general, they are a sufficient guard to the order of society. But superstition counteracts these principles, by holding forth men to one another as objects of divine hatred; and by putting them on harrassing, silenceing, imprissoning and burning one another, in order to do God service....Atheism is a sanctuary for vice, by taking away the motives to virtue arising from the will of God, and the fear of future judgment. But superstition is more a sanctuary for vice, by teaching men ways of pleasing God, without moral virtue; and by leading them even to compound for wickedness, by ritual services, by bodily penances and mortifications; by adoring shrines, going pilgrimages, saying many prayers, receiving absolution from the priests, exterminating heretics, &c....Atheism destroys the sacredness and obligation of an oath. But is there not also a religion (so called) which does this, by teaching, that there is a power which can dispense with the obligation of oaths; that *pious* frauds are right, and that faith is not to be kept with heretics.

"It is indeed only a rational and liberal religion; a religion founded on just notions of the Deity, as a Being who regards equally every sincere worshipper, and by whom all are alike favoured as far as they act up to the light they enjoy: a religion which consists in the imitation of the moral perfections of an Almighty but Benevolent Governor of Nature, who directs for the best, all events, in confidence in the care of his providence, in resignation to his will, and in the faithful discharge of every duty of piety and morality from a regard to his authority, and the apprehension of a future righteous retribution. It is only this religion (the inspiring principle of every thing fair and worthy, and joyful, and which, in truth is nothing but the love of God to man, and virtue warming the heart and directing the conduct). It is only this kind of religion that can bless the world, or be an advantage to society. This is the religion that every enlightened friend to mankind will be zealous to support. But it is a religion that the powers of the world know little of, and which will always be best promoted by being left free and open.[2] The following passage from the same author, deserves too much attention to be pretermitted: 'Let no such monster be known there, [in the United States] as human authority in matters of religion. Let every honest and peaceable man, whatever is his faith, be protected there; and find an effectual defence against the attacks of bigotry and intolerance. In the United States may religion flourish! They cannot be very great and happy if it does not. But let it be a better religion than most of those which have been hitherto professed in the world. Let it be a religion which enforces moral obligations; not a religion which relaxes and evades them....A tolerant and catholic religion; not a rage for proselytism....A religion of peace and charity; not a religion that persecutes curses and damns. In a word, let it be the genuine gospel of peace, lifting above the world, warming the heart with the love of God and his creatures, and sustaining the fortitude of good men, by the assured hope of a future deliverance from death, and an

---

[2] Price's observations on the American revolution, p. 28 to 34.

infinite reward in the everlasting kingdom of our Lord and Saviour.'[3]

"This inestimable and imprescriptible right is guaranteed to the citizens of the United States, as such, by the constitution of the United States, which declares,[4] that no religious test shall ever be required as a qualification to any office or public trust under the United States; and by that amendment to the constitution of the United States,[5] which prohibits congress from making any law respecting the establishment of religion, or prohibiting the free exercise thereof; and to the citizens of Virginia by the bill of rights,[6] which declares, 'that religion, or the duty which we owe to our Creator, and the manner of discharging it, can be directed only by reason and conviction, not by force or violence, and therefore all men are equally entitled to the free exercise of religion, according to the dictates of conscience: and that it is the mutual duty of all to practice christian forbearance, love, and charity, towards each other.' And further, by the act for establishing religious freedom, by which it is also declared, 'that no man shall be compelled to frequent or support any religious worship, place, or ministry, whatsoever, nor shall be enforced, restrained, molested or burthened in his body or goods, nor shall otherwise suffer on account of his religious opinions or belief; but that all men shall be free to profess, and by argument maintain their opinions in matters of religion, and that the same shall in no wise diminish, enlarge, or affect their civil capacities.'[7]

"2. Liberty of speech and of discussion in all speculative matters, consists in the absolute and uncontrollable right of speaking, writing, and publishing, our opinions concerning any subject, whether religious, philosophical, or political; and of inquiring into and, examining the nature of truth, whether moral or metaphysical; the expediency

---

[3] Ibid. p. 39.
[4] Art. 6.
[5] Art. 3.
[6] Art. 16. Revised code. Edi. of 1794, p. 4.
[7] Art. 16. Revised code. Edi. of 1794, c. 20.

or inexpediency of all public measures, with their tendency and probable effect; the conduct of public men, and generally every other subject, without restraint, except as to the injury of any other individual, in his person, property, or good name. Thought and speech are equally the immediate gifts of the Creator, the one being intended as the 'vehicle of the other: they ought, therefore, to have been wholly exempt from the coersion of human laws in all speculative and doctrinal points whatsoever: liberty of speech in political matters, has been equally proscribed in almost all the governments of the world, as liberty of conscience in those of religion. A complete tyranny over the human mind could never have been exercised whilst the organ by which our sentiments are conveyed to others, was free: when the introduction of letters among men afforded a new mode of disclosing, and that of the press, a more expeditious method of diffusing their sentiments, writing and printing also became subjects of legal coersion;[8] even the expression of sentiments by pictures and hieroglyphics[9] attracted the attention of the Argus-government, so far as to render such expressions punishable by law. The common place arguments in support of these restraints are, that they tend to preserve peace and good order in government; that there are some doctrines both in religion and politics, so sacred, and others of so bad a tendency, that no public discussion of them ought to be suffered. To these the elegant writer before referred to, gives this answer: 'were this a right opinion, all the persecution that has ever been practised, would be justified. For if it is a part of the duty of civil magistrates, to prevent the discussion of such doctrines, they must, in doing this, act on their own judgments of the nature and tendency of doctrines; and consequently, they must have a right to prevent the discussion of all doctrines which they think to be too sacred for discussion, or too dangerous in their tendency; and this right they must exercise in the only way in which civil power is capable of exercising it, by inflicting penalties on

[8] Stat. 13 and 14, Car. 2.
[9] 4 Blacks. Com. p. 150.

all who oppose sacred doctrines, or who maintain pernicious opinions.' [10]

"In England during the existence of the court of star
chamber, and after it's abolition, from the time of the long
parliament to the year 1694, the liberty of the press, and
the right of vending books, was restrained to very narrow
limits, by various ordinances and acts of parliament; all
books printed were previously licensed by some of the great
offices of state, or the two universities, and all foreign
books were exposed to a similar scrutiny before they were
vended. No shopkeeper could buy a book to sell again, or
sell any book, unless he were a licensed bookseller. By
these and other restrictions the communication of knowledge was utterly subjected to the control of those whose
interest led them rather to promote ignorance than the
knowledge of truth. In 1694, the parliament refused to
continue these prohibitions any longer, and thereby, according to De Lolme,[11] established the freedom of the
press in England. But although this negative establishment may satisfy the subjects of England, the people of
America have not thought proper to suffer the freedom of
speech, and of the press to rest upon such an uncertain
foundation, as the will and pleasure of the government.
Accordingly, when it was discovered that the constitution
of the United States had not provided any barrier against
the possible encroachments of the government thereby to
be established, great complaints were made of the omission, and most of the states instructed their representatives to obtain an amendment in that respect; and so sensible was the first congress of the general prevalence of
this sentiment throughout America, that in their first
session they proposed an amendment since adopted by all
the states and made a part of the constitution; 'that congress shall make no law abridging the freedom of speech,
or of the press.' [12] And our state bill of rights declares,
'that the freedom of the press is one of the great bulwarks
of liberty, and cannot be restrained, but by despotic gov-

[10] Price's Observations on the American Revolution, p. 19.
[11] Page 215.
[12] Amendments to C. U. S. Art. 3.

ernments.' [13]   And so tenacious of this right, was the convention of Virginia, by which the constitution of the United States was ratified, that they further declared, as an article of the bill of rights then agreed to, 'that the people have a right to the freedom of speech, and of writing and publishing their sentiments; that the freedom of the press is one of the greatest bulwarks of liberty, and ought not to be violated.' [14]   Nay, so reasonably jealous were they of the possibility of this declaration being disregarded, as not forming a part of the constitution, at that time, that the following declaration is inserted in, and forms a part of, the instrument of ratification, viz.   'That the powers granted under the constitution, being derived from the people of the United States, may be resumed by them, whensoever the same shall be perverted to their injury or oppression; and that, every power not granted thereby, remains with them, and at their will: that, therefore no right; of any denomination, can be cancelled, abridged, restrained, or modified by the congress, by the senate, or house of representatives, acting in any capacity; by the president, or any department, or officer of the United States, except in those instances where power is given by the constitution for those purposes: that among other essential rights, the liberty of conscience, and of the press, cannot be cancelled, abridged, restrained, or modified, by any authority of the United States.' [15]

"As this latter declaration forms a part of the instrument by which the constitution of the United States became obligatory upon the state, and citizens of Virginia; and as the act of ratification has been accepted in that form; no principle is more clear, than that the state of Virginia is no otherwise bound thereby, than according to the very tenor of the instrument, by which she has bound herself. For as no free state can be bound to another, or to a number of others, but by it's own voluntary consent and act, so not only the evidence of that consent, but the nature and

---

[13] State Bill of Rights. Art. 12.

[14] Bill of Rights agreed to by the convention of Virginia, by which the C. U. S. was adopted Art. 16.

[15] C. U. S. as ratified by the convention of Virginia.

terms of it, can be ascertained only by recurrence to the very instrument, by which it was first given. And as the foregoing declaration not only constitutes a part of that instrument, but contains a preliminary protest against any extension of the enumerated powers thereby granted to the federal government, it could scarcely have been imagined, that any violation of a principle so strenuously asserted, and made, as it were, the sole ground of the pragmatic sanction, would ever have been attempted by the federal government.

"But however reasonable such an expectation might have been, a very few years evinced a determination on the part of those who then ruled the public councils of the United States, to set at nought all such restraints. An act accordingly was passed by the congress,[16] on the fourteenth of July, 1798, whereby it was enacted, that 'if any person shall write, print, utter or publish any false and malicious writing against the government of the United States, or either house of congress, or the president, with intent to defame them, or either of them, or to bring them or either of them into contempt, or disrepute; or to excite against them or either of them, the hatred of the good people of the United States, then such person, being thereof convicted before any court of the United States having jurisdiction thereof shall be punished by a fine not exceeding two thousand dollars, and by imprisonment not exceeding two years.' The act was limited in it's duration to the third day of March, 1801, the very day on which the period for which the then president was elected, was to expire; and, previous to which the event of the next presidential election must be known.

"The consequences of this act, as might have been foreseen, were a general astonishment, and dissatisfaction, among all those who considered the government of the United States, as a limited system of government; in it's nature altogether federal, and essentially different from all others which might lay claim to unlimited powers; or even to national, instead of federal authority. The con-

---

[16] L. U. S. 5 Cong. c. 91.

stitutionality of the act was accordingly very generally denied, or questioned, by them. They alleged, that it is to the freedom of the press, and of speech, that the American nation is indebted for its liberty, it's happiness, it's enlightened state, nay more, for it's existence. That in these states the people are the only sovereign: that the government established by themselves, is for their benefit; that those who administer the government, whether it be that of the state, or of the federal union, are the agents and servants of the people, not their rulers or tyrants....That these agents must be, and are, from the nature and principles of our governments, responsible to the people, for their conduct. That to enforce this responsibility, it is indispensibly necessary that the people should inquire into the conduct of their agents; that in this inquiry, they must, or ought to scrutinize their motives, sift their intentions, and pentrate their designs; and that it was therefore, an unimpeachable right in them to censure as well as to applaud; to condemn or to acquit; and to reject, or to employ them again, as the most severe scrutiny might advise. That as no man can be forced into the service of the people against his own will and consent; so if any man employed by them in any office, should find the tenure of it too severe, because responsibility is inseparably annexed to it, he might retire: if he can not bear scrutiny, he might resign: if his motives, or designs, will not bear sifting; or if censure be too galling to his feelings, he might avoid it in the shades of domestic privacy. That if flattery be the only music to his ear, or the only balm to his heart; if he sickened when it is withheld, or turned pale when denied him; or if power, like the dagger of Macbeth, should invite his willing imagination to grasp it, the indigation of the people ought immediately to mark him, and hurl him from their councils, and their confidence forever. That if this absolute freedom of inquiry may be, in any manner, abridged, or impaired by those who administer the government, the nature of it will be instantly changed from a federal union of representative democracies, in which the people of the several states are the sovereign, and the administrators of the government their agents, to a consolidated oligarchy, aristocracy, or monarchy, according to the prevailing caprice of the constituted authorities, or of those who may usurp them. That where absolute freedom of discussion is prohibited, or restrained, responsibility vanishes. That any attempt to prohibit, or restain that freedom, may well be construed to proceed from conscious guilt. That the people of America have always manifested a most jealous sensibility, on the subject of this inestimable right, and have ever regarded it as a fundamental principle in their government, and carefully engrafted in the constitution. That this sentiment was generated in the American mind, by an abhorrence of the maxims and principles of that government which they had shaken off, and a detestation of the abominable persecutions, and extrajudicial dogmas, of the still odious court of star-chamber; whose tyrannical proceedings and persecutions, among other motives of the like nature, prompted and impelled our ancestors to fly from the pestilential government of their native country, to seek an asylum here; where they might enjoy, and their posterity establish, and transmit to all future generations, freedom, unshackled, unlimited, undefined. That in our time we have vindicated, fought for, and established that freedom by our arms, and made it the solid, and immovable basis and foundation both of the state, and federal government. That nothing could more clearly evince the inestimable value that the American people have set upon the liberty of the press, than their uniting it in the same sentence, and even in the same member of a sentence, with the rights of conscience, and the freedom of speech. And since congress are equally prohibited from making any law abridging the freedom of speech, or of the press, they boldly challenged their adversaries to point out the constitutional distinction, between those two modes of discussion, or inquiry. If the unrestrained freedom of the press, said they, be not guaranteed, by the constitution, neither is that of speech. If on the contrary the unrestrained freedom of speech is guaranteed, so also, is that of the press. If then the genius of our federal constitution has vested the people of the United States, not only with a censorial power, but even with the sovereignty itself; if magistrates are, indeed, their agents: if they are responsible for their acts of agency; if the people may not only censure whom they disapprove, but reject whom they may find unworthy; if approbation or censure, election or rejection, ought to be the result of inquiry, scrutiny, and mature deliberation; why, said they, is the exercise of this censorial power, this sovereign right, this necessary inquiry, and scrutiny to be confined to the freedom of speech? Is it because this mode of discussion better answers the purposes of the censorial power? Surely not. The best speech can not be heard, by any great number of persons. The best speech may be misunderstood, misrepresented, and imperfectly remembered by those who are present. To all the rest of mankind, it is, as if it had never been. The best speech must also be short for the investigation of any subject of an intricate nature, or even a plain one, if it be of more than ordinary length. The best speech then must be altogether inadequate to the due exercise of the censorial power, by the people. The only adequate supplementary aid for these defects, is the absolute freedom of the press. A freedom unlimited as the human mind; viewing all things, penetrating the recesses of the human heart, unfolding the motives of human actions, and estimating all things by one invaluable standard, truth; applauding those who deserve well; censuring the undeserving; and condemning the unworthy, according to the measure of their demerits.

"In vindication of the act, the promoters and supporters of it, said,[17] that a law to punish false, scandalous, and malicious writings against the government, with intent to stir up sedition, is a law necessary for carrying into effect the power vested by the constitution in the government of the United States, and consequently such a law as congress may pass. To which it was answered, that even were the premises true, it would not authorize congress to pass an act to punish writings calculated to bring congress, or the president into contempt or disrepute. Inasmuch as such

[17] See the report of a committee of congress, respecting the alien and sedition laws, Feb. 25, 1799.

contempt or disrepute may be entertained for them, or either of them, without incurring the guilt of sedition, against the government, and without the most remote design of opposing, or resisting any law, or any act of the president done in pursuance of any law: one or the other of which would seem necessary to constitute the offence, which this argument defends the right of congress to punish, or prevent.

"It was further urged in vindication of the act, that the liberty of the press consists not in a licence for every man to publish what he pleases, without being liable to punishment for any abuse of that licence; but in a permission to publish without previous restraint; and, therefore, that a law to restrain the licentiousness of the press, cannot be considered as an abridgment of its liberty.[18]

"To which it was answered that this exposition of the liberty of the press, was only to be found in the theoretical writings of the commentators on the *English* government, where the liberty of the press rests upon no other ground, than that there is now no law which imposes any actual previous restraint upon the press, as was formerly the case: which is very different from the footing upon which it stands in the United States, where it is made a fundamental article of the constitutions, both of the federal and state governments, that no such restraint shall be imposed by the authority of either.... That if the sense of the state governments be wanting on the occasion, nothing can be more explicit than the meaning and intention of the state of Virginia, at the moment of adopting the constitution of the United States; by which it will clearly appear that it never was the intention of that state (and probably of no other in the union) to permit congress to distinguish between the liberty and licentiousness of the press; or, in any manner to 'cancel, abridge, restrain, or modify' that inestimable right.

"Thirdly it was alleged, that the act could not be unconstitutional because it made nothing penal, which was not

---

[18] See the report of a committee of congress, respecting the alien and sedition laws, February 25, 1799.

penal before, being merely declaratory of the common law,[19] viz. of England.

"To this it was, among other arguments, answered. That the United States as a federal government have no common law. That although the common law of England, is, under different modifications, admitted to be the common law of the states respectively, yet the whole of the common law of England has been no where introduced: that there is a great and essential difference, in this respect, in the several states, not only in the subjects to which it is applied, but in the extent of its application. That the common law of one state, therefore, is not the common law of another. That the constitution of the United States has neither created it, nor conferred it upon the federal government. And, therefore, that government has no power or authority to assume the right of punishing any action, merely because it is punishable in England, or may be punishable in any, or all the states, by the common law.

"The essential difference between the British government and the American constitutions was moreover insisted on, as placing this subject in the clearest light. In the former, the danger of encroachment on the rights of the people, was understood to be confined to the executive magistrate. The representatives of the people in the legislature are not only exempt themselves, from distrust, but are considered as sufficient guardians of the rights of their constituents against the danger from the executive. Hence it is a principle, that the parliament is unlimited in it's power, or, in their own language, is omnipotent. Hence too, all the ramparts for protecting the rights of the people, such as their *magna charta,* their bill of rights, &c. are not reared against the parliament, but against the royal prerogative. They are mere legislative precautions against executive usurpations. Under such a government as that, an exemption of the press from previous restraints, by licencers from the king, is all the freedom that can be secured to it, there: but, that in the United States the case is altogether

---

[19] See the report of a committee of congress, respecting the alien and sedition laws, February 25, 1799.

different. The people, not the government, possess the absolute sovereignty. The legislature, no less than the executive, is under limitations of power. Encroachments are regarded as possible from the one, as well as from the other. Hence in the United States, the great and essential rights of the people, are secured against legislative, as well as against executive ambition. They are secured, not by laws paramount to prerogative; but by constitutions paramount to laws. This security of the freedom of the press requires, that it should be exempt, not only from previous restraint by the executive, as in Great-Britain; but from legislative restraint also; and this exemption, to be effectual, must be an exemption, not only from the previous inspection of licencers, but from the subsequent penalty of laws....A further difference between the two governments was also insisted on. In Great-Britain, it is a maxim, that the king, an hereditary, not a responsible magistrate, can do no wrong; and that the legislature, which in two thirds of it's composition, is also hereditary, not responsible, can do what it pleases. In the United States, the executive magistrates are not held to be infallible, nor the legislatures to be omnipotent; and both being elective, are both responsible. That the latter may well be supposed to require a greater degree of freedom of animadversion than might be tolerated by the genius of the former. That even in England, notwithstanding the general doctrine of the common law, the ministry, who are responsible to impeachment, are at all times animadverted on, by the press, with peculiar freedom. That the practice in America must be entitled to much more respect: being in most instances founded upon the express declarations contained in the respective constitutions, or bill of rights of the confederated states.[20] That even in those states where no such guarantee could be found, the press had al-

[20] See the Virginia bill of rights, Art. 12. Massachusetts, Art. 16. Pennsylvania, Art. 12. Delaware, Art. 23. Maryland, Art. 38. North-Carolina, Art. 15. South-Carolina, Art. 43. Georgia, Art. 61. The constitution of Pennsylvania, Art. 35, declares, "That the printing presses shall be free to every person who undertakes to examine the proceedings of the legislature or any part of the government. And the bill of rights of Vermont, Art. 15, is to the same effect.

ways exerted a freedom in canvassing the merits, and measures of public men of every description, not confined to the limits of the common law. That on this footing the press has stood even in those states, at least, from the period of the revolution.

"The advocates and supporters of the act alleged, fourthly; That had the constitution intended to prohibit congress from legislating at all, on the subject of the press, it would have used the same expressions as in that part of the clause, which relates to religion, and religious tests; whereas, said they, there is a manifest difference; it being evident that the constitution intended to prohibit congress from legislating at all, on the subject of religious establishments, and the prohibition is made in the most express terms. Had the same intention prevailed respecting the press, the same expression would have been used, viz. 'Congress shall make no law respecting the press.' They are not, however, prohibited, added they, from legislating at all, on the subject, but merely from abridging the liberty of the press. It is evident, therefore, said they, that congress may legislate respecting the press: may pass laws for it's regulation, and to punish those who pervert it into an engine of mischief, provided those laws do not abridge it's liberty. A law to impose previous restraints upon the press, and not one to inflict punishment on wicked and malicious publications, would be a law to abridge the liberty of the press.[21]

"To this it was answered, that laws to regulate, must, according to the true interpretation of that word, impose rules, or regulations, not before imposed; that to impose rules is to restrain; that to restrain must necessarily imply an abridgment of some former existing rights, or power: consequently, when the constitution prohibits congress from making any law abridging the freedom of speech, or of the press, it forbids them to make any law respecting either of these subjects. That this conclusion was an inevitable consequence of the injunction contained

[21] See the report of a committee of congress, to whom were referred several petitions for the repeal of the alien and sedition laws. February 25, 1799.

in the amendment, unless it could be shown, that the existing restraints upon the freedom of the press in the United States, were such as to require a remedy, by a law regulating (but not abridging) the manner in which it might be exercised with greater freedom and security. A supposition, which it was believed no person would maintain. That the necessary consequence of these things is, that the amendment was meant as a positive denial to congress, of any power whatever, on the subject.

"As an evidence on this subject, which must be deemed absolutely conclusive, it was observed, That the proposition of amendments made by congress, is introduced in the following terms: 'The conventions of a number of states, having, at the time of their adopting the constitution, expressed a desire, in order to prevent misconstruction, or abuse of its powers, that further declaratory and restrictive clauses should be added; and, as extending the ground of public confidence in the government, will best ensure the beneficent ends of it's institution:' which affords the most satisfactory and authentic proof, -that the several amendments proposed, were to be considered as either declaratory, or restrictive; and whether the one or the other, as corresponding with the desire expressed by a number of states, and as extending the ground of public confidence in the government. That under any other construction of the amendment relating to the press, than that it declared the press to be wholly exempt from the power of congress.... the amendment could neither be said to correspond with the desire expressed by a number of the states, nor be calculated to extend the ground of public confidence in the government. Nay more; that the construction employed to justify the 'Sedition Act,' would exhibit a phœnomenon without a parrallel in the political world. It would exhibit a number of respectable states, as denying first that any power over the press was delegated by the constitution; as proposing next, that an amendment to it should explicitly declare, that no such power was delegated; and finally as concurring in an amendment actually recognizing, or delegating such a power.

"But, the part of the constitution which seems to have been most recurred to, and even relied on, in defence of the act of congress, is the last clause of the eighth section of the first article, empowering congress 'to make all laws which shall be necessary and proper for carrying into execution the foregoing powers, and all other powers vested by the constitution in the government of the United States, or in any department or officer thereof.' [22]

"To this it was answered, that the plain import of that clause is, that congress shall have all the incidental, or instrumental powers, necessary and proper for carrying into execution all the express powers; whether they be vested in the government of the United States, more collectively, or in the several departments, or officers thereof. That it is not a grant of new powers to congress, but merely a declaration, for the removal of all uncertainty, that the means of carrying into execution, those otherwise granted, are included in the grant. Whenever, therefore, a question arises concerning the constitutionality of a particular power, the first question is, whether the power be expressed in the constitution. If it be, the question is decided. If it be not expressed, the next inquiry must be, whether it is properly incidental to an express power, and necessary to its execution. If it be, it may be exercised by congress. If it be not, congress cannot exercise it.... That, if the sedition law be brought to this kind of test, it is not even pretended by the framers of that act, that the power over the press, which is exercised thereby, can be found among the powers expressly vested in congress. That if it be asked, whether there is any express power, for executing which, that act is a necessary and a proper power: the answer is, that the express power which has been selected, as least remote from that exercised by the act, is the power of 'suppressing insurrections;' which is said to imply a power to prevent insurrections, by punishing whatever may lead, or tend to them. But it surely cannot, with the

[22] See the report of a committee of congress, Feb. 25, 1799; and the answer of the senate and house of representatives of Massachusetts. (Feb. 9th and 13th, 1799), to the communications from the state of Virginia, on the subject of the alien and sedition laws.

least plausibility, be said, that a regulation of the press, and the punishment of libels, are exercises of a power to suppress insurrections. That if it be asked, whether the federal government has no power to prevent, as well as punish, resistance to the laws; the proper answer is, that they have the power, which the constitution deemed most proper in their hands for the purpose. That congress has power, before it happens, to pass laws for punishing such resistance; and the executive and judiciary have a power to enforce those laws, whenever it does actually happen. That it must be recollected by many, and could be shown to the satisfaction of all, that this construction of the terms 'necessary and proper,' is precisely the construction which prevailed during the discussions and ratifications of the constitution: and that it is a construction absolutely necessary to maintain their consistency with the peculiar character of the government, as possessed of particular and defined powers only; not of the general and indefinite powers vested in ordinary governments. That if this construction be rejected, it must be wholly immaterial, whether unlimited powers be exercised under the name of unlimited powers, or be exercised under the name of unlimited means of carrying into execution limited powers.

"To those who asked, if the federal government be destitute of every authority for restraining the licentiousness of the press, and for shielding itself against the libellous attacks which may be made on those who administer it; the reply given was, that the constitution alone can answer the question: that no such power being expressly given; and such a power not being both necessary and proper to carry into execution any express power; but, above all, such a power being expressly forbidden by a declaratory amendment to the constitution, the answer must be, that the federal government is destitute of all such authority.[23]

---

[23] In the preceding sketch of the arguments used to demonstrate the unconstitutionality of the act of congress, I have extracted a few of those contained in the report of the committee of the house of delegates of Virginia, agreed to by the house, Jan. 11, 1800, and afterwards concurred in by the senate. This most valuable document is very long, and is incapable of being abridged, without manifest injury.

"This very imperfect sketch may be sufficient to afford the student some idea of the magnitude and importance of a question, which agitated every part of the United States, almost to a degree of convulsion : the controversy not being confined to the closets of speculative politicians, or to the ordinary channels of discussion through the medium of the press; but engrossing the attention, and calling forth the talents and exertions of the legislatures of several of the states in the union, on the one hand, and of the federal government, and all its branches, legislative, executive, and judiciary, on the other. For no sooner had the act passed, than prosecutions were commenced against individuals in several of the states : they were conducted, in some cases, with a rigour, which seemed to betray a determination to convert into a scourge that, which it had been pretended was meant only to serve as a shield.

"The state of Kentucky was the first which took the act under consideration, and by a resolution passed with two dissenting voices only, declared the act of congress not law, but altogether void, and of no force. The state of Virginia, though posterior to her younger sister in point of time, was not behind her in energy. The general assembly at their first session after the passage of the act, did 'explicitly and peremptorily declare, that it views the powers of the federal government, as resulting from the compact, to which the states are parties; as limited by the plain sense and intention of the instrument constituting that compact; as no further valid than they are authorized by the grants contained in that compact; and that in case of a deliberate, palpable, and dangerous exercise of other powers, not granted by the said compact, the states who are parties thereto have the right, and are in duty bound, to interpose for arresting the progress of the evil, and for maintaining within their respective limits the authorities, rights, and liberties appertaining to them'.... 'That a spirit hath, in sundry instances, been manifested by the federal government, to enlarge its powers, by forced constructions of the constitutional charter which defines them; and to expound certain general phrases (copied from the very limited grant of powers in the former articles of confederation, and therefore less liable to be misconstrued) so as to destroy the meaning and effect of the particular enumeration, which necessarily explains and limits the general phrases; so as to consolidate the states, by degrees, into one sovereignty.' That the 'general assembly doth, particularly protest against the palpable and alarming infractions of the constitution, in the two cases of the alien and sedition acts, passed at the last session of congress; the first of which exercises a power no where delegated to the federal government; and the other exercises, in like manner, a power not delegated by the constitution; but, on the contrary, expressly and positively forbidden by one of the amendments thereto; a power which, more than any other, ought to produce universal alarm; because it is levelled against that right of freely examining public characters and measures, and of free communication among the people thereon, which has ever been justly deemed the only effectual guardian of every other right.'

" 'That this state having by its convention, which ratified the federal constitution, expressly declared, that among other essential rights, "the liberty of conscience, and of the press cannot be cancelled, abridged, restrained, or modified, by any authority of the United States," and from its extreme anxiety to guard these rights from every possible attack of sophistry, or ambition, having, with other states, recommended an amendment for that purpose, which amendment was, in due time, annexed to the constitution; it would mark a reproachful inconsistency and criminal degeneracy, if an indifference were now shewn, to the most palpable violation of the rights, thus declared and secured; and to the establishment of a precedent, which may be fatal to the other.'

" 'That feeling the most sincere affection for their sister states; the truest anxiety for establishing and perpetuating the union; and the most scrupulous fidelity to the constitution which is the pledge of mutual friendship; and solemnly appealing 'to the like dispositions of the other states, in confidence that they will concur with this commonwealth in declaring, (as it does hereby declare,) that the acts aforesaid are unconstitutional; and that the necessary and proper measures will be taken by each, for co-operating with this state, in maintaining the authorities, rights and liberties, reserved to the states respectively, or to the people.' [24]

"Answers were received from the legislatures of seven states, disapproving of the resolutions of Virginia and Kentucky, which had also been transmitted with a similar proposition. The general assembly of Massachusetts, alone, condescended to reason with her sister states; the others scarcely paid them the common respect that is held to be due from individuals, to each other. The assembly of Virginia at their next session, entered into a critical review and examination of their former resolutions, and supported them by a train of arguments, and of powerful, convincing, and unsophistic reasoning, to which, probably, the equal cannot be produced in any public document, in any country.[25] They concluded this examination and review (which occupied more than eighty pages) with resolving, 'That having carefully and respectfully attended to the proceedings of a number of the states, in answer to their former resolutions, and having accurately and fully re-examined and re-considered the latter, they found it to be their indispensable duty to adhere to the same, as founded in truth, as consonant with the constitution, and as conducive to its preservation; and more especially to be their duty, to renew, as they do hereby renew their protest against the alien and sedition acts, as palpable and alarming infractions of the constitution.'

"Meantime, petitions had been presented to congress for the repeal of those obnoxious acts: on the 25th of February, 1799, congress agreed to the report of a committee advising them, that it would be inexpedient to repeal them. A majority of four members, only, prevailed on this occasion. During the session which succeeded, strenuous exertions were made for the continuance of the act commonly called the sedition act, (the other concerning aliens, having expired) : After a severe struggle, the attempt failed,

---

[24] See the sessions acts of 1798, ad finem.
[25] See the report of the committee, on this subject, agreed to in the house of delegates, Jan. 11, 1800.

and the act was permitted to expire, at the same moment that put a period to the political importance of those, for whose benefit, alone, it seems to have been intended.

"We may now, I trust, say with our former envoys to the republic of France: 'The genius of the constitution cannot be overruled by those who administer the government. Among those principles deemed sacred in America; among those sacred rights, considered as forming the bulwark of their liberty, which the government should contemplate with awful reverence, and approach only with the most cautious circumspection, there is none of which the importance is more deeply impressed on the public mind, than the liberty of the press.' [26]

"It may be asked, perhaps: is there no remedy in the United States for injuries done to the good fame and reputation of a man; injuries, which to a man of sensibility, and of conscious integrity, are the most grievous that can be inflicted; injuries, which when offered through the medium of the press, may be diffused throughout the globe, and transmitted to latest posterity; may render him odious, and detestable in the eyes of the world, his country, his neighbours, his friends, and even his own family; may seclude him from society as a monster of depravity, and iniquity; and even may deprive him of sustenance, by destroying all confidence in him, and discouraging that commerce, or intercourse with him, which may be necessary to obtain the means?

"Heaven forbid, that in a country which boasts of rational freedom, and of affording perfect security to the citizen for the complete enjoyment of all his rights, the most valuable of all should be exposed without remedy, or redress, to the vile arts of detraction and slander! Every individual, certainly, has a right to speak or publish, his sentiments on the measures of government: to do this without restraint, control, or fear of punishment for so doing, is that which constitutes the genuine freedom of the press. The danger justly apprehended by those states which in-

[26] See the letters from Messrs. Marshall, Binckney, and Gerry, to Mons. Talleyrand, minister of foreign affairs in France, 1798.

sisted that the federal government should possess no power, directly or indirectly, over the subject, was, that those who were entrusted with the administration might be forward in considering every thing as a crime against the government, which might operate to their own personal disadvantage; it was therefore made a fundamental article of the federal compact, that no such power should be exercised, or claimed by the federal government; leaving it to the state governments to exercise such jurisdiction and control over the subject, as their several constitutions and laws permit. In contending therefore for the absolute freedom of the press, and its total exemption from all restraint, control, or jurisdiction of the federal government, the writer of these sheets most explicitly disavows the most distant approbation of its licentiousness. A free press, conducted with ability, firmness, decorum, and impartiality, may be regarded as the chaste nurse of genuine liberty; but a press stained with falsehood, imposture, detraction, and personal slander, resembles a contaminated prostitute, whose touch is pollution, and whose offspring bears the foul marks of the parent's ignominy.

"Whoever makes use of the press as the vehicle of his sentiments on any subject, ought to do it in such language as to show he has a deference for the sentiments of others; that while he asserts the right of expressing and vindicating his own judgment, he acknowledges the obligation to submit to the judgment of those whose authority he cannot legally, or constitutionally dispute. In his statement of facts he is bound to adhere strictly to the truth; for any deviation from the truth is both an imposition upon the public, and an injury to the individual whom it may respect. In his restrictures on the conduct of men, in public stations, he is bound to do justice to their characters, and not to criminate them without substantial reason. The right of character is a sacred and invaluable right, and is not forfeited by accepting a public employment. Whoever knowingly departs from any of these maxims is guilty of a crime against the community, as well as against the person injured; and though both the letter and the spirit of our federal constitution wisely prohibit the congress of the

United States from making any law, by which the freedom of speech, or of the press may be exposed to restraint and persecution under the authority of the federal government, yet *for injuries done* the reputation of any person, as *an individual,* the state courts are always open, and may afford ample, and competent redress, as the record of the courts of this commonwealth abundantly testify."

This discussion of Blackstone's conception of mental constitutional freedom meets every issue so frankly and fairly as, in that respect, to make it a suitable model for judicial imitation. This edition of Blackstone, being published in 1803, must have been well known to Justice Kent in 1810, when he decided the Ruggles case. Likewise it must have been familiar to Justice Shaw when he decided the Kneeland case. That both of them should have ignored its existence *and its argument,* in deciding so important a problem as the meaning of constitutional religious liberty, speaks much more eloquently for their prejudices than it does for the maturity of their intellectual processes or of their conception of intellectual honesty.

In Conclusion.

In the foregoing discussion Judge Tucker has given us an exposition and justification of Jefferson's and Virginia's conception of the intelligent interpretation of constitutional intellectual liberty, religious or otherwise. In Reynolds vs. U. S.,[28] the Supreme Court of the United States has practically endorsed it. *Another authority still higher has also given it even a more specific approval. I refer to the people of the United States. Their interpretation of the constitution is higher than that of the court because they created both the court and the constitution. In the election of Thomas Jefferson to the presidency the dominant issue was his conception of constitutional intellectual liberty as against the Tory interpretation of it, which latter was a defense of the alien and sedition law. By the election of Jefferson on that issue, the people of the United States who had created the constitution, also declared its meaning. Jefferson accordingly pardoned all*

---

[28] Reynolds v. U. S., 98 U. S. 145.

*the convicts under the law[29] because it was uncon-
stitutional and void. The subsequent return of all
fines, by act of Congress, executed this popular
interpretation of the constitution and acknowledged
it upon the highest plane of authority that is possible in a republic. This view also placed the constitution in harmony with the Continental Congress which
had previously declared that we need liberty of the press
that "oppressive officials are shamed or intimidated into
more honorable and just modes of conducting affairs."[30]
So the United States of America as a nation and in the
most authoritative manner that is possible, has repudiated Blackstone's conception of mental freedom. Now intellectual liberty, according to this most authoritative interpretation, means that no man shall be punished for the
expression of ideas as such, or their tendency speculatively ascertained, no matter what they are or how expressed, but he may be punished for another resultant
overt act designed and efficient for inflicting an actual and
material injury, as distinguished from a mere psychologic
tendency.*

**This interpretation of mental freedom by
Jefferson and the American people was well
known in Connecticut before the adoption of
its constitution. Abraham Bishop, and the
others who led the movement for the Connecticut constitution were avowed supporters
and admirers of Jefferson and his doctrines.
Therefore when the Connecticut constitution
in 1818, provided for mental freedom, in language even more plainly and broadly libertarian than the Federal constitution it also
adopted the ideas thereby expressed and the
people's previous interpretation of these constitutional guarantees.**

[29] Booth vs. Ryecroft, 3 Wisc. Rep. 183.
[30] Journal of the Continental Congress, v. 1, p. 108, Edition, 1904.

XI.
ACADEMIC DISCUSSION OF THE MEANING OF FREE SPEECH.

In the preceding discussion reference was made to immature and defective intellectual processes as a means of promoting tyranny under the verbal guise of glorifying and defining liberty of speech and press. It was shown that pursuant to a conscious desire for restraining intellectual liberty, Blackstone defined freedom of the press "properly understood" to consist of the absence of only one mode of abridgment. Accordingly, all other methods of abridging the expression of thought and feeling are impliedly consistent with complete "freedom." Our courts following this mode of reasoning have sometimes intimated as much.

It is now proposed to apply this defective intellectual method to the other historic modes of curtailing the transmission of ideas. Thus the short-comings of this method will be made more evident, and we will be led quite automatically to a synthetic negation of *all* abridgments and to the focalization of our attention upon the achievement of an unabridged intellectual liberty rather than upon the mere abolition of any particular restraints. So it is believed that we will come to a more intelligent interpretation of our constitutional purposes than any which Blackstone can supply, and a more enlightened concept of religious liberty and human equality of intellectual rights, than any that has been given us by those courts which read Blackstone into our constitutions.

Liberty and Licensing the Printer.

"The press being introduced into this country [England] by Henry VII, an opinion prevailed that it was part of the prerogative of the King to govern it, and that opinion was not eradicated for many ages. This was perhaps not unnatural, the press being introduced by the King and the art of printing being by his munificence communicated

151

to his subjects, and he having at first licensed certain persons only to print."[1]

At that age, when few could read or write, the importance of the press as a vehicle of thought was not so generally understood, perhaps as was its importance as a tool of business. It is conceivable that at this time persons would define liberty of the press to consist in the equal freedom to use the press as a means of profitable business. Of course, those who monopolized the use of the press as an instrument of commerce, did not preserve for us any of the arguments of persons who opposed their monopoly.

Even in our time there are those who think and write of freedom of the press wholly from the viewpoint of commercial freedom for the use of the printing press as a tool of trade. Here I have in mind the numerous writings of Wilmer Atkinson. He endorses all existing restrictions on the press as a vehicle of thought, and seems willing to increase these restrictions.[2] Yet under the plea of "liberty of the press" he complains vigorously against those post office regulations which interfere with his profit making in the publishing business. In other words he is objecting to having publishers licensed to use the press in connection with mail privileges, and so far he is perfectly right. As to the tyranny of this he points out that the post office department has suppressed more periodical publications than it has allowed the use of second class mailing privileges. Liberty of the press includes the negation of all that and much more.

LIBERTY AND LICENSING THE BOOK.

From granting to a limited number of the friends of Royalty licenses as a printer's monopoly, the reformation made it seem desirable that the emphasis should be put upon the more direct control of the ideas that were to be printed. "In 1585 Whitgift obtained an order of the Queen that there should be no printing-press except in

[1] Scarlett's argument in: Memoir of the right honorable James first Lord Abinger, p. 297.
[2] The old battle renewed for the freedom of the press. Philadelphia. 1907 (See p. 52); Also: A bogy unveiled, argument against the adoption of * * * the Loud bill. [n. d.]

London and the two Universities, and no book should be printed that had not been read by the Archbishop or Bishop of London, or their chaplain. (Neal's Purit. 269; Strype's, Whitgift, 223.) And yet private and traveling presses were not unknown at that time, as was obvious from the trial of Knightley, who favored the Puritan party in attacking the church of England. (2 Camden, Eliz. 550; State Trials 1271.) It was near the eighteenth century before printing, which had previously been confined to London, became generally practiced in the country towns. Ghent's Life, 20."[3]

Thus came the transition from licensing the printer, to a licensing of the book. The freedom of the press as an instrument of commerce could be thus enlarged, without the least enlargement of intellectual freedom. Under this new dispensation another definition of freedom of the press might be attempted.

Manifestly from this point of view one might indulge in extravagant eulogies of freedom of the press as did Blackstone and in our day Wilmer Atkinson, and then perhaps paraphrase Blackstone and define it something like this: "Liberty of the press is indeed essential to the nature of a free state; but it consists in laying no previous restraint upon its use as a tool or trade, and not in freedom from censure for the publication of criminal matter when published. Every freeman has an undoubted right to own a printing machine if he pleases. To forbid this is contrary to the freedom of the press; but if he publishes what is improper, mischievous and illegal because disapproved by the censor he must take the consequence of his temerity. To subject the ownership of the press to the restrictive power of a licensor as was formerly done is to subject the freedom of the press to the prejudices and favoritism of one man and make him the infallible arbiter as to who shall be allowed to print discussions of controverted points in learning, religion and government. But to punish any dangerous and offensive writings, which upon a previous fair and impartial hearing by the intelligent censor shall have been adjudged of a pernicious tend-

[3] Patterson, Liberty of the Press, p. 44-45.

ency, is necessary for the preservation of peace and good order of government and religion, the solid foundation of civil liberty."

If one wished to return to the licensing of books, the foregoing definition of freedom sounds just as plausible as Blackstone's although in nearly his own language it expresses the very antithesis of his conception of it. Manifestly liberty of the press includes also something more than both of those combined.

FREE PRINTING AND RESTRAINED PUBLICATION.

The licensing act, against which John Milton wrote, as re-enacted September 20th, 1649, provided among its various abridgments of publication that "no person whatever should presume *to send by the post, carriers, or otherwise,* or endeavor to dispense, any unlicensed book," etc., on penalty of forfeiture, fine, and imprisonment. In addition every printer was required to give a bond to "the keepers of the Liberties of England" to insure against the violation of this licensing act.

Of course this is only a very remote restraint upon the liberty of the press, if we are thinking of that liberty from the viewpoint of mere commercial opportunity in the use of presses. However, it is quite different if we think of liberty of the press from the standpoint of intellectual intercourse. Then to restrain mankind from transmitting the printed page is a total destruction of the very essence of freedom in the interchange of ideas in print. Obviously the freedom of the press as an educational factor is still abridged, even though not totally destroyed, whenever one or more of the usual methods of conveying printed matter is prohibited, even though other methods of communicating ideas still remain. In either event intellectual freedom has been limited, that is abridged, and our constitutional guarantees violated.

The same is obviously true when, as in the time of Milton, the approved idea is allowed transmission and the conveyance of the contrary disapproved idea is penalized. In such matters one indispensable essence of intellectual freedom consists in the freedom of intercourse, unhampered by inequalities created by law. In other words, every legalized inequality of intellectual opportunity, whether in the receiving or expressing of ideas, may then be viewed as a violation of constitutional guarantees.

However, if we have only a narrow and partial view of liberty, or if we have an aversion or fear of mental freedom some essential factor of it will be ignored in our definition. So do we always unconsciously unmask our tyrannous desires. So always do we abridge liberty in the name of liberty. Thus one might say: thought is free. Any person can entertain any thought which pleases so long as he keeps it within his own head. But it might be said, no one can have a right to transmit by any mode of common carriage any idea suspected of an ill tendency. Any punishment inflicted for such conduct is wholly consistent with liberty of speech and of the press, "properly understood." Such definitions of mental freedom are always plausible in the eyes of all those who fear democratic freedom, which is the largest equal freedom for all persons of all shades of opinion. But from the standpoint of a courageous and self-confident democracy which will demand the largest intellectual opportunity, liberty of the press must negative *all* discrimination based upon *a priori* speculations about psychologic tendencies. That is only another way of saying that to inhibit the transmission of *some* printed matter, by any of the ordinary modes of conveyance, which discrimination is made according to the approval or disapproval of the idea to be carried is an abridgment of liberty of the mind and of the press. Milton did not conceive the press to be free with only this one restriction removed. That liberty includes more than the absence of this one mode of abridgment. It means the negation of all abridgment.

FROM PRIOR TO *ex Post Facto* CENSORSHIP.

Licensing the book was no more satisfactory than licensing the printer. In 1694 this licensing of the book was ended but without enlarging intellectual opportunity one particle. All that which the censors had formerly disapproved and made criminal to print was now penalized after printing, that is, at the point of distribution, without the possibility of getting authoritative advance information upon the right to publish. Thus tyranny had again changed the time and mode of applying its censorial authority without in the least curtailing censorial power. However, the demand for intellectual freedom, with liberty of the press as one means thereto, had been consciously formulated and that demand will never again be silenced.

After the repeal of the licensing act the enemies of mental liberty glorified the achieved reform and again denounced all further enlargement of liberty as dangerous to morality, church, and state. Of course, they framed definitions of freedom of the press to fit their tyrannous desires and to counteract the further demands of the friends of intellectual hospitality. Under these conditions Blackstone formulated the English practice and his conception of freedom of the press.[4] Others did likewise. "Each definition was in a legal point of view complete and accurate, but what the public at large understood by the expression was something altogether different—namely, the right of unrestricted discussion of public affairs."[5]

It is now believed that no person intelligently in earnest about insuring intellectual liberty could possibly imagine the securing of it, merely by prohibiting previous restraint in favor of an *ex post facto* censorship, especially where the latter censorship penalized publications according to *ex post facto* standards of judgment. Neither of these changes enlarges intellectual liberty and the latter enlarges the dangers of authors and publishers by creating unlimited uncertainties and corresponding potential and imminent tyrannies.

Those who, like Blackstone, conceive the absence of previous restraint to be the whole of intellectual liberty are mistaking a fragmentary means for an end, probably because more or less consciously they are opposed to that end. Liberty of the press includes the absence of previous

---

[4] Quoted on page 97 herein, and paraphrased on page 153.
[5] History of the Criminal law of England, v. 2, p. 70-71, second edition.

restraint, either by licensing the press or licensing the book, but it also includes the absence of *ex post facto* punishment of all ideas *as such,* and then includes still more.

TAXES ON KNOWLEDGE.

The next mode of abridging intellectual freedom was the taxing device which began in England in 1711. George Jacob Holyoake describes the situation thus: "Yet every newspaper proprietor was formerly treated as a blasphemer and a writer of sedition, and compelled to give substantial securities against the exercise of his *infamous tendencies;* every papermaker was regarded as a thief, and the officers of the Excise dogged every step of his business, with hampering, exacting and humiliating suspicion. Every reader found with an unstamped paper in his possession was liable to a fine of £20." Holyoake violated this law until, when the last warrant was issued against him the penalties amounted to $3,000,000. So the fight was won for enlarged freedom and thereby came cheaper newspapers and books, which the masses could better afford to buy. The story of this interesting fight for more liberty of the press needs to be better known than it is.[6] A similar controversy existed in the American colonies.[7]

Here again, one who is obsessed with the means of abridging human intercourse, instead of concentrating on the object of intellectual liberty, might easily have fallen into the error of saying that freedom of the press consists in levying no *special* taxes against the printing business *as such.* Careless thinkers and those wishing to find excuses for explaining away the beneficent provisions of our constitutions might adopt this definition and thereby seek to justify all other forms of abridging intellectual intercourse. The intelligent friends of educational progress and religious liberty will never be tricked into approving

[6] See: Collet's, Taxes on Knowledge, the story of their origin and repeal, London, 1899; also: Patterson's Liberty of the press, p. 57, for brief references.
Brougham and Vaux, Taxes on knowledge, London, 1834;
[Francis Place] A repeal of the stamp duty on newspapers, edited by J. R. Roebuck, London, 1855; Trial of George J. Holyoake.
[7] Clyde Augustus Duniway; Development of freedom of press in Massachusetts, p. 120-121.

this or any other definition of freedom which deals only with some one or two aspects of tyranny, nor will these act as if this constituted the whole essence of liberty. Intellectual freedom indeed precludes the levy of special taxes on intellectual intercourse, but it precludes also much more.

JURY AS JUDGES OF LAW.

In the eighteenth century and before (and sometimes since), the judges were very despotic, especially in dealing with those charged with seditious utterances, against either church or state. The courts uniformly held that whether or not a given publication was criminal was a question of law for the judge. This was particularly oppressive because then as now, the criteria of guilt for intellectual crimes had little existence except in the mind of the judges, whose whim, caprice, or superstition found *ex post facto* expression at the trial. Thus the only function of the jury was to determine whether or not the defendant said or published what was charged against him. Under such judges, not responsible to anyone except royalty, it was thought that even with the lawless uncertainty of the criteria of guilt the defendants would fare better if it were conceded that the jury had power to decide the law as well as the facts, or at least to render a verdict on the whole issue. The difference between these two propositions is of course, purely theoretical, and verbal.

This was the motive which prompted the demand for a return to the general criminal practice wherein juries return a general verdict which unavoidably gives them power to judge of both the law and the facts.

In England the matter was settled so far as libel is concerned by a declaratory act of Parliament. In America the same issue was several times brought before the courts. The power of juries received skillful defense by the opinion of Justice Kent in People v. Croswell.[8]

This inconclusive litigation was followed probably in all states by a declaratory constitutional provision, or statutes. In Massachusetts the constitution provides that in

---

[8] 3 Johnson's Cases, 337-363.

all criminal cases juries are judges of both law and fact. In some constitutions the declaration is limited to libels. If the opinion of Justice Kent in the Croswell case is to be followed by courts, as it seemingly has been by constitution makers and legislators, then it would seem that even in the absence of constitutional provision juries should be allowed to be judges of law and fact, at least in all intellectual crimes, that is, without distinction as to whether the offending words were spoken, written or printed.

The first case of seditious utterance which Erskine tried after the passage of the Fox Libel act resulted in a conviction. Where then was the enlargement of intellectual liberty? In this connection I am tempted to reproduce Sir James Fitzjames Stephens' interesting comment, on Lord Kenyon's eulogy of this kind of "liberty" of the press.

"The liberty of the press is dear to England," said his Lordship.[9] "The licentiousness of the press is odious to England. The liberty of it can never be so well protected as by beating down the licentiousness * * * I said that the liberty of the press was dear to Englishmen, and I will say that nothing can put that in danger but the licentiousness of the press." This is the very commonplace way of talking, by all those who desire to conceal their aversion to the democracy of unabridged intellectual opportunity. A little further on his Lordship defines liberty of the press thus: "It is neither more or less than this, that a man may publish anything which twelve of his countrymen think is not blamable, but that he ought to be punished if he publishes what is blamable." In this connection it might also be useful to re-read the criticism of Blackstone as made by Tunis Wortman, herein before republished.

Now comes Sir James with this comment on Lord Kenyon's remarks: "The definition is admirably terse and correct from a legal point of view, but how does it distinguish liberty from license? If the definition given is substituted for liberty of the press, the thing defined, the result is strange. 'The fact that a man is permitted to publish with impunity anything, which twelve of his country-

---

[9] R. v. Cuthill, 27 State Trials, 674.

men afterwards regard as not blamable, is dear to Englishmen, but that permission can never be so well protected,
as by punishing severely everyone who miscalculates what
juries will like.' In other words,—The jury are *ex post
facto* censors of the press. 'If they wish to make the
power of publishing without any other license really valuable, they ought to be severe censors. A severe censorship
is the best guardian of the liberty of the press.' A very
odd conclusion, practically not differing much from this—
the press ought to be put under severe censorship. This
may or may not be true, but it is inconsistent with the
doctrine that liberty of the press is dear to Englishmen."[10]

To authorize juries to put their arbitrary and lawless
check upon the arbitrary and lawless tendencies of judges
did not of necessity enlarge mental freedom, because jurors
often were dominated by the same immature lust for power,
the same psychologic imperative of religious and governmental superstitions, as the judges. However, on rare occasions, jurors do exhibit more sympathy with human
rights than judges, and then liberty is so far enlarged by
their spasmodic whim, when the law requires between the
judge and jury a concurrence of opinion as to the law of
liberty, before a conviction can be secured. Notwithstanding this, one must have strong prejudices against liberty,
or very immature intellectual processes, if this one opportunity for enlarging freedom is mistaken for the whole
essence of intellectual liberty. To me this seems in the
long run to have proven the least important of all the practical steps in that direction, and yet in past centuries it
was thought highly important. If there really existed a
conceded claim of right to intellectual liberty or if the
law defined the crime with the same precision as murder
is defined, then there never could arise any question as to
whether or not the rules of censorship, or the creation
of the criteria of guilt, was within the province of the
judge or of the jury, either to create or declare. Freedom
of speech meant much more than this, because it means
the absence of all penalization of the expression of ideas
as such.

---

[10] History of the Criminal Law of England, v. 2, p. 349.

TRUTH AND CRIMINALITY.

Since the eighteenth century courts held logically, but not consistently, to the pretense that to prevent disturbance of the peace as such, was the object of punishing libels and slanders. So came the doctrine that the greater the truth the greater the libel, since a bad man is more easily provoked to assault than a good one. The friends of larger liberty attacked this doctrine with much vigor by asserting the right to tell the truth and prove the truth in defense of a charge of libel or slander. Of course there were and still are varying degrees in which the right to hear and to tell the truth is defended. Again our definition of intellectual liberty will be determined by how much liberty and democracy we really believe in, or in what cases we think sham and pretense more sacred or useful than the right of others to know every claim of the truth. It was inevitable from the nature of the issue that truth should be held immaterial also in cases of blasphemy. One learned author states the case thus: "With regard, however, to writings affecting the Christian religion, supposing it to be considered as the object libelled, it is to be observed, that, here, the test of truth and foundation in reason of the matter published, fails us as a guide for ascertaining, in all cases, the motive of the publishers; the Christian religion not being demonstrable by mere human reason, either to be true or to be false. Faith in its truth is necessary to its belief; and if a man have such faith, no power of mere human reason can prove that his faith is mispleace." [11]

In the eighteenth century, one who was attempting to enlarge intellectual liberty and should confuse this one means to larger liberty with the end of a complete liberty, might say as did Justice Kent: "Liberty of the press consists in the right to publish with impunity, truth, with good motives and for justifiable ends." That doctrine did establish one aid to freedom, so far as personal libels were concerned, and it did repudiate the contention that peace as such was the end sought in prosecutions for libel. How-

---

[11] George, Treatise on Libel, 355.

ever, it has no practical value in dealing with academic questions of ethics and government or the metaphysical speculations about religion and its morality. What good would it have done for Taylor, or Ruggles to be conceded the right to prove that the Holy Ghost never took the Virgin Mary to the town clerk of Jerusalem to secure a marriage license? Or the right of Legat to prove the truth of his claim that Jesus is not to be prayed to? Or the right of Mockus to prove by seeming contradictions of Holy Writ, that the source of its inspiration was not possessed of absolute veracity? Such matters are not provable by such evidence as is usually accepted by courts, or by those dealing with the material universe according to the scientific method. For that reason alone all problems of religion, no matter in what vocabulary these are discussed, were constitutionally declared beyond the jurisdiction of the magistrate. In such matters the friends of freedom denied that the magistrate had any authority to make inquiry into the truth or utility of what was taught.

Conceding the right to prove the truth of one's statement as a special defense under particular circumstances, or even as a complete defense to all intellectual crimes, enlarges freedom somewhat, but woe be unto us if that is to be treated as the end and all of liberty for human intercourse. Liberty of speech and of the press must include even more than that, especially where blasphemy is the charge.

RESUME ON DEFINITIONS.

We have seen that liberty may be, and has been defined in various ways, according to that particular means of abridging intellectual liberty which for the moment obsessed the attention of the definer. Thus freedom of the press may be said to consist in the greatest equal liberty to use the press as an instrument of commerce, accompanied by any restriction upon its use as a factor of intellectual freedom. So also we may have thought of intellectual liberty as being merely the absence of some particular mode of its abridgment, such as previous restraint; or again, such as the absence of special taxes on the communication of ideas; or as consisting of the right to tell the truth, with or without good motives or justifiable ends; and by still another it is said to rest in a jury entitled to decide questions of law as well as of fact; or intellectual liberty may be defined as it was conceived by English tyrants after the licensing acts, as mere freedom from previous censorship; or later as conceived by Jefferson, and others who framed our American constitutions, as including all of these factors and the absence also of *ex post facto* censorship. Any of these definitions, except that of Jefferson and his followers, leave all but one means of abridging intellectual intercourse at the option of a ruling power. However, free speech defined from the viewpoint of securing unabridged intellectual liberty cannot consist merely in the negation of any particular mode or modes of abridging it, with a conceded claim of rightful authority to accomplish the same end by all other means of abridgment. That is merely a limited tolerance, to be withdrawn at will. Constitutional intellectual liberty as to religion can only mean the denial of legal authority to resort *to any of these or any other* modes of abridging mental freedom, so long as an expressed idea about a religious subject matter is the only factor involved. If the framers of our constitutions had intended less than this, they would have enumerated the particular abridgments which alone they intended to prohibit.

Manifestly if we are to enjoy the blessings of a constitution like that of Connecticut, which guarantees a separation of church and state, and guarantees that none, because of their religious opinions, are to have any discrimination or preference exercised for or against them (so precluding any special privileges or protection from scoffing or ridicule); and guarantees that every citizen may freely speak, write and publish his sentiments on all subjects; if no valid law can ever be passed to curtail or restrain the liberty of speech or of the press, then obviously *all* modes of abridgment must be destroyed—including *ex post facto* censorship as well as previous censorship.

If then we would acquire a synthetic concept of religious liberty perhaps we had better direct our attention away

from the old past or new future methods of abridging intellectual liberty and focus our interest upon abolishing
the jurisdiction of government to deal with mere religious
discussion and upon repudiating the excuses upon which
that jurisdiction had formerly been claimed. This is exactly what our constitutions sought to do. This will be
still more evident just as soon as we get away from our
quarrels about the acquired meaning of constitutional
phrases, to understand the real purposes sought to be accomplished, not only the purposes of those who recorded
the American verdict in our fundamental law, but also of
their predecessors, who fought the battles for intellectual
freedom through the preceding centuries. Without the
latter that verdict for liberty would never have been written. Without consulting the issues of that previous controversy our constitutions will rarely be properly understood.

XII.
THE ORIGIN, MEANING AND SCOPE OF BLASPHEMY.

We now come to the task of discussing the meaning of blasphemy and the scope of blasphemy laws. Aside from curiosity, this and the immediately succeeding narrative of prosecutions have a very important bearing upon the constitutional aspects of our problem. By exhibiting the scope, the origin and the changing theories of blasphemy prosecution we will be making clear what it was that the framers of our constitutions meant to destroy. Also it will exhibit the uncertainty of the statutory word "blaspheme." Thus we will come to a better understanding of constitutional religious and intellectual freedom. So we also prepare the way for an argument for the unconstitutionality of blasphemy laws upon the ground, of their uncertainty. A comparison of the various ancient conceptions of blasphemy shows them all to have had practical application under the common law of England.

PLATO ON BLASPHEMY.

All our laws concerning blasphemy are the outgrowth of the canon law, and this in turn was but a new formulation of what had preceded the advent of Christ. Since Erasmus called Plato a Christian before Christianity [1] we may begin with the latter.

"Plato distinguished Blasphemy into three sorts. I. Denying the Being of a God. II. Denying his Providence, or superintendency of Human Affairs. And III. Pretending that by Gifts and Sacrifices, he may be bribed into a Toleration of wickedness; or in other words, that God is not infinitely holy and an irreconcilable Enemy to Sin."[2]

THE CANON LAW ON BLASPHEMY.

The most widely used alphabetical work of references

---

[1] Revelation the best foundation of morals, v. 2, p. 107.
[2] Disney, John; A view of ancient laws against immorality and profaneness; * * * Cambridge, 1729, p. 204.

covering Canon Law and Moral Theology, current in Germany in the early 16th Century, is the Summa Angelica. It is the work of the Blessed Angelo Carletti di Chuvasso, a Franciscan friar who died in 1495. The first edition appeared in 1476 and down to the year 1520 it passed through 31 editions.[3] The article Blasphemia defines blasphemy as a certain derogation of the excellent goodness of *anyone* and especially of the Divine goodness. *Whoever therefore denies anything concerning God which is proper to God, or asserts anything concerning Him which is not proper to Him disparages* the Divine goodness; for God is the very essence of goodness.[4] The casuist then goes on to distinguish blasphemy of heart from oral blasphemy, and says that oral blasphemy is opposed to the confession of faith (creed), and to divine love. He quotes the theological works of Alexander Hales and of Thomas Aquinas on this point.

In paragraph I, Angelus asks what kinds of blasphemy there are, and he answers according to St. Ambrose, there are two. *First, when there is attributed to God that which is not proper to God, and second, when there is taken away from God that which is proper to God. To these two a third should be added, according to St. Thomas Aquinas, that when there is attributed to the Creature, that which is proper to the Creator alone.* Angelus, however, inclines not to insist on these fine distinctions.

In paragraph II, he asks whether the sin of blasphemy may be forgiven. He says it may not be forgiven when it was committed maliciously, and refers to Matthew 12, concerning blasphemy against the Holy Ghost. Then he discusses blasphemy against the Saints.

In paragraph III, he asks whether the blasphemous man may be absolved by his own Priest.

In paragraph IV, he deals with the case of blasphemous words in public. Here he cites Panormitanus and Hostiensis in their comments on the passage of the Canon Law which is fundamental for the treatment of blasphemy.

---

[3] Catholic Encyclopedia, v. 1, p. 484.
[4] According to Dionisius the Areopagite on the Divine Names.

This is c. 2. fff. De Maledicis 5, 26.[5] It begins: "We decree that if anyone should have presumed to loosen his tongue publically in blasphemy against God or any of his Saints, and especially of the Blessed Virgin, that he should thereby be punished." The gloss of the Canon Law on this chapter refers under the word blasphemy to the fact that it is far more serious to insult the eternal than the temporal majesty. By it, it means that it is far more dangerous to blaspheme against God than to commit the crimen laesse majestatis.[6]

DISNEY ON BLASPHEMY.

John Disney, the Vicar of St. Mary's in Nottingham, in 1729 published this definition: "Blasphemy in its strict and proper Sense is to deny, reproach, or insult the Being and Attributes of God, the person or character of Christ, the Operations of the Holy Spirit, or the truth and Authority of the Scriptures; to ascribe to any of these what is unworthy of them, and degrading; or to any Creature, an Excellence which only can belong to God." [7]

Although the wording here is a little more precise, the obvious purpose, I think, of this statement is essentially the same as that of Plato and the Canon Law. In making it more concrete we are already helped to see the uncertainty of the metaphysical speculations which one may not deny. For example: What are the operations of the Holy Ghost? Are Billy Sunday's performances and the war included? What are the "attributes of God" or of whose conception of God, that one may not deny or reproach? May we deny either the Unitarian, Universalist, Trinitarian, Mormon or Mohammedan conceptions of God? Let us be reminded that there are unnumbered varieties of these conceptions. Whose conception of the "character of Christ" is it that we may not deny? What degree of sensitiveness will determine what constitutes a "reproach" or an "insult?" By whose standard of "honor" is alleged

---

[5] Corpus juris canonici, ed. Friedberg II. 826 b.
[6] For this statement of the canon law I am indebted to Prof. Woodbridge.
[7] Disney, John. A view of ancient laws against immorality and profaneness, p. 201.

blasphemy to be judged? Such queries can manifestly be
multiplied indefinitely. It is the very vagueness which
makes this law so all inclusive that under it anything and
everything can be penalized which offends the most primitive and childish religious feelings. In this we see the
reason and the justification of the statement that all particular statutes upon the subject of religion were merely
declaratory of the common law.[8]

BLACKSTONE ON OFFENSES AGAINST RELIGION.

Blackstone of course wrote under the conditions when a
union of church and state prevailed. By bearing this unity
in mind it will be clear that all which follows comes clearly
within the canon law concerning blasphemy. One really
should re-read the whole of his chapter on "Offenses against
God and Religion" to understand what was sought to be
destroyed by our constitutional provisions for a separation
of church and state, and for intellectual equality and liberty. Because Blackstone's Commentaries are everywhere
accessible, we will here content ourselves with just a few
extracts. He classifies offenses into several groups and
then discusses each separately. Then he proceeds thus:

"First then, of such crimes and misdemeanors, as more
immediately offend Almighty God, by openly transgress-
ing the precepts of religion either natural or revealed; and
immediately by their bad example and consequences the
law of society, which constitutes that guilt in the action
which human tribunals are to censure."

Criminal heretics are defined as "teachers of *erroneous
opinions contrary to the faith* and blessed determinations
of the holy church." Also this is criminal: "Any person
educated in the Christian religion, or professing the same,
[who] shall by writing, printing, teachings, or advised
speaking, *deny any one of the persons of the holy Trinity
to be God* or maintain that there are more gods than one,
he shall undergo the same penalties and incapacities" as
apply to apostates.

"Another species of offenses against religion are those
which affect the *established church*. And these are either

---

[8] Blackstone's Commentaries, vol. 4, p. 50.

positive or negative: Positive as by *reviling its ordinances;* or negative by *nonconformity* to its worship. Or both of these in order." (Lord's Supper, Book of Common Prayer, Liturgy, Non-Conformist who absent themselves through mistaken or perverse zeal.)

"The fourth species of offenses, therefore, more immediately against God and religion, is that of blasphemy against the Almighty, *by denying his being or providence;* or by contumelous reproaches of our Saviour Christ. Whither also may be referred all profane scoffing at the holy scripture, or exposing it to contempt and ridicule * * * *. Somewhat allied to this, though in an inferior degree, is the offense of profane and common swearing and cursing. * * * *"

Then he deals with witchcraft and sorcery, and continues:

"Seventh species of offenders in this class are religious impostors, such as *falsely pretend an extraordinary commission from heaven;* or terrify and abuse the people with false denunciation of judgments. These as tending to subvert all religion, by bringing it into ridicule and contempt are punishable by the temporal courts with fine and imprisonment and infamous corporal punishment." [9]

In 1626, the King issued a proclamation, declaring: "That *neither in Doctrine nor Discipline of the Church, nor in the Government of the State will he admit of the least innovation,"* and, therefore, commanding that "neither by Writing, Preaching, Printing, Conferences, or otherwise, they raise, publish or maintain *any other Opinions concerning Religion,* than such as are clearly warranted by the Doctrine and Discipline of the Church of England, established by authority.—And enjoyneth his Reverend Archbishops and Bishops in their several Dioceses, speedily to reclaim and repress all such spirits, as shall in *the least degree* attempt to violate this Bond of Peace; and all the Ministers of Justice were required to execute his Majesty's Pious and Royal pleasure herein expressed; and if any shall take the boldness to neglect this

---

[9] Blackstone's Commentaries. Book 4, Chapter 4, especially pp. 43-50-55-61-62.

gracious admonition, His Majesty will proceed against such offenders with that severity as their contempt shall deserve, that by their exemplary punishment others may be warned, and that 'those that be studious of the peace and prosperity of this church and Commonwealth may bless God for his Majesty's pious, religious, wise and gracious Government."[10]

Under the reign of Henry VIII. "the bloody law of the six articles was made, which established the six most contested points of popery, transubstantiation, communion in one kind, the celibacy of the clergy, monastic vows, the sacrifice of the mass, and auricular confession; which points were 'determined and resolved by the most godly, study, pain, and travail of his majesty.' "[11]

"False and pretended prophecies, with intent to disturb the peace, are equally unlawful, and more penal; as they raise enthusiastic jealousies in the people, and terrify them with imaginary fears. They are, therefore, punished by our law, upon the same principle that spreading of public news of any kind, without communicating it first to the magistrate, was prohibited by the ancient Gauls, such false and pretended prophecies were punished capitally by statute 1 Edw. XI c. 12, which repealed in the reign of Queen Mary (A. D.　) and now by the statute of 5 Eliz. c. 151, The penalty for the first offence is a fine of 100 £ and one year imprisonment; for the second, forfeiture of all goods and chattels and imprisonment during life."[12]

"The duty and right of the civil power, I repeat, capitally to punish heretics, and blasphemers, and idolaters, (and let it be observed, that all these who dissented from the religion of the ruling party, were stigmatized as heretics, blasphemers, or idolators, or all three united,) were as firmly believed by the great majority of the reformers, as the New Testament itself. The solemn league and covenant, originally adopted in Scotland, and subsequently

---

[10] Rushworth's, Historical Collection of private passages of State, weighty matters in law, Remarkable proceedings, etc. Lond. 1721, v. 1, p. 412.

[11] Blackstone. Commentaries, v. 4, p. 47.

[12] Blackstone's Commentaries, v. 4, p. 149, 1st edition.

ordered by the British Parliament, during the civil war, to be taken by all the subjects of England, under severe penalties, went to the extirpation not merely of "popery," which was universally anathematized as rank idolatry, but of 'prelacy,' (i. e. episcopacy) 'superstition, heresy, schism, and whatsoever shall be found contrary to true godliness.' That is, in a word, every thing contrary to the Westminster Confession of Faith. On the 23rd of November, 1646, the parliament 'debated upon the ordinance against blasphemies and heresies, and the PUNISHMENT WAS VOTED TO BE DEATH.' "[13]

"By 1 Eliz. c. 2. Sect. 9, a severe Punishment is enacted for any Person who shall in any Interludes, Plays, Songs, Rhimes, or by other open Words declare or speak anything in derogation, depraving or despising the Book of Common Prayer—&c."[14]

"By 3 Jac. 1 C. 21. Whoever shall use the name of the Holy Trinity profanely or jestingly, in any stage, play, interlude or show shall be liable to a penalty of ten pounds."

"By Will. III. C. 18, sec. 17 [1689-1703] Whoever shall deny in his preaching or writing the doctrine of the blessed Trinity shall lose all benefit of the act for granting toleration. Etc. This act, in addition to depriving the offender of the privileges above mentioned, leaves the punishment of the offense, as for a misdemeanor at common law."[15]

In short the whole situation is summarized by Lord Holt, in his Law of Libels, 1816,[16] under the heading of "Offenses against Religion" when he includes: "All profane scoffing of the Holy Scripture or exposing *any part* to ridicule and contempt."

Hawkin's, Pleas of the Crown, seventh edition (1795), uses the same language above quoted from Holt. Thus

---

[13] Letters on religious persecution, * * * in reply to a libelous attack on the Roman Catholics * * * by a catholic layman. (Mathew Carey) Philadelphia, Jan. 1, 1827; p. 40, citing: Whitelock's Memorial, p. 232.

[14] Charge delivered to the grand jury * * * Westminster * * * June 1749 by Henry Fielding Esq. Lond. 1749. p. 32.

[15] Holt; Law of Libel, 1816, Second Edition, pp. 65-66.

[16] Second edition, p. 65.

again do we get back to the canon law as the source and
definition of all blasphemy.

Perhaps we can acquire a better view of these blasphemy
laws and of the state of mind that supports them by viewing them in actual operation through the judicial instructions to Grand Juries. The simple childlike reasoning
must surely have been outgrown and repudiated by our
constitutions. These instructions exhibit the plain reason
of the law, and of the discredited relations of church and
state, and something of the theories on which the resultant institutions were founded. If we get behind the words
of these instructions to juries, and those of our constitutional guarantees of religious and intellectual, equality
and liberty to understand the states of mind which these
words symbolized, then there can remain no doubt of their
incompatibility.

A SEVENTEENTH CENTURY MAGISTRATE'S INSTRUCTIONS.

Whitelocke Bulstrode (1650-1724) was an important
personage of his time, a controversialist, a mystical and
philosophical writer of much note. He had been prothono-
tary of the marshal's court, and commissioner of excise.
He had been a justice of the peace, and several times chair-
man of the Quarter Sessions. His charges to the grand
jury and other juries have been printed and reprinted "by
request" for the enlightenment of the magistrates. I use
the edition of 1718.

"Blasphemy is in its general sense, an evil speaking of
any one; Maledicentia: But by use and custom (the governor of the Sense of Words) it is appropriated to an evil-
speaking of God; and sometimes it is taken for profane
cursing and swearing (p. 4).

"God Himself pronounced Judgment against the Blasphemer, and bid Moses bring forth him that cursed, that
he might be stoned to Death, which was accordingly done
(p. 4).

"Under this head [blasphemy] I think prophane cursing
and swearing, by the name of God, may be well compre-
hended, for the Divine Majesty has so adjudg'd it. Blasphemer and Curser, are synonymous terms in the language
of Holy Writ (pp. 4-5).

"The Jew that was ston'd to Death by the command of God for prophane cursing was in a great passion, was contending with another person, and might have had some provocation to curse, which though not excusable, yet might mitigate somewhat the fault, in respect of humane Frailties (p. 7).

"But many Christians in their common and ordinary conversation, invoke God to damn them, when they ask what o' th' clock 'tis, or even one how the other does (p. 7).

"The most senseless Practice in the World, and which nothing but the Excess of Folly and Wickedness could make mankind even be guilty of (p. 7).

JUDGMENTS ON PROFANE SAILORMEN.

"The sin of prophane cursing and swearing is so very great, and become so general amongst the common People, the soldiery and Mariners, Hackney-Coachmen and Carmen especially, that 'tis much to be feared, if there is not some stop put to it, it will draw down Veangeance from Heav'n upon us: *No wonder that our ships so often miscarry when our Mariners curse and damn themselves through the Sea to Hell.*

"When the moral World is so much out of order, why should we expect a calm in the Material? The storm arose for Jonah's sake, and even the Heathen idolatrous mariners (who did not curse and swear as ours do in a storm, but called upon their several Gods) by the Light of Nature found out the Cause by the Effect, and adjudg'd Jonah's crime to be the Cause, before God's Providence had confirm'd it.

"*Why should not the Elements, made to serve us, oppose and resist our Designs, turn their Point and Edge against us,* when we rebel against their Creator in so vile a manner, as by blasphemous Oaths and Curses, even affront the Divine Majesty to his Face.

"An habitual Swearer is a common Nuisance to the Place where he lives, worse than a Dunghill before one's Door. He has no right to Credit, in whatever he says or Swears: This Sin comes not alone, for these People let themselves loose to Lewdness and other Vices in the highest Degree.

"They breathe Contagion wherever they come, they defile Human Bodies by their corrupt and filthy emanations, and they taint humane Souls by their execrable Oaths and Curses, which is the worst sort of Plague.

"For the common Plague infects only the Body, which is only the Case or Instrument of the Soul; but these miscreants taint even the Soul, the very Man himself; they teach by their vile Example even Women and Children to Curse and Swear. There are particular laws provided against this great and crying sin. * * * If you have any regard for your Country, for the honour of God, or for your own Souls, set your Faces against this Sin.

"You ought to complain of these vile Wretches to the Magistrates, that they may be brought to condign Punishment; so that where the love of Virtue cannot restrain them the fear of Punishment may" (pp. 7-10).

THE SABBATH BREAKER DENOUNCED.

A long tirade against the Sabbath-Breaker has its presumed motive explained by saying that such persons "may justly be said to be guilty of Sacriledge, in robbing God of the public Honour, more particularly due to his Majesty that day" (p. 11).

"That great man, the Lord Chief Justice Hale, made it his Observation, that *the more strictly he kept that Day, the better success he had the Week following*" (p. 11).

"Take care of Religion, and suppress Vice; Present the authors of Books writ against Religion; as for Atheism, such as that of *Spinoza, and other detestable Authors,* or that are contra bonos Mores, or that revile the Scriptures; *Authors that deny their Creator and yet swear by him; or if they acknowledge a God they confine his majesty to heav'n and exclude a Providence,* or that God governs the World, or presides over Humane affairs. Whereas the Scriptures assert, and good sense asserts, that not a sparrow (one of the lowest in value of the animal creation) falls to the ground without a permissive or directive Providence" (p. 12).

"Zeal in these matters will never sink or deprave itself into superstition. A lukewarmness herein is a very great sin, a sort of indifferency for the honour of God, for which there can be no excess of zeal.

"Gentlemen, you will not act so in your own affairs; have but the same zeal for the Creator of the World, as you have for the World, and you will not act amiss, tho the balance ought to turn on the Creator's side" (p. 13).

"Thus wise laws duly executed prevent much evil. As for witchcraft, sorcery or enchantments, which were anciently the common topicks under this head of Offences against God, by the Learned of old; I shall not trouble you with them, there being no such practice now, blessed be God within this Kingdom" (p. 15).

HIGHER WAGES WERE HIGH TREASON.

Next he proceeds to offenses against the king, etc. "I. As to his Majesty and Royal Family. To compass, or even imagine the Death of the King, Queen or Prince, and declaring the same by some Overt Act, is High Treason. This law comes the nighest to the Divine Law of any of our laws; for the Divine law punishes the evil thoughts, and evil intentions of the heart. For from thence is the spring of all our actions. * * * *The Overt-Act is but the means whereby the wickedness of the heart in known and discovered* by the short capacity of man; but *the sin is in the thought* or intention of the heart, to contrive the death of the King. The King is the life and soul of the Kingdom. Therefore the utmost care is to be taken for the preservation of his Royal Person" (pp. 16-17).

"A raising a force to burn, or throw down a particular inclosure, is only a riot; but if it is to go from town to town, and cast in all inclosures; *or to change religion; or to* ENHANCE THE SALARIES OF LABOURERS, *these are respectively by construction of law, a levying of War, because the design is general."* (p. 18).

"They that maintain the authority of the Bishop of Rome, by writing or printing in the King's Dominions; for the first offense incur a *Praemunire*, and for the second offense (a conviction being had of the first) if they do it only by words, its High Treason.

"The bringing in of bulls or putting them in execution,

or reconciling any to the See of Rome, is high treason by 13 Eliz." (p. 22).

"And so do they incur a *Praemunire* who conceal an offer of absolution from, or conciliation to, the Church of Rome.

"They who bring into this realm a thing called an *Agnus Dei or any crosses, Pictures or beads*, from the Bishop of Rome, or from any persons having authority derived from the See of Rome, and shall deliver them to any subject of this realm, incur a Præmunire." (p. 22).

"In the days of popish ignorance, the foolish people were made to believe that these things wore by them would fright away the Devil and other Evil Spirits; but the true use of them was for the crafty Priests, to gull the people out of their money for them. . . . (p. 23).

PENALTIES OF POPERY.

"Putting in practice to persuade any person, or to absolve him from his obedience to the King, or to reconcile a person to the See of Rome, is high treason in both; and so it is in all aiders and procurers. * * * It is high treason to maintain that the King and Parliament cannot bind the descent of the Crown. And so it is if any person by writing or printing, maintains that the pretender hath right to the Crown; and if by words, the party incurs a Præmunire." (p. 27).

"The speaking of ill words of his Majesty for they are punishable at common law. The King not being within the statute of Scandalum Magnatum. Libels that are made public against the ministry, or other great men; present the printers and publishers as well as the Authors." (pp. 30-31).

In commenting on the suppression of the theatre the learned judge uses this moralistic reasoning and has it all put in italics: *"Men should not make themselves monkeys to get money; or taint the morals of those who see or hear them: It's below the dignity of humane Nature; revere yourself is a good rule. What person ever frequented the company of the actors of either sex, but what was ruined in his morals, person and estate. One Play House ruins more souls, than fifty churches are able to save."* (p. 35).

If more such information is desired it will be found in "A summary of the penal laws relating to nonjurors, papists, popish recusants, and nonconformists, and the late statutes concerning the succession, riots, and imprisonments of suspected persons. * * * to which are added, several adjudged cases, and notes upon the most material points. * * * London, 1716."

The above instructions exhibit to perfection the kind of intellect in which the censorship germ develops. The aristocratic devotion to privilege is exhibited by the laws which penalize the claim that the people have anything to say about the descent of the crown and by that law which makes it a levying of war to attempt to enhance the wage earners pay. Likewise the monopoly of a special priestcraft and if emoluments are equally preserved by excluding competitive creeds, and by making it an act of war to attempt to change the official religion. The sceptre and mitre are symbols of mutual support in privileged parasiting.

The intellectual development is further revealed by the suggestion that prosperity can be promoted by keeping the sabbath, that shipwrecks are produced by sailor's profanity, and that it is the province of government to punish blasphemy, for *the honor of God and the protection of the human soul.* This anti-democratic attitude, the metaphysics upon which it was founded and the privileges which such laws maintain are all incompatible with the culture of our time as that is expressed in our constitutions. Which will now prevail?

XIII.
PROSECUTIONS FOR CRIMES
AGAINST RELIGION.
1600-1636

The Connecticut statute against blasphemy was first enacted in 1642, and except as to its death penalty, it has been little modified since. It now penalizes "every person who shall *blaspheme* against *God*, either of the persons of the *Holy Trinity*, the *Christian religion* or the *Holy Scripture.*" Each of the italicised words symbolize a great variety of contradictory concepts, according to the varying metaphysical theories of competing sectarians as well as of many independent and unorganized mystics. Which of these mutually destructive meanings are we to adopt as a matter of law? The statute nowhere makes the choice. If we confine ourselves to one body of theological factors, and assume that the court may enact *ex post facto* tests of criminality, then these words may now be made to mean what we may at present think were the concepts of the dominant theologians of Connecticut in 1642. Let us not forget that these theologians left England to get away from the conceptions of Christianity which had prevailed there, and which were being there imposed by the aid of penal laws. From the viewpoint of the common law, we must ignore speculations about the vagaries of *colonial* theologians, and read into their statute some of those conflicting conceptions of *blasphemy*, of the *Trinity* and of the *Christian religion*, which were hated in Connecticut, but which at different times were "established" according to the changing religious fashions of the political machinery of England.

For the moment we will assume that this statute is not void for uncertainty in the criteria of guilt, and that therefore, in each blasphemy case each court may be a law unto itself, for the enforcement of some personal theologic and legal concepts in the promotion of a personal theory

178

of the general welfare, as distinguished from a legislative standard. Since the statute does not enlighten us about colonial theology, we may ignore the colonist's well-known aversion to England's established interpretation of Christianity, and proceed with our researches in juridical lore. If we are to interpret a statute of 1642 by English precedents we must begin their examination at a time much earlier. Thus we may arbitrarily choose the year 1600, as the starting point of our inquiry.

Those who are more curious, about the antecedent savagery by which priests satisfied their sadistic lust for murder, may look elsewhere.[1]

OPENING THE SEVENTEENTH CENTURY.

In our day it has become difficult to understand the thought, and much more difficult to understand the feelings entertained by the few intelligent libertarians of a few centuries ago. Unfortunately the present space limits preclude all effort to portray the condition upon which

[1] See, James Fitzjames Stephen—History of the criminal law of England, v. 2, p. 412, to end of volume, Edition of 1883,
Fox's, Book of martyrs;
Neal,—Rev. Daniel, History of Puritans.
Reese, Richard—A Compendious Martyrology, containing an account of the sufferings and constancy of Christians, in the different persecutions, which have raged against them under the pagan and popish governments. By Richard Reese. London, 1812. 3 vols.
Andrews, William Eusebius—An examination of Fox's calendar of protestant saints, martyrs * * * contrasted with a biographical sketch of catholic missionary priests and others executed under protestant penal laws, from 1335-1684 abridged from Parson's, Examen and Challoner's Memoirs, with additional remarks. London 1826.
Letters on religion persecution, by A Catholic Layman. [Mathew Carey.] (4th ed. Phila. 1827, and authorities cited.
Burn's Ecclesiastical Law;
Oldcastle's Case, (1413) v. 1, State Trials;
Master Thorpe. (1407) v. 1, State Trials, p. 17.
Keyser's, John—Case, v. 3, Coke's Institutes, 41. This man doubted that excommunication would effect the wheat crop. The spiritual court proceed against him but the court of Kings Bench released him on writ of habeas corpus.
Besse has written two folio volumes of 14 and 15 hundred pages filled with details of the suffering of the Quakers. It is estimated that between 12,000 and 15,000 Quakers were imprisoned at different times between 1660 and 1684. In the latter year there were 1,460 Quakers in the jails of England.
Maitland's Collected works, v. 1, p. 385-406; "The deacon and the Jewess or apostacy at common law."
Burnett's, History of the reformation.

those feelings were founded. With the opening of the seventeenth century the worst of the savagery was passing. In just a few paragraphs, I wish merely to give a suggestive hint of these facts.

"Were it possible to increase the abhorence and detestation which every upright mind must feel on a contemplation of the horrible scenes above depicted, one feature remains to be considered, calculated to produce this effect. While the punishment for harbouring or aiding a priest, was hanging—the most atrocious murderer, who had sent a dozen wretches to their final account, 'with all their imperfections on their heads,' was only hanged for his offence, however aggravated by circumstances—whereas the punishment of a priest, whatever his piety or merits might be, was—HANGING—CUTTING DOWN ALIVE—CUTTING OFF HIS PRIVY MEMBERS—SCOOPING OUT HIS BOWELS—BURNING THEM BEFORE HIS FACE—CHOPPING OFF HIS HEAD—CUTTING THE BODY IN QUARTERS—WHILE THE FLESH WAS STILL QUIVERING UNDER THE BUTCHER'S KNIFE!!—the quarters were hung up in different places in terror to others, to force them to apostatize and renounce the religion of their fathers, and profess a religion which they probably abhorred. A wonderful plan for spreading the mild spirit of the gospel, and making proselytes! Could a congress of devils from the bottomless pit of hell, devise anything more atrocious?" [2]

"A madman, who called himself the Holy Ghost, was in the same reign BURNED ALIVE." [3]

1605 July 2nd. "Seventeen Scottish ministers, contrary to the King's express command, held a solemn assembly at Aberdeen in Scotland; who, being for the same convented before the Council of Scotland, utterly denied not only their lordships' authority in that behalf, but also the king's * * * for which riot, and for denying the king's supremacy in causes ecclesiastical, six of the chief, the

[2] [Mathew Carey] Letters on Religious Persecution * * * in reply to a libelous attack on the Roman Catholics * * * by a Catholic Layman, Phila. Jan. 1, 1827. (p. 42.)
[3] [Mathew Carey] Letters etc. p. 43, citing Hume's England, vol. 3, p. 371. edition not given.

10th of January following, were ARRAIGNED AND CONDEMNED OF HIGH TREASON." [4]

Quite true, these were not charges for blasphemy. They were only gentle Christian amenities in anticipation and for the prevention of blasphemy and for preventing even the advocacy of tolerance for such dangerous tendencies. If we concede to the State a jurisdiction to punish blasphemy, then it may indeed be dangerous to wait till the blasphemy has poisoned innocent minds. Far better protection against this heinous offence is given if the heretic predisposed to blasphemy and tolerance is put out of the way before he has a chance to infect others.

With just these hints as to that which was passing we will now proceed to a study of the relatively few cases of which any record remains. Often the record will be incomplete. To the best of our facilities we will portray as near as may be the essence of the offence and as completely as may be possible and useful the official or judicial action. To each case discussed a bibliography is attached. Occasionally this includes books which were not accessible. The cases will be reported in their chronological order.

ATWOOD'S CASE—1605. [5]

In Atwood's case the indicted language was: "Your religion is a new religion, within fifty years; preaching was but prating, and hearing of service more edifying than two hours of preaching." Held: "Car les parolls son seditious parolls encontre le State de nottre Esglise & encontre le peace del Relme & coment que ils sont spiritual parols, uncore *ils trahe un temporall consequent*, scillicet le disturbance del peace."

BARTHOLOMEW (LEGATE OR LEGATT)—1612. [6]

This heretic was "of bold spirit, confident carriage, excellently skilled in the scriptures; and well had it been

---

[4] [Mathew Carey] Letters etc. p. 42-43, citing Stowe's Chronicles. 870.

[5] Atwood's case, vol. 2, Rolle's Abridgment, p. 78;
Croke's Report, James I, p. 421.
Digest Law concerning Libels, [1765] p. 56.
Starkie: Law of Slander and Libel, 5th ed. p. 615.

[6] 2 Howell's State Trials, p. 727;
British Review, v. 5, p. 208-210;
Dictionary of National Biography, v. 32, p. 405.

for him if he had known them less or understood them
better. His conversation very unblamable, and in the position of heretical doctrine is never more dangerous than
when served up in clean cups, and washed dishes * * *
Before we set down his pestilent opinions; may the writer
and reader fence themselves with prayer to God,
against the infection thereof; lest otherwise, touching such
pitch (though but with the bare mention) defile us,
casually tempting a temptation in us, and awakening some
corruption which otherwise would sleep silently in our
souls. And if notwithstanding this our caution, any shall
reap an accidental evil to themselves, by reading his damnable opinions, my pen is none more accessory to their
harm, than that apothecary is guilty of murder, if others,
out of a liquorish curiosity, kill themselves with that
poison, which he kept in his shop, for sovereign use to make
antidotes thereof."

Having now prepared your soul according to the above
injunction you may proceed to read the thirteen "divers
wicked Errors, Heresies, and Blasphemous Opinions
holden, affirmed, and published by the said Bartholomew
Legat, and chiefly in these thirteen Blasphemous Positions
following, viz:—

"1 That the Creeds called the Nicene Creed and
Athanasius's Creed, contain not a profession of the true
Christian Faith, or that he will not profess his Faith ac-
cording to the same Creeds.

"2. That Christ is not God, of God begotten, not made,
but begotten and made.

"3. That there are no persons in the Godhead.

"4. That Christ was not God from everlasting, but began to be God when he took Flesh of the Virgin Mary.

"5. That the world was not made by Christ.

"6. That the Apostles teach Christ to be Man only.

"7. That there is no Generation in God, but of creatures.

"8. That this assertion, God to be made Man, is contrary to the rule of Faith, and monstrous Blasphemy.

"9. That Christ was not before the fullness of time except by Promise.

"10. That Christ was not God otherwise than an anointed God.

"11. That Christ was not in the form of God, equal with God, that is, in substance of God, but in righteousness and giving Salvation.

"12. That Christ by his Godhead wrought no miracle.

"13. That Christ is not to be pray'd unto."

For these "dangerous and blasphemous" speculations against the dogma of the trinity "as a zealot of justice and a defender of the Catholic Faith", in the name of the King Legatt was "burned to ashes" at Smithfield in 1612.

EDWARD WIGHTMAN—1612. [7]

A month after the burning of Legatt the same fate befell Edward Wightman at Litchfield. The pious reporter tells us the latter suffered for far worse opinions (if worse might be) than Legatt maintained. * * * The wicked heresies of the Ebionites, Corinthians, Valentinians, Arian, Macedonians, of Simon Magnus, of Manes, Manichees, of Photinus and Anabaptists and of other heretical, execrable, and unheard of opinions, by the instinct of Satan, by him excogitated and holden, viz.:

"1. That there is not the trinity of persons, the Father, the Son, and the Holy Ghost, in the unity of the Deity.

"2. That Jesus Christ is not the true natural Son of God, perfect God, and of the same substance, eternity and majesty with the Father in respect of his Godhead.

"3. That Jesus Christ is only man and a mere creature, and not both God and man in one person.

"4. That Christ, our Saviour, took not human flesh of the substance of the Virgin Mary his Mother; and that, that Promise 'The Seed of the Woman shall break the serpent's head,' was not fulfilled in Christ.

"5. That the person of the Holy Ghost is not God co-equal, coeternal, and coessential with the Father and the Son.

"6. That the three creeds, The Apostles Creed, the Nicene Creed, and Athanasius's Creed, are the heresies of the Nicolaitanes.

---

[7] R. v. Wightman, 2 Howell's State Trials, 734-735.

"7. That he the said Edward Wightman is that prophet spoken of in the eighteenth of Deuteronomy in these words, 'I will raise them up a prophet,' &c. And that, that place of Isaiah, 'I alone, have troden the winepress;' and that place, 'Whose fan is in his hand,' are proper and personal to him, the said Edward Wightman.

"8. And that he the said Wightman is that person of the Holy Ghost spoken of in the Scriptures; and the Comforter spoken of in the 16th of St. John's Gospel.

"9. And that those words of our Saviour Christ of the Sin of Blasphemy against the Holy Ghost, are meant of his person.

"10. And that, that place, the fourth of Malachy, of Elias to come, is likewise meant of his person.

"11. That the soul doth sleep in the sleep of the first death, as well as the body, and is mortal as touching the sleep of the first death, as the body is: And that the soul of our Saviour Jesus Christ did sleep in that sleep of death as well as his body.

12. That the souls of the elect saints departed, are not members possessed of the triumphant Church in Heaven.

"13. That the baptizing of infants is an abominable custom.

"14. That there ought not to be in the church the use of the Lord's Supper to be celebrated in the Elements of Bread and Wine; and the use of Baptism to be celebrated in the Element of Water; as they are now practiced in the Church of England: But that the use of Baptism is to be administered in water, only to converts of sufficient age of understanding, converted from infidelity to the faith.

"15. That God has ordained and sent him, the said Edward Wightman, to perform his part in the work of the Salvation of the world, to deliver it by his teaching, or admonition, from the heresy of the Nicolaitanes; as Christ was ordained and sent to save the world, and by his death to deliver it from sin, and to reconcile it to God.

"16. And that Christianity is not wholly professed and preached in the Church of England, but only in part."

These two last cases are a perfect illustration of the meaning of our constitutional guarantees for unabridged free speech, according to some judicial interpretations of it. There was no previous restraint, and only such subsequent punishment according to law, for "dangerous or offensive writings which when published were on a fair and impartial trial adjudged of a pernicious tendency". Of course, this is always done "for the preservation of peace and good order of government and religion, the only solid foundation of civil liberty." At least so says Blackstone and some other "learned" judges.

These heretical and blasphemous opinions, or some equally dangerous contrary ones, might be punishable under the Connecticut blasphemy law, if we knew what conception of the Trinity the legislature meant to protect against blasphemy. A practical question is: Did our constitution in such cases leave the concept of the Trinity to be determined by the whim or convictions of each jury? Does constitutional religious liberty mean only the substitution of a milder penalty? or the abolition of all penalty for such or any blasphemy?

JOHN OGELVIE—1615. [8]

In Scotland Feb'y. 1615 John Ogelvie was tried for "treason, declining the king's authority, alleging the supremacy of the Pope, hearing and saying mass," &c. In order to secure confessions he was prevented from sleep. Finally he said:

"I deny any point raised against me to be treason, for if it were treason it would be treason in all places and in all kingdoms; but that is known not to be so, as for your acts of parliament, they are made by a number of partial men, the best of the land not agreeing with them, and of matters not subject to their forum or judication for which I will not give a rotten fig."

On the king's prerogative he said: "I know no other authority he hath but that which he received from his predecessors, who acknowledged the Pope of Rome his Jurisdiction. If the King will be to me as his predecessors were to mine, I will obey and acknowledge him for my King; but if he do otherwise, and play the runagate from

---

[8] Narrative of Criminal Trials in Scotland, vol. 2, p. 143-147.

God, as he and you all do, I will not acknowledge him more than this old hat."

Adopting Presbyterian ground he said: "For declining of the King's authority, I will do it still in matters of religion, for with such matters he hath nothing to do;—neither have I done anything but that which the ministers did at Dundie; they would not acknowledge his majesty's authority in spiritual matters, more than I. * * *

"That if the King offended against the Catholic Church the Pope might punish him as well as a shepard, or the poorest fellow in the country, that in abrogating the Pope's authority the Estates of parliament had gone beyond their limits and that the King in usurping the Pope's right had lost his own." Was hung——

THOMAS DIGHTON AND JOHN HOLT—1616.[9]

In September, 1616, the Court of High Commissioners set at Ashby to examine certain witnesses against Mr. Hildersham and his friends Dighton and Holt. One of them had been imprisoned in the Gatehouse, the other in the Fleet. They were brought to the court under guard and received the following sentence:

"It appeared to the court that the said Dighton and Holt, being laymen had, in opposition to the State Ecclesiastical, kept sundry conventicles, or exercises of religion in private houses, * * * * * and held public disputations against the orders, rites and ceremonies of the church, and disuated others from conformity to the same. * * * Leaving their own parishes went to other parishes to hear unconformable ministers and carried many of the parish of Ashby after them, to the great encouragement of schismatical and refractory persons; * * * and having made common purses, and sundry collections, for maintaining, abbetting, and encouraging such schismatical persons in their obstinacy and disobedience to his majesty's laws ecclesiastical, they are therefore pronounced schismatics and schismatical persons, and worthy to be severely punished, and were accordingly fined, a thousand pounds a piece, pronounced excommunicate, ordered to be publicly

⁹ Richard Reese, Compendious martyrology, v. 3, p. 426.

denounced, to make their submission in three severaly places, condemned in costs of suit, and sent back to prison."

RICHARD MOKET (MOCKET or MOQUET)—1617.[10]

Richard Mocket (1577-1618), was a graduate of Oxford and a clergyman of some distinction. In 1616, in London, Moket published a volume in Latin, containing the writings of others, and adding a work of his own entitled, "Doctrina et Politia Ecclesiae Anglicanae" which was a general view of ecclesiastical jurisdiction in the English church. The book gave offence, and by public edict the king condemned it to be burnt in 1617. Heylyn was of the opinion that the real offence was the omission of the first clause in the translation of the twentieth article of the thirty-nine articles which runs: "The Church hath power to decree rites or ceremonies and authority in controversies of faith." Evidently because the offence was negative, that is an omission, no criminal prosecution followed. May we not legitimately infer, however, that if the denial of ecclesiastical jurisdiction had been expressed, it would have been treated as being also a criminal offence?

TRASKE'S CASE—1618.[11]

"In the Star Chamber likewise one John Traske, a Minister that held opinion that the Jewish Sabbath ought to be observed, and not ours, and that we ought to abstain from all manner of swines' flesh; being examined upon these things he confessed that he had divulged these opinions, and had laboured to bring as many to his opinions as he could. And had also written a letter to the King wherein he did seem to tax his Majesty of Hypocracie, and did expressly inveigh against the Bishop's high Commissioners, as bloody and cruel in their *proceedings against him and a Papal Clergy.*"

"Now being called Ore tenus, was Sentenced to Fine

---

[10] Vickers, Robert H. Martyrdoms of literature, p. 373.
Dictionary of national biography, vol. 38, p. 91.
General biographical dictionary, Lond. 1815, vol. 22, p. 207-9.
[11] Hobart's Report, 236.

and Imprisonment, not for holding these opinions, (for those were examinable in the Ecclesiastical Courts and not here) but for *making of Conventicles and Factions* by that means, *which may tend to sedition* and commotion, and for *scandalizing* the King, *the Bishops and the Clergy.*"

Among other things we see here that an argument for toleration and denunciation of intolerant bishops, is penalized because it "may tend" to sedition.

REGINALD (or REYNOLD) SCOT (or SCOTT) bet. 1603-1625.[12]

Reginald Scott (1538?-1599) was a man of social position and financial comfort, and the scholarly author of books. He also held several creditable public offices. He was a member of the parliament of 1588-9 representing the constituency of New Romney. In 1584 he first published his most notable book about witchcraft which for our purpose has an important history. Its lengthy title page is very illuminating and is now herewith given in full, and with the other comment quoted shows this condemned book to be undoubtedly the most enlightened book about witchcraft that had been written up to the time of its burning which occurred before 1625. Here, then, follows the title page:

"Scot's discovery of witchcraft, proving the common opinions of witches contracting with devils, spirits, or familiars; and their power to kill, torment, and consume the bodies of men, women, and children or other creatures by diseases or otherwise; their flying in the air, &c. to be but imaginary erronious conceptions and novelties; wherein also the lewd unchristian practices of witchmongers, upon aged, melancholy ignorant, and superstitious people in extorting confessions, by inhumane terrors and tortures is notably detected. Also the knavery and confederacy of conjurors. The impious blasphemy of inchanters. The imposture of soothsayers, and infidelity of atheists. The delusion of pythonists, figure-casters, astrologers, and vanity of dreamers. The fruitlesse beggerly art of alchimistry. The horrible art of poisoning

---

[12] Dictionary of national biography, v. 51, p. 64.

and all the tricks and conveyances of juggling and lieger-demain are fully deciphered. With many other secrets opened that have long lain hidden; though very necessary to be known, for the undeceiving of judges, justices, and juries and for the preservation of poor, aged, deformed, ignorant people; frequently taken, arraigned, condemned and executed for witches when according to a right under-standing, and a good conscience, physic, food, and neces-saries should be administered to them. Whereunto is added a treatise upon the nature and substance of spirits and devils, &c. all written and published in Anno 1584 by Reginald Scot, Esquire," reprinted in London, 1654.

As showing the erudition of the man it is worthy of note that he enumerates 212 authors whose works in Latin he has consulted and 23 authors who wrote in English. Many editions, in the English and European languages, have been published.

"With remarkable boldness and an insight that was far in advance of his age, he set himself to prove that the be-lief in witchcraft and magic was rejected alike by reason and religion, and that spiritualistic manifestations were wilful impostures or illusions due to mental disturbance in the observers. He wrote with the philanthropic aim of staying the cruel persecution which habitually pursued poor, aged, and simple persons, who were popularly cred-ited with being witches. The maintenance of the super-stition he laid to a large extent at the door of the Roman Catholic Church * * * Scot performed his task so thor-oughly that this volume became an exhaustive encyclo-pædia of contemporary beliefs about witchcraft, spirits, alchemy, magic, and legerdemain."

Of course, the book was vigorously attacked by the ad-herents of superstition. Among these was James VI of Scotland. In his "Daemonologie" (1597) he character-ized the opinions of Scot as "damnable." After his acces-sion to the English throne, he ordered all copies of Scot's "Discoverie" burnt. Scot himself was already dead and beyond reach of prosecution.

James VI of Scotland became James I of England in 1603 and died in 1625. The burning of Scot's book must have occurred between those dates. After his accession to the English throne he immediately manifested his preference for the High Church view. This is as much as I have had time to unearth as to the date and circumstances of the burning of Scot's book against witchcraft. We shall later see that this precedent is of interest and importance in construing the Connecticut state against blasphemy, as applicable to those who deny witchcraft.

DAVID PARE (PAREUS)—1622.[13]

David Pare (Pareus; 1548-1622), was a distinguished German protestant divine born in Selicia. His writings were collected and published at Frankfort in 1647 making four volumes folio.

"In 1622 David Pare's [Pareus'] Commentary on the Epistle to the Romans was burned in London, Oxford and Cambridge, by order of the privy council." It was also burnt by the common hangman on the order of James I. The author was on the continent and beyond the reach of prosecution.

RICHARD MOUNTAGU—1626.[14]

Richard Montagu (or Mountague; 1577-1641), was a controversialist of note, and was appointed the bishop of Chichester, being later transferred to Norwich. But these honors came after much trouble. Montagu was of the high church party and under suspicion of too close an affection for Romanism. This, of course, enabled him to count bishop Loud and the king among his staunch supporters. Doubtless this approval prevented his being prosecuted and secured his promotion to a bishopric, as will be seen presently.

"Some popish priests and Jesuits were executing their mission at Stamford-Rivers, in Essex, of which he was

[13] Vickers, Robert H. Martyrdoms of literature, p. 374.
Rose, Hugh James. A new general biographical dictionary, vol. 10, p. 472-3.
Algemeine deutsche biographie, vol. 25, p. 167.
[14] General biographical dictionary, Lond. 1815, vol. 22, p. 478-484.
Dictionary of national biography, vol. 38, p. 266-270.
Vickers, Robert H. Martyrdoms of literature, p. 373.
Rushworth, John. Historical collections, vol. 1, p. 212.
Howell's, State trials, vol. 2, p. 1258-1266.

then rector; and to secure his flock against their attempts, he left some propositions at the place of their meeting, with an intimation that, if any of those missionaries could give a satisfactory answer to the queries he had put, he would immediately become their proselyte.   In these, he required of the papists to prove, that the present Roman church is either the catholic church, or a sound member of the catholic church; that the present church of England is not a true member of the catholic church; and that all those points, or any of those points which the church of Rome maintains against the church of England, were, or was, the perpetual doctrine of the catholic church, the decided doctrine of the representative church in any general council, or national approved by a general council, or the dogmatical resolution of any one father for 500 years after Christ.   On their proving all this in the affirmative, he promised to subscribe to their faith.   Instead, however, of returning any answer, a small pamphlet was left at last for him, entitled 'A new Gag for the old Gospel.'   To this he replied, in 'An Answer to the late Gagger of the Protestants,' 1624, 4to, which gave great offence to the Calvinists, at that time a very numerous and powerful party in the church, and thus drew upon him enemies from a quarter he did not expect: and their indignation against him ran so high, that Ward and Yates, two lecturers at Ipswich, collected out of his book some points, which they conceived to savour of popery and Arminianism, in order to have them presented to the next parliament. Mountagu, having procured a copy of the information against him, applied to the king for protection, who gave him leave to appeal to himself, and to print his defence. Upon this, he wrote his book entitled, 'Appello Cæsarem; a just Appeal against two unjust Informers;' which, having the approbation of Dr. White, dean of Carlisle, whom king James ordered to read, and give his sense of it, was published in 1625, 4to, but addressed to Charles I.   James dying before the book was printed off.

"In this work many of the acknowledged doctrines of the church of England are undoubtedly maintained with great force of argument, but there are other points in which he afforded just ground for the suspicions alleged against him; and that this was the opinion of many divines of that period appeared from the numerous answers. * * *

"The controversy, however, was not to be left to divines, who may be supposed judges of the subject. The parliament which met June 18, 1625, thought proper to take up the subject, and Mr. Mountagu was ordered to appear before the House of Commons, and being brought to the bar July 17, the speaker told him, that it was the pleasure of the House, that the censure of his books should be postponed for some time; but that in the interim he should be committed to the custody of the serjeant at arms. He was afterwards obliged to give the security of 2000l. for his appearance. The king, however, was displeased with the parliament's proceedings against our author; and bishop Laud applied to the duke of Buckingham in his favour; Mr. Mountagu also wrote a letter to that duke, entreating him to represent his case to his majesty; and this application was seconded some few days after by a letter of the bishops of Oxford, Rochester, and St. David's, to the duke. In the next parliament, in 1626, our author's 'Appello Cæsarem' was referred to the consideration of the committee for religion, from whom Mr. Pym brought a report on the 18th of April concerning several erroneous opinions contained in it. Upon this it was resolved by the House of Commons, 1. 'That Mr. Mountagu, had disturbed the peace of the church, by publishing doctrines, contrary to the articles of the church of England, and the book of homilies. 2. That there are divers passages in his book, especially against those he calleth puritans, apt to move sedition betwixt the king and his subjects, and between subject and subject. 3. That the whole frame and scope of his books is to discourage the well-affected in religion from the true religion established in the church, and to incline them, and, as much as in him lay, to reconcile them to popery.' And accordingly articles were exhibited against him; but it does not appear, that this impeachment was laid before the House of Lords, or in what manner the Commons intended to prosecute their charge, or how far they proceeded. * * *

"This prosecution from the parliament seems to have recommended him more strongly to the court, for, in 1628, he was advanced to the bishopric of Chichester, on the death of one of his opponents, Dr. Carleton. On August 22, 1628, the day appointed for his confirmation, a singular scene took place. On such occasions it is usual to give a formal notice, that if any person can object either against the party elected, or the legality of the election, they are to come and offer their exceptions at the day prefixed. This intimation being given, one Mr. Humphreys, and William Jones, a stationer of London, excepted against Mountagu as a person unqualified for the episcopal function, charging him with popery, Arminianism, and other heterodoxies, for which his books had been censured in the former parliament. Fuller tells us, 'that exception was taken at Jones's exceptions (which the record calls 'prætensos Articulos)' as defective in some legal formalities. I have been informed,' continues he, 'it was alledged against him for bringing in his objections *viva voce,* and not by a proctor, that court adjudging all private persons effectually dumb, who speak not by one admitted to plead therein. Jones returned, that he could not get any proctor, though pressing them importunately, and profering them their fee to present his exceptions, and therefore was necessitated *ore tenus* there to alledge them against Mr. Mountagu. The register mentioneth no particular defects in his exceptions; but Dr. Rives, substitute at that time for the vicar-general, declined to take any notice of them, and concludeth Jones amongst the contumacious, "quod nullo modo legitime comparuit, nec aliquid in hac parte juxta Juris exigentiam diceret, exciperet, vel opponeret." Yet this good Jones did bishop Mountagu, that he caused his addresses to the king to procure a pardon, which was granted unto him, in form like those given at the coronation, save that some particulars were inserted therein, for the pardoning of all errors heretofore committed either in speaking, writing, or publishing, whereby he might hereafter be questioned.' "

ALEXANDER LEIGHTON—1630.[15]

Alexander Leighton (1568-1649) was a physician and divine, descendent from an ancient and wealthy family. He graduated at the University of St. Andrews as M. A. and Leyden University as M. D. He was interdicted practicing medicine mainly because "being perverse as to ecclesiastical affairs." In 1624 he published " 'Speculum Belli Sacri or the Looking Glass of the Holy War,' a book against Romanism which involved him in much trouble. Some years later he prepared a petition to parliament against episcopacy to which he secured many influential signatures. He took this to the continent and expanded it into a book, 'An Appeal to the Parliament, or Sion's Plea against Prelacie' which was published in Holland in 1628. * * * * The book was not only a virulent attack on prelacy, but 'an appeal to political presbyterianism to take the sword in hand.' * * * Besides his strictures on episcopacy, his violent abuse of the queen [separate from the above book I judge], whom he styled the 'daughter of hell, a' cananite, and an idolatress' made Leighton a marked man." He was arrested Feb. 17, 1630, on a warrant from the High Commission Court. In the June following he was tried in the Star Chamber Court, during his absence on account of illness, and sentenced to fine, whipping, pillory, slitting

---

[15] Bibliography on Alexander Leighton's Case. Speech of Sir R. Heath * * * in the case of Alexander Leighton in the Star Chamber, June, 4th, 1630 London, Camden Miscellany, v. 7, 1847.
A brief account of Archbishop Laud's cruel treatment of Dr. Leighton. See, Benson (G.) D.D. A collection of Tracts etc. 1748.
An epitome or brief discovery from the beginning to the end of the great troubles that Dr. Leighton suffered in his body, estates, and family, wherein is laid down the cause of those sufferings, namely, that book called Sion's Plea against prelacie. London, 1646.
Dictionary of National Biography, vol. 33, p. 1-2.
Reese. Richard, A compendious Martyrology, containing an account of the sufferings and constancy of Christians in the different persecutions which have raged against them under pagan and popish governments. London, 1815, vol. 3, pp. 433-438.
Rushworth. John, Historical Collections, vol. 3, Appendix, p. 29.
Appendix Star Chamber Reports.
An appeal to the Parliament; or Sion's plea against prelacie, 1628.
Speculum Belli Sacri, or looking glass of the holy war. 1624.
Digest of the law concerning libels, (1765), p. 72.
Macaulay's Hist. of Eng., v. 2, p. 98.
Howell's, State Trials, v. 3: 383 to 387.

of nose and cutting off of ears, and branding in the face, and degraded from orders.

Leighton once escaped, was rearrested and remained in prison till 1640 when a change in political situations insured his release by the Long Parliament. It is said that: "He was a puritan of the narrowest type and in controversy a man of 'violent and ungoverned heat.'" In 1642 he was rewarded for his zeal by an appointment as keeper of Lambeth House, then turned into a state prison.

This Leighton case well illustrates the rule that "it is in the power of the prosecution to call the offence what he pleases"—in this case sedition or blasphemy. Bishop Laud, one of the judges of Leighton, called it both blasphemy and high treason. Attorney General Sir R. Heath called it sedition.

The case of Leighton excited much interest at the time and accordingly there has been preserved a more complete record than is usual. This then affords an opportunity for a better portrayal of the spirit which engendered prosecutions for religious offences than is commonly the case. Accordingly there will now be reproduced a rather detailed account of all that happened, so we may make the better comparison of the spirit behind such prosecutions with the spirit that inspired our constitutional guarantees for intellectual liberty. Such a comparison will enable us to make a better decision as to whether our constitutions were merely designed to change the name of such crimes and ameliorate the penalty, or were designed to destroy the jurisdiction upon which such prosecutions rested.

"On February 29, 1629, Dr. *Leighton,* coming out of Blackfriars church, was seized by a warrant from the high commission court; and, by a multitude of men armed, was dragged to Bishop Laud's house. From thence, without any examination, he was carried to Newgate, and there clapt in irons, and thrust into a loathsome dog-hole, full of rats and mice: and the roof being uncovered the rain and snow beat in upon him, having no bedding, nor place to make a fire, except the ruins of an old smoky chimney; where he had neither meat nor drink from the Tuesday night till Thursday noon. In this loathsome and miserable place he continued fifteen weeks, not any of his friends, or even his wife, being permitted to come near him, and was denied a copy of his commitment. On the fourth day after his imprisonment, the pursuivants belonging to the high commission went to his house, and laid violent hands upon his distressed wife, using her with the most shameful and barbarous inhumanity; and holding a pistol to the breast of a child five years old, threatening to kill him, if he would not inform them where the books were, by which the child was so frightened that he never recovered. They broke open presses, chests, boxes, &c. though his wife was willing to open all. They carried away all the books, manuscripts, apparel, household stuff, and other things, leaving nothing they wished to possess. During his confinement in Newgate, it appeared from the opinion of four physicians, that poison had been given him; for his hair and skin came off. As he lay in this deplorable situation, sentence was passed upon him in the star-chamber, even without hearing a single word he had to say, though a certificate from four physicians and an attorney was given of the dreadful state of his complaint.

CHARGES AGAINST LEIGHTON.

"But it will be requisite to give a particular account of the charges brought against this unhappy man. June 4, 1630, an information was exhibited again Dr. Leighton in the star-chamber, by attorney-general Heath, when he was charged with having published and dispersed a scandalous book against the king, peers, and prelates, entitled, 'Sion's Plea against the Prelacie;' in which, among other things, he sets forth these false and seditious assertions and positions following:

"1. 'That we do not read of greater persecution, and higher indignity done upon God's people in any nation professing the gospel, than in this our island, especially since the death of Queen Elizabeth.'

"2. 'He terms the prelates of this realm *men of blood,* and enemies to God and the state; and saith, that the maintaining and establishing of bishops within this realm, is a main and master sin established by law, and that ministers should have no voices in council deliberative and decisive.

"3. 'He avows the prelacy of our church to be antichristian and satanical, and terms the bishops ravens and magpies, that prey upon the state.

"4. 'He terms the canons of our church, made in 1603, *non-sense*-canons.

"5. 'He disallows and contemns the ceremony of *kneeling* in receiving the sacrament, alleging that this spawn of the *beast* was brought forth by the prelates to promote their own unlawful standing.

"6. 'He affirms that the prelates have corrupted the king, forestalling his judgment against God and goodness, and most audaciously and wickedly calleth his majesty's royal consort, our gracious queen, the *daughter of Heth*.

"7. 'He most impiously seems to commend him who committed the barbarous and bloody act of murdering the late Duke of Buckingham, and to encourage others to second him in the like wicked and desperate attempt, to the destruction of others.

"8. 'He layeth a most seditious scandal upon the king, state, and kingdom, wickedly affirming, 'That all who pass by us spoil us, and we spoil all who rely upon us.' And amongst other particulars, instanceth the black pining death of the famished *Rochellers,* to the number of fifteen hundred, in four months. By which passages and wicked assertions, he doth as much as in him lay, scandalize his majesty's sacred person; his religious wise and just government; the person of his royal consort, the queen; the persons of the lords and peers of the realm, especially the reverend bishops.

"9. 'That in another place in the said book, endeavoring not only to slander his majesty's sacred person and government, but to detract from his royal power, in making laws and canons for ecclesiastical government, he saith, 'That the church hath its laws from the *scripture,* and that no king may make laws in the house of God; for if they might, then the scripture would be imperfect.'

"10. 'And he is further charged in another place in the said book, with these words following, thinking to salve all with an expression of his sacred majesty; 'What a pity it is, and indelible dishonour it will be to you, the states representative, that so ingenuous and tractable a king should be so monstrously abused, to the undoing of himself and his subjects.'

"These ten particulars contain all the charges brought against Dr. Leighton, and we may be sure they were the worst that could be collected out of his book, his enemies being judges. * * * Dr. Leighton, in his answer to the above charges, confessed, that when the parliament was sitting, in the year 1628, he drew up the heads of his book; and having the approbation of five hundred persons under their own hands, some of whom were members of parliament, he went into Holland to get it printed. Also, that he printed betwixt five and six hundred only for the use of the parliament; but they being dissolved before the work was finished, he returned home, not bringing any of them into the kingdom, but made it his special care to suppress them. He confessed his writing the book, but with no such ill intention as suggested in the information. His only object was to remonstrate against certain grievances in church and state, under which the people suffered, that the parliament might be induced to take them into consideration, and give such redress as might be most for the honour of the king, the advantage of the people, and the peace of the church.

LEIGHTON'S DEFENCE.

"When the cause was heard, the doctor's defense was read at length, and the various particulars contained in his charges were read out of his book. In answer to the first charge, viz. 'That we do not read of greater persecution of God's people, in any nation professing the gospel, than in this our island, especially since the death of Queen Elizabeth;' he confessed the words, and said, 'The thing is too true, by the prelates taking away the life and livelihood from many ministers and private men, many of whom have been pined to death in prison; and many have wandered up and down their families being left desolate and helpless: and besides this, the blood of souls hath been endangered, by the removal of the faithful shepherds from their flocks.' This was a most cutting truth; at which Laud was so exceedingly enraged, that he desired the court to inflict the heaviest sentence that could be inflicted upon him. This they did to his lordship's fullest satisfaction. For Leighton was condemned to be degraded from his ministry, to have his ears cut, his nose slit, to be branded in the face, to stand in the pillory, to be whipped at a post, to pay ten thousand pounds, (although they knew he was not worth so much) and to suffer perpetual imprisonment. The grateful sentence being passed against him, Laud pulled off his hat, and holding up his hands, GAVE THANKS TO GOD, WHO HAD GIVEN HIM THE VICTORY OVER HIS ENEMIES. A certain knight having moved one of the lords relative to the dreadful nature of the censure, intimating that it opened a door to the prelates to inflict the most disgraceful punishments and tortures upon men of quality; *that* lord replied, that it was designed only for the terror of others, and that he would not have any one to think the sentence would ever be executed. This worthy lord, however, was greatly mistaken; for Laud and his adherents caused the dreadful sentence to be executed with the utmost rigour and severity."

The argument of Sir Robert Heath the Attorney General has been preserved to us, and lengthy quotations will be made even at the risk of duplication of sentiment. It all helps us to understand the spirit in which censorial laws were conceived and by contrast helps us to understand what our constitutions were meant to prevent. Now comes the language of the learned prosecutor.

ARGUMENT AGAINST LEIGHTON.

"The matter of the book is a bitter invective against the reverend Bishops of this Church and Kingdoms of England; but this not against ther persons or any personall fault of thers, but against ther functions, against ther calling, against the prelacy. * * * To sclaunder the Kynge by his ministers, or in his ministers is all one as without that circumlocution to sclaunder the Kynge himself, for that's the meaning of it in other terms. * * * I make bold to affirme that whoever lives under a monarchye and would reject the dicipline of the Church under the Bishops, would if they durst, reject the government of a kynge and interteyn a popular government. * * *

"This brainsick man and his complices, whose religion is never to be contented with the present times, hath indevoured, with as much malice as cann be imagined, to defame and to destroy the whole prelacye. He hates them himself, and desires that all men else should hate them, *et quem quisque odit, periisse expetit;* and thes are the degrees he goes by.

"And this hatred I may thus distinguish of. It is reall, it is not personall; for uppon his examinations he confesseth for the honour of thes reverend Bishops that he knoweth noe ill by any of ther persons; but ther calling is such as is not to be indured.

"To come to the booke it selfe. It is directed to the Court of Parliament in the intitleing therof. And the last conclusion of it is thus:

> High must you soar, but glory gives thee wings,
> Noe lowe attempt a starlike glorye brings.

"And this pitch of pride he himself beginns with; for in the preface to his books, in the first page, he doth arrantly and impudently sclaunder the sacred persons and happy government of his Majesty that nowe is, and of our late soveraign of ever blessed memory, in thes false and sclaunderous words: 'We doe not reed of greater persecution, higher indignitie, and indemnitie done unto God's people in any nation professinge the Gospell then in this our island, specially since the death of Queen Elizabeth.'

"And we are bound to preserve the honour of our King and Princes, and of the State we live in, not only from the malice of the present times, but of the future ages also. And in the same preface to his booke, however he pretends he hateth not the persons of the Bishops, yet he expresses his love to them in this hatefull manner; he states them men of bloud, enemyes to God and the State, and the prelacye he calls anti-christian and satanicall.

"These 2 things I observe to your Lordships in the preface, wherby he ushers in an ill opinion of the State in which he liveth, and a perfect hatred, as himself termes it, to the persons of the Bishops.

"From the preface I come to the booke itself, wherin, to omitt a multitude of idle, wicked, and malitious passages, whereof every leaf is full, I have made choise to single out only 14 severall places.

"1. The first is page 3d. That he might the better worke on the consciences of weake and silly men, he layeth this downe as a position, That this is the maine and master sinn which is established by a lawe to maynteyne and continue Bishops.

"2. Next to introduce the plausible doctrine of parity in the Church amongst his discontented disciples, and of a parity by consequence a confusion, page 7th, he lays down another position, That all ministers have voyce in counsell, both deliberative and decisive.

"3. That he may the better prevaile herein, he indeavours next to bring the persons of the Bishops into contempt by terming them ravens and pye magotts, which prey upon the State. 35. Thes sorts of men have the humility that Diogenes had, he contemned Platoes pride *fastu majore.*

"4. In the fourth place he discovers that infinite pride of hart which lurks in men of this stamp, and withall the gross ignorance that cannot distinguish betwene a reverent devotion at the receaving of the Communion and an idolatrous adoration of the Mass, expressed fol. 70, in thes words: 'The suggestion of false feares to the King, and the seeking of ther owne unlawfull standinge, brought forth that revived spawne of the beast, kneeling in receaving of the sacrament, for the greater reverence thereto, wherby the Papists had contentment.'

"5. Then he comes holme to the Kinge himself, and, at the first stepp, he takes uppon him to *crye downe the King's powre in causes ecclesiasticall,* which besides the inherent right therof in the Crown, is established by Parliament. See pages 42 and 43. Thus he saith: 'That statute 1 Eliz. cap. 1, giving powre to the Queen to constitute and make a commission in causes ecclesiastical is found inconvenient, because abusing that powre given to one or more they wrong the subject, wheras by virtue of the statute powre only ecclesiastical is graunted, yet by letters patents from the King, unsoundly grounded on the words of the statute, *they fine, imprison, &c., which is a great grief and a wrong to the subject.'*

"A bold and an ignorant censure of the powre of the Kinge and of the lawes of the kingdome, which he understandeth not.

"6. But this is not enough unless with a proud scorne he did deride the ecclesiasticall cannons, which have ther life from the Kinge, terming them, page 63, 'nonsence cannons.'

"7. Next in plaine termes thorough the sides of the Bishops he wounds the honour of the King himself, for, speaking of the Bishops, page 118, he saith this: 'They corrupt the King, forstalling his judgment against the good and goodness.'

"8. In the 8th place, that he might shewe more despite and irreverence to the person of the Kinge, he speaks scornfully of the person of His Royall Consort the Queen; for, speaking of the mariage of the King, page 172, he saith thus: 'That God suffred him, to our heavie woe, to match with the daughter of Heth, though he mist an Ægyptian.'

"9. But yet he is not at the hight, but he wickedly and trayterously indevoureth to traduce the Kinge on his very abilitye of governinge. For, page 175, he hath thes words: 'Consider then what a pittie it is to all, and an indelible dishonour it will be to you,'—speakinge to the Parliament, —'the State representative, that soe ingenuous and tractable a King should be so monstrously abused by the bane of Princes,'—meaning the Bishops,—'to the undoinge of himself and of his subjects.'

"10. My Lords, one would thinke this wicked man could not rayse his malice to a higher pitch, but he doth it; for a little after, speaking of the late Duke—this sort of people spare neather livinge nor dead—he doth impiously and prophanly give countenance to the barbarous murder of that noble Lord, and irreligiously termeth it to be God's blowe, and excites others to the like; and wher he ment that second blowe should light, God knowes. His words are thes: 'A fourth reason is from God's offring of him-self to guide you by the hand, as we have shewed, who by giving of the first blowe hath in mercye removed the great-est nayle in all ther tent, and will not you followe holme?' Page 176.

"11. The next thing I shall observe to your Lordships is that which moves a doubt in me, wheather the Jesuits or the Protestants, frayed out of ther witts, be the greatest enimys to a monarchical government. I raise my doubt out of thes words in his book, page 191: *'But the Church hath her lawes from the Scriptures, neather may any King make lawes in the howse of God, for if they might the Scripture should be imperfect.'* Thes words spoken by a discreet man as D. Whitacre was, out of whom he citeth the words, may have a good sence applied to matters of faith and doctrine in religion, for then *sola Scriptura est norma fidei.* But being spoken by Mr. Leighton, who ap-plieth them to Church discipline, they are full of pride and aversenes from government.

"12. In the 12th place I shall observe a passage in his booke which will aske some payne to distinguish from a traytor. His words, page 208, are thes: 'But put the case that the good, harmless King be a captivated Joash by Athaliah's Arminianised and Jesuited crewe, or a misledd Henry the Sixth dispossest of his faithfullest frends and best counsell by the pride of the French, or a Henry the Third overawed by a divilish dominering favourite, or an Edward the Sixth overpoysed and borne downe from his good purposes to God's glorie and the good of the State by the halting and falshood of the prelats and ther Romish confederats, soe that such a King, though he hold the scepter, yet he sweyeth not the scepter, neather cann he free himself and execute deseignes, because the sonns of the mann of sin are toe hard for him.'

"Whether this be a language fitt for a subject to speake but by way of supposition of his soveraign, I submitt to your judgments.

"13. But next, my Lords, for his commendation, I shall say this, that he is very indifferent, for he speares neather; fot, page 202, he hath thes words:—'Our King, counsel,

nobles, ministers, and all sortes of people are wofully cor-
ruptly by that Romish dross.' Now, my Lords, you have
your shares in plain termes.

"14. But, for the 14th and last thing which I shall observe out of his book, I am soe far from commending him
that I cann not forgive him, for in that, like an ingrate
viper, he indevors to render the King and the kingdome
and the whole nation a scorne and a reproch to the whole
world; for, page 269, speaking of our assistaunce to our
neighbours of the religion, he hath thes words:—'All that
pass by spoile us, and we spoile all that relye uppon us.
To omitt many instances which, being too well known,
makes us odious to the world, lett us touch upon the last,
namely, the black pining death of the famished Rochellers,
to the number of 15,000 in 4 moneths, besids thos that had
formerly perished, proclaimeth to the world the vanetye,
if not the falshood, of our helpe.'

"Thus stands this defendant convicted, not by a decade
of arguments only, as he devided his book, but by a grand
jurye, of severall crymes, whereof every single one wher
enough to condemne. * * *

"I come nowe to his pretences for an excuse.

"1. That he did it out of conscience.

"A blind zeale and a misledd conscience are noe excuse
for a seditious pamphlett. All the hereticall scismatikes,
nay all the traytors in the world, may say the like.

"2. That he intended to present it to the Parliament.

"This a lay heresye, and fitt to be condemned by this
great Counsell; as if it were lawfull or tollerable to sclaunder the King or the Government in Parliament.

"*The Parliament is a great Court, a great Counsell, the
great Counsell of the Kinge; but they are but his Counsell,
not his governours.* But this also is an irregular and in-
sufferable way, growen too frequent of late, to put all informations, petitions, breviatts intended for the Parliament, in print.

"I humbly move it, and offer it to your judgments, as a
fitt thinge to be suppressed for the future.

"If this had been brought to the Parliament, I make noe
doubt but the success therof would have been the severe

punishment of the author: for I find the judgment of Parliament in the like case, W. 2, cap. 33; 2 R. 2, cap. 5; 1 and 2 P. and M."

Now we come to the sequel, the barbarous punishment and the final vindication by resolution of parliament.

"The sentence, so grateful to the remembrance of Laud, was inflicted in the following most shocking and barbarous manner: he was carried to Westminster, where he had one of his ears cut off, then one side of his nose slit; he was branded on the cheek with a red-hot iron, with the letters S. S. for a *sower of sedition;* he was put in the pillory, and kept there nearly two hours in frost and snow; he was then tied to a post, whipped with a triple cord to that cruel degree, that every lash brought away the flesh; and he himself affirmed, ten years after, that he should feel it to his dying day. And after this shocking barbarity, he was not permitted to return to his quarters in the Fleet in a coach prepared for the purpose; but was compelled, in that lamentable condition and severe season, to go by water. On that day sevennight, his nose, ear, face, and back not being yet cured, he was taken to the pillory in Cheapside; when the other ear was cut off, the other side of his nose slit, and the other cheek branded; he was then set in the pillory, and whipped a second time. He was then carried back to the Fleet, where he was kept ten weeks in dirt and mire, not being sheltered from the rain and snow. He was shut up in close prison, and not suffered to breathe in the open air for ten or eleven years, until the meeting of the long parliament. And when he came forth from his long and miserable confinement, he could neither *walk, see* nor *hear.* The sufferings of this learned divine greatly moved the compassion of the people; and, surely, the records of the *inquisition* can hardly furnish an example of similar barbarity.

"The long parliament having assembled, Dr. Leighton presented a petition, November 7, 1640, to the house of commons, complaining of the hard usage he had met with; which the house could not hear without several interruptions with floods of tears. The petition being read, an order passed the house. "That Dr. Leighton shall have liberty by the warrant of this house, to go abroad in safe custody, to prosecute his petition here exhibited; and that he be removed out of the common prison, where he now is, into some more convenient place, and have the liberty of the Fleet." A committee was at the same time appointed to take his case into mature consideration.

LEIGHTON VINDICATED.

"Through the innumerable complaints from all quarters, and a multitude of other concerns which came before the house and the committee, some time elapsed before the result of the examination of Dr. Leighton's case came forth. But, April 21, 1641, Mr. Rouse having delivered the report of the committee, the house came to the following resolution:

1. "The the attaching, imprisoning, and detaining Dr. Leighton in prison, by warrant of the high commission, is illegal.

2. "That the breaking up of Dr. Leighton's house, and taking away his papers by Edward Wright, then sheriff of London, and now lord mayor, is illegal.

3. "That the said Edward Wright ought to give reparations to Dr. Leighton, for his damages sustained by breaking open his house, and taking away his papers and other goods.

4. "That the Archbishop of Canterbury, then Bishop of London, ought to give satisfaction to Dr. Leighton, for his damages sustained by fifteen weeks imprisonment in Newgate, upon the said bishop's warrant.

5. "That the great fine of ten thousand pounds laid upon Dr. Leighton, by sentence of the star-chamber, is illegal.

6. "That the sentence of the corporal punishment imposed upon Dr. Leighton; the whipping, branding, slitting the nose, cutting off his ears, setting in the pillory, and the execution thereof, and the imprisonment thereupon, are illegal.

7. "That Dr. Leighton ought to be freed from the great fine of ten thousand pounds, and from the sentence of perpetual imprisonment, and to have his bonds delivered to him, which he entered into for his true imprisonment.

8. "That Dr. Leighton ought to have good satisfaction and reparation for his great sufferings and damages sustained by the illegal sentence in the star-chamber."

This Leighton case illustrates very well several important contentions. To criticize the function and jurisdiction of the prelates is to criticize the King. In other words, church and State are but different aspects of the same thing. Blasphemy against the bishops is treason against the government, and is punishable under either or both heads. What shall come under these designations depends upon the kind of government that exists. What is blasphemous treason against an episcopal regime may not be such under the dominance of presbyterian or catholic rule and vice versa, because the meaning of God, of the Holy Scriptures and of the province of government changes as the official religion changes. We may add that logically such offences should disappear when all established religion disappears.

With the change in administration, Leighton was liberated and honored, although much of his offence consisted in a provocative literary style. Will it now be said that our constitutional guarantees are less inclusive in this respect than the House of Commons in 1641?

WILLIAM PRYNNE—1633.[16]

William Prynne (1600-1669) was a Puritan pamphleteer and a member of the bar. In the light of what happened to him later it is interesting to remember that in the preface to one of his earlier pamphlets "he appealed to parliament to suppress anything written against Calvinistic doctrine and to force the clergy to subscribe the conclusions

[16] Howell's State Trials, v. 3, pp. 563-566-574-579-584-585.
"Histrio—Mastix, the players scourge & actors tragedy." [Rushworth]
Rushworth, John. Historical Collections, v, 2, p. 380-471, Edition 1721; also: Appendix, p. 69 and 117-133.
A new Discovery of the prelates Tyranny in their late prosecutions of Mr. Wm. Prynne, Dr. John Bastwick and Mr. H. Burton. 1641.
Wm. Laud's Works, v. 3, p. 221; v. 6, pp. 35-82.
Dictionary of national biography, v. 46, p. 432.
As to Burton see: House of Commons Journal, v. 2: 22, 102, 112, 124, 171;
Bastwick, H. C. Journal, v. 2: 22, 25, 90, 92, 125;
Prynne, H. C. Jour., v. 6. 111, 112, 115.

of the synod of Dort." That those who love persecution
may become the victims of persecution has a double illustration in this man's career.

William Pryn as the author, Michael Spark's as printer,
and William Buckner for licencing were tried in the Star
Chamber Court on a book entitled "Histrio-Mastix, or a
scourge for stage players," a volume of over 1,000 pages.
It is said that in this book "he exposed the liberties of the
stage, and condemned the very lawfulness of acting. * * *
Because the Court became now more addicted to these
ludicrous entertainments, and the Queen herself was so
fond of the amusement that she had bore the part of a
pastoral in her own royal person. * * * This book of
Prynn's was shewed her as levelled at her, there being a
reference in it 'women actore notorious whores'; though in
truth the book was published six weeks before the queen's
acting."

All this of course, had in it an element of pretence.
Prynn was a religio-political disturber and must be punished and any pretence was adequate. The charge was
labelled sedition, but manifestly was aimed at his puritanism. Mr. Attorney General Noy pointed out many reflections upon *the established church and clergy* and hoped
the Court of High Commission would also take notice of
the book in its blasphemous aspects. The comments of the
judges show a dominance of religious motive for the convictions and the technical demarkation of the offenses of
blasphemy and sedition are wholly ignored. I supply some
of their comment.

Francis Lord Cottington said: "That which hath been
more remarkable is, his spleen against the Church and
Government of it. * * * Surely he was assisted [in writ-
ing] immediately by the Devil himself, or rather he hath
assisted the Devil. *He hath written a book against due
reverence and honor, which all Christians owe to our
Saviour, Jesus, this doth convince my judgment against
him.* * * * He liketh nothing, no state or sex; music, dancing, &c., unlawful even in Kings."

L. C. J. Richardson in passing sentence said: "I be-
seech your lordships to give me leave but in a word to read

unto you what he writes of dancing, &c. 'It is the Devils profession; and he that entereth into a dance, entereth into a devilish profession, and so many paces in a dance so many paces to hell.' This is that which he conceiveth of Dancing, 'The woman that singeth in the dance, is the prioress of the Devil and those that answer are clerks, and the beholders are the parishioners, and the music are bells, and the fiddlers are the minstrels of the Devil.' "   Of course, thus to describe a church whose prelates allowed such things and whose political coadjutors attended at such places, must be treason against both God and his divinely appointed government.   "For Mr. Prynn, I do judge you by your book to be an insolent spirit and one that did think by his book to have got the name of a Reformer, *to set up the Puritan or separatist faction.*"

The Earl of Dorset spake to this effect: "This brittel Conscience Brother, [Prynne] that perhaps starts at the sight of the Corner-Cap, sweats at the Surplice, swoons at the sign of the Cross, and will rather die than put on Woman's apparel to save his life, yet he * * * misapplies texts with false interpretations, * * * and yet this man is a pillar of the church. * * * You seemed by the title of your Book to scourge Stage-Plays, yet it was to make people believe that there was an apostasy in the Magistrates."

Now listen to this fiction like unto our fictions about a psychologic tendency to a disturbance of the peace: This judge continued: "It is not Mr. Attorney that calls for judgment against you, but it is all mankind that are parties agrieved, and they call for judgment. Mr. Prynn I do believe you to be a Schism-Maker in the Church, a Sedition Sower in the Common-Wealth, a Wolf in sheeps clothing; in a word omnium malorum nequissimus," and much more intense and vulgar vituperation. Prynn was fined 10.000£, imprisoned for life, his ears cut off, his nose slit, his forehead branded and all copies of his book burnt.

From the Jail, in 1636, he caused to be published an anonymous attack on Bishop Wren entitled "News from Ipswich" for which he was again brought before the Star Chamber Court. On June 14, 1637, Prynn was again sen-

tenced to 5.000£ fine and imprisonment for life, and to
loose whatever stump of an ear he might have left, and
to be branded on the cheek SL. meaning "seditious li-
beler." (See, Burton's Case, following.)

The Long parliament declared Prynn's conviction illegal gave him liberty, restored his honors and voted him
pecuniary reparation. When Laud's turn came to go to
the gallows, it was Prynn who managed the prosecution.
Again, those who love persecution may become the victims of persecution. This was true both of Prynn
and his persecutor. All is easy if guilt under an uncertain statute may be predicted upon the mere disapproval of
ones opinions. That emotional disapproval always sup-
lies the conviction of a dangerous psychologic tendency as
the quality of that which is disapproved.

Which conception of schism-maker are we to punish
under the Connecticut blasphemy law? That of Laud and
others who condemned Prynn? Or that of the Long Parliament which honored Prynn? Does our constitution
provide for less liberty than the resolution of the Long
Parliament as to indulging one's "spleen against the
church" and one's "insolent spirit"?

JOHN HAYDEN—1634.[17]

I reproduce in its entirety the only reference to this case
that was found.

"John Hayden was minister in Devonshire, and most
grievously persecuted for non-conformity. Having spoken
in his sermon *against setting up images in churches*, he
was forced to quit the county, and was afterwards apprehended in the diocese of Norwich by Bishop Harsnet, who,
taking from him his horse, his money, and all his papers,
caused him to be shut up a close prisoner in the common
jail of Norwich for thirteen weeks, where he was in danger
of starving for want. When the justices at the quarter
sessions would have admitted him to bail, his lordship refused, and sent him under the guard of a pursuivant to
the high commission in London. Having been kept under
confinement two whole terms, or more, he was brought

---

[17] Reese, Richard. Compendious martyrology, v. 3, p. 432.

before the high commission in the consistory of St. Paul's, when he was deprived of his ministry, degraded from the sacred function, required to pay a fine, and sent back to prison. Being at length released from confinement, and venturing, in the year 1634, to preach occasionally, without being restored, he was again apprehended and sent to the Gatehouse by Archbishop Laud, and from thence to Bridewell, where he was whipt and kept for some time to hard labour; then he was confined in a cold dark dungeon during the whole of winter without fire or candle, being chained to a post in the middle of the room, with heavy irons on his hands and feet, having no other food than bread and water, and only a pad of straw to lie upon. Before his release could be obtained, he was obliged to take an oath, and give bond, that he would preach no more, but depart out of the kingdom in a month, and never more return. All this was done without any exception against his doctrine or his life."

The New England Puritans were very much opposed to images in churches. Did their blasphemy statute of 1642 adopt the common law conception of blasphemy and so penalize some of their own number? If this statute is valid isn't it a crime now to preach against images in churches? Can such a statute by any possibility be constitutional?

XIV.
PROSECUTIONS FOR CRIMES AGAINST RELIGION.

1637-1642

HENRY BURTON, ET AL.—1637.[18]

The prosecutions of Burton, Prynn and Bastwick make so conspicuous a page in the history of religious persecution that we will quote the story quite in full, first in the language of a sympathetic historian and then state the cause of complaint quite in detail and in the language of Bishop Laud's judgment against the defendants.

Henry Burton was born in Yorkshire, and educated in St. John's College, Cambridge. He was made clerk of the closet to Prince Henry, and after his death to Prince Charles. In 1623 he was appointed to attend the young prince to Spain; but for reasons unknown, he was set aside.

Mr. Burton was a person of a most heroical spirit, and never feared the appearance of an enemy, as appears from the account he gave of himself. Speaking of his various citations before Laud, his courage was such, that he says, "I was not at any time before him, but methought I stood over him, as a school-master over his scholars; so great was the goodness of God towards me. Being convened before the high commission for my book, entitled, 'Babel no Bethel,' Harnet, Archbishop of York, having run himself out of breath with railing against me and my book; and saying, that I had dedicated my book to the parliament, to incense them against the higher powers, (meaning the king,) I answered, 'No, my lord, I am none of those who divide the king and parliament, but I pray God unite them together!'"

He afterwards describes the prelatical innovations and usurpations, and how he set himself to oppose them, say-

---

[18] Reese, Richard. Compendious martyrology. V. 3, pp. 440-451. Howell's, State trials, V. 3, pp. 714-742.

ing, "I more and more disliked the prelates' usurpations, and tyrannical government, with their attempts to set up popery. Therefore I purposely preached upon the second chapter to the Colossians, crying down all will-worship and human inventions in God's service. I began in my practice, as in my judgment, to fall off from the ceremonies. Only I watched for an occasion to try it out with them, either by dint of arguments, or force of law, or by the king and his council, resolving to foil my adversaries, though I had no great hope of success; or, at least discover the mystery of iniquity and hypocrisy, which, like a white veil, they had cast over all their foul practices. This discovery I took to be of no small importance." * * *

Mr. Burton was a great sufferer in the cause of non-conformity. In the year 1626, he was convened before the high commission, when he would have received the censure of the ruling ecclesiastics, had not the judges interposed and granted a prohibition, which they might do according to law, by which he was at that time rescued from his cruel oppressor. Mr. Burton having published a book, entitled, "The Baiting of the Pope's Bull; or, an Unmasking of the Mystery of Iniquity, folded up in a most pernicious Breave or Bull, sent from the Pope lately into England, to cause a Rent therein, for his Re-entry," 1627; though the book was wholly against the pope and his dangerous bull, and was licensed by Dr. Goad, he was called before the council by the instigation of Laud, who spoke vehemently against the book, calling it a libel. Afterwards, he published another work against popery, entitled, "The Pouring out of the Seven Vials," 1628; for which he was prosecuted in the high commission by this prelate, and the book suppressed. And when he published his book, entitled, "Babel no Bethel," wholly against the church of Rome, this prelate employed his pursuivant to apprehend him; committed him to the Fleet, refusing bail when offered, contrary to the petition of right; suspended him from his benefice; and suppressed the book. About the same time, his "Trial of Private Devotions," 1628, against Dr. Cosins; and his "Plea to an Appeal, in refutation of divers Arminian and Popish Errors broached by Mountague in his *Appello Cæsarem,*" were both called in and suppressed.

How long Mr. Burton remained under the above suspension, and a prisoner in the Fleet, we have not been able to learn. He was afterwards released. This, however, was to him only the beginning of sorrows. November 5, 1636, he preached two sermons at his own church in Friday-street, from prov. xxiv. 21, 22, "My son, fear thou the Lord and the king, and meddle not with them that are given to change," &c. in which he laid open the late innovations in doctrine, worship, and ceremonies, and warned his hearers against them. Dr. Laud, now archbishop of Canterbury, hearing of this, caused articles to be exhibited against him in the high commission, and summoned him to answer them, out of term, before Dr. Duck. On his appearance, he was charged with having "spoken against turning communion tables into altars, against bowing to them, against setting up crucifixes, against saying the second service at the altar, and against putting down afternoon sermons on the Lord's day." He was, moreover, charged with having said, "that ministers might not safely preach upon the doctrines of grace without being troubled for it: and that the ministers in Norfolk and Suffolk were suspended for non-conformity to the rites and ceremonies, imposed upon them contrary to the laws of the land." These charges, amounting, it is said, to *sedition,* he was required to answer upon his oath, and so to become his own accuser: but he refused the oath; and, instead of answering, appealed to the king. Notwithstanding his appeal, within fifteen days he was summoned, by the direction of the archbishop, to appear before a special high commission at Doctors' Commons; when, in his absence, he was suspended from his office and benefice, and attachments were given out to apprehend him.

Under these oppressive proceedings, Mr. Burton kept himself close shut up in his own house; and, to give an impartial public a fair opportunity of deciding upon his case, he published his sermons, entitled, "For God and the King; the Summe of two Sermons preached on the fifth of November last in St. Matthewes, Friday-street, 1636;" with "An

Apologie for an Appeale," addressed to the king, the lords of the council and the learned judges.[19] The pursuivants of the high commission not daring to break open Mr. Burton's doors, the archbishop and the bishop of London, with several others, drew up a warrant to one Dendy, a serjeant at arms, to apprehend him. By virtue of this warrant, Dendy, accompanied by the sheriff of London, and various other armed officers, went the same evening to Mr. Burton's house in Friday-street and between ten and eleven o'clock at night, violently broke open his doors, took him into custody, and seized his books and papers, as many as they pleased. The next day, instead of being brought before the lords, as the warrant expressed, he was, by another warrant and without any cause assigned, committed close prisoner to the Fleet.

During Mr. Burton's close confinement, two anonymous publications came forth, the one entitled, "A Divine Tragedy, containing a Catalogue of God's late Judgments upon Sabbath-breakers;" the other, "News from Ipswich," discovering the innovations and severities of the prelates, especially Bishop Wren of Norwich. These were supposed to have been written by Mr. William Prynne, the lawyer. Dr. John Bastwick, a physician, having published a book, entitled, *Apologeticus ad præsules Anglicanos,* and a pamphlet, called, "The New Litany;" these three, Mr. Burton, Mr. Prynne, and Dr. Bastwick, now confined in prison, were prosecuted in the star-chamber, for "writing and publishing seditious, schismatical, and libellous books against the hierarchy, and to the scandal of the government." This was the substance of the indictment. *They had warmly reflected upon the bishops, taxed them with inclinations to popery, and exclaimed against the severity and injustice of the proceedings of the high commission.* The persons then in power were of too impatient and revengeful a temper to let such reflections and invectives go unpunished.

When the three defendants had prepared their answers to the indictment, they could not obtain counsel to sign them, through fear of the prelates; upon which they peti-

---

[19] Mrs. Burton his wife, venturing to present copies of these sermons to several of the lords in parliament, was committed to prison.

tioned the court to receive them from themselves, which was rejected. However, Mr. Prynne and Dr. Bastwick, having no other remedy, left their answers at the office, signed by their own hands, but were, nevertheless, proceeded against *pro confesso*. Mr. Burton prevailed upon Mr. Holt, a learned and an aged bencher of Gray's-inn, to sign his answer; but the court, instead of receiving it, even when signed, ordered the two chief justices to expunge what they deemed unfit to be brought into the court. Accordingly, they struck out the whole answer, consisting of forty sheets of paper, except a few lines at the beginning, and a few more at the end: and because Mr. Burton would not acknowledge it thus purged, he was, in like manner, proceeded against *pro confesso*.

The three prisoners were brought to the bar June 14, 1637, when they offered to defend their several answers at the peril of their lives; but the court, finding them not filed on record, would not receive them. The prisoners at the bar cried aloud for *justice,* and that their answers might be read; but, however reasonable their request, it was peremptorily denied.

Upon the petition of Sir Thomas Jermin, governor of Jersey, being presented to the king, in behalf of Mr. Prynne, he was allowed to attend divine service, and receive the sacrament in the castle, and to walk with his keeper in the gardens. But as soon as the archbishop heard of the royal indulgence, he fell into a violent rage, and sent a messenger for one Mr. Hungerford, who had been employed in procuring it, and convened him before the council.

In the above year, the prisoners were called home by order of the parliament. For, November 7th, Mrs. Burton and Mrs. Bastwick having presented petitions to the house of commons, in behalf of their husbands, complaining of their heavy sentence in the star-chamber, the house immediately ordered, "That their said husbands shall be forthwith sent for, in safe custody, by a warrant of the house, directed to the governors of the islands where they are prisoners, and to the captains of the castles there; that the cause of their being detained may be here certified."

This warrant is dated November 7, 1640. A petition was also presented in behalf of Mr. Prynne, when the house gave a similar order for his return.

Mr. Burton and Mr. Prynne coming in the same vessel, arrived at Dartsmouth on the 22d of November, where they were received and entertained with extraordinary demonstrations of affection and joy. As they approached the metropolis, the road betwixt Brentford and London was so full of coaches, horsemen, and persons on foot, come to meet them, and congratulate them on their safe arrival, that it was with difficulty they could ride one mile an hour. As they entered London, there was so immense a concourse of people, that they were nearly three hours in passing from Charing-cross to their lodgings in the city. The numerous crowds who escorted them into the city, in token of their great joy, carried lighted torches before them, strewed the road with herbs and flowers, put rosemary and bays in their hats, and, as they went along, with loud acclamations for their deliverance, shouted, *Welcome home, welcome home! God bless you, God bless you: God be thanked for your return.*

On November 30th, being two days after his arrival in London, Mr. Burton appeared before the house of commons, and, December 5th, presented his petition to the house, entitled, "The humble Petition of Henry Burton, late Exile, and close Prisoner in Castle-cornet, in the Isle of Guernsey." In this petition he gives a sketch of his numerous and painful sufferings, and concludes by recommending his case to their impartial consideration. On the presentation of the petition, with many others of a similar kind, the house appointed a committee for their examination; and on the 12th of March following, Mr. Rigby delivered their report to the house, when the house passed the following resolutions:

1. "That the four commissioners, Dr. Duck, Dr. Worral, Dr. Sams, and Dr. Wood, proceeded unjustly and illegally in suspending Mr. Burton from his office and benefice, for not appearing upon the summons of the first process.

2. "That the breaking up Mr. Burton's house, and arresting his person without any cause shewed, and before

any suit depended against him in the star-chamber, and his close imprisonment thereupon, are against the law and the liberty of the subject.

3. "That John Wragg hath offended in searching and seizing the books and papers of Mr. Burton, by colour of a general warrant dormant from the high commissioners; and that the said warrant is against law and the liberty of the subject; and that sergeant Dendy and alderman Abel have offended in breaking open the house of Mr. Burton, and ought respectively to make him reparation for the same.

4. "That Mr. Burton ought to have reparation and recompence for the damages sustained by the aforesaid proceedings of Dr. Duck and others, who suspended him from his office and benefice.

5. "That the warrant from the council-board, dated at Whitehall, February 2, 1637, for committing Mr. Burton close prisoner, and the commitment thereupon, is illegal, and contrary to the liberty of the subject.

6. "That the Archbishop of Canterbury, the Bishop of London, the Earl of Arundel and Surrey, the Earl of Pembroke and Montgomery, Sir H. Vane, Sir J. Coke, and Sir Francis Windebank, do make reparations to Mr. Burton for his damages sustained by this imprisonment."

The 24th of the same month, Mr. Burton's case being again brought before the house, it was further resolved:

1. "That the sentence in the star-chamber against Mr. Burton is illegal, and without any just ground, and ought to be reversed, and he ought to be freed from the fine of £5000, and the imprisonment imposed upon him by the said sentence, and to be restored to his degrees in the university, orders in the ministry, and to his ecclesiastical benefice in Friday-street, London.

2. "That the order of the council-board for transferring Mr. Burton from the castle of Lancaster to the isle of Guernsey, and his imprisonment there, are against law and the liberty of the subject.

3. "That the said Mr. Burton ought to have reparation and recompence for the damages sustained by the said im-

prisonment, loss of his ears, and other evils sustained by the said unjust and illegal proceedings."

On the 20th of April, the house of commons voted Mr. Burton to receive *six thousand* pounds for his damages sustained; but the confusions of the times prevented the payment of the money. And by an order of the house, dated June 8, 1641, he was restored to his former ministry and benefice in Friday-street. Mr. Prynne and Dr. Bastwick also presented their petitions to the house, when their cases were taken into consideration, and the house passed similar resolutions in their favour.

Fortunately Bishop Laud has given us a very detailed statement of the defendants treasonable utterance. I quote this in full but omit the Bishops answering argument. Upon critical view it will be seen that the whole matter simmers down to a dispute as to what is true christian doctrine and duty.

In this case it was held that in Ecclesiastical Court's process may issue in the names of the bishops, and that citations need not be in the name of the King or under his seal of arms and that "Patent under the Great Seal is not necessary in any of these cases," of "correction of Ecclesiastical offences."

Burton and the others, denied the apostolic succession and divine right of the Bishops, claiming they were resurping the authority that rightly belonged to the King, and were introducing innovations tending toward Romanism.

These words following are the accusations against the defendants in the language of Bishop Laud of the Star Chamber Court.

"*Mr. Burton* in his Answer, set forth the substance of his Sermon which he preached the 5th of November in his parish church in Friday-street, touching the innovations brought into the church.

"*Dr. Bastwick* in his Answer termed the Prelates Invaders of the king's Prerogative, Contemners of the Scriptures, advancers of Popery, superstition, idolatry, profaneness, oppression of the king's subjects, in the impious performance whereof they shewed neither wit nor honesty; Enemies of God and the king and servants of the Devil.

"Mr. *Prynn's* Answer was much against the Hierarchy, but in more moderate and cautious expressions.

"The Information, which was read being very large, and having these five Books thereto annexed, Dr. Bastwick's Latin 'Apology,' his Litany, Mr. Burton's book entitled, 'An Apology for an Appeal to the king's most excellent majesty, with two Sermons for God and the King,' preached on the 5th of November last: The News from Ipswich, and the Divine Tragedy, recording God's fearful Judgments against Sabbath-Breakers.—The king's counsel being five, took each of them a several Book."

After a brief statement of the argument of attorneys the report gives us, in the language of archbishop Loud speaking for the court, a concise summary of the offences. of the defendant. Loud's statement of the position for which the defendants were prosecuted will be given in full. The court's self defence against the seditious or blasphemous utterances will usually be omitted. Only enough is presented to suggest the fundamental theory of the court, which will later be contrasted with the contrary concepts expressed and implied in our constitutions.

"And I said well, 'Quis tulerit Gracchos?' for it is most apparent to any man that will not wink, that the intention of these men, and their abettors, was, and is, to raise a Sedition; being as great incendiaries in the state (where they get power) as they have ever been in the Church; Novatian himself hardly greater.

"Our main crime is (would they all speak out as some of them do) that we are Bishops; (Burton Apol. p. 110.) were we not so, some of us might be as passable as other men. And a great trouble it is to them, that we maintain that our Calling of Bishops is *Jure Divino,* by divine right; of this I have said enough, and in this place, in Leighton's Case; nor will I repeat. Only this I will say, and abide by it, that the Calling of Bishops is *Jure Divino,* by divine right, though not all adjuncts to their calling. And this I say in as direct opposition to the Church of Rome, as to the puritan humour. And I say further: That from the apostles times, in all ages, in all places, the Church of

Christ was governed by Bishops; and Lay Elders never heard of till Calvin's new-fangled device at Geneva.

"Now this is made by these men, as if it were *contra regem,* against the king, in right or in power. But that's a mere ignorant shift; for our being bishops *Jure Divino,* by divine right, takes nothing from the king's right or power over us. For though our office be from God and Christ immediately, yet may we not exercise that power, either of order or jurisdiction, but as God hath appointed us, that is, not in his majesty's, or any Christian king's kingdoms, but by and under the power of the king given us so to do.—And were this a good argument against us, as Bishops, it most needs be good against Priests and Ministers too; for themselves grant that their calling is *Jure Divino,* by divine right; and yet I hope they will not say, that to be priests and ministers is against the king or any his royal prerogatives.

"Next suppose our callings as Bishops, could not be made good *Jure Divino,* by divine right; yet *Jure Ecclesiastico,* by ecclesiastical right, it cannot be denied. And here in England the Bishops are confirmed, both in their power and means, by act of parliament. So that here we stand in as good case, as the present laws of the realm can make us. And so we must stand, till the laws shall be repealed by the same power that made them.

"Now then, suppose we had no other string to hold by (I say suppose this, but I grant it not) yet no man can libel against our Calling (as these men do) be it in pulpit, print, or otherwise, but he libels against the king and the state, by whose laws we are established. Therefore, all these Libels, so far forth as they are against our calling, are against the king and the law, and can have no other purpose than to stir up Sedition among the people. If these men had any other intention, or if they had any Christian or charitable desire to reform any thing amiss; why did they not modestly petition his majesty about it, that in his princely wisdom he might set all things right, in a just and orderly manner? * * *

"For the main scope of these Libels is, to kindle a jealousy in men's minds, that there are some great plots in hand, dangerous plots (so says Mr. Burton expressly p. 5.) to change the Orthodox Religion established in England; and to bring in I know not what, Romish Superstition in the room of it. As if the external decent Worship of God could not be upheld in this kingdom, without bringing in of Popery.

"Now by this art of theirs, give me leave to tell you that the King is most desperately abused and wounded in the minds of his people; and the Prelates shamefully.

"The King most desperately: for there is not a more cunning trick in the world to withdraw the people's hearts from their Sovereign, than to persuade them that he is changing true Religion and about to bring in gross Superstition upon them.

"And the Prelates shamefully: for they are charged to seduce, and lay the plot, and be the instruments. * * *

"They say, there are great Innovations brought in by the Prelates; and such as tend to the advancing of Popery. Now that the vanity and falsehood of this may appear, I shall humbly desire your lordships to give me leave to recite briefly the Innovations charged upon us, be they of less or greater moment; and as briefly to answer them. And then you shall clearly see, whether any cause hath been given of these unsavory Libels; and withal, whether there be any shew of cause to fear a Change of Religion. And I will take these great pretended Innovations in order as I meet with them.

"First, I begin with the 'News from Ipswich.'

"Where the first Innovation is, (p. 2), 'That the last year's Fast was enjoyned to be without Sermons in London, the suburbs, and other infected places, contrary to the orders for other Fasts in former times: whereas Sermons are the only means to humble men,' &c. * * *

"2. The second Innovation is, (p. 3.) 'That Wednesday was appointed for the Fast-day, and that this was done with this intention, by the example of this Fast without preaching, to suppress all the Wednesday-Lectures in London.' * * *

"3. The third Innovation is, (p. 3.) 'That the Prayer for seasonable weather was purged out of this last Fast-book, which was (say they) one cause of Shipwrecks and tempestuous weather.' * * *

"4. The fourth Innovation is, (p. 3.) 'That there is one very useful Collect left out, and clause omitted in another.' * * *

"5. The fifth Innovation is, (p. 3.) 'That in the sixth Order for the Fast, there is a Passage left out concerning the Abuse of Fasting in relation to merit.' * * *

"6. The sixth Innovation is, (p. 3.) 'That the lady Elizabeth and her princely children are dashed' (that is their phrase) 'out of the new collect, whereas they were in the Collect of the former Book.' * * *

"7. The seventh Innovation is, (p. 3.) 'That these Words' (who art the father of thine elect and of their seed) 'are changed in the preface of that collect, which is for the prince and the king's children.' And with a most spiteful inference, that 'this was done by the prelates to exclude the king's children out of the number of God's Elect.' And they call it 'an intolerable impiety, and horrid treason.' * * *

"8. The eighth Innovation is, That in the Epistle the Sunday before Easter, we have put out 'In,' and made it, 'At the Name of Jesus' every knee shall bowe: which alteration, he saith, is directly against the act of parliament. (Burton's Apology, p. 2.) * * *

"9. The ninth Innovation is, 'That two places are changed in the Prayer set forth for the fifth of November; and ordered to be read (they say) by act of parliament. The first place is changed thus, from, root out that Babylonish and antichristian sect which say of Jerusalem, &c.' Into this form of words; 'root out that Babylonish and antichristian sect, (of them) which say, &c.' The second place went thus in the old: 'Cut off those workers of iniquity, whose Religion is Rebellion. But in the book printed 1636, 'tis thus altered: Cut off those workers of iniquity, who turn Religion into Rebellion, &c.' * * *

"10. The tenth Innovation is, (p. 3.) 'That the Prayer for the Navy is left out of the late Book for the Fast.' * * *

"11. The 11th Innovation is, (p. 105.) 'The reading of

the second Service at the Communion-Table, or the Altar.'
* * *

"12. One thing sticks much in their stomachs, and they call it an Innovation too. And that is, 'bowing, or doing reverence at our first coming into the church or at our nearer approaches to the holy table, or the altar,' (call it whether you will) in which they will needs have it, that we worship the holy table, or God knows what. (P. 105).
* * *

"13. The thirteenth Innovation is, The placing of the holy Table altar-wise, at the upper end of the chancel; that is, the setting of it North and South, and placing a rail before it, to keep it from profanation, which Mr. Burton (P. 4, 5, 105,) says, is done to advance and usher in Popery."

The gist of this offending is that the defendants promulgated unorthodox views as to theology, ecclesiastical organization, and religious duties toward God. In short these defendants ascribed desires to God, which the established church authorities deemed false. But this is blasphemy under the canon law and common law. However this particular blasphemy was of such a character as to discredit the prelates of the established church. Therefore it had a speculative tendency to discredit the government. Manifestly then it could be called either blasphemy or sedition. This illustrates what is meant by a previous statement that church and state under the old system were but different aspects of the same thing, and that words against an archbishop are therefore words against the government. Also, blasphemous utterances are likewise essentially seditious in their tendency.

THOMAS WILSON—1637? [20]

What follows is all that was found in relation to this prosecution.

"Thomas Wilson, A.M. was born at Catterly, in Cumberland, in the year 1601, and educated in Christ's college, Cambridge; where he was greatly admired for his indefatigable industry, and great progress in useful learning.

[20] Reese, Richard. Compendious martyrology, v. 3, pp. 453-457.

Upon his leaving the university, he taught school for some time at Chartwood in Surrey; then entered into the ministry at Capel, in the same county. Here, by his judicious preaching and holy example, he directed the people in the way to eternal life. Though he received little or nothing for his pains, he was not the less faithful and laborious in promoting the welfare of souls, and was greatly beloved by his people. His great popularity and usefulness soon awakened the envy of profane sinners, and several neighbouring ministers; but he went on undismayed, the Lord blessing his labours.

"Notwithstanding his labours and usefulness, he was at length silenced for refusing to read the Book of Sports. In the month of April, 1634, he was inhibited by Archbishop Laud's vicar-general from part of his public ministerial exercises. But, upon the publication of the Book of Sports, he refused to read it, when the archbishop sent for him to Lambeth; and, April 29, 1635, no less than *fourteen* charges were exhibited against him, to each of which he gave his answer, May 28th following. The substance of these articles, together with Mr. Wilson's answer, was as follows:

"1. That canonical obedience is due by your oath, taken at your institution.

"*Answer.* It is true, as I understand the oath, it is according to the canons of the church of England.

"2. That a minister must have a popular election, as necessary to hold his place.

"*Ans.* I never held such an opinion, nor ever spoke it, privately or publickly.

"3. That there is little comfort for a minister instituted and inducted, without the approbation of the people.

"*Ans.* I know and believe the contrary.

"4. You have held conventicles in your house, and in other houses in the town of Otham, within these two years, and used exercises of religion by law prohibited.

"*Ans.* I deny that I have holden conventicles, and used exercises of religion by law prohibited.

"5. Within these four years you have collected in private houses, or caused to be collected, forty or fifty persons, and to them repeated sermons, expounded scripture, made tedious extemporary prayers, full of tautologies, and delivered dangerous doctrine, to the perverting and corrupting of his majesty's subjects.

"*Ans.* I protest against such doctrine and any such effect. I also deny that I collected, or caused to be collected, any such persons.

"6. You refused to read the King's Declaration for Sports on Sundays, and spoke disdainfully to the apparitor and officer of the court.

"*Ans.* I said to the apparitor, 'Remember the sabbath-day to keep it holy;' and I said no more. I refused to read the book, not out of contempt of any authority, being commanded by no law. The king's majesty doth not in the book command or appoint the minister to read it, nor it to be read, but published. And seeing there is no penalty threatened, nor authority given to any one to question those who refuse to read it, my refusal to read it was upon sufficient grounds of law and conscience; which, for the satisfaction of this high court, and to clear myself from contempt, I shall briefly express myself thus: His majesty's express pleasure is, that the laws of the realm, and the canons of the church be observed in all places of the kingdom; and therefore at Otham in Kent: but this book as I conceive, is contrary to both.—It is contrary to the statute laws.—It is contrary to the ecclesiastical laws. —It is contrary to the scriptures.—It is contrary to the councils.—It is contrary to divines, ancient and modeern.—It is contrary to reason.

"7. In 1633, when the commission was granted for repairing St. Paul's you said, to build sumptuous temples is to justify antichrist.

"*Ans.* I deny this altogether.

"8. In 1634, you bade the people, in scorn and derision, to take heed of dealing with high priest's servants.

"*Ans.* I deny both the time and the words.

"9. At Boxley, June 29, 1632, you said, No man can have a broken heart, who hath two steeples; meaning two benefices, alleging Acts xx. 20.

"*Ans.* I never spake such words. But at the funeral of

a grave and learned minister, I entreated the ministers present to prepare to give an account of their lives and livings, shewing the vanity of those who plead for pluralities, saying, 'That if a man's heart were broken, it would not be with the weight of three churches;' and herein I followed no new opinion, but the general opinion of learned divines, both ancient and modern.

"10. You have scandalized the governors and government of the church of England, as persecutors of God's faithful ministers and people.

"*Ans.* This is not true, in the whole or in any part.

"11. In April, 1633, you delivered a dangerous doctrine, even that if a subject suffer the penalty of the law from the civil magistrate, he is free from sin.

"*Ans.* I deny the time, and words, and doctrine. I never taught, nor read, nor heard of this doctrine, till I heard this article; and I abhor it, and disclaim it as dangerous.

"12. April 22, 1634, you lectured and expounded, after inhibition by the vicar-general.

"*Ans.* This is not true. I did not preach, excepting on Lord's days and holidays; neither did I expound. Yet I had a license to expound and was not forbidden expounding. I constantly instruct by question and answer, in the catechism, such as come to prayers, for which I had my institution and license, and from which I never received any prohibition; nor, so far as I understand, is it any sin against God or man.

"13. You are accounted an enemy to the church of England, and draw others into schism after you.

"*Ans.* I deny the whole of this, and every part.

"14. You are to promise, by your word and honour, to speak the truth.

"*Ans.* I believe what I have confessed, and deny what I have denied in every part.

"Mr. Wilson's answers, in which, he declared his refusal to read the book, were no sooner given, than the archbishop replied, *I suspend you for ever from your office and benefice till you read it:* and he continued suspended for the space of four years. About the same time he was com-

mitted to Maidstone jail for non-conformity, but how long
he remained in confinement does not appear. At the expiration of the above period, he was brought into the high
commission court by means of the archbishop; and, to his
great cost and trouble, was again prosecuted for the same
crime.

"Mr. Wilson, remaining under suspension, and being
dissatisfied with the ministry of his successor, removed to
Maidstone, where he gave private instructions among his
friends. His adversaries, at the same time traduced his
character, and slandered him as a favourer of schism.
Therefore, to wipe off the reproach, he addressed a letter
to the parishioners of Otham, exhorting them 'to fear God
and honour the king, and walk in love one towards another.' For the information and satisfaction of all, this
letter was read to the public congregation on the Lord's
day. The news of this however, soon reached London,
when Mr. Wilson and Dr. Tuck, who had read the letter,
were cited to appear before the high commission. Mr.
Wilson was charged in the court with having sent a scandalous and offensive letter to Otham, to nourish schism,
and to confirm the people in the dislike of government;
upon which he acknowledged his writing a letter, but
denied its *evil tendency,* saying, 'I know that it was to
exhort the people to fear God and the king, and to meddle
not with those that are given to change; to walk in faith
and love and to call upon God: but I utterly deny all occasion of derogating from the church of England, or confirmation of any in a dislike of the governments, and protest against all aspersions and imputations of schism or
scandal: neither did I direct any one to read it, nor intended or desired it should be read in the church.' Notwithstanding all they could alledge in their own defence,
they were enforced to continue their attendance no less
than *three* years, to their great cost and trouble.

"In the year 1639, the Scots having entered England, and
a parliament being called, Laud took off Mr. Wilson's
suspension. But his troubles and sufferings were not
ended; for, September 30, 1640, he was cited to appear before the archbishop's visitors at Feversham, together with

other ministers in Kent, to answer for not reading the prayer against the Scots. Upon their appearance, Mr. Edward Bright, being called first, was asked whether he had read the prayer; and when he said he had not, the archdeacon instantly suspended him from office and benefice, without admonition, or even giving him the least time to consider of it. Mr. Wilson who witnessed this rash proceeding, was next called. When he was asked whether he had read the prayer, he answered in the negative; 'because, (said he) in the rubrick of the Common Prayer, it is enjoined that no prayer shall be publickly read excepting those which are contained in the Book of Common Prayer, and that prayer against the Scots is not.' This unexpected answer so confounded the archdeacon that he did not know what to say. It cooled his fury, and caused him to proceed more deliberately with Mr. Wilson than he had done with Mr. Bright. He gave him fourteen days to consider of it, and then deliver his answer at Canterbury.

"About the same time a warrant was issued from the lords of the council, among whom were Archbishop Laud and the Bishop of London, to apprehend Mr. Wilson. With this warrant a pursuivant was sent to bring him to London. It does not appear for what crime this prosecution was designed; yet no doubt it was the sin of non-conformity. The pursuivant, having received his warrant, hastened without delay to Otham; where, though he heard Mr. Wilson preach, and was afterwards in the same room with him in his own house, he let him slip out of his hands. Mr. Wilson, suspecting him as soon as he entered the room, retired and hid himself, and so escaped the snare. The pursuivant was enraged at his loss, and said he had been employed in this service *thirty-six* years, and he had never been served so before. Mr. Wilson, having escaped the snare, withdrew from the storm till the meeting of the long parliament, when he went to London, and presented his case and petition to the house of commons. The house appointed a committee to take his case into consideration; and, November 30, 1640, Mr. Rouse, who was one of this committee, reported to the house, 'That Mr. Wilson had been suspended four years from his

living, worth sixty pounds a year, only for not reading the
Book of Recreations on the Lord's day; that the archbishop
himself had suspended him; and that for three years he
had attended upon the high commission.' The house therefore resolved, 'That Mr. Wilson had just cause of complaint; and that there was just cause for the house to afford him relief.' Upon the presentation of his petition,
Sir Edward Deering, one of the members for Kent, said,
'Mr. Wilson, your petitioner, is as orthodox in doctrine,
as laborious in preaching, and as unblemished in his life,
as any minister we have. He is now separated from his
flock, to both their griefs: for it is not with him as with
many others, who are glad to set a pursuivant on work,
that they may have an excuse to be out of the pulpit; it
is his delight to preach.' Sir Edward further observes of
Mr. Wilson, 'He is now a sufferer, as all good men are,
under the general obloquy of a puritan. The pursuivant
watches his door, and divides him and his cure asunder, to
both their griefs. About a week since, (he adds) I went to
Lambeth, to move that great bishop (too great indeed) to
take this danger from off this minister, and to recall the
pursuivant. And I did undertake for Mr. Wilson, that
he should answer his accusers in any of the king's courts
at Westminster. The bishop made me answer, 'I am sure
that he will not be absent from his cure a twelve-month
together.'

"Upon the above resolution of the house, he was released
from all his troubles, when he returned to his charge and
wonted labours at Otham. In the year 1643, he was nominated one of the assembly of divines; and, though at so
great a distance, he constantly attended. In the assembly
he was much esteemed. * * * Having continued some time
at Otham, he removed to Maidstone, where he remained
to the day of his death."

JOHN POCKLINGTON—1640.[21]

John Pocklington (d. 1642), graduated at Cambridge
(B. A. 1598—B. D. 1610—D. D. 1621). He was credited

---

[21] Howell's. State trials, vol. 5, p. 747.
Sunday no sabbath. A sermon preached before the Lord bishop of

at Cambridge with being a high churchman.   Much later he was charged with being "a chief author and ring leader in all those [ritualistic] innovations which have of late flowed into the Church of England."

Feb. 12, 1640 he was sentenced by the House of Lords never to come within the verge of the court, to be deprived of all his preferments, and to have his two books, "Altare Christianum" and "Sunday No Sabbath" publicly burnt in the city of London and at Cambridge and Oxford, by the hand of the common executioner.   When Pocklington was deprived of his preferments, William Bray, D.D., who licensed his works was enjoined to preach a recantation sermon in St. Margaret's Church Westminster.

The specification of delinquencies is fortunately preserved.   If the actual enactment of erroneous ritual is thus penalized, of course, the advocacy of such practices must come within technical blasphemy, as can readily be seen by comparison with the definition of blasphemy and the adjudicated cases.

Here then are the charges against Pocklington:

1. "He hath within these few years, in his church at Yelton turned the communion table alterwise.

2. "He bows to or before this altar, very low; as often as either he passeth by it, or makes his approach therunto.

3. "He shews more outward reverence to the altar, than to the name of God: for one time in the church protesting before God, and his holy altar, when he made mention of the altar, he turned himself towards it, and made low obeysance before it, but at the name of God he shewed no such respect.

4. "He hath placed a cross in a cloth behind the altar, called the altar cloth.

5. "He useth much to magnify the cross; and once in his sermon speaking of Moses his prayer against Amalek,

Lincolne at his lordship's visitation at Ampthill * * * Aug. 17, 1635. London 1636 [two editions].
Altare christianum; or the dead vicar's plea. Wherein the vicar of Go [antham] being dead. yet speaketh, and pleadeth out of antiquity against him that hath broken downe his altar'. London 1637.
Vickers, Robert H.   Martyrdoms of literature, p. 377.
Dictionary of national biography, vol. 45, p. 450.

he said, that Moses spread forth his arms in the form of a cross, and that that posture of his was more available with God than his prayer.

6. "He hath caused a bell to be hung up in his chancel, called a sacring-bell, which the clerk always rings at the going up to second service, which he performs with variety of postures, sometimes turning his face towards the South, sometimes towards the East, and sometimes towards the West.

7. "He hath caused two cloaths to be made, which he calls corporals, and these he useth to lay over the bread in the Sacrament; and each of these hath five crosses on it, one at each corner, and one in the middle.

8. "That he refused to give the Sacrament on Easter-day, anno 1638, to twelve or fourteen of his parishioners, though they had acquainted him before, that they intended to receive on that day, according to their usual custom; and though at the time of the administration of the Sacrament, even from the beginning thereof to the end, they kneeled at the rails, for otherwise he would not administer it to them at any time, yet he still passed them by, and sent them away without it, to their great reproach and discomfort: having no just cause so to do.

9. "He hath also composed and published two books or pamphlets, the one intituled "Sunday no Sabbath," the other "Altare Christianum," wherein he justifies and defends all those innovations in religion that have been unhappily introduced into this church, which also he practices by himself; and besides, in those books he asserts and maintains divers wicked, Popish and Antichristian points, to the great danger and damage of this church and state; justifies sundry popish canonized saints for true saints and Martyrs of God, and censures for our own English Martyrs (mentioned in Master Fox's Calendar, before his book of Acts and Monuments, set forth by the public authority, and approved by the whole convocation anno 1579), for traitors, murderers, rebels and heretics.

"May it therefore please this honourable house, to take the premises into your just and pious consideration, and to convent the said Doctor Pocklington before you, to answer the same, that so he may receive such condign and exemplary punishment, as may deter all others from the like dangerous attempts and innovations: and your Petitioner [22] shall ever pray, &c."

The first eight of these Articles being evidently proved against him, and also acknowledged by himself; the ninth was thus managed against him, as follows:

"A Discovery and Declaration of divers wicked, Popish and Antichristian innovations and doctrines, published and taught, and peremptorily affirmed and defended by JOHN POCKLINGTON, D. D., to the great dishonour of God, the great reproach and scandal of true religion, and to the great hurt and danger of the Church of England: collected word for word out of his own books, viz. "Altare Christianum," and "Sunday no Sabbath;" and humbly presented to the knowledge, consideration, and just sentence of the right honourable the Lords of the higher house of parliament.

1. Touching Churches.

"1. He affirms and maintains the dedication and consecration of them by prayers: and that, as he saith, from the doctrines and decrees of Popes of the first and best times, and confirmed by the doctrine and practice of the holy Catholic church.   And he censures the Centurists for bold and impious, because they condemn and brand such kind of Popish consecration of wood and stones, for the mystery of iniquity, Alt. Chr. c. 10, p. 52.

"Now such consecration is contrary to the statute of Ed. 6, c. 10, and 1 Eliz. c. 2, and 8 Eliz. c. 1, which abolisheth and inhibits all other rights and ceremonies and forms of consecration (with all Popish ceremonies and pontificals, wherein the manner of consecreting churches, chapels, and church-yards is prescribed) but such as are only prescribed in the books of Common Prayer and ordination, wherein there is not one word touching any such

---

[22] See Oldmixon's Hist. of England under the Stuarts, vol. 1, p. 165, where it is said that for the rare doctrine of "Sunday no Sabbath," he (Harvey) was made the king's chaplain.

consecration of churches, chapels, and altars, as this man would have.

"2. He teaches and affirms, that the distinction of places in the church is very ancient, and observed even from the Apostles times; and that several places in the church were appointed for the Clergy, and for the Laity, Alt. Chr. c. 8, p. 43, 44. And these several places had several degrees of holiness. Auditorium was the place for the laity, and that was less holy; but Presbyterium was the place for the clergy, and this was more holy. And in the holy place, namely the Chancel or Presbytery, there was a throne or chair placed.

"3. But he bethinks himself, and saith, that this chair was not in all churches, but only in the churches of bishops; and that such a chair was in the church of Jerusalem and Rome; and then after affirms that the succession of bishops in such a chair, was one thing that kept Saint Augustine from departing out of the bosom of the Catholick church; for he brings him in, saying thus, The succession of priests from Saint Peter keeps me of right in the church: the name of this Catholic see, that is, of Rome, keeps me in, Alt. Chr. p. 47.

"And again, Sunday no Sabbath, p. 2, he saith, that the succession of bishops from the seat of Peter is that which keeps us in the church's lap.

"Moreover, he saith touching this succesion in the chair, that the very note whereby heretics were known from catholics, was, that the catholics could shew their churches and the very chairs in them; wherein there was not only a moral succession in purity of faith and manners, but a local succession of bishops continued, Alt. Chr. p. 47.

"Again, he saith, that they that say there were no material churches till 200 years after Christ, are more injurious to the church than they are aware; for if in all this time there were no material churches, then there could be no material chair, then no real inthronization, then no personal succession from the apostles, whereby the right faith was derived from God the Father to his Son, and from the Son to his apostles, and from the apostles to succeeding bishops, Alt. Chr. p. 49. And a little after he saith, they that deprive us of the benefit of this apostolical tradition, pluck one staff out of our hands, whereby we stay ourselves from falling from the true catholic church, and beat all heretics out of our communion. "Miserable were we, if he that sitteth now archbishop of Canterbury could not derive his succession from St. Augustine, St. Augustine from St. Greyory, St. Gregory from St. Peter.[23] What a comfort is this to his Grace, and to all those that receive consecration from him, and to all those that they shall ordain, when they remember that his Grace can say, 'Ego sum hæres apostolorum,' &c. here I and my predecessors have kept possession, here are my evidences that I have to show, that I have received the right faith from the true owner. All this he saith, Alt. Chr. c. 9, p. 50.

[23] The uninterrupted succession by imposition of hands of the Clergy of the Church of England from the Apostles (which is by some supposed to give particular efficacy to their ordination, and, indeed, to be essential to the validity of Orders) has been much litigated. See the Church Histories and "Brett's Divine Right of Episcopacy," &c. Lond. 1728. "Williams's Succession of Protestant Bishops asserted, &c." also his 'Translation of Le Courayer's Defence of the Validity of the English Ordinations. and of the Succession of the Bishops in the Church of England, 2d ed. Lond. 1728," and his translation of "Le Courayer's Defence of his former Treatise,", published in the same year: together with the other books mentioned in these words. Le Courayer for his part in this controversy was persecuted in France. and took refuge in England, where the University of Oxford conferred on him, by Diploma, the degree of Doctor in Divinity. In Ward's Errata of the Protestant Bible, printed in 1688, and lately republished in Ireland, it is asserted that Bishops, Priests and Deacons, being Protestants, are without consecration. ordination, mission, succession, and pastoral jurisdiction; and that all those and their flocks are guilty of sacrilege. See also "Certain Accusations brought recently by Irish Papists against British and Irish Protestants of every denomination, examined by Thomas Kipling, D. D. Dean of Peterborough," London. 1809. In the Church of Rome, Orders are one of the Seven Sacraments. At the time of the Reformation, their sacramental character was much disputed. In the "Institution of a Christian Man" Orders, Matrimony, Confirmation and Extreme Unction are recognised as Sacraments, but declared to be of inferior consideration to the other three, viz.: Baptism, the Eucharist, and Penance. It was at length determined that none but Baptism and the Lord's Supper are Sacraments. See the twenty-fifth of the Thirty-nine Articles of Religion. In the Church's Catechism, however, it does not seem to be absolutely affirmed that these two are the only Sacraments. but rather that no others are generally necessary to salvation. The sacramental character of Orders was discussed in both houses of parliament during the debates upon the bill for removing doubts respecting the eligibility of persons

"So that he makes succession to evidence faith, and not the true faith to evidence succession, which is downright Popish.

"And in his 'Sunday no Sabbath,' p. 48, he speaks to the same purpose in these words:—In this sort Augustine confounds the Donatists and Sectaries of his time, saying, 'Numerate Sacerdotes,' &c. reckon up your Priests, who succeeded one another after St. Peter in his chair; if you will be esteemed members of the Church. Hereby we may by God's mercy make good the truth of our Church; for we are able lineally to set down the succession of our Bishops, from St. Peter to St. Gregory, and from him to our first Archbishop St. Augustin, and so downward to his Grace that now sits in his Chair, Primate of all England and Metropolitan.

"So that he makes the succession of Bishops from St. Peter and the See of Rome, to be a sure and infallible sign of the true Church, and herein shews himself to be a perfect Papist.

"All this he speaks by occasion of the Bishop's chair, which he saith is placed in the Chancel, which is a degree holier than the body of the Church.

"4. But yet he affirms a holier place than both these and that he calls 'Sacrarium,' or 'sanctum sanctorum,' the holy of holies, and this he thus describes; it is a place at the upper end of the Chancel, inclosed and railed in from the rest of the Chancel, whereinto none may enter but the Priests themselves, and none else, no not the King, without a dispensation. This he clears, as he saith, out of the history of Theodosius the Emperor, who when the time

---

in Holy Orders to sit in the House of Commons, (st. 41 G. 3, (U. K.) c. 63,) and upon a motion for the issue of a new writ for the Borough of Old Sarum, made in the House of Commons, May 4th, 1801, see Cobb. Parl. Hist. See also upon the sacramental nature of Orders and the indelible character of the Priesthood, (which seems to be derived from it) Campbell's Lectures upon Ecclesiastical History.

The objection to the English Orders derived from the story of the *Nag's Head* ordination (as it is called, perhaps consecration or episcopation would be a more exact name) seems to be extremely refined and subtle; since it does not appear to be questioned that Parker and his brethren had been apostolically ordained Deacons and Priests.

of offering gifts was come, rose up, and with tears went into the holy place, and after his oblation stood within the rails: but St. Ambrose, saith he, put him in mind of the difference of places, and told him that that part of the Sacrarium or Chancel within the rails, was only for Priests, and no other might enter in there, or so much as touch them.   And so he, fair and mannerly, bad the King go forth, and stand with the rest of the common people, which accordingly he did.   Alt. Chr. p. 81.

2. TOUCHING ALTARS.

"1. He affirms, that we ought to have in the Church a real, material, proper Altar, Alt. Chr. p. 13.   And again he saith, we have an earthly Altar here over earth, on which tithes, and offerings, and such earthly things were at first dedicated and consecrated, to maintain the earthly bodies of Priests, whose bodies serve at God's Altar.   Alt. Chr. p. 9.

"2. For the manner how Altars came into the Christian Church, he saith that no man of judgment or learning, though he looked over antiquity, as the devil looked over Lincoln, will say, and justify, that Altars crept into the Church, but the governors of Christ's Church, and the true and only successors of the Apostles (sure he means the Pope of Rome) brought them in by the special direction of God's holy spirit, Alt. Chr. c. 21, p. 141.

"To affirm that God's spirit directed the bringing in of material and proper altars into the Christian Church, is to slander the Holy Ghost, seeing the spirit of God never taught any man in any age, any other thing but that which Christ taught in the days of his flesh; as appears Joh. 14, 26.   Now Christ never taught any thing of earthly and material altars in the Christian Church; and therefore that spirit that teacheth any such thing is not the spirit of Christ, but of Antichrist.

"3. For the necessity of Altars, he would make that appear in this regard, because without them, he saith, there can be no consecration; the Eucharist, saith he, cannot elsewhere be consecrated but on an Altar, Alt. Chr. p. 27.

"This he affirms stoutly in his Sunday no Sabbath, p. 48, and in his Alt. Chr. c. 12, p. 75, 76, that where there is no Altar there çan be no consecration. And he saith touching the Primitive Church, that if they had no Altar, then they had no Eucharist to deliver; or if they delivered it, they gave it before it was consecrated; for they had no Church nor Altar to consecrate the same upon, and 'Eucharistia in Altari consecratur,' we are sure out of all antiquity, that the Eucharist must be consecrated on an Altar.

"From which desperate assertion, it must needs follow, that Christ did not deliver the Eucharist to the Apostles, nor they to the faithful, or else that it was not consecrated, as he saith, when he delivered it, seeing it is most evident by Scripture that Christ and his Apostles had no altars, but tables, and did institute and administer the Sacrament on a table in an upper chamber, and not at an altar in a church. And again, according to this doctrine the Church of England for this fourscore years hath had no Sacraments, for it hath had no altars, and without altars, saith he, no Sacraments.

"Again, he speaks farther, St. Cyprian tells you, saith he, that the use of altars is to sanctify the Eucharist upon, and that without an altar it cannot be consecrated, and therefore Heretics have no Sacraments among them, because they have no altars, Alt. Chr. c. 24, p. 17.

"Here he affirms that the altar doth sanctify the Sacrament, which is no less than *blasphemy*: for as by Christ's own words it is plain, that which sanctifies the offering, is greater than the offering which is sanctified; and so he makes a wooden or stony altar greater than Christ, which is, as he saith, the sacrifice offered.

"Again, he saith, Heretics have no altars, whereby he intimates that the Church of England is heretical, because that hath no altars.

"4. For the place of the altar, he saith, it is Sacrarium or the Holy of Holies, and that the altar is not to stand in the body of the church, among the people; but, saith he, let it stand as the governors of our church appoint it, at the upper end of the quire, or in the highest or most

eminent place of the chancel, where reason and piety ever
placed it, in the Eastern Church, the practice whereof
Englishmen and Britons ought to follow, to express thereby
their concord and agreement with the Primitive Church,
where St. Peter's chair was set, except some diptiches can
he produced for the derivation of our faith and religion,
more ancient and authentical than from St. Elutherius
and St. Gregory.

"So that this man derives our faith and religion not
from Christ the Son of God, but from two Popes,
Elutherius and Gregory; and this Christian faith and
religion, he makes to consist in the placing the Communion-table altar-wise, at the upper end of the chancel.

"5. For the matter of altars, he saith, these altars are
some of them of stone; 'quia Christus est lapis angularis,'
because Christ is a corner-stone: and some of them of wood,
the better to express his death on the tree.   Sund. no
Sab. p. 43.

"6. For the ornaments of them, he saith; they are to
have their carpets, corporals, veils and rails, Alt. Chr. p.
15.

"And touching corporals, he saith thus, Pope Pius
maketh mention of altars and of a linen cloth or corporal
spread upon altars: whereunto the practice of the church
agrees (sure he means here, as in other places, the church of
Rome; for it is not the practice of the church of England)
for 'Corpus Domini non in sericis sed in syndone munda
consecratur:' and to strengthen this, he adds the constitution of Pope Sylvester, who ordained (saith he) that
the sacrifice of the altar should not be consecrated in
silk or dyed cloth, but only in linen, as his dead body was
buried in clean linen.   And thus he makes way to Christ's
corporal presence in the Sacrament.   Alt. Chr. p. 7.

"7. For the praise of alters, he saith, that they are the
seats and chairs of state, where the Lord vouchsafeth to
place himself among us; for what is the altar but the seat
of the body and blood of Christ?   And these have been
in all ages greatly honoured and regarded of the most wise,
most learned, and most blessed Saints of God, Alt. Chr.
c. 22, p. 143, and 159.

"8. For the reverence and worship of altars, he saith, that when the church was consecrated, the altar was the chiefest place, which with most ceremony and devotion was hallowed; and so tithes of the greatest sanctity were given to the altar, Alt. Chr. c. 21, p. 141, 142. And that the priests themselves durst not ascend thither, without doing lowly reverence three several times; yea, some, he saith, did willingly fall down and kiss the holy altar. All which he propounds to our imitation; and when all this is done, he saith, altars are no otherwise used in our church than the most holy fathers that ever lived, used them, Alt. Chr. c. 21, p. 144.

"And again, c. 22, p. 152, he saith, if the types of these altars were had in singular honour among the Jews, then the substance ought to be had in much more honour among Christians.

"The Jews never bowed to or before their altars, though erected and consecrated by God's own institution; much less then should we do it, to or before altars set up and hallowed by men, contrary to Christ's institution.

"So that he makes these material altars of wood and stone, superstitiously set up in the church, to be the substance which the Jewish altars did typify, to the great reproach of Christ and Christian religion.

"Again, 'Sunday no Sabbath,' p. 50, he saith, if we do only bend or bow our body to his blessed board or holy altar (here he clearly declares, that the worship he gives, is to the altar itself, which is plain idolatry) but fall flat on our faces before his foot-stool, so soon as ever we approach in sight thereof; what Patriarch, Apostle, blessed Martyr, holy or learned Father would condemn us for it? Or rather would not be delighted to see their Lord so honoured, &c. and concludes it thus, blessed are the servants whom the Lord when he comes shall find so doing, that is, bowing to the altar.

"9. Lastly, he gives God thanks for an altar set up at Grantham, p. 121, affirms that there is no doubt but they put salvation in great hazard, that undermine altars, p. 150, and for his own part, he saith, he would be glad at his heart to be sacrificed for altars, p. 34, and exhorts, that for as much as God had put into the hearts of the Governors of our Church,[24] to restore the Lord's Table to its ancient and true place it had in the Primitive Church, and also to the honor and reverence which of right belongs unto it; in regard of the presence of our Saviour, whose chair of state it is upon earth, and to inclose it with rails, not only to keep it from all manner of profanation, but to strike the minds of all beholders with some reverence and respect, to keep their true distance, and to make a difference between place and place, that therefore no sacrilegious [25] and factious persons should disturb so holy and godly a purpose, c. 24, p. 175.

"3.   Touching the Service of the Church.

1. He teaches a first and second service, and saith that the first service is to be read in Auditorio or body of the church, and the second service ought to be read only in Sacrario, or in the chancel at the holy altar, if the practice of holy Church be enquired after, Alt. Chr. p. 86.

"Whereas the Epistle and Gospel which is part of his second service, in Durand's time was read in the pulpit, and reading pew, and by Edward the Sixth's Injunction, at the beginning of reformation, was to be read in the pulpit.

"2. He saith, that this second service consisteth in consecrations, oblation and orisons, made unto God the Father only by priests, p. 103.

"3. For the postures of his second service, he saith thus; when supplication, intercession, consecration and giving of thanks unto God the Father were finished by the priest, with his face unto the East; and the next office he performed, being to bless the people, who always kneeled below him, and were divided from him, and did not stand about or above him and the holy altar itself.   Is it not fit he turn him, after reverence done to the holy altar, and with his face unto the West, bless the congregation of the Lord, and do it upon this ground, 'Aperui os in medio

---

[24] That is, our Popish and superstitious prelates.
[25] See how this wicked man hath bent his bow against the face of the Parliament.

Ecclesiæ,' I have opened my mouth in the midst of the church, Alt. Chr. c. 17, p. 118.

"All the prayers in the canon of the mass itself are 'pro circumstantibus,' for those who stood round about the altar, and priest when he consecrated.

"Here he expounds the Scripture, not according to the mind of God, but according to his own carnal mind.

"4. For the time when second service is to begin, he saith, that St. Ambrose began not the second service as our church calls it, at the altar, before the first service in the body of the church was finished, which still is the custom in our church, and none will ever go about to put that sweet harmony which we keep with the Primitive Church out of tune but schismatics and sectaries. Sund. no Sab. p. 29.

4. Touching Confession, Penance and Absolution.

"1. He affirms and maintains Popish Confession, for he thus describes it, to be an act wherein, we confess our fault to God, not as if he were ignorant thereof; but so far forth as by this confession, the mind is set in readiness for satisfaction; our repentance springs out of it, and by our penance God is appeased, Alt. Chr. p. 54.

"So he makes God to be appeased not by the death of Christ but by a man's own penance.

"2. He teaches Popish Penance; for he saith it is a discipline used for the humbling and casting down of men, imposing on them such a manner of conversation, as may move pity and commiseration; it giveth law to food and raiment, orders men to lie in sackcloth and ashes; to humble ourselves before the priests, and to fall down upon our knees before God's altars. Penance works all this. And after in the same tenth chapter, 'To this purpose' saith he 'a solemn day was set apart for taking of public penance for open faults, by imposition of hands and sprinkling of ashes, viz. Ash-Wednesday: this' saith he 'is the godly discipline whereof our church speaks in the Commination, of putting notorious sinners to open penance in the beginning of Lent, and wish that it might be restored again, p. 58.

"3. For Popish absolution, he saith, that as Ash-Wednesday was appointed for putting notorious sinners to open penance; so Maundy-Thursday was set apart for their absolution: and this absolution they took on their knees, by imposition of the priests hands. And this he commends, though he saith, he knows it is not pleasing, and they that read it will say, that therein they have endured long penance, p. 58.

5.   TOUCHING THE SACRAMENTS.

"1. In Alt. Chr. c. 25, p. 181, he speaks thus—Come we to the Sacraments, and of two which remain as generally necessary to salvation, we shall not have one at all left us, if they and the rites and the ceremonies about them must not be maintained by the authority, practice and tradition of holy church.

"So that he grounds the sacraments not on the Scripture, but on the tradition of holy church, which is plain popery.

"2. Touching baptism, he saith, that baptism is not rightly performed, 'nisi signum crucis adhibeatur,' unless the sign of the cross be used.

"Though it be evident that the Apostles of Christ never used it, and therefore by his doctrine did never rightly baptise.

"3. Touching the Supper of the Lord, he saith, that the Protestant hath the abuses and novelties only which are crept into the Roman church in detestation, not the things themselves, no not the name of the very Mass itself, Alt. Chr. c. 20, p. 138.

"Whereas the very name of the Mass is obliterated and expunged out of the book of Common Prayer, the Articles of Religion and the book of Homilies, and is in truth a mere barbarous word.

"Again, he saith, c. 16, p. 108, that the people were not so profane and unchristian, to press rudely into the Lord's house, and not to perform their humble and most lowly reverence towards the holy and most sacred altar, where Christ is most truly and really present in the blessed sacrament.

"And that we may know that by real presence he means
corporal presence, he saith, as he tells us out of Irenæus,
that when Christ took the bread and the wine, he gave
thanks, and said, that the bread was his body, and confessed the wine to be his blood, and taught a new oblation
of the New Testament which the church receiving from the
apostles, doth offer unto God in all the world, c. 18 p. 122.

"Again, he saith, the priest offers a true and full sacrifice to God the Father, and that when the priest doth use
the bread, and pour wine into the chalice, and doth not consecrate water only without wine, he doth offer a pure sacrifice, as Christ himself did, p. 123.

"This is just the sacrifice and popish doctrine of the
Mass, and indeed pure nonsense; for Christ in the sacrament doth give himself to us, we do not offer him to God;
he bids us take and eat the bread, and take and drink of
the cup; he doth not bid us offer the bread and the wine.

"And yet further, he saith, this sacrifice, the priest standing at the altar, offers unto God for all the world, for
bishops, for the church, &c. according to our collect on
Good-Friday, and prayer for the whole estate on Christ's
church militant here on earth, p. 124.

"Whereby it appears that he would fain screw our church
into this popish doctrine and practice.

"Also that he may make good his Mass, he calls the
sacrament the sacred Host, p. 124, and the sacrifice of the
altar, p. 127, and p. 128, he saith, Thus you see altars,
oblations and sacrifices were in common use among the
most holy saints of God that ever lived.

6.   Touching Prayer for the Dead.

"He saith, that because Geminius did appoint a clergyman his executor, whereby he was withdrawn from the
altar and sacrifice, therefore it was ordered, that they
should not sacrifice for him, nor celebrate a sacrifice for
his death.

"But on the other side, he saith, that the same holy
martyr is careful to have the names of such confessors,
who died in prisons to be brought to him, and the particular days of their departures, that sacrifices and obla-

tions might be celebrated for them, c. 18, p. 123. And a little after in the same chapter, he saith, when the sacrifice in our Mediator is offered, it cannot be denied but the souls of the faithful are hereby eased, p. 126, plainly teaching a purgatory.

7. TOUCHING THE CROSS AND PICTURES.

"1. For the cross, he saith, that the cross ever used to stand on the altar, and that Rhenænus saith, that in those times Christians had no other images in their churches, but only the cross of Christ, which stood on the altar; and accordingly he hath placed a cross in the midst of his altar, in the church of Yelden.

"2. Touching pictures, he saith, that pictures in a chapel cannot but strike the beholders with thoughts of piety and devotion, at the entering into so holy a place, c. 13, p. 87. Whereas St. Paul saith, Christ is not to be known after the flesh, according to which these pictures only represent him, if so be that they were true pictures of him.

8. TOUCHING OBEDIENCE.

"He maintains popish and blind obedience: for he would have the decrees, constitutions and canons of holy church, absolutely obeyed before scanned and disputed upon, cap. 25, p. 187, and p. 190, he saith, that what canons and laws the lords archbishops and bishops, and the whole convocation house frame and devise, and the king's majesty gives assent unto, under his broad seal, ought not to be banded up and down by vicars, parsons, and parishioners, and questioned at their pleasures, but saith, he believes, that they ought to be allowed and believed, and that before they maintained *rationibus cogentibus.*

"Therefore the last canons and new oath and benevolence, ought to be obeyed, and neither disputed nor debated, much less renounced and censured, if this be good doctrine.

9. TOUCHING PREACHING.

"1. He teacheth, that reading is preaching; for (saith he) reading of lessons, and of Epistle and Gospel, is preaching; and the reader is a preacher. Sunday no

Sabbath, p. 34. And a little after, Reading then is preaching, nay, heavenly preaching, and there is nothing more profitable for the church and more powerful to make the most perfect men of God, even to make martyrs, p. 34.

"He saith, that when Paul preached at Troas, mentioned Acts xx. and continued his speech till midnight, he did but read a homily; and he saith, it is hard for him to say, whether St. Paul made it himself and pronounced it, or whether some other made it, and he only read it. But yet after, he absolutely concludes, that St. Paul's preaching. there till midnight, was only the reading the Apostle's decrees, and saith thus: Wherefore I take it for a clear truth, that St. Paul read the decrees, and sure I am that when he read them, and did no more but read them, without adding or diminishing, that he preached by way of homily. Reading of homilies then is preaching, and so is adjudged by the learned bishops in the Council of Rhemes, (which was a Popish Council) Sunday no Sabbath, p. 32, 33.

"2. Touching lectures, he saith, that the plot of setting up lectures in every good town, was but a dull device of a foggy brain and willing blunderer, that light upon it in a mist, wherein the brethren were at first involved, Alt. Chr. c. 24, p. 172.

"Though Origen and others in the primitive church were lecturers, and lectures in divinity were commonly used, within 300 years after Christ, both in Antioch and other Christian churches.

"3. Touching afternoon sermons, he saith, that our Saviour came not to break the law, but to fulfil it, and he being at Capernaum on a sabbath day, preached but once, for he went immediately from the synagogue to Simon's house to dinner, and went no more to the synagogue to preach in the afternoon. The law that enjoined afternoon sermons for the keeping the sabbath, was not then known to the Pharisees themselves, who else were apt enough to have laid it in his dish at supper: no, nor to these men's progenitors, for 1565 years after, Sunday no Sabbath, p. 31.

"Though bishop Hooper, bishop Latimer, Adam Damplip, and sundry others of our martyrs preached twice every

Sunday; and St. Chrysostom, Ambrose, Augustine, and others of the Fathers preached twice every day.

2. TOUCHING THE SABBATH.

"He most wickedly and vilely reproaches the Sabbath. He saith the Sabbath is old leven to be cast out of the church, and that it hath soured the affections of too many towards the church, and disturbed the peace, and hindered the pious devotion thereof, c. 22, p. 155.

"Again, he saith, It was anabaptized after the mind of some Jew, hired to be godfather thereof, and to call it the Sabbath. Sunday no Sabbath, p. 6.

"Though the Lord's day be called a Sabbath by sundry Fathers, Councils and ancient writers, both Protestant and Popish, by the homilies of our church, acts of parliament, proclamations of the king, and by the very canons then selves.

"And a little after he saith, for this name Sabbath is not a bare name, like a spot in their foreheads, to know Laban's sheep from Jacob's, but indeed it is a mystery of iniquity intended against the church; for allow them but their Sabbath, and you must allow them the service that belongs to their Sabbath, which saith he, is nothing but preaching, Sunday no Sabbath, p. 6, 7.

"And again, p. 20. Hence it is, saith he, that some for want of wit, some for too much, adore the Sabbath as an image dropped down from Jupiter, and cry before it as they did before the golden calf; This is an holy day to the Lord: whereas it is indeed the great Diana of the Ephesians, as they use it.

"And a little after, yet to die they will call it a Sabbath; presuming in their zealous ignorance or guileful zeal, to be thought to speak the scripture phrase, when indeed the dregs of Ashdod flow from their mouths; for that day which they nickname the Sabbath, is either no day at all, or not the day that they mean.

"Whereas *sabbatum* signifies a day of sacred rest consecrated to God; whence all such days are in scripture, called sabbaths as well as the seventh day. Therefore the Lord's day may be so termed without any danger of

Judaism, as well as Easter is still called Pasca, and Whitsunday Pentecost, though Jewish words and institutions.

11. TOUCHING MARTYRS AND WITNESSES OF THE CHRISTIAN FAITH AND TRUTH.

"He reproaches and slanders all those blessed martyrs that have resisted and withstood the cursed heresies of the church of Rome, in all ages, and particularly our own English martyrs, as appears in a most remarkable passage that he sets down in his Altare Christianum, c. 16, p. 114. The words are these, 'This was the holy and profitable use of these diptiches, much unlike the list of persons censured by holy church, called with some reproach of truth and Christian religion, *Catalogus testium veritatis.*'

"[This book was set forth by Illyricus, and is thus intituled, A Catalogue of the Witnesses of the Truth, which before our time, have opposed and resisted the primacy of the bishops of Rome, and divers superstitions, errors and deceits of popery; as namely, John Hus, Jerome of Prague, Luther, with divers others, which the church of Rome therefore condemned; which Romanish church, this great champion thereof, terms holy church; and these faithful Christians and true martyrs and confessors, he saith were censured by holy church, that is, the church of Rome, for that only censured them; and therefore he saith, they are called witnesses of the truth, to the reproach of truth and Christian religion.   Where he plainly and openly declares himself to fight for the church of Rome, against the true church of Christ.]

"And then for our own English martyrs, he goes on thus: And as unlike a calender that I have seen, wherein the holy martyrs and confessors of Jesus Christ, who not only had place sometimes in these diptiches, but whose name are written in heaven, are erased out, and traitors, murderers, rebels, and heretics set in their room, if the best of our chronicles deserve credit, that if Penry, Hacket or Legat, had come in time, they might have challenged as orient and scarlet coloured a dye as some of them.

"[This he speaks of the calender prefixed to the book of martyrs, where the popish saints are omitted, and our

English martyrs names inserted, whom he terms traitors, murderers, rebels and heretics. And that this he means, is most evident, because there is no other calender but it alone, and one almanack taken out of it, of this nature; and because he refers to our English chronicles, and to our English sufferers.]

12.   Touching Saint Paul.

"He reproaches and slanders this blessed apostle; for he saith, that Saint Paul in setting things in order among the Corinthians, crossed the order used by Christ, and forbad the Corinthians to take their supper before the sacrament, which is utterly false, as appears by the apostle's own words, 1, Cor. 11, 22, and 34; Alt. Chr. p. 163; Sunday no Sabbath, p. 3; he saith, that Saint Paul, contrary to his own rules given to the Corinthians, did administer the sacrament, and preach, where men did both eat and drink (wherein again he slanders the apostle: for he never gave any such rule to the Corinthians, as it is evident by the text itself) and he saith he continued preaching out of order till midnight.

"So that he affirms, 1. That Saint Paul crossed Christ's order.   2. That he crossed his own orders, and 3. That he did things out of order.

"These among other corrupt, false wicked and popish points, are gathered out of his own books, and out of his own words, and here presented to the right honourable the Upper House of Parliament.

"Seeing then it is most evident, that this wretched man hath come forth as a fierce enemy against Jesus Christ, and his everlasting truth; and as a great and a bold agent and factor for the Devil and Antichrist; may it therefore please this right honourable Assembly of Parliament, that by that strength which Almighty God hath given into your hands, he may be cast forth of the church of England, as dirt and dung, as one of the chief banes and pests thereof, who hath been one busy cause of all those wicked doctrines and Popish rites, and of all those horrible disorders and confusions that are among us, under the heavy burden whereof this whole kingdom groans and sighs for deliverance, that all others by his example may fear, and do no more any such thing.

"When many of the chief points here expressed (for the time would not suffer the producing of them all) were brought forth in judgment against the Doctor, at a Committee of many lords, in the Painted Chamber, Feb. 11, the man was not able to make any reasonable Defence; for his parts and learning had quite forsaken him, if ever he had any, and he had nothing left in him but anger and passion to manage his cause; which provoked all good Christians to praise God, who had given his truth such a weak enemy; and error such a foolish patron.   Whereupon, the day following, the House sentenced him, as follows:[26]

"12 Feb. 1641.—The Upper House of Parliament did Sentence and resolve upon the question:

"1. That Doctor John Pocklington is by the Judgment of the House prohibited ever to come into the verge of the king's court.   2. That he is deprived of all his ecclesiastical livings, dignities, and preferments.   3. That he is disabled and held uncapable hereafter to hold any place or dignity in the church or commonwealth.   4. That his two books, one intituled, "Altare Christianum," the other, "Sunday no Sabbath," be publicly burnt in the city of London, and the two Universities, by the hand of the common Executioner."

"Ordered by the Lords, that all whom it concerns, shall put in execution the Judgment of this House against the said Doctor Pocklington.

"Certain Articles against Master Pocklinton, found in the records of the University of Cambridge, and truly transcribed by Master Tabor, which shew that the seed which brought forth all this cursed fruit, had taken root in him long ago.

"1. After words of consecration, the body of Christ is

---

[26] "Dr. Bray, one of the Archbishop's chaplains, who had licensed Pocklington's books, acknowledged his offence at the bar of the House, confessed that he had not examined the books with that caution that he ought, and made a public recantation in the church of Westminster.   But Pocklington refusing to recant about thirty false proposititions, which the Bishop of Lincoln [Williams] had collected out of his books, was sentenced by the Lord Keeper," &c. Neal's Hist. of the Puritans, vol. 2, p. 314, ed. 1759.

so essentially, and inseparably present in the sacrament, as that *Hoc est corpus meum* must be taken plainly as it sounds, not drawing any manner of trope or figure therein, not thinking that the spirit in so great a mystery should play the vain and idle rhetorician.

"2. Hereof being reprehended by master Belcanquall, he more peremptorily defended it; affirming, that except the bare word alone of transubstantiation, he could find no fault at all in Bellarmine's doctrine of the sacrament.

"3. He was much offended that this question should be propounded in our schools, 'Secessio ab Ecclesia Romana fuit necessaria.'

"4. He wondered at one of our fellows, who having opportunity, would not be present at Mass, it being a thing both requisite and lawful, in as much as there was a lawful ministry, giving no other thing than what we have in our sacrament.

"5. He affirmed it to be an evident sign how acceptable the Romish religion was to God in former ages, because there were not then in the times of popery, so many murders, adulteries, robberies, &c., as since have been in the time of protestancy.

"He counselled younger men beginning to study divinity, wholly to rely upon Cassander's Consultations, as himself there had done, as the safest author for resolution about the true church.

"7. On a Gun-powder Treason day, he was offended at an oration made by a scholar, wherein traitor Faux was with fitting terms detested, and his matchless impiety execrated: He said it was a great offence of our church to speak evil of any that are dead.

"8. By the masters not regarding it, our College is very ill reported of abroad, for corruption in religion, and scandalous opinions, which is occasioned by the master's deputy, who oftentimes useth, and that before young gentlemen, and other young students, with great earnestness of words and countenance, to argue for pontifical doctrines, never drawing to any contrary conclusion whereby to inform them otherwise.

"9. He held that Christ's righteousness could not be imputed to us.

"10. That our sins were no way imputed to Christ.

"11. That interpretation of Scripture should be made, not by Scripture, but the exposition of holy men.

"12. That Bellarmine and Baronius in all worth, far exceeded all protestant divines, wishing that our religion were as well defended by our men, as theirs is by them.

"13. That Tortura Torti, and Responsio ad Apologiam Bellarmini were works of small worth, solidity and gravity.

"14. He professed also in his sermon, the like belief of the bread and wine in the sacrament, to be verily turned into the flesh of Christ, as he believed Moses rod to be verily turned into a serpent, though the sensible mutation were not there.

"15. He laboured also therein to answer the objection which the protestant divines make against the pontifical doctrines of the sacrament.

"16. At a public disputation with us, where he maintained 'Romanam Ecclesiam esse veram, visibilem Christi Ecclesiam;' being admonished by master Belcanquell respondent, that doctor Whittakers, doctor Fulke, doctor Abbott, doctor Downham, master Calvin, monsieur de Plessis, Sadael, Moulin, and many more of our divines held the contrary; he notwithstanding with great vehemency slighted all that so said, 'impios, sceleratos, perniciosos atque in ipsum Christum blasphemos,' with other words to that effect: whereof the master when he was publicly admonished, would take no notice.

"17. The college also from whence he came had some jealousies of him, and publicly in a divinity act *pro gradu,* he was so offensive, that for fear he should lose his degree, he afterwards, whether by command or counsel we know not, made an apologetical retraction in a public sermon, of those offences that he had given in that act of his."

JOHN GOODMAN—1640.[27]

John Goodman in 1640 merely for being a Romish Priest was ordered killed.

---

[27] Rushworth's Historical collections (Book 4) Vol. 1, part 3, p. 166. Howell's, State trials, v. 4, p. 59-64.

NATHANIEL BARNARD—1640.[28]

What follows is all that was found concerning this case. "Nathaniel Bernard, having preached a sermon at Cambridge which gave offence, was cited before the high commission, when the following passages were deemed objectionable.

" 'It is not the single *having* of God's ordinances of public worship, but having them in their purity, that dignifies a nation.   God's ordinances in their purity are a sure shield to a nation from public ruin and desolation.   For the proof of this, I challenge all records, both human and divine, to produce one instance wherein God punished any part of his church, with any national ruin and destruction, before they had departed from, or corrupted his ordinances.   The gospel, which is the power of God to salvation, is the means by which God manifesteth his omnipotent power in the conversion and salvation of all those that believe.   Is there not a generation of profane men among us, who are afraid and ashamed to preach twice on a Lord's day; to preach plainly, powerfully, and spiritually to the souls and consciences of their people, lest they should be accounted puritans?'

"But the principal exception was the conclusion of his sermon, as follows: 'It is impossible, I say, that any should be saved living and dying without repentance, in the doctrine and idolatrous worship of the church of Rome, as the late Tridentine council hath decreed.   My reason is, that he who thinks of going to heaven in any other way than by faith in Christ only, shall never come there. Furthermore, if God's ordinances of public worship, in their divine purity, be the glory of a nation; then it follows, that they who go about to deprive a nation of them, either wholly, or of their purity, go about to make the nation base and inglorious, and are the enemies and traitors of that nation.   Let us then pray these men either to conversion, if it be the will of God, or to destruction. And let us use that prayer against them, which David used against Ahithophel, with which I will conclude: O

[28] Reese, Richard. Compendious Martyrology, v. 3, pp. 428-429.

Lord, turn the council of all these Ahithophels into folly, who go about to lay the honour of this church and nation in the dust, by depriving us of the purity of thy ordinances of public worship, which are the glory of this our nation.'

"For these expressions in his sermon, Mr. Bernard was most cruelly censured in the high commission. He was suspended, excommunicated, fined one thousand pounds, condemned in costs of suit, and committed to New Prison; where, for six months, he was most barbarously used, and almost starved for want, of which he complained in sundry letters and petitions which he sent to the bishop; but the good man could obtain no relief, unless he would defile his conscience by a public recantation. Whether this severe and heavy sentence was disproportionate to his crime, the impartial reader will easily determine.

"The degrading recantation enjoined upon Mr. Bernard, was as follows: 'Whereas in a sermon made by me, in this place, the 6th of May last, upon this text, "The glory is departed from Israel, because the ark of God was taken," 1 Sam. iv. 21; I had this passage: 'The gospel, which is the power of God unto salvation, is the means by which God manifesteth his omnipotent power in the conversion and salvation of all that believe.' 'And I do here publicly acknowledge, that hereby, contrary to his majesty's command in his declaration lately published with the articles of religion, I did go beyond the general meaning of that place of scripture, and of the said articles; and drew the same to maintain the one side of some of those ill-raised differences, which his majesty's said declaration mentioneth. And this I did rather out of a desire to thrust something into my said sermon in affirmation of one side of the said differences than was any way occasioned by the text I preached from. For which I here publicly profess my hearty sorrow, and do humbly crave pardon of Almighty God, of his majesty, and of this congregation.'

" 'And whereas in the said sermon, I had this passage: "If God's ordinances of public worship, in their purity, be the glory of a nation; then it follows, that they who go about to deprive a nation of them, either wholly or of their purity, go about to make the nation base and inglorious, &c." 'I do now, upon better information, find that many erroneous and dangerous assertions and consequences, unfit to be here expressed, may be collected and inferred from the said words. I do, therefore, hereby publickly recant all the said words, as they were used or may be inferred, to be very rashly and inconsiderately uttered, and to be very undutiful to his majesty. I do humbly refer and submit myself to his majesty's clemency and gracious acceptance, for the interpretation of my meaning; and I am heartily sorry, and do humbly ᴄrave pardon, that words and applications, so scandalous and dangerous to the present state of the church of England, proceeded from me.' &c. &c.

"Mr. Bernard was required to make this recantation publickly before the congregation where he had delivered the sermon; but he absolutely refused. Though in his numerous letters and petitions to Bishop Laud, he professed his sincere sorrow and repentance for any oversights and unbecoming expressions in his sermon, he could obtain no relief. He must either recant according to the above form, or be ruined." He died in prison.

CONNECTICUT STATUTE—1642.

This brings us to the time of the first law concerning religion, which was enacted by the colonists in Connecticut. The juridicial record prior to 1642, which has just been reproduced, has two important bearings upon our present problem.

First: It is in part from this record that we must extract, *if we can*, the common-law meaning of the words, *blasphemy, God, God* the *Father*, the *Son*, and the *Holy Ghost*, as these were used in the law of that time, and after. Also: the meaning of the *Christian Religion* and of *Holy Scriptures* as used in the later amendments.

Secondly: In part THIS PREVIOUS RECORD EXHIBITS TO US JUST WHAT WAS TO BE PREVENTED BY OUR CONSTITUTIONAL GUARANTEES FOR FREE SPEECH AND FOR EQUALITY AND LIBERTY IN RELATION TO RELIGION.

By the following statute of 1642 it was sought to protect the dignity and the reputation of God, (or did they think he also had vanity?) Doubtless these pious souls hoped that from gratitude the omnipotent one might bestow upon them more heavenly rewards for thus preserving Him against that change in the worshiping habits of the human animal which is the product of criticism and other factors of normal intellectual development.

"1. If any man after legal conviction, shall have or worship any other God but the Lord God, hee shall bee put to death. Deut. 13.6-17.2—Exodus 22.20.

"2. If any man or woman bee a Witch, that is hath or consulteth with a familliar spirritt, they shall bee put to death. Exodus 22.18.—Levit. 20.27.—Deut. 18.10,11.

"3. If any person shall blaspheme the name of God the ffather, Sonne or Holy Ghost, with direct, express, presumptuous or highhanded blasphemy, or shall curse in the like manner, hee shall bee put to death. Lev. 24. 15, 16."

XV.
PROSECUTIONS FOR CRIMES AGAINST RELIGION.
1643—1677.

It is now proposed to continue the narative of religious prosecutions in England from 1642 to 1818, the date of the Connecticut constitution guaranteeing religious liberty, equality, and freedom of speech and press. Again it is the purpose to the supply data for a more thorough study of the meaning and motives of blasphemy laws. It is also the purpose to exhibit the evils against which the constitutional guarantees were directed. This will enable us to interpret the constitution with better understanding.

PAUL BEST—1643.[23]

Paul Best (1590-1657) was an educated gentleman, a soldier in Poland and a facile controversialist. While traveling on the continent "he unhappily disputed with some anti-trinitarians, and more adhering to carnal reason than to the mysteries of faith, he was drawn to the dangerous opinion, the denial of our Saviour's divinity." Later he studied unitarian theology in Germany.

Having written out his conclusions on the doctrine of the Trinity he submitted his manuscript to the Rev. Roger

---

[23] Rushworth, John. A continuance of historical collections (book 6) part IV, v. 1, p. 635. July 24, 1647.
Mysteries discovered. Or a mercurial picture pointing out the way from Babylon to the holy city, for the food of all such as during that night of general errour and apostasie * * * have been so long misled with Rome's hobgoblins. By me Paul Best prisoner in the gatehouse, Westminster. Printed in the yeare, 1647.
Dictionary of national biography, v .4, pp. 417-418.
Journal of the House of Commons, Mch. 2. 1645-6, July 24, 1647, v. 5, p. 257. Also: Sept. 8, 1647, v. 5, p. 296.
Farrer, James Anson. Books condemned to be burnt, pp. 107-109. To certain noble and honorable persons of the House of Commons assembled in Parliament (the petition of P. B. prisoner in the Gatehouse in Westminster) [Lond. Aug. 13, 1646].

Ley (a supposed friend), "for his Judgment and advice only." This pious parson turned the manuscript over to the authorities as blasphemous. One of Best's opponents represents the document as having applied "the most profane epithets to the doctrine of the Trinity," calling it *"a mystery of iniquity, a three-headed monster, a figment, a tradition of Rome,"* etc. For this he was committed to Gatehouse, Feb. 14, 1644. After several examinations, on March 28, 1645, the House of Commons voted that he be hanged for this offence. The dispute about the lawfulness of hanging for this offence was not settled until May 2, 1648. In 1647 he published a pamphlet from jail, in his own vindication so that he might not seem "an accessory to the false accusation of those that blast me [Paul Best], with the most odious infamy of blasphemy (to deny the heavenly Trinity, and Jesus Christ to be our blessed Saviour), and the truth of the sacred Canonicall Scriptures."

Best declared that he could not by his best friends or those appointed by parliament secure the presentation of a petition in his behalf, although he had written and printed 100 of them. He also reported that some had declared him "distracted and mad."

From this pamphlet it appears that his chief item of dispute about the Trinity is verbal. On the dispute "whether the sonne * * * be in himself coequal to the King" he contends, depends upon an adverb meaning "of like quality and not equality." Now he proceeds with a lot of metaphysical speculation as to whether "the great King" in addition to unity also has "his supremacy and majority." He expressed his own conclusions, omitting bible references, thus: "I believe the Father to be God himself * * * and that the Sonne is our Messiah * * whom God made Lord and Christ, * * * Prince and Saviour. * * * And that the holy spirit is the very power of God or the Father God essentially, the Sonne vicentially the holy Spirit potentially or the Father God above all, * * * the Son of God with us, * * * the holy Spirit God within us. * * * But for the Son to be coequal to the Father, or the holy Spirit a distinct coequall person, I cannot finde, and I believe that these three are one or agree and conspire in the substance of the same truth to salvation," and more such.

On March 2, 1645 the House of Commons ordered that "all the lawyers of the House be enjoined to attend the Committee of plundered Ministers tomorrow in the Afternoon concerning the ordinance for punishing the Blasphemies of Paul Best." On September 8, 1647, Paul Best is again mentioned in the Parliamentary proceedings, but nothing is done. He had been in jail since February, 1644. It is said that at the end of 1647 he was quietly released, no one knows how. It is surmised that Cromwell may have interfered, perhaps thinking he had suffered enough.

Here we have a case where the mere metaphysical speculation which did not deny the trinity but in the gentlest of language defended an unorthodox conception of the trinity, was held to be blasphemy. This is the common law adjudged and applied soon after the passage of the colonial statute against blasphemy. What attitude toward the trinity is now penalized? Is the catholic conception blasphemous, or the presbyterian? Are all unitarians criminals? If not where has the common law been amended by our statutes? Is this statute with this common-law interpretation constitutional?

REV. HANSERD KNOLLES—1644.[24]

Hanserd Knolles (1599-1691) was a Baptist divine. He left England for America about 1637, to escape the High Commission Court. The exact nature of his offence is not known. A warrant from that court caused his arrest in Boston but he was soon discharged. Cotton Mather enumerates him among "godly anabaptists." In December, 1641, he returned to London, the revolutionary spirit probably making it safer for him. Did "blasphemy" have a different meaning in New England than in old England?

His sermons were twice the subject of parliamentary inquiry, but he seems to have escaped without punishment

---

[24] Commons Journal, v. 2, 1642-1644, p. 585. Dictionary of national biography, v. 31, pp. 279-280.

or perhaps without a final decision. The record shows that he "did preach openly" as follows:

"Retaining the baptism of children was one of the greatest sins in the land. * * * One Mr. Simson once prohibited by the House [of Commons] to preach, . . . said that Jesus Christ is in Hogs and Dogs or sheep yea, that the same Spirit that ruleth in the Children of God ruleth in the Children of Disobedience: and diverse abominable Doctrines . . . Mrs. Randall, he holds. Though a Woman (though wicked) if married to one that is godly, that she is thereby snactified. These things will admit of no longer suffrance." So Mr. Marshall informed the House. Thereupon it was resolved that it be referred to a committee "to examine them upon the informations and to secure them by imprisonment if they shall see cause."

This condition suggests that it was a matter of doubt not determinable by statutory criteria of blasphemy whether such language was criminal or not. Manifestly a different whim or desire could have found this language sufficient to sustain a conviction especially in view of the fact that this man's sermons had actually been instrumental in creating "riots and tumults." The offending doctrine seems to be that of a "purposeful divine immanence in the universe" which opinion is today entertained by some of the best and wisest of men. Is it a crime to express such a view under the Connecticut blasphemy statute? Is a statute constitutional which leaves this in doubt? Could a law be constitutional which penalized these opinions?

KING JAMES—1644.[25]

"King James' famous 'Book of Sports,' published in 1618 gave great offense to the godly puritans. This work was issued on the advice of Morton, bishop of Chester; and was occasioned by the dull visit of King James to Lancashire. The people did not make holiday enough on Sundays for the royal taste. The people are therefore enjoined to practise dancing, archery, leaping, vaulting,

[25] Vickers, Robert H. Martyrdoms of literature, p. 377-8.

whitsunales, morris dances, and others. The baiting of animals being at all times prohibited to the meaner sort of people and playing at bowls were also forbidden. Some time afterward recreations were forbidden until after evening prayer; and those not godly enough to attend prayers; either morning or evening were excommunicated from the baitings, and 'incapable of such his royal indulgence at all.' This foolish production was ordered to be read in all churches throughout England. The lengthened face, and 'rigid feature' of the puritans relaxed at the consignment of the 'Book of Sports' to the flames. Chief Justice Richardson had published an order forbidding the observance of village feasts and wakes on Sundays. The king and clergy resented this interference with ecclesiastical authority, and the Book of Sports saw the light. The Chief Justice was summoned before the Council and 'received such a rattle,' that as he declared 'he had almost been choked by a pair of lawn sleeves.' At length when puritan influence became supreme in 1644, both houses adopted a resolution ordering the Book to be burned by the justices of the peace in Cheapside, and at the Exchange. May 10 the Sheriffs of London and Middlesex were gravely required to see the order carried into effect. All persons possessing copies were ordered to surrender them. All that could be seized were destroyed."

JOHN ARCHER—1645.[26]

No biography of John Archer was found. He appears to have been a preacher at Allhallows, Lombard Street, and the author of some books. After his death some admirers published a manuscript founded on the text of John 14 : 1 to 4, which book was entitled as follows: "Comfort for believers about their sinnes and troubles in a treatise

---

* The personal reign of Christ upon Earth. In a treatise wherein is proved that Jesus Christ * * * shall visibly possess a monarchiacall state and kingdome in this world. London, 1642.
A short declaration of the Assembly * * * by way of detestation of this abominable * * * opinion * * * mentioned in a book intituled, Comfort for believers about their sinnes and troubles * * * 1645. Comfort for believers about their sinnes and troubles, a sermon, [on John XIV, 1-4] London, 1645.
Farrer, James Anson, Books condemned to be burnt, pp. 106-107.

shewing that true believers, how weake soever in faith, should not be opprest, or perplext in heart, by anything whatever befalls them; either in sinne or affliction. Together with divers other comfortable observations; gathered out of that counsell, given by Christ to his apostles and in them to all believers.   Lond. 1645."

Parliament condemned the book and directed a committee of divines to counteract its evil influence.   The result of their deliberations was published under the title following: "A short declaration of the assembly of divines by way of detestation of this abominable and blasphemous opinion, that God is, and hath an hand in, and is the author of the sinfulnesses of his people; mentioned in a book intituled 'Comfort for believers, about their sins and troubles' together with the Order of both Houses of Parliament for the burning of the said Book by the hand of the common hangman.   London, July 25, 1645."

This parliamentary committee of clergymen express themselves partly as follows: "As it hath pleased the Honorable Houses of Parliament, out of their pious care for preserving Religion pure, from the leaven of pernicious and Blasphemous Doctrine, to order the burning of this most scandalous Book; so have they further appointed us to declare the abominableness thereof unto the people. And we doubt not but that every good Christian, as soon as he shall hear the scope and contents of it, will, together with us, detest the horrid Blasphemie therein asserted, and acknowledge the godly zeal, wisdom and justice of Authority in commanding it, as an execrable thing to be taken away."   Thus begins the "short declaration of the assembly of divines."

Archer seems to have believed in predestination and foreordination, and that apparently was the whole of his offending.   Our pious committee characterized it as a "most vile and Blasphemous assertion" which Archer "openly in express Termes, and in a very foul manner propounded, maintained and purposely at large prosecuted to wit:

"a. That God is, and hath an hand in, and is the Author of the sinfulnesse of his people.

"b. That he is the Author, not of those actions alone, in and with which sin is, but of the very Pravity Ataxy, Anomy, Irregularity and sinfulnesse itself, which is in them.

"c. That God hath more hand in men's sinfulnesse then they themselves.

"d. That the Creature's sin doth produce the greatest good, either in God's glory, or in the Creature's happinesse, as the next cause thereof and that all that good is onely brought about by sin.

"e. That it is as Incongruous and Inconvenient to make God the Author of the Afflictions of the Creature, as of the sins.

"f. That by sins Believers are as much nurtured and fitted for Heaven as by anything else.

"g. That God fits Believers for service in this world, by leading them into sins.

"h. That no course is so full, to remove or prevent sinfull or pernicious troubles for sin, as this looking on God the Author of it and the good which he brings about by it; which, because it is rarely done by Believers, and indeed hardly known, he therefore professeth to have himself enlarged upon it" (p. 5-6).

I have compared these charges with the original book of Archer. Thus it appears that the asembly of divines are not at all copying Archers language but state in their own language what they hope to be the logical import of the words used by Archer. The result is hardly fair to the author because their blunt statement was meant to be a reduction to absurdity, of that which Archer had really contended for. Furthermore they do not even attempt to answer his careful argument, which was based upon holy writ. Let me illustrate the unfairness of the committee's statement of Archer's contentions. The divines make him say "That by sins Believers are as much nurtured and fitted for Heaven by their various sinning heere: Not only as Sinnes make way for Afflictions, but also as they make way for God's free Grace, Christ's mercy, and the exercise of diverse Graces, etc."

They resorted to the same tactics that other judges

sometimes fall into. That is, a seeming novel conclusion, or one that does violence to some conventional sentimentalism is stated in complete dissociation from the reasons which might prove plausible, if not convincing. Thus stated it seems absurd to the unenlightened and the judge also seems quite justified in his condemnation, whereas, if the justifying argument had been stated at its best the stupid crowd might have become enlightened and the judge's conclusion would not have looked so well in the eyes of intelligent persons.

The main scope of Archer's book is alleged to be to persuade men "Not to be oppressed or perplexed in heart, for anything whatsoever befalls them either in sin or affliction." For this Archer had quoted Jesus, "Let not your heart be troubled." In such doctrines was "both danger and scandall * * * exceeding injurious to the Gospel of Christ, and to the power of godlinesse." The above characterization of this doctrine, of course, has some color of truth and yet in effect is false. It was called blasphemy and doubtless Archer would have been severely punished, were he still living when the matter came to the attention of parliament.

In that benighted age it was thought better to drive people insane by artificial fears than to incur the danger to "morality" which comes from knowing the truth. Now a large school of psychiatrists restore mentally sick persons by relieving them of artificial fears. Is an American court in 1917 going to say that we must still drive people insane to protect God and moral sentimentalism? Will it say that a statute with such an object directed against blasphemy is constitutional?

A single passage will convey the drift of the seventy-six pages devoted to this difficult problem: "Who hinted to God, or gave advice by counsel to Him, to let the creature sin? Did any necessity, arising upon the creature's being, enforce it that sin must be? Could not God have hindered sin, if He would? Might He not have kept man from sinning, as He did some of the angels? Therefore, it was His device and plot before the creature was that there should be sin. * * * It is by sin that most of God's

glory in the discovery of His attributes doth arise. * * *
Therefore certainly it limits Him much to bring in sin by
a contingent accident, merely from the creature, and to
deny God a hand and will in its being and bringing forth."

Are such sentiments as these blasphemous because we
must resort to the common law for a definition of this
crime?   Has the legislature now power to penalize such
opinions?

JOHN BIDDLE—1647-8.[27]

The Rev. John Biddle (1615-1662) was a precocious
youth and became the "father of Unitarianism."   He was
an Oxford graduate, and later became a teacher.   With
Presbyterian ascendency he was deemed heretical and
dangerous and summoned before the magistrate.   After
interrogation a form of confession under three heads was
submitted for his signature.   He signed it with modifications, in May 1654.   This being unsatisfactory to the
authorities, he made another to avoid imprisonment, and
he pursued his studies and literary work.   In this "he
confessed, that there were three in the divine essense com-

[27] Twelve arguments drawn out of the scripture wherein the commonly received opinion touching the Deity of the Holy Spirit is
clearly and fully refuted. To which is prefixed a letter tending to
the same purpose written to a member of the honorable House of
Commons. And to which is enjoyed an exposition of five principal
passages and scripture alleged by the adversaries to prove the
Deity of the Holy Spirit; together with an answer to their grand
objection touching the supposed omnipresence of the Holy Spirit.
By John Biddle, Master of Arts, printed in the yeare 1647.
God's glory vindicated and blasphemy confuted being a brief and
plain answer to that blasphemous book intituled, Twelve arguments
against the deity of the Holy Ghost, written by [Theo. (John)
Biddle] Master of Arts, and now burnt by special command from
Parliament on Wednesday the eight of this present September, by
the common hangman * * * London, 1647, 12 p.
Confession of Faith touching the Holy Trinity according to Scrip-
ture. Lond. 1648.
The Testimonies of Irenaeus, Justin Martyr, Tertullian, Novatianus,
Theophilus, Origin (who lived in the two centuries after Christ
was born, or thereabouts), as also, Arnobius, Lactantius, &c., con-
cerning that one God and the persons of the Trinity, with observations on the same. Lond. 1650.
A two fold catechism, the one simply called a scripture catechism,
the other a brief scripture catechism for children, 1654.
Dictionary of national biography, v. 5, pp. 13-16.
Reese, Richard. Compendious martyrology, v. 3, pp. 468-471.
Two letters of Mr. John Biddle late prisoner in Newgate but
now hurried away to some remote island. One to the Lord Protector, the other to the Lord President Lawrence. London, 1655.

monly called persons." In 1647 "having made up his mind
more fully upon this subject [he] drew up his thoughts
upon a paper entitled 'Twelve Arguments' etc."

A treacherous "friend" stole the manuscript and submitted it to the parliamentary commissioners, and the
magistrates of Gloucester. The blasphemer was forthwith
ordered to jail by the magistrates. Later he was bailed
and given opportunity to repent and correct his errors,
with some assistance from Archbishop Usher. Failing in
this he was cited before a parliamentary committee.

Biddle frankly avowed his disbelief in the Divinity of
the Holy Ghost and expressed a readiness to debate his
opinions with any theologian whom they might appoint.
Now Biddle published "Twelve questions or arguments
drawn out of Scripture, wherein the commonly received
Opinion touching the Deity of the Holy Spirit is clearly
and fully refuted," 1647. Prefixed to this was a letter
to Sir Henry Vane, who was a friendly member of the
committee. At the end was "An exposition of five principal Passages of the Scriptures alleged by the Adversaries to prove the Deity of the Holy Ghost." Called
to the bar of the House, he acknowledged responsibility for
the book, was remanded to prison, and on September 6,
1647, the "Twelve Arguments," etc., was ordered to be
burnt by the hangman, as being blasphemous. Biddle remained under restraint for five years. In the meantime
the matter was referred to the assembly of divines.

Journal of House of Commons, Sept. 8, 1647. See: v, 5: 293,
296; 7: 400, 416. See also: notes under Racovian catechism.
Neal, Daniel. History of the puritans, v. 4, p. 122.
Goodwin, Commonwealth, v. 3, pp. 510-513.
Register and Chronicle, p. 761.
The faith of one God, who is only the father, and of one mediator
between God and man, who is only the man Christ Jesus; and
of one the gift, and sent of God, asserted and defended in several
tracts contained in this volume. London, 1691.
Ditchfield, P. H. Books fatal to their authors, pp. 55-56.
Toulmin, Jushua. Review of the life character and writings of
Rev. John Biddle. London, 1789.
The spirit of persecution again broken loose, by an attempt to put
in execution against Mr. J. Biddle an abrogated ordinance of the
Lords and Commons for punishing blasphemies and heresies. To-
gether with a full narrative of the whole proceedings upon that
ordinance against the said Mr. J. B. and Mr. W. Kiffen. Lond.
[July 26] 1655.

The book was republished the same year, and some answers to the argument also appeared. The Presbyterians were now in full control. Upon the appearance of Biddle's book (1648) they secured the passage of an ordinance which among other things inflicted the death penalty upon those who denied the doctrine of the Trinity. "But the act was directed to so many objects, and so various, and meeting with considerable opposition of the army, and because there was a dissention in the parliament itself, it lay unregarded."

Notwithstanding, Biddle immediately published his "Confession of Faith touching the Holy Trinity according to Scripture." Soon after also appeared his "The Testimonies of Irenæus, Justin Martyr, Tertullian, Novatianus, Theophilus, Origin (who lived in the two centuries after Christ was born, or thereabouts), as also Arnobius, Lactantius, etc., concerning that One God and the persons of the Trinity, with observations on the same."

Upon the publication of the "Testimonies" the assembly of divines sitting at Westminster made their appeal to the parliament for Biddle's death. Parliament did not confirm the divines' appeal. He never was brought to trial and friends again secured his release on bail. Biddle soon became a preacher. Tidings of this having been conveyed to the Lord President Bradshaw, Biddle was once more imprisoned. Thomas Firmin appealed to Cromwell for the release from Newgate. Bishop Kennet thus reports the Protector's answer: "You curl-pate boy, do you think I'll show any favour to a man who denied his Saviour, and disturbs the government?"

On February 10, 1652 parliament passed a general act of oblivion which restored Biddle and others to liberty. Again he published in England and Holland some Socinian books and soon began to preach.

In 1654 he was again arrested, now for publishing "A Two-fold Catechism, the one simply called A Scripture Catechism, the other A Brief Scripture Catechism for Children." Early in 1654 the author was arraigned before the bar of parliament, and refused to answer incriminating questions. Parliament voted that this book contained many impious and blasphemous opinions against the Deity of the Holy Ghost. After debate and resolution he was "committed a close prisoner to the Gatehouse * * *.and all the copies of his books which could be found were ordered burnt." After six months, the protector dissolving the parliament, he obtained his liberty at the court of the Upper King's Bench, May 28, 1655.

Within a month he had a debate with one John Griffen. He was indicted and arrested. Cromwell soon after interposed his authority and stopped the proceedings. An entanglement ensued, as the upshot of which Biddle was "banished to the Scilly Islands, October 5, 1655, to remain in close custody in the Castle of St. Mary's during his life."

On the day previous there came out "Two Letters of Mr. John Biddle, late Prisoner in Newgate but now hurried away to some remote Island. One to the Lord Protector, the other to the Lord President Lawrence, 1655." He expressly separates himself from Socinus as to the personality of the Holy Ghost. The Protector allowed him 100 crowns per annum but he remained in jail until 1658. Many influential friends interceded for his liberation, but in vain. At length he was conveyed by a writ of *habeas corpus* to the Upper Bench at Westminster, and no accuser appearing, he was ordered discharged by Lord Chief Justice Glynn.

Again he resumed preaching and teaching, continuing until the death of Cromwell, September following. Before the parliament summoned by Richard Cromwell met, Biddle was advised to retire into the country "by it is believed, the Lord Chief Justice. It was a prudent step." A parliamentary committee was appointed to examine into the state of religion, and one of its first acts was to institute an inquiry into Biddle's liberation. The matter subsided and he returned to London.

In June, 1662, he was again arrested "with a few of his friends who were assembled for divine worship. All were sent to prison without bail." Biddle was found guilty of being the author of another blasphemous book, fined 100£s. and to stand committed till paid. He died in jail, having spent all told, over seven years in confinement.

His fatal book was entitled "The Faith of one God, who is only the Father, and of one Mediator between God and man, who is only the man Christ Jesus; and of one Holy Spirit, the gift, and sent of God, asserted and defended in several tracts contained in this volume" (London, 1691). This work was also publicly burnt.

In all Biddle's troubles, the gist of the offence was a mere difference of opinion about theology. In psychologic terms this meant that for him the words "Holy Trinity" symbolized a different mental content than was entertained by his orthodox neighbor. Here as in several other cases, the mere unorthodox product of dignified metaphysical speculation, even though founded upon the Bible, was held to be blasphemous.

LAURANCE CLARKSON (OR CLAXTON)—1645-1650.[28]

Laurance Clarkson, later calling himself Claxton, (1615-1667) was one of those restless religious spirits who was in turn a member of nearly all the dissenting sects. He died a Muggletonian. He was baptised as an anabaptist in Nov. 1644 and in January, 1645, was cast into prison at Bury St. Edmunds. He was released July 15, 1645. The only clue as to the cause of his confinement is found in the condition of his release which was by formally renouncing the practice of "dipping." From this we infer that it was his opinion upon baptism, or the practices in accordance with that opinion that were the basis of the prosecution.

Later he published what the House of Commons designated as an "impious and blasphemous" tract called, "The single eye, all light no darkness, or light and darkness one." (1650, 4to. 16 pp.) For this he was condemned by the House of Commons to be sent to prison for one

---

[28] The single eye, all light no darkness, or light and darkness one, 1650. 16pp.
Dictionary of national biography, v. II, pp. 5-6; House of Commons Journal, v. VI, pp. 427, 474-475. Laurance Clarkson, 27th Sept., 1650
A Paradisical dialogue betwixt faith and reason, 1660, said to be autobiographical of Claxton, was not located.

month and from that time to be banished out of the commonwealth and the territories thereof, and not to return upon pain of death. The book itself was burned by the common hangman and all persons ordered to deliver all copies thereof up to the nearest Justice of the Peace.

Are baptist opinions now dangerous and blasphemous, because they were generally so considered at common-law? The statute has not altered the crime since then.

WILLIAM ERBERY—1646.[29]

William Erbery (1604-1654) in 1634 was pronounced a "schismatical and dangerous preacher" by Bishop Laud, and "after a judical admonition" from the court of high commission, he was forced to resign his vicarage. In 1638 he became an itinerant preacher. He "declared himself for general redemption; that no man was punished, for Adam's sin should be imputed to no man. He said also that within a while God would raise up apostolical men, who should be extraordinary, to preach the gospel; and after that shall be the fall of Rome. He spake against gathering churches, the anabaptists' rebaptising, and said men ought to wait for the coming of the Spirit, as the apostles did. 'Like as in the wilderness they had honey and manna, but not circumcision and the passover till they came into Canaan, so now we may have many sweet things, conference and prayer, but not a ministry and sacraments. And then, after the fall of Rome, there will be new heavens, and a new earth; then shall be new Jerusalem; and then shall the church be one, one street in that city and no more'." He declared "that Adam's sin could not be imputed to Adam and denied the divinity of Christ."

In the parliamentary army Erbery became a chaplain and after the surrender of Oxford, 1646, he continued to preach these doctrines, and disputed with presbyterians.

"Although very popular with the soldiers, he was about this time on account of his Socinian opinions directed to

---

[29] Dictionary of national biography, vol. 17, pp. 383-5.
The testimony of W. E. left upon record for the saints of succeeding ages. Being a collection of the writings of the aforesaid author * * * Whereunto is added the honest heretic, being his trial at Westminster, a piece never printed before. London, 1658.

leave Oxford, when he went to London * * and preached * * *until his tenets caused him to be summoned before the committee for plundered ministers at Westminster in 1652, when he made orthodox profession of faith. The committee refused to accept this as genuine, and are believed to have committed him to prison." According to Wood, "he vented his blasphemies in several places."

"His widow, Dorcas, became a quakeress, and in 1656 was apprehended for paying divine honours at Bristol to James Nayler, when she alleged that Nayler was the son of God and had raised her to life after she had been dead two days. She was liberated after a few days confinement." Here there seems to have been more intelligence used than in the trial of Nayler himself, though of course the letter of the law was violated.

Are all universalists now to be punished under the statute against blasphemy because that doctrine was officially declared "dangerous" and "blasphemous" and because the colonists undoubtedly considered it both? Was it not to preclude the punishment of all blasphemous opinions, only speculatively "dangerous" that intellectual liberty was guaranteed in our constitutions?

REV. ABIEZER COPPE—1650.[30]

Abiezer Coppe (1619-1672) is described as a grossly immoral student who left the university without a degree at the opening of the civil wars. Also as a fanatic, first a presbyterian and then an anabaptist who was a "preacher and leading man" of that sect. Then he became a ranter and is said to have preached stark naked. There is much to show him a mad man. He now jointed a sect "of the worst type known among themselves as 'My own flesh.'" Some associate him with Muggleton, others with Lawrence Claxton or Clarkson, mentioned hereinbefore.

In 1649 he published: "A Fiery Flying Roll: a word from the Lord to all the great ones of the earth whom this may concern: being the last warning piece at all the dread-

[30] Vickers, Robert H. Martyrdoms of literature. p. 377.
Dictionary of national biography, v. 12, p. 190.
Farrer, James Anson, Books condemned to be burnt, p. 114.

full day of Judgment * * * With another flying roll ensuing (to all the inhabitants of the earth)" (Lond. 1649).

On Feb. 1, 1650, Parliament issued an order that this book be burnt by the hangman because containing "many horrid blasphemies." This book is said to have been the immediate occasion for an ordinance of Aug. 9th, 1650, for the "punishment of atheistical, blasphemous, and execrable opinions."

"His tenets are the ordinary mistical views of the ranters who are charged with holding that there is no God and no sin. His denial of sin in the elect was a distorted antinomianism." Some types of the insane are prone to claim for themselves such divine qualities as place them above human moral codes.

"Perfectionism" is a doctrine often entertained by religious zealots, who consider themselves "blessed" and "redeemed" and is sometimes accompanied by sexual irregularities as among the Bible Communists of Oneida, and the Adamites. As an abstract doctrine, entirely dissociated from overt act, it is a proclamation of holiness or sinlessness. Should such a doctrine now be declared blasphemous merely because of a speculative tendency to disturb the peace and sexual morality?

JOHN FRY—1650.[31]

Our knowledge of this case rests wholly upon the record made in Parliament, and fortunately that gives us suf-

---

[31] Journal of the House of Commons, Feb. 20-22nd, 1650, v. 6, pp. 539-540.

The accuser shamed or a pair of bellows to blow off that dust cast upon John Fry a member of parliament, by Colonel John Downs, likewise a member of parliament, who by the confederacy and instigation of some, charged the said J. F. of blasphemy and error to the * * * House of Commons. Whereunto is annexed, a word to the priests, lawyers, royalists, self-seekers, and rigid presbyterians. Also a brief ventilation of that chaffie and absurd opinion of three persons and substances in the God head. By the accused J. F. London 1648.

The clergy in their colors; or a brief character of them. Written from a hearty desire of their reformation and great zeal to my countrymen, that they may no longer be deceived by such as call themselves the ministers of the gospel, but are not. By John Fry, a member of the parliament of England. * * * London, 1650, p. 60.

Collection of Acts of Parliament. 1648-1658, v. 2, pp. 1293-1297.

Vickers, Robert H. Martyrdoms of literature, p. 377.

ficient detail to enable us to know what religious discussions were prohibited at common law. Here is the record:

"Mr. Millington reports from the Committee of plundered Ministers, the Exceptions taken to the Book, intituled, 'The Clergy in their Colours,' and to the Book, intituled, 'The Bellows,' &c.: With the Opinion and Resolutions of the said Committee thereupon: * * * were this Day read.

"Exceptions taken by the Committee for plundered Ministers, against the Book, intituled, 'The Accuser shamed,' &c. by the accused John Fry, Februarii 13, 1650.

"1. THAT he, the said John Fry, hath published, in Print, the Accusation that was made against him, *viva voce* only, in the House of Parliament, by a Member of Parliament; often particularly naming and reproaching the said Member, in the said Book, Title Page, and Page 14, 15, 16, 17.

"2. That he denies the Trinity, calling it, 'A chaffy and absurd Opinion of Three Persons, or Subsistences, in the Godhead,' Title Page, and Page 15; and especially, Page the 22, Line the 14; *viz.* 'Persons, and Subsistences, are Substances, or Accidents. As for the Word *Person,* I do not understand that it can properly be attributed but to Man. It is out of Doubt with me, that, if you ask the most Part of Men, what they mean by a *Person,* they will either tell you 'tis a Man, or else they are not able to give you any Answer at all: And, for the Word *Accident,* I suppose none will attribute that to God; for, according to my poor Skill, that Word imports no more, but the Figure or Colour, &c. of a Thing: And certainly no Man ever saw the likeness of God; as the Scriptures abundantly testify: And therefore neither of the Words, *Persons* or *Subsistences,* can hold forth such a Meaning as *Accidents* in God. *Athanasius,* in his Creed, faith, 'There is one Person of the Father, another of the Son, and another of the Holy Ghost:' Others say, That there is Three distinct Subsistences in God: Well these Three Persons, or Subsistences, cannot be Accident; neither do I think it is the Meaning of any: Then certainly they must be *Substances*: If so, then they must be created or uncreated; limited or unlimited:

If created, and limited; then the Person of the Father is a
Creature, the Person of the Son a Creature, and the Person of the Holy Ghost a Creature; which I think none will
affirm: If they are not created, or limited, then they must
be uncreated and unlimited; for I know no Medium between created and uncreated, limited and unlimited: If
they are uncreated and unlimited, then there are Three uncreated and unlimited Substances; and so, consequently,
Three Gods. For my Part, I find no Footing for such Expressions in Scripture; and I think them fit only to keep
ignorant People in carnal and gross Thoughts of God:
And therefore I do explore them out of my Creed.'

"Resolved, by the Committee, That the aforesaid Second
Exception be reported to the House, as containing Matter
of Blasphemy.

"Exceptions taken by the said Committee against the
Book, intituled, 'The Clergy in their Colours,' printed
under the Name of *John Fry,* a Member of the Parliament
of *England.*

"THAT the said Committee do except against the
Clause in the Book, Page 39, Line 17, as scandalous; *viz.*
'I cannot let pass one Observation: And that is, The
strange Posture these Men put themselves into, when they
begin their Prayers before their Sermons: Whether the
Fools and Knaves in Stage Plays took their Pattern from
these Men, or these from them, I cannot determine, *&c.*
What wry Mouths, squint Eyes, screwed Faces, do they
make.' And Page 41, Line 3; *viz.* 'Again, how like a
Company of Conjurers do they mumble out the Beginning
of their Prayers, that the People may not hear them, and,
when artificially they have raised their Voices, what a
Puling do they make.'

"This Committee being of Opinion, That the aforefaid
Passages are fit to be excepted against, in regard they are
scandalous.

"That the said Committee do further except against the
Clause, Page 49, Line 1; *viz.* 'I must confess, I have heard
much of believing Things above Reason; and the Time
was, when I swallowed that Pill: But I may say, as *St.
Paul, &c. When I was a Child, &c.* Every Man that

knoweth any thing, knoweth this: that it is Reason that distinguisheth a Man from a Beast: If you take away his Reason, you deny his very Essence: Therefore, if any Man will consent to give up his Reason, I would as soon converse with a Beast as with that Man: And whatsoever Pretence some may make of Religion; in this Particular, certainly there is nothing else in it but Ignorance and Policy.'

"The said Committee do further except against the Clause, Page 11; Line 14, to the End of the Thirteenth Page; 'I have for some Years past entered into a serious Consideration of my latter End, and of a Saint's Life in this World: And, being convinced, that I should not be saved by an implicit Faith, I took Example by the *Bereans,* to search the Scriptures, whether such Things as I heard and read of God, and his Attributes, Heaven, Hell, Angels both good and bad, Man, Prayer, Sin, were so or no: And, upon a narrow Scrutiny, I found such Contradictions, Absurdities, and Inconsequences, in many considerable Things, that I wondered I had been so long blind, &c. After I had a full Sight of these Things; and that from mine own Experience, I concluded, that Men greedily swallow down such Doctrines; and that some of the Teachers, as well zealously, through ignorance and otherwise, held them forth.'

"That it appears to this committee, that the whole scope of the book doth tend to the Overthrow of the Preachers and Preaching of the Gospel.

"That both said Books, throughout, are against * * * Doctrine and assertions of the true Religion."

The books were ordered burnt and Fry "disabled to sit as a Member of this House" of parliament.

Here again is the highest authority to the effect that it is a violation of law to deny the trinity or to promote any doctrines that "are against doctrines and assertions of true religion." It is that meaning that must be ascribed to the blasphemy definition. It is with that meaning that we must determine the constitutionality of the blasphemy statute.

ROBERT NORWOOD—1651.[32]

As to this man no biographical data was found except that contained in his own pamphlets. He seems to have been identified with political, military and religious activities, during the turbulent period of England's history. He claims to have spent a considerable fortune to accomplish reforms that he deemed important. A postscript to a pamphlet devoted to his trial shows that he was under suspicion of disloyalty to the government of 1651 and doubtless this was the real motive for his prosecution.

So far as preserved, the story of his prosecution is as follows: Some acquaintances of Norwood called upon him to repudiate some "false" doctrines ascribed to him. Instead he offered publicly to defend whatever he believed. A meeting was arranged at which he read a carefully prepared paper. He invited his pastor, the Rev. Shidrack Simpson, to discuss the merits of his contention "in love, peace and quietness," and sent him a copy of the

[32] A brief discourse made by Capt. R. Norwood in the upper-bench court at Westminster. With some argument by him then given, in defense of himself, and prosecution of a writ of errour by him brought upon an indictment found and adjudged against him upon an act against blasphemy, at the sessions in Old Bayly, Jan. 28, 1651, London, 1652.
The case and trial of Capt. R. Norwood * truly * stated. Together with some observations upon the law and its professors. [London, 1651]
The form of an excommunication against Capt. R. Norwood, examined and answered, by Capt. R. Norwood, 1651.
Simpson, S. A declaration or testimony given by * * R. Norwood under his own hand * * April 21 * * together with several of his answers and desires, proposed * * after his excommunication, 1651.
Capt. Norwood's declaration proved an abnegation of Christ. See Graunt (J) of Bucklerbury. Truth's defender and error's reprover; or a briefe discoverie of feined Presbyterie, etc., 1651.
A pathway unto England's perfect settlement, and its centre and foundation of rest and peace, London, 1653.
An additional discourse, relating unto a treatise * * * by Capt. R. Norwood, intituled "a pathway to England's perfect settlement." * * * with something concerning the Jewish civil constitutions. With a brief answer to Mr. J. Spittlehouse, in the book bearing the title: The first addresses to his excellencie, etc., London, 1653.
Proposal for propagation of the gospel, offered to the parliament. [London 1651? o. s.]
Norwood also wrote a preface to a book by T. Tany, 1651.
As to Shidrack Simpson see: Dictionary of national biography, v. 32, p. 278.

paper. Simpson was a man of some importance, being a member of the Westminster Assembly of Divines.

A second paper was sent by Norwood to Simpson with a letter more challenging than before and both papers were published. Thereupon Simpson caused Norwood to be excommunicated for "blasphemous heresy" of pantheistic stamp. Simpson also broke into print with his "The form of an excommunication against Captain R. Norwood." Norwood replied in "Excommunication Excommunicated." The parson was also a member of a society for preserving the laws of the nation, and in that capacity caused Norwood to be arrested for his blasphemy.

Two items were alleged, first, "that the soul of man is of the essence of God, and second, that there is neither heaven nor hell but what is here."

Norwood tells us that the charges in the criminal court were substantially the same as for his excommunication from the church. There is much discussion as to this blasphemous matter which however seems to be chiefly about the meaning of words. Norwood insists that he shall be tried upon the exact words used by him. His opponents characterize them according to their own detestation of them. Let me illustrate.

Norwood identified himself with Francis Rous, one of the most conspicuous puritans of his time. Rous had published a book on "Mystical marriage" which according to Norwood expressed doctrines like unto his own. Norwood writes: "This gentleman [Rous] whom they have already wounded through my sides, may now also expect (such are the present times) an indictment at the Sessions house for same as well as myself, he being guilty of the same truth, as saying, the soul came or was breathed into man from God, is of a divine and heavenly essence, or of the essence of God." So Norwood claims that by denying the truth of this doctrine his prosecutors "deny the immortality of the soul."

When this innocent doctrine was transformed into the language of the indictment by adding to it the dangerous tendencies and implications existing in the feverish brain of the Attorney General it read thus: "Robert Norwood

being one most monstrous in his opinions, loose, wicked
and abominable in his practices, not only to the notorious
corrupting and disordering, but even to the dissolution
of all humane society, rejecting the use of any Gospel-
Ordinances, doth deny the necessity of civil and moral
righteousness amongst men." When Norwood protested
his innocence of such iniquity he was told from the Bench
"that was no part of the charge but was only a preamble."
Such things happen if crime is predicted upon mere speculation about psychologic tendency instead of overt act to
inflict actual and material injury.

More detail of his trial is not vouchsafed us except indirectly. Norwood tells us the criminal charges were the
same as on his excommunication. This we must believe
because Simpson was responsible for both. The latter's
published justification of the excommunication will therefore illumine us still further. He says:

"The crimes that he is charged withal are, First of all,
Lying in a matter of trust. Secondly, Apostacy from the
Truth, to blasphemous errors; as that there is neither
Heaven nor Hell, but all the Hell that there is, is the light
of God burning up the darkness that is in Man; and that
the soul of man is the Essence of God. These have been
proved to him, and before him; in Lying in matters of
trust, by two witnesses; his blasphemous errors by many
more. The question being put to him, whether he spake
these things as his judgment, he made answer and said,
he did utter them as his judgment; and that which he
must say except he should lye befor God."

Much scripture is cited in the excommunication to prove
that Hell is a place, and not a psychologic condition.
Likewise he deals with the controversy as to the nature
of the soul. Here again Norwood's accusers declare his
offending doctrine. "What the witnesses have affirmed,
his Paper now holds out, and as he hath now printed holds
out; that the soul of man is the Essence of God; and there
be three in men, the Soul, that is God, the Spirit, that is
the Devil, and the Body, that is the Beast; * * * He hath
added to all these errors, this error more, that it was one
of the greatest blasphemies to teach and exhort people to

pray when God was angry; and that upon faith and repentance God would be well pleased again; and together withal, that Jesus Christ did not die to pacifie any wrath and displeasure of God against sinfull man."

Norwood disclaimed these interpretations of his words and offered to confess belief in hell, heaven, damnation and salation, but this did not satisfy. Accordingly he received a sentence of six months imprisonment.

Norwood makes interesting technical defences for his position, but only persuades us that the whole controversy is merely a metaphysical quibble about the interpretation of scripture. His disagreement with the official interpretation was all there was to his "blasphemous error." To blaspheme the holy scriptures therefore is sufficiently accomplished by denying the legalized interpretation of it. What is the present statutory meaning of "blaspheme" of "Christian religion" and of "Holy Scripture" under the Connecticut statute?

RACOVIAN CATECHISM—1652.[33]

The famous *Racovian Catechism,* was first published in Polish at Racow in 1605, and in Latin in 1609. In it two anti-Trinitarian divines reduced to a systematic form the whole of the Socinian doctrine. A special interest attaches to it from the fact that Milton, then nearly blind, was called before the House in connection with the Catechism, as though he had had a share in its translation or publication. It was condemned to be burnt as "blasphemous, erroneous and scandalous" (April 1st, 1652). In the Journals of the House copious extracts are given from the work, from which the following may serve to indicate what chiefly gave offense:—

"What do you conceive exceedingly profitable to be known of the Essence of God?

"It is to know that in the Essence of God there is only

---

[33] Journal of the House of Commons, See Vol. 7: 86, III, 112, 114, 144, 1652.
Racovian Catechism: Chatechisis ecclesiarum quae in regno Poloniae et magno Ducatu Lithuaniae * * * affirmant Christi, neminem alium praeter Patrem Domini nostri Jesu esse * * * 1609. (A translation of the Racovian Cathechism has been ascribed to Biddle.)
Farrer, James Anson. Books condemned to be burnt, pp. 110-114.

one person * * * and that by no means can there be more persons in that Essence, and that many persons in one essence is a pernicious opinion, which doth easily pluck up and destroy the belief of one God * * *

"But the Christians do commonly affirm the Son and Spirit to be also persons in the unity of the same Godhead.

"I know they do, but it is a very great error; and the arguments brought for it are taken from Scripture misunderstood.

"But seeing the Son is called God in the Scriptures, how can that be answered?

"The word God in Scripture is chiefly used two ways: first, as it signifies Him that rules in heaven and earth * * *; secondly, as it signifies one who hath received some high power or authority from that one God, or in some way made partaker of the Deity of that one God. It is in this latter sense that the Son in certain places in Scripture is called God. And the Son is upon no higher account called God than that He is sanctified by the Father and sent into the world.

"But hath not the Lord Jesus Christ besides His human a Divine nature also?

"No, by no means, for that is not only repugnant to sound reason, but to the Holy Scripture also."

This is doubtless enough to convey an idea of the Catechism, which was again translated in 1818 by T. Rees. Whether Biddle was the original translator or not, he must have been actuated by good intentions in what he wrote; for he says of the Twofold Catechism, that it "was composed for their sakes that would fain be mere Christians, and not of this or that sect, inasmuch as all the sects of Christians, by what names soever distinguished, have either more or less departed from the simplicity and truth of the Scripture."

JAMES NAYLOR—1656.[34]

This blasphemer (1616-1660) was a Quaker of Bristol, suffering from harmless delusions of grandeur. Before

---

[34] Hume, Commentaries on the Laws of Scotland, v. 1, p. 571.
5 Howell's State trials, pp. 801-842.
Goodwin's, Commonwealth, v. 4, p. 320, cited.

the House of Commons he was charged with claiming equality with God and allowing himself to be adored as God or Christ. In his examination he professed that Christ dwelt in him in the flesh and that he was "set up as a sign to summon this nation, and to convince them of Christ's coming. The fulness of Christ's coming is not yet, but he is come now. * * * As I have dominion over the enemies of Christ, I am King of Israel, spirtually. * * * He that has a greater measure of Christ than 10,000 below him the same is the fairest of 10,000," and so he was called. He confessed that some of the women who waited on him had kneeled to him; but he denied that in doing so they paid him worship or adoration as a creature, and professed his abhorrence of such a thing and of all adolatry.

Entering Bristol on horseback followed by a multitude, he explained that this "was born in upon him against his will and mind," and could not be resisted. "It was the Lord's will to give it into me, to suffer such things to be done in me; and I durst not resist it, though I was sure to lay down my life for it." His general attitude toward God and Christ was orthodox.

After several days spent in debate as to whether or not this amounted to blasphemy, etc., Naylor was found guilty of "horrid blasphemy," sentenced to be repeatedly set in the pillory, and scourged; to be branded with the letter "B" on the forehead, and to have his tongue bored with a red-hot iron; as also to be confined afterwards in Bride-well, at hard labour, without any society and with "no

Memoirs preceding the trial of James Naylor. Report from the Committee, 80, p.

Memoirs of the life, ministry, tryal and sufferings of that very eminent person James Nailor, the quaker's great apostle. Who was try'd by the High Court of parliament for blasphemy, in the year 1656. London 1719.

House of Commons Journal, v. 7, pp. 468-775.

Law Magazine and Review, v. 9, pp. 163-164.

C. Bradlaugh in "The laws relating to blasphemy and heresy." p. 11-12.

Bonner, Hypatia Bradlaugh, Penalties upon opinion or some records of the laws of heresy and blasphemy. London, 1912.

Diary of Thomas Burton, Esq., member of the parliaments of Oliver and Richard Cromwell, from 1656 to 1659; now first published * * * edited * * * by John Towill Rutt. * * * London 1828.   Vol. 1, pp. 46, 158, 246.

relief but what he earns by his daily labour." He escaped
death by a vote of 96 to 82.

Naylor was again scourged, on Jan. 17, 1657, at Bristol
sitting "upon a horse bareridged, with his face backwards."
It is said that at one of his scourgings "there was no skin
left between his shoulders and his hips." Later he was
confined in Bridewell, without pen, ink, or paper, fire or
candle. He was kept there till 8th September, 1659, and
was then discharged by the Long Parliament, at that time
revived.

The Lord Commission Whitelocke in giving judgment,
attempted to discriminate between blasphemy and heresy.
He said: "I think it not improper first to consider the signification of the word 'blaspheme', and what it comprehends in the extensiveness of it; and I take it to comprehend the reviling or cursing the name of God or of his
neighbor." He further said: "They are offences of a
different nature: heresy is *Crimen Judicii,* an erroneous
opinion; blasphemy is *Crimen Malitiae,* a reviling the
name and honor of God."

BENJAMIN KEACH—1664.[35]

Keach (1640-1704) was minister of the Armenian Baptists. He began to preach in 1659. He expressed his
theology in poetry as "The Glorious Lover," and published
over fifty items, some mystical, but mostly controversial,
and expository.

In 1664 he was arrested for preaching at Winslow, Buck-
inghamshire. He was not long at liberty when indicted
for "certain damnable positions" contained in his "Child's
Instructor," or a "New and Easy Primmer," a Baptist
catechism which maintained that infants ought not to be
baptised, "contrary to the doctrine and ceremonies of the
Church of England." The trial occurred Oct. 8, 1664, before Sir Robert Hyde, who sentenced him to a fine of £20
and a fortnight's imprisonment, with the pillory, where

[35] Dictionary of national biography, v. 30, p. 254.
Howell's, State trials, vol. 6, pp. 702-710.
Stephen, James Fitzjames; History of the criminal law of England,
v. 1, p. 375.
Cobbett's, State trials, v. 3, pp. 701-710.

his book was burned before his eyes. He was also required
to give sureties for his good behavior.

Fortunately, the indictment has been preserved so that
we may judge what gave offence. Here it is as read to the
defendant by the clerk:

"Thou art here indicted by the name of Benjamin Keach,
of the parish of Winslow, in the county of Bucks: For
that thou being a seditious, heretical, and schismatical
person, evilly and maliciously disposed, and disaffected
to his majesty's government, and the government of the
Church of England, didst maliciously and wickedly, on
the 1st day of May, in the 16th year of the reign of our
sovereign lord, the king, write, print, and publish, or
cause to be written, printed, and published, one seditious
and venomous book, entitled, 'The Child's Instructor; or,
A New and Easy Primmer'; wherein are contained by
way of Question and Answer, these damnable positions,
contrary to the book of Common Prayer, and the Liturgy
of the Church of England; That is to say, in one place
you have thus written; 'Q. Who are the right subjects
of baptism? A. Believers, or Godly men and women only,
who can make confession of their faith and repentence.'
And in another place you have maliciously and wickedly
written these words: 'Q. How shall it then go with the
Saints? A. O, very well. It is the day they have longed
for: Then they shall hear that sentence, Come, ye blessed
of my Father, inherit the kingdom prepared for you; and
so shall they reign with Christ on the earth a thousand
years, even on Mount Sion, in New Jerusalem; for there
will Christ's throne be, on which they must sit down with
him.' Then follows this Question, with the Answer thereto,
in these plain English words: 'Q. When shall the wicked
and the fallen angels, which be the Devils, be judged? A.
When the thousand years shall be expired, then shall the
rest of the devils be raised, and then shall be the general
and last judgment, then shall all the rest of the dead and
devils be judged by Christ and his glorified saints; and
they being arraigned and judged, the wicked shall be con-

demned, and cast by angels into the lake of fire, there to be burned for ever and ever.'

"In another place thou hast wickedly and maliciously written these plain English words: '*Q.* Why may not infants be received into the Church now, as they were under the law? *A.* Because the fleshy seed is cast out: Though God under that dispensation did receive infants in a lineal way by generation, yet he that hath the key of David, that openeth and no man shutteth, that shutteth and no man openeth, hath shut up that way into the Church; and hath opened the door of regeneration, receiving in none but believers. *Q.* What then is the state of infants? *A.* Infants that die are members of the kingdom of Glory, though they be not members of the visible Church. *Q.* Do they then that bring in infants in a fleshly and lineal way, err from the way of truth? *A.* Yea, they do; for they make not God's holy word their rule, but do presume to open a door that Christ hath shut, and none ought to open.' And also in another place thou has wickedly and maliciously composed 'A short Confession of the Christian Faith'; wherein thou hast affirmed this concerning the second person in the Blessed Trinity, in these plain English words: 'I also believe that he rose again the third day from the dead, and ascended into Heaven above, and there now sitteth on the right hand of God the Father; and from thence he shall come again at the appointed time of the Father to reign personally upon the earth, and to be judge of the quick and dead.' And in another place thou hast wickedly and maliciously affirmed these things concerning true Gospel-Ministers, in plain English words following: 'Christ hath not chosen the wise and prudent man after the flesh, not great doctors and rabbies; Not many mighty and noble, saith Paul, are called: but rather the poor and despised, even tradesmen, and such-like, as was Matthew, Peter, Andrew, Paul, and others. And Christ's true ministers have not their learning and wisdom from men, or from universities, or human schools for human learning. Arts and sciences are not essential to making of a true minister, but the gifts of God, which cannot be bought with silver and gold; and also as they have freely received the gift, so they do freely administer; They do not preach for hire, for gain and filthy lucre; They are not like the false teachers, who look for gain from their quarter; who eat the fat, and clothe themselves with the wool, and kill them that are fed; those that put not into their mouths, they prepare war against: Also they are not Lords over God's heritage, they rule them not by force and cruelty, neither have they power to force and compel men to believe and obey their doctrines, but are only to persuade and intreat; for this is the way of the Gospel, as Christ taught them.'

"And many other things hast thou seditiously, wickedly, and maliciously written in the said book, to the great displeasure of Almighty God, the scandal of the liturgy of the Church of England, the disaffection of the king's people to his majesty's government, the danger of the peace of this kingdom, the evil example of others, and contrary to the statute in that case made and provided. How say you, Benjamin Keach; are you Guilty or Not Guilty?"

Keach plead not guilty, was tried and found guilty except that in one place the indictment used the word "devils" for dead in the phrase where book read "then shall the *dead* be raised."

Here then is a clear case where difference of opinion about baptism and of the relations of the several members of the trinity was a crime both seditious and heretical. The jury were given a copy of the Book of Common Prayer with the appropriate passages marked for comparison with Keach's Primmer. There, comparisons were also made by the Judge in his instructions. How trifling the differences can be seen by reading the account in Howell's State Trials.

TAYLOR'S CASE—1675.[36]

Lord Hale presided in Taylor's Case. The record reads thus: "An information by Attorney Jones for saying:

---

[36] 1 Ventris, 293.
3 Kebble, 607.
2 Strange, 789.

'Christ is a whore-master, and religion a cheat, and profession a cloak, and all cheats, all are mine, and I am
a king's son and fear neither God, devil nor man. I am
Christ's younger brother (proved by three witnesses),
and that Christ is a bastard, and damn all Gods of the
Quakers,' etc., *in distruction* of society and religion, and
contempt, etc., 'none fear God but an hypocrite,' proved
by one.'

According to one report, a part of these quoted words
were denied, another part explained. What was neither
denied, nor explained is thus reported: "Religion was a
cheat, and that he neither feared God, the devil nor man."
The partial denial and explanation will account for the
fact that all the accused words are not used in both reports, and perhaps explains why Lord Hale did not repeat
all of them. He said:

"These words, though of ecclesiastical cognizance, yet
that religion is a cheat *tends to a dissolution of all governments, and therefore punishable here,* and so of contumelious reproaches of God, or the religion established;
which the court agreed and adjudged. An indictment lay
for saying the Protestant religion was a fiction; *for taking
away religion, all obligation to government by oath,* etc.,
ceaseth, and Christian religion is part of the Law of itself:
therefore injuries to God are as punishable as to a King or
any common person."

LODOWICK MUGGLETON—1653-1676.[37]

Lodowick Muggleton (1609-1698) was one of that numerous band of religious enthusiasts who consider them-

Digest of the law concerning libels, pp. 57-117.
Folkard's Starkie on libel and slander. 5 Ed. p. 615.
Law Magazine and Review, v. 9, p. 164.
[37] Dictionary of national biography, v. 39, pp. 364-267.
A transcendent spiritual treatise on several heavenly doctrines from
the man Jesus the only true god, sent unto all his elect as a token
of love unto them by the hand of his own prophet being his last
and witness and forerunner of the visible appearing of the distinct
personal God in power and great glory in the clouds of heaven with
his ten thousands of personal saints to separate between the elect
world and reprobate world to all eternity * * * John Reeve and
Lodowick Muggleton the last witnesses and true prophets of the
Man Jesus the only Lord of life and glory. [1652]
Muggleton revived or new news of the grand impostor being a nar-

selves more favored of God than we ordinary mortals. Muggleton's religious career began about 1651. His partner in the enjoyment of special divine prerogatives was his cousin, John Reeve (or Reeves), both being tailors by trade. Between them they claimed to have been vested with certain divine powers and prophetic gifts. In these matters of course they became competitors of those who had a legally established monopoly on divine truths. What made them the more obnoxious is that as " kid-

rative of his late behaviour since his sentence and standing in the pillory. With the substance of several discourses had with him he still persisting in his blasphemous tenets, and damning people as formerly with allowance. London, printed for D. M. 1677.
A remonstrance from the eternal God and declaring several spiritual transactions unto parliament and commonwealth of England: until his excellency, the lord general Cromwell the council of state and the council of war * * * Printed in the year 1653 and reprinted in the year 1719, pp. 13-14.
A volume of spiritual epistles * * *. This printed by subscription in the year 1755 * * * was reprinted * * * 1751—1752—1753 * * *.
News from the sessions-house in the Old Bayley being a true account of the notorious principles and wicked practices of the grand impostor Lodowick Muggleton, who has the impudence to style himself one of the two last commissionated witnesses and prophets of the most high God Jesus Christ. Collected out of his own writings, for which damnable heresies being bound over, he made his appearance at the sessions this 14th of December, and gave such security in order to his future trials * * *. London, 1676.
True narrative of the proceedings at the sessions-house in the Old Bayly, at a sessions there held on Wednesday the 17th of January 1676/7. Giving a full account of the true tryal and sentence of Lodowick Muggleton for blasphemous words and books. London. 1676/7.
A looking glass for George Fox, Quaker, and other Quakers, wherein they may see themselves to be right devils * * *.
A letter presented unto alderman Fowke; page 264 of a book that appears to be without title page but is bound in with one entitled A volume of Spiritual epistles * * *. This re-printed by subscription in the year 1755 * * * had been previously printed * * * 1751, 1752, 1753 * * * Farrer, James Anson. Books condemned to be burnt, pp. 115-116.
Hyde, James. The Muggletonians; New Church Review, v. 7, pp. 215-227.
Powell, ..., True account of trial. 1677. [?]
Discourse * * * on a charge of blasphemy. 1652. [?]
Letters to colonel Phaire. 1681.
Harleian Miscel, vols. 1 and 8.
A remonstrance from the eternal God declaring several spiritual transactions unto parliament and commonwealth of England unto his excellency the Lord General Cromwell the council of State and the council of war. * * * Printed in the year 1653 and reprinted in the year 1719.
A true interpretation of the eleventh chapter of the revelation of St. John.

nappers of souls" they were successful. It is said that the sect founded by them is still in existence.

William Reeve, a cousin, converted Muggleton to Puritanism. In 1650 he was attracted to John Robins, "a ranter," and Thomas Tany, "a predecessor of the Anglo-Israelites." Soon he began to receive inward revelations. John Reeve, another cousin, also became infected and claimed communications "by voice of words" from Jesus Christ. The two came forward as prophets of a new dispensation, with authority to pronounce upon the eternal fate of humans. They held that the devil was a human being, witchcraft a delusion; and that narratives of miracles were mostly parables.

CRIME TO DENY TRINITY.

In 1652 they published their "commission book" entitled "Transcendent Spiritual Treatise." In September, 1653, they were arrested for this "charging them with blasphemy in denying the trinity." They were tried before Lord Mayor John Fowke and committed to Old Bridewell for six months, being released April, 1654. It will illuminate the situation if we will enquire a little more in detail into the blasphemous doctrines of their treatise.

In this book Muggleton speaks of: "the Man Jesus, the only true God." Himself and Reeve he designates as "the Lord's two last witnesses and prophets that ever shall declare the mind of God, the Man Jesus."

A phrase used in that book is: "the Lord Jesus the only wise God." Again: "the invisible Creator of all life and spirits was a God of glorious substance, a Spiritual Body in the form and likeness of a man from all eternity." Also: "the holy angels are spiritual bodies, in their persons formed like men," and are inferior to "elect men," like Muggleton and Reeve. Further: "You may understand that God, the Father, was a spiritual Man from eternity, and that in time His righteous spiritual body brought forth a righteous natural body; that the Father, to show his infinite love and humility, and to bring forth a new transcendent glory to Himself, might become a son, yea and a servant, unto His creatures, in the very condition of a creature for a season."

Regarding the words "I and my Father are one," the explanation is: "His spirit living within His body, that was the Father; and his visible body, that was the Son, both God and Man in one person and so but one personal God, the Man Christ Jesus."

"They teach that the Father to whom the Lord prayed was Elijah. It was Elias that spake these words, 'this is my beloved Son in whom I am well pleased.'"

To disparage another view of the Deity, they said: "A God of words only, without substanial form, a bodiless form, a bodiless God which they imagine was in heaven when the Lord Jesus was personally on this Earth," whereas the "true" doctrine is: "The immortal, eternal Creator for a season became an absolute mortal man or creature, sin only excepted." An appendix by Reeve is entitled "A Cloud of Unerring Witnesses, plainly proving that there neither is, nor ever was, any other God but Jesus Christ, the Lord." In this Reeve says: "It is impossible for any man, from Scripture record, or any way else, to prove the Creator to be two or three distinct essences, because of His threefold name of Father, Son and Holy Ghost, or Lord Jesus Christ, as it is to prove a man's body may live without a soul, or that a man is two or three distinct essences, because he is styled in scripture records by a three fold name of body, soul and spirit."

Thus it appears that Muggleton's anti-trinitarianism was little more than a war of words, quite void of objective or pragmatic significance.

In one of his published letters Muggleton eternally curses a judge for blasphemy in denying his anthropomorphic God in favor of one that is more mystical and spiritual.

CRIME TO ADVOCATE TOLERATION.

In a letter to a recorder who sentenced them, these defendants denied his jurisdiction, declaring that God had chosen them and only them "to be judges of Blasphemy against the Holy Spirit because no man clearly knew the

Lord until we were commissioned by Voice of Words from
Heaven to declare what the true God is; yet notwithstanding your Honour, with the Jury, gave Sentence against
us, as Blasphemers because we declared Jesus Christ to
be the only God, in heaven or in earth, but the Man
Jesus only * * * Whoever tries us by the Law of the
Land, it is allowed as if he tried his God by the Civil Law
as the Jews did." In vain the judge was commanded to
reverse the judgment of the jury or suffer eternal damnation.

During one of his trials Muggleton was questioned about
his God, and his answers were declared *blasphemous* by
the judge. Muggleton had said: "We told you that you
had no Commission from our God to be the judge of
spiritual things. * * * That you [the judge] by your
Commission from men are the judge of temporal things
only in this perishing world, and we [Muggleton and
Reeve] only are the judges of Spiritual Things, that are
eternal in the World to come, by a Commission from the
Throne of Glory, from the glorious Mouth of our Lord
Jesus Christ."

In his book, "A Looking Glass for George Fox," Muggleton says that reason is the devil, and that the magistrates who sentence him are reasonable men. He adds:
"But this I must tell you, that when reasonable men do
judge rightly between man and man in things temporal,
this is highly esteemed by me, and warrantable in the
sight of God; but for reasonable men to meddle with the
Conscience of Men that breaketh no temporal law, this is
altogether condemned by me and God also."

Although in Muggleton's case the motive and intellectual process by which he arrived at his conclusion for
mental freedom are not of a high order, yet his views are
sound as to the want of proper criminal jurisdiction in
the courts over spiritual (that is mere psychologic) concerns. Later it will appear that this was in harmony
with the general contention of dissenters. Expressed in
modern terms it means that secular courts cannot sit in
judgment for crime over purely psychologic issues.

These statements by Muggleton bring into bold relief

the conflict of the personal lust for power which is always involved in the issue between intellectual freedom and censorship, when our desires are functioning on the lower evolutionary levels. The demand for censorship is always psychogenetically based upon such an immature lust for power. In Muggleton's case, it appears that the demand for tolerance was similarly conditioned. In others, the demand for tolerance may find its justification at the highest evolutionary level of desire and mental processes. When so conditioned it will be based upon a desire for social service and for progressing democratization. Our constitutional guarantees of free speech and religious liberty were designed to compel tolerance among the relatively undeveloped in order to promote the higher order of tolerance, which is complete intellectual freedom as a conceded and constitutionally guaranteed right.

When we come to summarize all prosecutions for blasphemy it will be shown that *the mere advocacy of toleration is blasphemy* under the common law conception of that offence. These incidents in connection with the trials of Muggleton exhibit human aversion to toleration to be grounded in a competition for divine prerogatives, and "spiritual" vanity. The orthodox spiritual aristocrats believed in censoring those heretics who evidently desired to supercede them. The first believers in tolerance, such as Muggleton, opposed censorship mainly because they claimed in themselves more of the divine authority than they conceded to the established clergy. This conflict between aristocratic contestants for spiritual priveleges has been, in modern times, superceded by a demand for free speech as essential for the further democratization of the world. When this larger viewpoint is generally attained by our judges then our constitutional interpretation will exhibit the larger interest and confidence in democracy and its growth.

Muggleton and Reeve seem to have suffered a second arrest for blasphemy in the same year and appear to have been tried before Recorder Steel, October 14th and 15th, 1653.

Muggleton says: "The recorder and the jury did pronounce us [Muggleton and Reeve] to be blasphemers, for our declaring the Man Jesus that died at Jerusalem and arose from Death to Life by his own Power, to be the only God and Everlasting Father. For this glorious Truth's sake which they call Blasphemy, they have committed us to Old Bridewell, there to remain six months without bail or main-prize."

Muggleton's third arrest occurred at Chesterfield in 1663 at the instance of John Coope on the charge of denying the Trinity. He was imprisoned and released on bail. The account does not state what became of the case. In 1670, Muggleton's books were seized in London, but he evaded arrest.

In his "Looking Glass for George Fox," Muggleton informs us that he was acquitted at Darby after justifying himself to the Magistrate. He tells us that the thing he was accused of at Darby was his claim of power to damn and to save, and the claim that he was one of the two witnesses spoken of in Revelation and that the people's believing the Scripture now, they being damned by Muggleton, would do them no good. Perhaps the magistrate had a sense of humor not possessed by the judge in the next case.

Muggleton's chief controversies were with the Quakers whose "bodiless God" was the antithesis of his own conception of divinity.

In 1675 as executor to Deborah Brunt he brought suit for some property. This made it necessary for him to appear in the spiritual court and he was at once arrested on the charge of blasphemous writings. His trial took place at the Old Bayley, Jan. 17, 1677, before Sir Richard Rainsford, chief justice of the King's Bench. He was convicted on the book "Neck of the Quakers Broken," it being held by the court that it was falsely dated as if published before the Act of Indemnity of 1674, though in fact printed after. His attorney refused to make any other defense, for shame of being associated with Muggleton's doctrines. Sentence was passed by Recorder George Jeffreys. Muggleton was amerced 500£, condemned to the pillory on three several days and his books ordered to be burned before his face. He was imprisoned in Newgate in default of the fine, and released in July, 1677.

Two so-called accounts of this trial have been published. One author tells us "it makes my hair stand on end to rake thus in the Naucious Dunghill of his horrid ·Blasphemies. His whole volume is nothing but a promiscuous composition of Heresie, Delusion and Blasphemy." This explosion was a climax following upon a quotation in which Muggleton claims divine authority to curse humans in the name of God. His words are: "As for my mouth being full of cursing, that is my commission. * * * Full of his Cursing I confess my mouth is, and I do rejoice in it, too. I know that God is well pleased in the damnation of those I have cursed and I am wondrous well satisfied in giving judgment upon them according to the Tenelt of my condition."

Here then blasphemy of the most offensive type consists in a frank and open avowal of a commission to pronounce divine wrath in competition with the "established" monopolists. Let us read another similar paragraph requoted from this same pamphlet. These are perhaps the most offensive samples and doubtless for that reason were selected from among those upon which the criminal charge was based.

"Neither (says he) will God give this power to any after me, neither can any man come to the assurance of the favour of a God now in these days but in believing that God gave this power to John Reeve and myself. For there is no coming to know God or see God, but by the faith in this Commission of the spirit, for I having the Keys of Heaven and Hell, none can get into Heaven unless the witness of this spirit doth open the Gate. * * * Neither doth any man know the Scripture, neither can any man interpret them truly, but myself. * * * God hath put the two-edged Sword in my mouth, that whosoever I pronounce cursed, is cursed to Eternity." All this was, of course, an outrageous challenge to the legalized claims of the clergy, just emerging from the dark ages. From that background, it was extremely blasphemous. Is a statute now constitutional which sought to perpetuate the punishment for such harmless pretentions of mental illness?

The other chronicler of Muggleton's troubles tell us of the seizure and that "many wicked passages out of them being recited in the indictment, but so horrid and blasphemous, that we think fit to spare the Christian modesty of each pious ear, by not repeating the same."

Muggleton upon this trial was found guilty and "sentenced to stand three days in the Pillory at three most eminent places of the City, with Papers showing his Crime; and his Books so seized, divided into three parts, to be burnt over his head upon the Pillory: And besides, to be fined five hundred pounds, and to continue in Gaol until the same be paid, and afterwards for his life, unless he procured good Bail, such as the court should accept of, and not of his own Gang, Faetion or Sect, for his being of the good Behaviour."

In his "Divine Looking-glass or Heavenly Touchstcne," first printed in 1656 and reprinted in 1760, Muggleton intimates that Cromwell has a secret divine appointment, through Muggleton himself one may suppose.

"The perfidious usurper, conscious to himself that Muggleton could not be greater impostor in the church than he was in the state, upon consideration of fratres in malis restored him to his liberty."

XVI.
PROSECUTIONS FOR CRIMES AGAINST RELIGION.
1678—1706.

ONE OF THE SOCIETY OF LOVE—1678.[38]

This defendant was convicted at Stepney and sent to Newgate, May 28, 1678. She was a servant of "proper body and good countenance." From childhood she had been religious, drifting from one sect to another. She finally became a member of the "Society of Love," by others styled ranters. "They soon instilled wild notions into her head, which she has ever since retained impressions of, and upon all occasions would be venting their bold Impious Expressions in her Discourses and Conversations. * * * Always a great Exclaimer against the established Church, and a haunter of private Conventicles. * * * The devil at last screwed her up to that height of Impiety as to pretend to a personal and familiar Communion with the Deity so that she began to take upon herself to pronounce whom she list Damn'd and those that pleased her Sav'd. And to justifie these pretentions ('tis said) assum'd to herself the Sacred Attributes of God, and sometimes gave out, That she was the Virgin Mary; at other times *Blasphemously* taking upon her other adorable Names and Tytles. But that which particularly and immediately caused her present Commitment was this: On Wednesday, the 29th of May, the Festival justly celebrated with publique Divine Worship, as the Anniversary of our Sovereign Lord the King's Happy Birth and miraculous Restoration; this Woman came into the Church-Yard at Stepney and there beginning an Harangue as if she

---

[38] News from Newgate: or the female Muggletonian being an account of the apprehension and commitment of a certain fanatical woman, charged with speaking several horrid blasphemous words. Taken at Stepney the 29th of May, 1678 * * * London, printed for P. B. 1678, 8p.
A true narrative of the proceedings at Sessions-house in the Old Bailey on Oct. 3, and 4 day of July, 1678 * * * London, printed, for D. M. 1678, 8p.

would preach to them, soon got a company of people about
her, to whom she uttered several *blasphemous and detest-*
able expressions, not fit here to be related, since they must
needs be grevious in the repetition to any good Christian's
ears; at first they concluded her to be distracted, but upon
several peoples discoursing with her, finding Coherence
in her talk, and offers of pretended Reasons, sometimes
Texts of Holy Scripture truly cited and readily abus'd
to maintain her sayings, and that no argument could
reclaim her, or Admonitions persuade her to desist, they
seized her and carried her before a Majestrate, where persisting in her impious Language, and pretending to Damn
the people, &c., she was committed to Newgate.

"Next day after she came in there, a Minister went to
see her, to whom she recounted several of her horrid
speeches, and told him, He was certainly Damn'd if he
did not believe her; He told her she was Mad, and seemed
to pitty her; Whereupon she Replyed: Pitty thy self and
thine own soul, I am not Mad, but bear witness to the
truth, and thou shalt hear me affirm the same things when
I come before the Bench; To another, asking her if she
were not acquainted with Muggleton, she said, Muggleton was not worthy to unloose the Latches of her Shoes,
and that he was a Deceiver, and she would Damn him.

"By this poor Creature's lamentable delusion, we may
observe the danger of an unsettled Faith in matters of
Religion, and to what pernitious Ends the following of
New-fangled Sects and Heresies brings may weak Melan-
cholly heads, which may caution all to learn to be wise
unto Sobriety; not to perplex their brains with Notional
Extravagances, but in an humble, though not Implicite
Faith, to submit to the Establisht Church of England, as
directing all her children in the soundest Path of Doctrine, and most sober form of Discipline in the World.
To which whoever joyns a Holy, Humble, and Charitable
Conversation, need not doubt of everlasting Happiness;
without which pious life all Religion is vain: And therefore as we should endeavor to avoid Heresies, so we should
also forsake Debaucheries, and gross Impieties."

This then ends the story of this unnamed blasphemer, a

poor demented woman. I have added the homily of the
pious reporter because it furnishes a good sidelight on the
spirit of the times and its ignorance.

It is reported that on a subsequent day she confessed
"her having taken upon her to be God," the judge gravely
advised her to repent and committed her to jail till she
should furnish a bond for her good behavior.

This case illustrates that part of the blasphemy law as
stated by Disney thus: "To ascribe * * * to any creature
an Excellence which only can belong to God."   Naylor's
case was of the same sort. If this blasphemy law were
now so enforced, it would cause a great shrinkage in the
population of our asylums.

JOHN MORGAN—1679.[39]

"One John Morgan was Indicted on the Statute, for
that being born a Subject of England, and having received
Orders from the See of Rome, yet he came into and remained in England. There was very good Evidence that
proved he was a Priest, and had said Mass, but as formerly, so now at Bar he freely confest that he was a
Priest. Some say he was heretofore a little crazed in his
Understanding, which was probable enough by his Behavior: However, the Offence being evident, according to
Law, he was found Guilty of Felony and High-Treason
and received a Sentence to be Drawn, Hanged and Quar-
tered."

No, technically this was not a prosecution for blasphemy. It was a precaution against probable future blasphemy. If our constitutions permit punishment for blasphemy, then it must also permit the anticipation of that
offence in those who give evidence of being stubbornly so
inclined. Then we may of course apply that one ounce of
prevention which is superstitiously believed to be always
better than a pound of cure.

---

[39] A true narrative of the proceedings at the sessions for London
and Middlesex Begun April 30th, 1679 giving an account of the
tryal of a popish priest condemned for high treason * * *. London,
1679.

HENRY CARR—1680.[40]

In 1680, in the case of Henry Carr, he was convicted of High Treason to destroy the King, the government, "and the sincere religion of God within this Kingdom of England well and piously established, to destroy and subvert, and the Romish religion within this Kingdom of England to introduce." The word so offensive to church and state were only these: "There is lately found out by an experienced physician, an incomparable medicament, called 'The Wonder-working Plaister—truly Catholic in operation, somewhat of kin to Jesuits' Powder, but more effectual. The virtues of it are strange and various. It will make justice deaf as well as blind, takes out spots of deepest treasons, more cleverly than Castile-soap does common stains. It alters a man's constitution in two or three days, more than the virtuous transfusion of blood in seven years. Is a great alexipharmic, and helps poisons, and those that use them. It miraculously exalts and purifies eyesight, and makes people behold nothing but innocence in the blackest malfactors. It is a mighty cordial for a declining cause, stifles a plot as certainly as the itch is destroyed by butter and brimstone. In a word it makes fools wise men, and wise men fools, and both of them knaves. The colour of this precious balm is bright and dazzling, and being applied privately to the fist in decent manner, and a competent dose, infallibly performs all the said cures and many others not fit here to mention."

In the judicial opinion I find this: "When, by the King's commandment we were to give in our opinion what was to be done in print of regulation of the press; we did all subscribe, that to print or publish any news-books or pamphlets *of news whatever, is illegal; that it is a manifest intent to the breach of the peace,* and they may be proceeded against for an illegal thing. Suppose now that this thing is not scandalous, what then? *If there had been no reflection in this book at all,* yet it is *illicite,* and the author ought to be convicted for it."

40 Howell's State Trials, v. 7: 1111-1130.
Digest of the law concerning libels [1765] p. 32-72.

Underlying all such reasoning is the tacit though unconscious assumption of approximate or relative omniscience in the privileged ruling caste, whose divine right no one may question with impunity, even by offering well meant but unsolicited advice. Before the rebellion we find the same unconscious assumptions made in some slave states where all effort to teach the negro how to read or write was penalized. Some people there are even in our relatively democratic time and country who still resent the education of both negro and white laborers. Especially is this so, if that education tends to induce the laborer to question the perfect justice of our wage system. In all these cases we find a dominant emotional attitude, which is never consciously so formulated and yet amounts to this: those who are the beneficiaries of things as they are have something akin to a divine property right in the maintenance in *statu quo* of the sustaining public opinion. Thus the King's Judges argued that all unauthorized printing "of news whatever is illegal," even though "it is not scandalous." Then to invent a theory to justify the King's desires, the judges created a fiction, and declared it as a theory in these words: "that it is a manifest intent to a breach of the peace." So blindly are we lawyers habituated to precedent that many follow this fiction even to this day, and instead of determining the psychologic tendency of an accused idea by the actual and visible resultant facts, we are still content to indulge our feelings with the pretence that we have found the intent and tendency manifest in the words. The legal theory seems to have made little progress. Censorship even in our day is still justified by the bald assumption of an evil psychologic tendency, toward an imaginary and prospective breach of the peace. Although we have become ashamed to apply this constructive breach of the peace as freely as formerly, the very bringing of such a prosecution as that now before the court assumes that our judges are still willing to follow the mediaeval fiction as a justification for upholding the constitutionality of this blasphemy law.

THOMAS DELAUNE and MR. RALPHSON—1683.[41]

These defendants were arrested Nov., 1683, for "Plea for the Nonconformists," written by Thomas Delaune.

He attempted to make his case wholly from the Scriptures and all was written in the best conceivable temper. But, of course, in basing his demand for tolerance upon Holy Writ, he necessarily came in conflict with the official interpretation thereof. The indictment reads that the defendant, "not regarding his due allegiance, but contriving and intending to disquiet and disturb the peace and common tranquility of this kingdom * * * to bring the said Lord the King into the greatest hate and contempt of his subjects, machinating and further intending to move, stir up, and procure sedition and rebellion, and to disparage and scandalize the book of common prayer," etc.

The following were the most offending words that could be found to place in the indictment: "The Church of Rome and England also are great transgressors to presume to vary from Christ's precepts, in altering or adding to the form of words, expressed by Christ, in this 11th of Luke, for so they have done: they say, forgive us our trespasses as we forgive them who trespass against us; when there are no such words in Christ's prayer, his words are, *forgive* us our sins or debts, for we also forgive every one that is indebted to us."

"And [says the indictment again] in another part of the said libel are contained these false, fictious, seditious and scandalous sentences following *viz*. 'And may we not say, that in these following particulars, we do not symbolize with idolatrous Rome herein? First, By enjoin-

---

[41] A plea for the non-conformists showing the true state of their case: and how far the conformists separation from the church of Rome, for their popish superstitions & introduced into the service of God, justifies the non-conformists separation from them. * * * By Thomas De Laune. See especially pages 195-6-200, Edition of 1800.

A narrative of the sufferings of Thomas De Laune for writing and printing and publishing a late book called A plea for the nonconformists; with some modest reflections thereon, directed to Dr. Calamy, in obedience to whose call, that work, was undertaken. By Thomas De Laune, Printed 1712.

Dictionary of National Biography, v. 14, p. 316.

Farrer, James Anson, Books condemned to be burnt, p. 130 to 134.

Eikoon Tou Therou or the image of the Beast, p. 111.

ing and imposing this *viz.* meaning the book of common prayer aforesaid, as a set form; as they do with penalties, contrary to the Scripture. Secondly, By an often repetition of the same form in the same exercise, three or four times at least; insomuch, that in the cathedral churches, it is said, or sung, ten or twelve times a day, contrary to Christ's express words, that, *when* we pray, we do not make vain repetitions as the heathen do, for they think they shall be heard for their much speaking. Thirdly, By enjoining the whole congregation, men and women, to repeat the same after the priest, though no such direction by Christ: nay, he forbids women to pray or prophesy in the church. Fourthly, In singing this prayer in the cathedrals by responses of the people, without the least warrant from Christ for such song-praying'."

The Chief Justice refused to allow the context of these extracts to go the Jury, and upon mere admission of the act of publication the Jury was instructed that they must find the defendant guilty; the question of its being a libel being one purely for the court. The defendant was fined 100 marks a sum he could not pay, and to be imprisoned till paid and to good security for his good behavior for one year.

The judge said that out of respect for their education, the defendants (being teachers) as scholars, should not be pilloried though he believed they deserved it.

"His books (for he also wrote *The Image of the Beast,* wherein he showed, in three parallel columns, the far greater resemblance of the Catholic rites to those of Pagan Rome than to those of the New Testament) were condemned to be burnt; and his judges, humane enough to let him off the pillory in consideration of his education, sent him back to Newgate notwithstanding it. There, in that noisome atmosphere and in that foul company, he was obliged to shelter his wife and two small children; and there, after fifteen months, he died, having first seen all he loved on earth pine and die before him. And he was only one of eight thousand other Protestant Dissenters who died in prison during the merry, miserable reign of Charles II.! Of a truth, Dissent has something to forgive the church; for persecution in Protestant England was very much the same as in Catholic France, with, if possible, less justification.

"The main argument of Delaune's book was, that the Church of England agreed more in its rites and doctrines with the Church of Rome, and both Churches and Pagan or preChristian Rome, than either did with the primitive Church or the word of the Gospel—a thesis that has long since become generally accepted; but his main offence consisted in saying that the Lord's Prayer ought in one sentence to have been translated precisely as it now has been in the Revised Version, and in contending that the frequent repetition of the prayer in church was contrary to the express command of Scripture. On these and other points Delaune's book was never answered—for the reason, I believe, that it never could be. After the Act of Toleration (1689) it was often reprinted; the eighth and last time in 1706, when the High Church movement to persecute Dissent had assumed dangerous strength, with an excellent preface by Defoe, and concluding with the letters to Dr. Calamy, written by Delaune from Newgate. Defoe well points out that the great artifice of Delaune's time was to make the persecution of Dissent appear necessary, by representing it as dangerous to the State as well as the Church."

RICHARD BAXTER—1684.[42]

Many of the older members of every English speaking community must have come somewhat under the influence of Baxter's "Saints Everlasting Rest" and many will no doubt be surprised to find that this super-pious author's

[42] King v. Baxter, 3 Modern Reports, 68-69.
Life of the Reverend Mr. Baxter, third part, pp. 123, 175, 198.
The certainty of the world of spirits. Fully evidenced by unquestionable histories of apparitions and witchcrafts, operations, voices, etc., proving the immortality of souls, the malice and miseries of the devils and the damned and the blessedness of the justified. Written for the conviction of Sadduces and infidels. London, 1691.
Howell's, State trials, vol. 11, p. 493.
Digest of the law concerning libels, (1765) pp. 10, 11, 118.
Life of Richard Baxter, (American Tract Society), pp. 105-114.
Elisha's cry for Elisha's god, p. 15.
A paraphrase upon the new Testament.
Vickers, Robert H. Martyrdoms of Literature, p. 381.

religious opinions could and did make him a criminally seditious person. Baxter was a voluminous controversialist. He was an intimate friend of Sir Mathew Hale, and wrote a book defending witchcraft, in which both evidently believed.

Baxter often came into conflict with the conventicle law against the Dissenters. However, these cases nominally did not concern his religious opinion. Those laws did not make the criteria of guilt depend upon the tendency of the opinion, but such a tendency was still the justification for the statute against the right of assembly. The case with which we are concerned deals more directly with the religious opinions of Baxter and their dangerous tendency toward sedition. The prosecution was founded upon "A Paraphrase upon the New Testament." He wrote this book partly to explain an earlier one, his "Treatise of Episcopacy," which had been much misunderstood. To be impartial in his criticism of opponents he attached "two pieces against Dr. Sherlock that ran quite into the contrary Extremes, unchurching almost all Christians as Schismaticks." He adds: "I wrote so sharply against him as must needs be liable to blame with those who know not the man, and his former and later Virulent and ignorant Writings."

The information charged the defendant with writing "A Paraphrase upon the New Testament", intending thereby to bring the protestant religion and likewise the Bishops of England into contempt. He was found guilty, fined 500£ and required to give security for good behaviour. He was unable to pay his fine or thought it useless, because new excuses for his re-arrest would be invented. So he served about two years of his sentence when he was released as larger liberty was accorded to Dissenters generally.

Baxter was tried by the blood-loving Jeffries. Calamy has preserved for us a good pen-picture of this trial. One may well wonder if this was Jeffries at his worst. It is difficult to conceive of a more malignant spirit than he exhibited on this occasion. His associates however, prevented the penalty of whipping.

In this case Baxter's blasphemies were not against God but against the orthodox established conception of Christianity and its Bishops, so Jeffries called it sedition.

Another author comments thus on this case: "There was just room in Baxter's case for the defendant pretending that he meant not Protestant Bishops, but Popish." But that did not save him. "It is observable with what Discernment the Managers of this prosecution proceeded. In a Book of Controversy, as this was, there was Scope to punish the Author for a Schismatical Libel, a new Term of Art which some People have attempted to bring into use; but they very wisely thought the religious Dispute unfit for the Cognizance of Lay Heads, and only urged against the Defendant the Satyr upon the Bishops, who are, in our State, great Officers, and make up a part of our Constitution."

Baxter's "Holy Commonwealth or Political Aphorisms opening the true principles of government," London, 1659, was also burned at Oxford, in 1688.

Words against the Bishoprics are words against the government as well as against God. If we are possessed by sympathetic emotions toward any church our desire to suppress critics will be proportionately strong. Much desire and lively imagination will create in such persons a necessity for believing that the offensive doctrine tends to a disturbance of the peace. Whether now you call it sedition or blasphemy is utterly unimportant except as a matter of efficiency in securing the approval of others by adjusting the intellectualization of our desire to the dominant prejudices of others.

Does constitutional free speech now mean that perhaps under some name other than blasphemy, the legislature may still penalize the theologic offence of criticising the offices of bishops or priests without such criticism having resulted in any actual or material injury to person or estate of any particular ecclesiast?

ARTHUR BURY—1690.[43]

Arthur Bury (1624-1714) was a graduate of Exeter and received degrees at Oxford. In 1648 he learned to know what it was to be led from his college by a file of musketeers and forbidden to return to Oxford or his fellowship under pain of death, because he had the courage in those day to read the prayers of the church. On the recommendation of Archbishop Sheldon, he became rector of Exeter College, 1866. He was ousted with approval of the House of Lords, Dec. 10, 1694.

"Oxford University has always tempered her love for learning with a dislike for inquiry, and set the cause of orthodoxy above the cause of truth. This phase of her character was never better illustrated than in the case of *The Naked Gospel*, * * * A high value attaches to the first edition of this book, wherein the author essayed to show what the primitive Gospel really was, what alterations had been gradually made in it, and what advantages and disadvantages had therefrom ensued. * * * His motive was the promotion of that charity and toleration which breathes in every page."

Like most of the religious libertarians of his time he made the emphasis on the absence of state jurisdiction rather than considerations of expediency. He said: "No King is more independent in his own dominions from any foreign jurisdiction in matters civil, than every Christian is within his own mind in matters of faith."

It must have been his advocacy of tolerance that gave offence. This is inferred from the fact that in the second edition, evidently to minimize or eliminate his offence he omitted such passages as this: "The Church of England, as it needs not, so it does not forbid any of its sons the use of their own eyes; if it did this alone would be sufficient reason not only to distrust but to condemn it."

Bury sums up the doctrine of his book "in two precepts—believe and repent." So simple and tolerant a re-

[43] Dictionary of National Biography, v. 8, p. 22.
Farrer, James Anson. Books condemned to be burnt. 141-143.
An historical evidence of the naked gospel.
Vickers, Robert H. Martyrdoms of literature, p. 383.

ligion, was so offensive that its expression was destroyed
by fire. Must we still express our aversion by now declaring such doctrines to be blasphemous?

CHARLES BLOUNT—1693.[44]

Charles Blount (1654-1693) had for a father "Sir Henry
Blount, the Socrates of the age." The son was clever,
scholarly in a sense, and a "most unscrupulous plagiar-
ist", an extreme whig and a deist. As a deist, however,
he was extremely conservative, believing deism true but
unsafe without an admixture of Christianity.

In 1675 he published "Anima mundi." He professes to
present nothing on his own authority, but acts as a reporter. "As the lustre of an Oriental Diamond is more
clearly perceived, when compared with counterfeit Stones;
so Christianity appears in its greatest Glory and Splendor,
when compared with the obscurity of Paganism," so he
began. "If any had stronger Arguments to Justify their
Opinion than the other, blame not me who deliver them
but recitative, and am as it were their Amenuensis, without ever concerning myself with the intrinsick value of
their Doctrine," so he explains in the preface.

That is the spirit in which the book was conceived,
though, of course, there was a "dangerous tendency" in
thus presenting fairly the contentions and supporting

---

[44] Blount, Charles. A just vindication of learning and the liberty
of the press. London 1605, 24p.
Reasons humbly offered for the liberty of unlicensed printing [to
which is appended:] A just and true character of Edmund Bohum
[the licenser of the day].
Vie d'Apollonius * * * avec les commentaries donnes en Anglois
par C. B., etc.
Gorton, John. A general biographical dictionary.
An account of Mr. Blount's late book entitled King William and
Queen Mary Conquerors, ordered by the house of commons to be
burnt. London, 1693.
Dictionary of national biography, v. 5, p. 243.
Biographical dictionary, vol. 5, pp. 418-422.
Vickers, Robert H. Martyrdoms of literature, p. 383.
Leland, John. A view of deistical writers that have appeared in
England in the last and present century * * * London, 1754-56.
Macaulay, Thomas B. History of England, Chap. XIX; vol. 4,
pp. 282 to 289, Phila. 1877 edition.
Anima mundi, or, an historical narration of the opinions of the
ancients concerning man's soul after this life; according to unen-
lightened nature. London, 1675. Also 1679.

arguments of the ancients whose views conflicted with legalized orthodoxy. Doubtless this deist also hoped that such enlightenment would have its natural effect, toward rationalizing Christianity. Compton, the bishop of London, was quick to scent the danger and ordered the book suppressed. It was subsequently publicly burnt.

In 1680 Blount published the most celebrated of his works, a translation: "The Life of Apolonius Tyaneus", in folio, extracted from the two first books of Philestratus, with his own notes. "This too was considered so dangerous a work that its suppression was at once determined on." Unfortunately this book was not accessible, so cannot now be described. The offence probably consisted in some hints against the miracles of Jesus.

"It was held to be the most dangerous attempt, that had been ever made against revealed religion in this country, and justly thought so, as bringing to the eye of every English reader a multitude of facts and reasonings, plausible in themselves, and of the fallacy. of which none but men of parts and learning can be proper judges."

This exhibits to perfection the undemocratic attitude of all those who oppose intellectual liberty. Because the common people cannot be entrusted to reach orthodox conclusions, therefore they must be denied opportunity for that development which depends on practice.

These conflicts with the censorship made Blount an aggressive, as he proved an efficient opponent of the system and of Bohum the censor. Accordingly, Blount wrote his "King William and Queen Mary Conquerors," but anonymously. In it he cleverly defended the extremely conservative toryism of the censor. Blount the republican succeeded in personating a high tory; Blount the deist effectively personated a high churchman. The licenser joyously authorized the publication, and so fell into the trap that had been cleverly baited for him.

Only four days after its publication the House of Commons took up the matter, and not knowing the author, proceeded against the licenser. The King was requested to remove Bohum, the Commons imprisoned him, and the book was ordered burnt. It could not be tolerated that

a licenser should authorize anything that savored of
popery.

Next came "A Just vindication of Learning" and then
"Reasons for Liberty of Unlicensed Printing." In 1693
this latter book was also ordered to be burnt by the hangman. This too is now inaccessible to me. The facts suggest the religious fear of arguments for enlarging tolerance.

Blount's work was an important factor toward killing
the licensing statute.

THOMAS AIKENHEAD'S (OR AIKEN'S) CASE—1695.[45]

This is the single instance to be found of capital punish-
ment for blasphemy under the Scotch statutes. The indictment there was said to be founded "on the law of
God, the law of this and all other well governed realms,
and specially the 21st Act, 1st Parl. Ch. 2, and the 11th
Act, 5th Sess. of 1st Parl. Will. iii;" and it charged (inter
alia) that the defendant (pannel) had called the Old
Testament Ezra's Fables (profanely alluding to Aesop's
Fables). Christ an imposter, who had learned magic in
Egypt, etc.; that he rejected the mysteries of the Trinity
and Incarnation; maintained that God, the world, and
nature, were the same thing; preferred Mohomet to Jesus;
hoped he should see Christianity extirpated, etc. The
court found "Cursing and railing upon any of the Persons of the blessed Trinity relevant to infer the pains of
death; and the other crimes likewise relevant to infer an
arbitrary punishment;" The accused was hung.

Hume comments upon his case as follows: "It appears
to have been tried with vigorous disposition, not on the
part of the Court but of the Assize, who found the pannel
guilty of railing at and cursing Christ, without proof of

[45] Howell's State Trials, v. 13, pp. 917-938.
Hume on crimes, v. 2, c. 19, p. 570.
Coulson, H. J. W. The law relating to blasphemy, Law Magazine
and Review, v. 9, p. 165.
Gordon, John. Thomas Aikenhead. A historical review in relation
to Mr. Macaulay and the witness.
Macaulay, Thomas B. The history of England, v. 5, pp. 226-229,
Chicago 1890. Citing also Postman, Jan. 9-19, 1696-7.
MacLauren's arguments and decisions in remarkable cases, p. 12,
A. D. 1774.

his having done so, and only upon inference from opinions occasionally vented."

Macaulay gives this account:

"A student of eighteen, named Thomas Aikenhead, whose habits were studious and whose morals were irreproachable, had, in the course of his reading, met with some of the ordinary arguments against the Bible. He fancied that he had lighted on a mine of wisdom which had been hidden from the rest of mankind, and, with the conceit from which half-educated lads of quick parts are seldom free, proclaimed his discoveries to four or five of his companions. Trinity in unity, he said, was as much a contradiction as a square circle. Ezra was the author of the Pentateuch. The Apocalypse was an allegorical book about the philosopher's stone. Moses had learned magic in Egypt. Christianity was a delusion which would not last till the year 1800. For this wild talk, of which, in all probability, he would himself have been ashamed long before he was five and twenty, he was prosecuted by the Lord Advocate. The Lord Advocate was that James Stewart who had been so often a Whig and so often a Jacobite that it is difficult to keep an account of his apostasies. He was now a Whig for the third, if not for the fourth, time. Aikenhead might undoubtedly have been, by the law of Scotland, punished with imprisonment till he should retract his errors and do penance before the congregation of his parish; and every man of sense and humanity would have thought this sufficient punishment for the prate of a forward boy. But Stewart, as cruel as he was base, called for blood. There was among the Scottish statutes one which made it a capital crime to revile or curse the Supreme Being or any person of the Trinity. Nothing that Aikenhead had said could, without the most violent straining, be brought within the scope of this statute. But the Lord Advocate exerted all his subtlety. The poor youth at the bar had no counsel. He was convicted and sentenced to be hanged and buried at the foot of the gallows. It was in vain that he with tears abjured his errors and begged piteously for mercy. Some of those who saw him to his dungeon believed that his recanta-

tion was sincere; and indeed it is by no means improbable
that in him, as in many other pretenders to philosophy
who imagine that they have completely emancipated themselves from the religion of their childhood, the near prospect of death may have produced an entire change of
sentiment. He petitioned the Privy Council that, if his
life could not be spared, he might be allowed a short respite to make his peace with the God he had offended.
Some of the Councillors were for granting this small indulgence. Others thought that it ought not to be granted
unless the ministers of Edinburgh would intercede. The
two parties were evenly balanced; and the question was
decided against the prisoner by the casting vote of the
Chancellor. The Chancellor was a man who has been
often mentioned in the course of this history, and never
mentioned with honour. He was that Sir Patrick Hume
whose deputations and factious temper had brought ruin
on the expedition of Argyle, and had caused not a little
annoyance to the government of William. In the Club
which had braved the King and domineered over the Parliament there had been no more noisy republican. But a
title and a place had produced a wonderful conversion.
Sir Patrick was now Lord Polworth: he had the custody
of the Great Seal of Scotland: he presided in the Privy
Council; and thus he had it in his power to do the worst
action in his bad life.

"It remained to be seen how the clergy of Edinburgh
would act. That divines should be deaf to the entreaties
of a penitent who asks, not for pardon, but for a little
more time to receive their instructions and to pray to
Heaven for the mercy which cannot be extended to him
on earth, seems almost incredible, yet so it was. The
ministers demanded not only the poor boy's death, but
his speedy death, though it should be his eternal death.
Even from their pulpits they cried out for cutting him
off. It is probable that their real reason for refusing him
a respite of a few days was their apprehension that the
circumstance of his case might be reported at Kensing-
ton, and that the King, who, while reciting the Coronation Oath, had declared from the throne that he would

not be persecutor, might send down positive orders that the sentence should not be executed. Aikenhead was hanged between Edinburgh and Leith. He professed deep repentence and suffered with the Bible in his hand. The people of Edinburgh, though assuredly not disposed to think lightly of his offence, were moved to compassion by his youth, by his penitence, and by the cruel haste with which he was hurried out of the world. It seems that there was some apprehension of a rescue, for a strong body of fusileers was under arms to support the civil power. The preachers, who were the boy's murderers, crowded round him at the gallows, and while he was struggling in the last agony, insulted Heaven with prayers more blasphemous than anything that he had ever uttered. Wodrow has told no blacker story of Dundee."

Do our constitutional guarantees of free speech and religious liberty leave open the door of legislative power, so that such conduct can again be thus punished or punished at all?

PATRICK KINNYMOUNT—1697.[46]

In this case of blasphemy the court stated the law in part as follows: "That whoever shall deny God, or any of the persons of the blessed Trinity, and obstinately continue therein, shall be in like manner punished by death; * * * Whosoever shall in their wryting or discourse deny, impugne, or quarrel, argue or reasone, against the Being of God or any of the persones of the blessed Trinity, or the authority of the Holy Scriptures, or the providence of God, in the government of the World, shall be punished with the paines contained in the said act."

The defendant denied having used the words alleged against him and vehemently expressed his horror of such sentiments. He also plead drunkenness and the insufficiency of the indictment. For the present purpose the statement of the court as to the law is the only matter of interest.

---

[46] Law Magazine and Review, v. 9, p. 165.
Howell's, State trials, vol. 13, p. 1274.

Rev. John Toland—1697.[47]

John Toland (1670-1722) is believed by many to have been the illegitimate son of a priest. Raised a catholic he became a deist of great distinction. Educated by dissentors he graduated from Edinburgh and finished at Leyden. He wrote considerable, edited the works of Milton and Harrington and wrote a biography of each. He was on terms of intimacy with many of the great men of his time.

In 1696 Toland published his: "Christianity not mysterious." It is said that Toland attacked only the superstructure, not the foundations of orthodox Christianity.

In a letter on his *Vindicius Liberius* he says: "As for the Christian religion in general, that book is so far from calling it in question that it was purposely written for its service, to defend it against the imputations of contradiction and obscurity which are frequently objected by the opposers."

One paragraph will exhibit the spirit of the offensive contention and the author as well. "The Christians," he says, "were careful to remove all obstacles lying in the way of the Gentiles. They thought the most effectual way of gaining them over to their side was by compounding the matter, which led them to unwarrantable compliances, till at length they likewise set up for mysteries. Yet not having the least precedent for any ceremonies from the Gospel, excepting Baptism and the Supper, they strangely disguised and transformed these by adding to them the pagan mystic rites. They administered them with the strictest secrecy; and to be inferior to their adversaries in no circumstances, they permitted none to assist at them but such as were antecedently prepared or initiated."

The book above referred to "produced an outburst of controversy, the first [?] act of the warfare between deists and the orthodox which occupied the next generation. Toland did not openly profess disbelief in the orthodox doctrines, though the tendency of his argument was obvious. The

[47] Dictionary of national biography, v. 56, pp. 438-442.
Farrer, James Anson. Books condemned to be burnt, pp. 149-152.
Christianity not mysterious: or, a treatise showing that there is nothing in the gospel contrary to reason nor above it; and that no Christian doctrine can be properly called a mystery.

book was presented by the grand jury of Middlesex. Toland went to Ireland." At one time feeling ran so high that it was dangerous to be seen speaking with him. He found it difficult to secure food and clothing.

On Sept. 9, 1697, after some sharp discussion the Irish House of Commons voted that the book should be burnt by the common hangman and the author arrested and prosecuted. In the discussion one member went as far as to advocate the burning of Toland himself. Toland disappeared to escape arrest. In the third volume of his sermons (1698) he congratulated the parliament upon having made the kingdom too hot for him.

SUSANNAH FOWLER—1698.[48]

"On Saturday the 7th of May, 1698, Susannah Fowler of the Parish of Hammersmith in the County of Middlesex, was indicted at the Session-House in the Old Bailey, for uttering blasphemous Words against Jesus Christ, and Cursing and Damning the Lord's Prayer." The account of the trial is as follows:

"The first Evidence depos'd, that the Prisoner's Husband came to him, and told him that his wife was possesst with a Devil: Upon which he asked him if she had been guilty of any heinous Sin? and was answered, That upon some Discontent she wished several unlawful wishes, such as That the Devil might fetch her, cursed herself if she would live such a Life, &c. And upon her being visited she said, she saw an Apparition in the shape of a Man; and afterwards seemed to be possesst with a Devil, and had seemingly dreadful Fits, and made a great noise at prayers; and when she was out of her fits, she told the spectators that she saw the Apparition sometimes in one shape sometimes in another; and at one time said it was one Mr. Thomas, and then making a great sqeek, said, Now he is gone out of me; That she used to make a sqeek at the end of every Fit, sometimes two Sqeeks, and sometimes three; and one of the Ministers who visited her,

---

[48] The trial of Sussanah Fowler of Hammersmith for blaspheming Jesus Christ and cursing the Lord's prayer, and who also pretended to be possest with the devil.

being jelous of her being a Cheat, said that at the end of
the next Fit she would make four Sqeeks, which she did.
It was also observed, that as soon as Prayers begun, she
took her Fits, and pretended to be altogether senseless;
at another time he said, she saw a short Man with a long
Beard, which her Handkerchief was a fool to for length;
and it was taken notice of, that she never altered her
Countenance in the time of her Fits; which together with
divers Methods which were us'd to make her believe they
were at Prayers when they were not, increased the belief
that she was a Cheat: And being questioned if she dis-
sembled, she said, if she did, it were just with God to strike
her dead: and upon its being declared to her she was a
Cheat, she and all her Family spoke not a word. Afterwards at another visiting, she seem'd to be in a great Fit,
lifting up her hands as if she would have done herself
some mischief; but upon speaking the words *Tie her,* she
let them rest. It was likewise observ'd, that when she
was in her Fits, she never cursed nor blasphemed, as those
who are possesst with the Devil do, until she heard some
of the Ministers take notice of it; and then she did.

"At another time the Visiters read and prayed with her
from morning to night, when she seemed to be in agony;
and being forced on her knees at Prayer, she swore she
would go with him on Friday, naming the Devil frequently; and on the Friday following she said, One of the
Windows above-stairs was open, and the Devil was come
to fetch her, making a great noise and lighting a great
many Candles: and search being made for the open Win-
dow, it could not be found.

"On the 3d of January last, upon one of the Visiters
repeating the words *Lords save us,* she said, *I'll save you;*
and frequently upon repeating the Lord's Prayer to her,
she said, *Curse it, damn it, sink it;* and upon repeating
the words *I believe in God the Father Almighty,* she said,
that's me; and at repeating the words, *and in Jesus Christ
his only Son,* she said *that's my Son.* At another time
when the words *Lord save us* were again repeated to her,
she said, *I'll save you, I came to save you all, for which I
shed my Blood.* And at other times, on repeating the

Lord's Prayer, she inverted the expressions; and instead of the words, *Lead us not into temptation;* and at the words, *Deliver us from evil,* she said, *bring evil into us.* And upon repeating the words, *Glory to the Father and to the Son,* she said, *that's me and my Son,* after the words *Blessed be the Name of Jesus,* she would say, *Curse him."* Here the broadside from which I am copying at the New York Public Library is mutilated and I must skip a little.

"The Evidence also deposed that the Prisoner said she had a Needle and a Paper in writing given her by the Devil; and that she had a Spell given her to put about her Neck by one Jorden a Papist, some of which profession she said had sent to her several times, and told her she would never be cured till the man with the hair Coat and bare Legs came from the Portugal Embassadors."

There is more of this which a partial mutilation again prevents my copying. This demented woman was found guilty of blasphemy and sentenced to imprisonment, fine, the pillory and required to give a bond for good behavior.

This, like the Bulstrodes instructions to the jurors elsewhere herein quoted, gives us an intimate view of the real workings of the minds of those who have upheld and do uphold blasphemy prosecutions. Then, and now, the judges of more important courts, may invent more plausible formulas to justify the same result, but these will not be founded upon the facts of human experience. They will be more astute intellectualizations of the same fears working in the same manner though a little further below the surface of consciousness. The fundamental ignorance of the impulses that make for punishing the blasphemer is just as great as ever. Those who still believe in blasphemy laws, at present are a little more careful to conceal their ignorance behind phrases more acceptable to the intelligence of our time.

Today we may measure the intelligence of a man by the nature of his desires. In the case at bar it amounts to this: At one grade of intelligence new excuses will be sought to justify persecution as of old, and the constitutional guarantees for equality, religious liberty and free speech will be so misinterpreted as to permit punishment for a Susannah Fowler of our day. At another grade of intelligence a judge will interpret the constitutional guarantees according to the historic and synthetic method. Then blasphemy statutes will be annulled and Susannah Fowler will be more intelligently dealt with.

DANIEL DEFOE—1703.[49]

Defoe (1661-1731) perhaps needs no introduction. He was from dissenting ancestors, but, while believing in more liberty than generally obtained, he did not favor complete religious liberty. His contention was for a liberalizing modification of test laws rather than their repeal. On this account dissenters held him to be a deserter. To put himself right as to his attitude toward a pending bill affecting dissenters, "he pretended to justify the extirpation of all dissenters."

"Defoe's pamphlet so exactly accorded with the sentiments of the High Church party against the Dissenters that the extent of their applause at first was only equalled by that of their subsequent fury when the true author and his true object came to be known. Parliament ordered the work to be burnt by the hangman."

For expressing this interest in toleration, "Defoe was soon afterwards sentenced to a ruinous fine and imprisonment, and to three days' punishment in the pillory," and to be imprisoned during the queen's pleasure, and to find security for good behavior for seven years.

JAMES DRAKE—1705.[50]

James Drake (1667-1707) was a vigorous tory pamphleteer, who graduated from Cambridge with "unusual honors." Later he studied medicine and became a Fellow of the Royal Society and was elected a Fellow of the Col-

[49] Dictionary of national biography, v. 14, p. 283.
Towers, Joseph. Observations on the right and duty of juries in trials for libels, Dublin, 1785, p. 95.
The shortest way with dissenters. 1702.
Farrer, James Anson. Books condemned to be burnt, pp. 152-156.
[50] Vickers, Robert H. Martyrdoms of literature, p. 385.
Farrer, James Anson. Books condemned to be burnt.
Dictionary of national biography, vol. 15, p. 446.

lege of Physicians. An early pamphlet dealing with the succession received notice in Parliament. A second pamphlet (anonymous), very offensive to Presbyterians, was ordered burnt.

In the year 1705 much public effervescence was created by a pamphlet called "The Memorial of the Church of England humbly offered to consideration of all true lovers of our Church and Communion." The name of the author was not published. A reward of 1,000£ was offered for the apprehension of the author. All that could be elicited was that two women, one of them masked, brought manuscripts to David Edwards, the printer, with directions to print 350 copies. These were delivered to four persons sent to receive them. Every copy of this pamphlet could be got hold of was destroyed. It was afterward reprinted in Dublin, and audaciously dedicated to the Lord Lieutenant. That edition was totally destroyed.

The Tory author was indignant that the House of Lords should have rejected the Bill against Occasional Conformity, which would have made it impossible for Dissenters to hold any office by conforming to the Test Act; he complained of the knavish pains of the Dissenters to divide Churchmen into High and Low; and he declared that the present prospect of the Church was "very melancholy," and that of the government "not much more comfortable." Long habit has rendered us callous to the melancholy state of the Church and the discomfort of Governments; but in Queen Anne's time the croakers' favourite cry was a serious offence. The Queen's speech, therefore, on October 27th, 1705, expressed strong resentment of this representation of the Church in danger; both Houses, by considerable majorities, voted the Church to be "in a most safe and flourishing condition"; and a royal proclamation censured both the book and its unknown author, a few months after it had been presented by the Grand Jury of Middlesex, and publicly burnt by the hangman, before the court and again before the Royal Exchange and in the palace yard.

It is difficult at this to find a legal explanation for this act. Motives are usually complex. The pamphlet doubtless afforded some one an excuse for expressing personal and political animosity. But how are we to find a legalistic theory for justification when the author was such an extreme Tory and the Government moderate Tory? The official religion was "low church." That is to say, it interpreted holy writ so as to allow of more tolerance than the author approved. He denounced the Dissenters for their efforts to divide the Church into high church and low church parties and proclaimed low churchmen dangerous to the true faith of the high churchmen and, therefore, unworthy defenders of the faith. In other words, here was a general denial of something officially believed to be orthodox. That, of course, is blasphemy in that by implication it denies something which the othodox find in the Holy Scriptures. So it had a dangerous tendency.

JOHN ASGILL—1707.[51]

John Asgill (1659-1738) was a mystical writer, lawyer and also dabbled with problems of statecraft. In 1700 was published his best known work and the one with which we are concerned. Its title page reads: "An argument proving that according to the covenant of eternal life revealed in the Scriptures, man may be translated from hence into that eternal life without passing through death, altho the human nature of Christ Himself could not be thus translated till he had passed through death. Anno Dom. 1700."

---

[51] Dictionary of national biography, .v. 2, pp. 160-161.
An argument to prove that death is not obligatory on Christians, by the celebrated John Asgill, Esq., M. P. with introductory essay,. memoir. notes and ministerial testimony by the Rev. Tresham D. Greeg, D.D. Chaplain of St. Nicholas within, Dublin.
Mr. Asgill's defense upon his expulsion from the house of commons of Great Britain in 1707. London 1881, p. 79. Heywood.
An argument proving that according to the covenant of eternal life revealed in the scripture, man may be translated hence into that eternal life without passing through death, although the human nature of Christ himself could not be so translated till he passed through death.
Journal of House of Commons of Ireland. 1702, v. 111, pp. 15-16, 46.
Journal of House of Commons of England. 1707. Nov.-Dec., v. 15, pp. 440, 445, 449, 455, 473-4.
Digest of Law concerning Libels, 1765, pp. 40, 44.
Farrer, James Anson. Books condemned to be burnt, pp. 144 to 147.

About this time he went to Ireland where professional opportunities seemed alluring. Asgill's printer thought him mad and the reputation was, as he said, useful to him in Ireland by increasing his notoriety. He was elected a member of the Irish House of Commons.

That body ordered the above pamphlet to be burnt by the hangman. The resolution adopted Sept. 21, 1703, reads in part as follows: "Resolved, nemine contradicenti, that the said book contains in it several heretical and blasphemous doctrines and positions contrary to the Christian religion and the established doctrine of the Church of Ireland and destructive of human society."

Asgill, not being present, was ordered, at a time fixed, to be dealt with by the House. At the appointed time, Oct. 10, 1702, he was heard in his own behalf, after which it was: "Resolved, nemine contradicente, that John Asgill, Esq., a Member of this House, be expelled this House, and be ever hereafter incapable of being chosen, returned or sitting a Member in any succeding Parliament in this Kingdom."

Soon he returned to England, was elected to Parliament, and sat from Oct., 1705, until Dec. 18, 1707. At that time his troublemaking book having been again investigated and a committee reporting such passages as are contrary to and reflect upon the Christian religion, Asgill was expelled and the book for the third time ordered burnt. Following is part of the committee's report:

"Then the committee took into consideration what passages are used in said book contrary to and reflecting upon the Christian religion; which they find to be as followeth, viz:

"*Page 7th.* 'Now the assertion of Christ concerning Himself was that man by Him may live forever. And this is that magnetick which hath drawn all the world after Him.'

"*Page 8th.* 'Now if these words of his are words only, then was He an impostor and His doctrine is false.

" 'But if this assertion of Himself be true, that, man by Him may live forever, then all our attempts beneath

this are mean and cowardly, as counting ourselves unworthy of eternal life.'

"*Page 24th.* 'Such was the death of Christ, without
a precedent, without a name, without a reason, without a
cause: 'They hated Me without a cause.' But they were
all against him because God was against Him.'

"*Page 35th.* 'Had Christ thus become man, and died,
and rose again, all voluntarily to try an experiment, He
had only saved His own life, and left all the world to
shift for themselves.

" 'But this would have been Knight-errantry in tempting God—against which He hath sufficiently declared
Himself.'

"*Page 36th.* 'The Devil told Eve, that, they might eat,
and not die.

" 'And these were the first words spoken to man by
God or the Devil; upon the truth or falsehood whereof the
very Beings of them both were to depend forever; for
which ever of them could maintain the truth of his word
against the other, he must have been God, and the other
the Devil.

" 'And, therefore, God having turned the lie upon the
Devil, he is from thence called a liar from the beginning,
and the father of it, and will never be believed again forever.

" 'God could not have dispensed with his word without
complimenting the Devil with his Godhead in taking the
lie upon himself. And this he could not do—for God
cannot lie without undeifying himself; and this he can't
do, because all his qualities being of his essence he can't
change them.'

"*Page 51st.* 'And after that it was no matter to man
whether Christ had ever given satisfaction to God or not.
We might have said to God, *Look thou to that.*'

"*Page 78th.* 'We don't think ourselves fit to deal with
one another in human affairs till our age of one-and-
twenty. But to deal with our Maker thus offended, to
counter-plot the malice of fallen angels, and to rescue
ourselves from eternal ruin, we are generally as well

qualified for before we can speak plain as all our life time after."

"*Page 82d.* 'But what is it that you do, or would believe of him, or in him?'

" '*Why, we believe him for our Saviour.*'

" 'Save you from what?''

" '*Why! from our sins.*'

" 'Why, what hurt will sin do you?'

" '*Why, it will kill us.*'

" 'How do you know?'

" '*Why, the law of God saith so: 'In the day thou eatest thereof thou shalt die!*'

" 'Why, but then will not the Saviour save you from this law, and from this death?'

" '*No, no. He'll save us from sin?*'

" 'Why, then it seems you've got a pardon for horse stealing, with a *non obstante* to be hanged.'

" 'Do but see now, what a jest you have made of your faith. And yet I defy the order of priesthood to form a better creed than this, without admitting the truth of my argument; or to make sense of their own faith without adding mine to it.

" 'It is much easier to make a creed, than to believe it after it is made.'

"*Page 95th.* 'But when that is done, I know no business I have with the dead; and, therefore, do as much depend that I shall not go hence by returning to the dust —which is the sentence of that law from which I claim a discharge—but that I shall make my exit by way of translation, which I claim as a dignity belonging to that degree of the science of eternal life, of which I profess myself a graduate, according to the true meaning and intent of the covenant of eternal life revealed in the Scriptures.'

" 'And if, after this, I die like other men, I declare myself to die of no religion.'

"*Page 98th.* 'Therefore, to be even with the world at once, he that wonders at my faith, I wonder at his unbelief.'

" 'And, stare at me as long as you will, I am sure that neither my physiognomy, sins, nor misfortunes, can make me so unlikely to be translated as my Redeemer was to be hanged."

"Then John Asgill, Esquire, was heard in his place in relation to the said report concerning the said book.

"And the title of the said book was read.

"Resolved, that in the book intituled, 'An argument proving that according to the Covenant of Eternal Life revealed in the Scriptures, man may be translated from hence into that eternal life without passing through death, although the human nature of Christ Himself could not be thus translated till He had passed through death,' are contained many *profane and blasphemous* expressions highly reflecting upon the Christian Religion.

"Ordered, that the said book be burnt by the hands of the common hangman, in the new Palace yard, Westminster, upon Saturday next, between the hours of 12 and 1, and that the Sheriffs of London and Middlesex do assist the Sergeant-at-arms attending this House in seeing the same done."

"Resolved, that John Asgill, Esquire, having in his place owned himself to be author of said book, be expelled this House."

Our blasphemer now published "Mr. Asgill's defense upon his expulsion from the House of Commons of Great Britain in 1707." In his account of the discussion it appears that the doctrines of his book constituted "a crime higher than high treason." While in the Irish House the vote was unanimous, in England it stood 165 to 109 against Asgill.

In 1875, Ennis Bros., of New York City, republished in one volume all of the above documents, together with some biographical data from Chamber's Encyclopaedia and an endorsement of Asgill's main position by Rev. Tresham Dames Gregg, D.D.

Do our constitutions now permit of the prosecution of these publishers because those doctrines were declared blasphemous under the common law?

XVII.
PROSECUTIONS FOR CRIMES
AGAINST RELIGION.
1707-1818.

READ'S CASE—1707.[52]

In Queen against Read, there is only this brief memoranda: "Par Curiam. *A crime that shakes religion,* as profaneness on the stage, &c., *is indictable,* but writing an obscene book, as that entitled, 'The Fifteen Plagues of a Maidenhead,' is not indictable, but punishable in the spiritual courts." Lord Holt presided in this case and arrested judgment after conviction.

JOHN CLENDON—1709.[53]

In this case the book ordered to be burnt deal with the subject of the Trinity, and bore the following title: "Tractatus Philosophico-Theologicus de Persona; or a Treatise of the Word Person * * * London, 1710." It was said to be "a libellous reflection on the trinity." In this case no further biographical or other information was found.

JOHN HUMPHRIES—1709.[54]

John Humphrey (1621-1719), an ejected minister, says the Dictionary of National Biography, had "his pamphlet on the sacramental tests burned by the hangman, but on

---

[52] 11 Modern Reports, 142.
Fortescue 98. This is the fuller report.
Howell's, State trials, vol. 17, 157, note.
2 Strange, pp. 789-790. Read's case cited.

[53] Queen v. Clendon, cited 2 Strange 780.
Tractatus philosophico-theologicus de persona.
Farrer, James Anson. Books condemned to be burnt, p. 159.
Digest of law concerning libels (1765).
Folkard's, Starkie, Law of Libel and slander, 5th edition, p. 615.

[54] Dictionary of national biography, vol. 28, pp. 235-6.
Wilson, Walter. Memoirs of the life and times of Daniel Defoe, * * * Lond. 1830, vol. 3, p. 52.
Farrer, James Anson. Books condemned to be burnt, p. 154.

admitting the authorship at the bar of the House of Commons he was dismissed without further censure."

Farrer states the case thus:

"Parliament ordered to be burnt by the hangman a pamphlet against the Test, which one John Humphrey, an aged Noncomformist minister, had written and circulated among the members of Parliament. There seems to be no record of the pamphlet's name; and I only guess it may be a work entitled, *A Draught for a National Church accommodation, whereby the subjects of North and South Britain, however different in their judgments concerning Episcopacy and Presbytery, may yet be united* (1709). For, to suggest union or compromise or reconciliation between parties is generally to court persecution from both."

To argue for more tolerance tends to disturb the tyrannous peace of government and is a denial of Holy Writ which commands persecution. Therefore, it may be called either sedition or blasphemy.

HALL'S CASE—1709.[55]

Rex v. Hall was "an information for a libel against the doctrine of the Trinity." Beyond this information and the statement that the defendant was the author, the legal report gives nothing. According to Holt, the book involved was, "Sober reply to the Merry Argument about the Trinity." A conviction was secured. No biographical data was found, but doubtless this is the same man and the same book mentioned hereafter, Joseph Hall, 1720.

MATHEW TINDAL—1710.[56]

Mathew Tindal (1653?-1733) graduated from Oxford B. A., 1676, B. C. L., 1679, D. C. L., 1685, and elected to a

[55] 1 Strange Reports, p. 416.
Holt on libel, 2nd edition, p. 67.
Digest concerning the law of libels [1765].
Folkard's Starkie, Law of libel & Slander, 5th edition, p. 616.
[56] Dictionary of national biography, v. 56, pp. 403-5.
The rights of the Christian Church asserted against the Romish and other priests who claim an independent power over it. With a preface concerning the Church of England, second edition, 1706. Third edition, 1707.
A second defence of the rights of the christian church, occasioned by two late indictments against a bookseller and his servant for

law fellowship at All Souls' in 1678.   In the reign of
James II. Tindal became for some time a Roman Catholic,
returning to the Church of England in 1687, becoming
later a deist. "Tindal was admitted as an advocate at
Doctors' Commons on 13 Nov., 1685, and after the Revolution was consulted by ministers upon some questions of
international law." He was the author of many pamphlets.

After publishing his book, "The Rights of the Christian
Church," Tindal "became one of the most hated antago-
nists of the high church party." The book was ordered by
the House of Commons to be burnt March 1710.

Before this (Dec., 1707) Richard Sare, a bookseller, and
his journeyman, Mr. Williams, together with the author
of the last named book (third edition) were presented by
the grand jury. Later the case was removed to the King's
bench by Certiorari and there a new indictment was preferred against Mr. Sare.

He wrote a "Second Defence" and therein reproduced
the offending passages from the first. Fortunately this
is accessible in the material parts will now be quoted.

"And now we will examine the Passages themselves,
and the first is, p. 78. *A Clergyman, 'tis said, is God's*

selling one of said books. In a letter from a gentleman in London
to a clergyman in the country * * * London, 1708. .
A letter to a friend: occasioned by the presentment of the grand
jury for the county of Middlesex, of the author, printer and publisher of a book entitled the rights of the christian church asserted.
London, 1708.
Blasphemy as old as the creation, or, the Newgate divine * * * A
satyr [in verse, against M. Tindal] by a gentleman and a christian
[1730].
Hillard, S. A narrative of the prosecution of Mr. Sare and his
servant for selling the "Rights of the christian church" in answer
to what relates to that prosecution in the second part of the De-
fence of the said book, 1709.
The religious, rational and moral conduct of Matthew Tindal, LL.D.,
late fellow of All Souls College in Oxford. In a letter to a friend.
By a member of the same College. London, 1735, p. 65.
Memoirs of the life and writings of Matthew Tindall.
General biography, composed by John Aiken and William Johnston.
London, 1814, vol. 9, p. 434.
The general biographical dictionary. London, 1816, vol. 29, pp.
391-400.
Farrer, J. Anson. Books condemned to be burnt, p. 159.
Leland John. A view of the principle deistical writer, fifth edition.
London, 1798, v. 1, p. 124.

*Embassador, therefore, the People neither Collective or
Representative can make one, because they have no Power
to send Embassadors from Heaven. But taking Embassadors in that sense, it will, I'm afraid, prove there are now
no Clergymen, since they who pretend to the sole Power
of making 'em, can as little send an Embassador from
God, who alone chuses his own Embassadors. Christ, and
his Apostles, as they were commissioned by God, so they
brought their Credentials with 'em visible to Mankind,
viz. the Power of working Miracles: But what Credential,
or what Mission can these Gentlemen pretend to? or what
Gospel, never before known to the World, are they to discover? Are they not at the best only Commentators, Note-
makers, or Sermon-makers on those Doctrines which the
Embassadors of God once deliver'd to the Saints? which
many of 'em have render'd by their absurd Glosses and
false Comments so perplext and intricate, that only a new
Commission from Heaven seems able to set 'em in their
due Light; yet they do not scruple to call their Pulpit-
Speeches, the* Word of God, *and apply those Texts to themselves, which belong only to the Embassadors of God.*
* * *

"The next Passage I shall take notice of is in p. 108.
*Among Christians, one no more than another can be reck-
on'd a Priest from Scripture, because the only Sacrifices
of our Religion are* Prayers, Praises, *and* Thanksgivings;
*which every one of the Congregation offers for himself:
and there's no more reason to affirm that the Minister offers
up the Peoples' Prayers, than they his; unless it can be
suppos'd that God hears him only who talks loudest, in
that he's the Servant of the Congregation, being imploy'd
by 'em to speak with an audible Voice, that all may join
together in offering up the same Prayers. And the Clerk
has as good a Title to the Priesthood as the Parson; since
the People join with him in offering up their Sacrifices of
Spiritual Songs, Hymns, and Thanksgivings. To make
this pertinent to the present purpose; Does not every one
as well as the Minister equally apply the Bread and Wine
to the same Holy and Spiritual Use, in commemorating
the Benefits receiv'd by our Saviour, and in offering up*

the same Prayers, and desiring the same Blessings? And whoever does this with a due Application of Mind, rightly consecrates the Elements for himself, since this is the only Consecration they are capable of: Any thing further than this may rather be call'd Conjuration than Consecration. * * *

"The next Passage that I shall consider is recited in the first Indictment only, and is taken from pag. 151. The words are: *The Jews when they came out of the Land of Bondage were under no settled Government, till God was pleas'd to offer himself to be their King, to which all the People expressly consented; and upon the Covenant's being ratify'd after the most solemn manner as could be, God gave them those Laws, which bound no Nation except those that had agreed to the* Horeb *Contract.*"

It may be worth while to quote a little of the comment made by the author, in order to make plainer the democratic issues involved. After quoting Grotius, Erasmus and others in his support, our author continues thus:

"As this Opinion allows the Magistrate (the Scripture being wholly silent in this Matter) to appoint for the National Church after what manner the Sacrament shall be receiv'd; so likewise it permits private Churches to agree amongst themselves about the way and method of taking the Sacrament, as they judge most proper for their Circumstances. And nothing, as I know, can be said against it, but what is urg'd by the learned Mr. *Dodwel* in his Premonition to his Discourse of the Natural Mortality of the Soul.

"If Judges and Jurys can think that the end of instituting the Sacrament was to subject the Laity to the Clergy, under the pain of being depriv'd of the ordinary means of Salvation; then indeed the Publisher of the *Rights* may be in some danger: But if they are not of that opinion, they will hardly think themselves oblig'd to their own Clergy for not showing (as I know none of them that has; the least dislike to this absurd Hypothesis. And the Abetters of this Prosecution seem to have no other design in having this Passage of the Rights condemn'd, than to obtain a Judgment against 37 *H*. 8. *cap*. 17. and the rest

of the Laws which make the Prince the Fountain of all
Ecclesiastical as well as Civil Jurisdiction; who can upon
an Appeal not only revoke the spiritual Censures of any
Bishop or Archbishop, but likewise for just causes excommunicate them.

"The next Passage I shall consider is *Pag.* 105, and in
the first Indictment (it's left out in the second) runs thus:
*To which Christ, who instituted no new Rites, superadded
the Remembrance of his Sufferings, and directs his Disciples as often as they did this, that is, celebrate such Festivals, and close them with the Postcœnium.* Here the
Promoter of the Prosecution begins and ends in the middle of a Sentence; and all the Conclusion which can be
drawn from it is, That he, if he knew how, would have
something to present; and will make nonsense of what
he presents, rather than not present at all. What he
should have presented, as it stands intire in the *Rights,* is,
*The Passover and other Festivals among the Jews were
never celebrated in the Temple or Synàgogue, but in their
private houses, where, as* Grotius *observes, they invited
their Kindred, Friends and Neighbors, to the number of
above ten, but under twenty; which* Josephus *calls a Fra-
ternity: and at the close of the Supper, the great Meal
with them, the Master of the Feast distributed among his
Guests small Pieces of the finest Bread; and having first
drank of the Grace-Cup, deliver'd it to be handed about.
All this was accompany'd with Thanks to God for having
created Bread and Wine, which was follow'd by some Relation suitable to the Festival, and the Eucharisty or Hymn
of Thanksgiving; to which Christ, who instituted no new
Rites, superadded the Remembrance of his Sufferings, and
directs his Disciples as often as they did this, that is, celebrate such Festivals, and close them with the* Postcœnium,
to commemorate him after this manner. Had the Informer
put this down at length, and withal mention'd it as a
Quotation from *Grotius,* he had done fairly; but he apprehended that a Jury would not upon his Authority present
as criminal what the ablest Commentator on the Scripture
had said in a Point relating to the Jewish Customs: And
I defy the Informer to produce any one Person compe-

tently skill'd in Jewish Antiquitys that contradicts *Grotius.* * * *

"The next Passage I shall take notice of is in *P.* 80. *What's more requir'd to give one a Right to exercise the Office of a Minister in any particular Congregation, than an Agreement amongst them to chuse a Person capable and willing to take upon him that Function, and consent to hear him say Prayers, preach, and administer the Sacraments? And what is depriving or deposing him, except agreeing not to hear him any longer, or own him any more for their Minister? And this private Churches may do by a Right natural to all Societys whatever, since it's only a Liberty of their own Actions in hearing or not hearing such a Person pray or preach, and in receiving or not receiving the Sacraments from him.* * * *

"But to make the Rights to be against the State as well as the Church this Passage in p. 233 is inserted in the Indictment: *The Reason why the People may on just Grounds withdraw their Allegiance from the Civil Magistrate, is, Because all the Power he has is given him by them, in order to act for their Good; and they who depute him, must needs reserve to themselves a Power to Judg, whether their Deputy acts according to the Trust lodg'd in him.*

"The word *Magistrate,* in this Passage, can't upon any fair Construction be apply'd to the Person, to whom by our Constitution Allegiance is due; because the Author, in the beginning of his Book, declares in what sense he uses that word in the ensuing Discourse; and says, *By Magistrate I mean him or them who have the Supreme or Legislative Power:* and consequently Allegiance is not due to any such, but where the Legislative and Executive Power is in the same hands. But were this out of the Case, if any thing is criminal in this Passage, it must be supposing either that the Magistrate derives his Power from the People, or that there are no Causes which can justify them in withdrawing their Allegiance; or else tho there are such Causes, yet they have no Right to judg when they happen.

"If Mankind have not a sufficient Power from God (as

everything they have is from him) to form themselves
into Political Societys, and entrust some of their Body
with the Administration of their Affairs; then (since
there is no Medium) God himself, without any Consent of
the Partys, must have miraculously form'd all the Civil
Governments which have been in the World; and all those,
whether in Elective or any other Governments, which have
had the whole or any share in the Legislative Power, must
have had it without any human Intervention, by an immediate Commission from God.

"But if this be Infinitely absurd, then it is evident, that
the People are sufficiently authoris'd by God to chuse their
own Governors, and that all Political Power must be de-
riv'd from the Consent of the Partys concern'd: who, as
'tis impossible they sho'd desire their own Hurt, or not
act (especially in so important a Matter) but for their
own good; so it's impossible that they shou'd be willing
to pay Allegiance to any Person, except they thought it
for their Good, or continue to give it him any longer than
they judg'd so. And tho it be said, that it is never for
their good to withdraw their Allegiance, for fear of the
great mischief of Resistance; yet whether this be true or
no, it's unavoidable but they must judg of it.

"But if this were true, it would equally hold true with
relation to every other Invader: since there is no other
difference, than that the Oppression would be more intolerable from one who had all the Obligation in the world
to defend the People from all Oppression. Nay, if the
Mischief of Resistance were too great, it would be Folly
and Madness in every body to defend themselves against
all Highway-men and House-breakers.

"Were this allow'd as a Principle, That tho the People
had Rights, yet they had no Right to defend those Rights
against a Person who had no Right to take them away; all
distinction between Free and Arbitrary Governments
would be lost, and Men would hold their Propertys, Liber-
tys and Lives, as precariously in one place as in another;
since their *All* would depend alike on Will and Pleasure."

We have quoted the offending passages and a little of
the author's anonymous self-defence to make the practical

issues clear. It was all a matter of loaves and fishes, under a system where church and state presented only different aspects of the same thing. Whoever sought to promote change or more democracy was dangerous to the peace of the realm, that is the beneficiaries of legalized injustice and vested wrongs. Under our constitutions there can be no place for penalizing psychologic tendencies.

JOSEPH HALL—1720.[57]

On February 12th, 1720, the Lords condemned a work which, it is said, in a daring, impious manner, ridiculed the doctrine of the Trinity and all revealed religion, and was called, "A Sober Reply to Mr. Higgs' Merry Arguments from the Light of Nature for the Tritheistic Doctrine of the Trinity, with a Postscript relating to the Rev. Dr. Waterland." This work, which was the last to be burnt as an offence against religion, was the work of one Joseph Hall, who was a gentleman and a serjeant-at-arms to the King, and in this way won his small title to fame.

DR. MEAD—1723.[58]

"In 1723, a prominent physician named Dr. Mead purchased from the Landgrave of Hesse a copy of the Christianismi Restitutio of Servetus. This copy was reputed to have belonged to Colodon, one of the unhappy man's accusers. Dr. Mead took measures to publish the work in quarto; but before the completion the sheets were seized by order of Dr. Gibson, bishop of London, and burned May 27. One copy that escaped is now in the library of the Medical Society of London. In 1770 a reprint was issued, but was all destroyed except a very few copies. Dr. Mead's volume found its way into the collection of the Duc de la Valliere; and at the sale of this library was purchased for the Imperial Library of France."

[57] Farrer, James Anson.   Books condemned to be burnt, p. 172.
[58] Vickers, Robert H. Maryrdoms of Literature, p. 387-8.

BERNHARD MAUDEVILLE—1723-1728.[59]

Bernhard Maudeville (1670- ?) was interesting, face-tious, paradoxical and satirical. One of his performances, "The Fable of the Bees," was attacked by many prominent literary men, and has been published probably in more than a dozen editions. A few praised it. One said: "The most remarkable philosophical work of its time." The Grand Jury of Middlesex presented the book as a nuisance in July, 1723, and twice after that. However, I cannot find that any record of the trial has been preserved. It is possible that the sacriligious features were not sufficiently pronounced or partisan to make it blasphemous, and there was no precedent to make it punishable purely for its "immorality" as such.

However, one of the presentments and some discussion of it have been preserved and parts thereof perhaps are worth reproducing, as further exhibiting the workings of the censorial minds of that time. This same grand jury of 1728 also presented the case against Woolston here-inafter reported.

"So restless have these Zealots for Infidelity been in their diabolical Attempts against Religion, that they have,

"First, Openly blasphemed and denied the Doctrine of the ever-blessed Trinity, endeavoring by specious Pre-tences to revive the *Arian Heresy, which was never intro-duc'd into any Nation, but the Vengeance of Heaven pur-su'd it.*

"Secondly, They affirm an absolute Fate, and deny the Providence and Government of the Almighty in the World.

"Thirdly, They have endeavoured to subvert all Order and Discipline of the Church, and by vile and unjust Reflections on the Clergy, they strive to bring Contempt

---

[59] Allibone, Dictionary of authors. (Maudeville B. de) pp. 1211-12.
Dictionary of national biography, v. 36, pp. 21-22.
A cordial for bow spirits, being a collection of tracts * * *. By Gordon, p. 257.
Wickliffe, John. Remarks upon two late presentments of the grand-jury of the country of Middlesex, * * *, London, 1729.
The presentment of the grand-jury of the county of Middlesex. 1723, p.

on all Religion, that by the Libertinism of their Opinions, they may encourage and draw others into the Immoralities of their Practice.

"Fourthly, That a general Libertinism may the more effectually be established, the Universities are decried, and all Instructions of Youth, in the Principles of the Christian Religion are exploded with the greatest Malice and Falsity.

"Fifthly, The more effectually to carry on these Works of Darkness, studied Artifices, and invented Colours, have been made use of to run down Religion and Virtue, as prejudicial to Society, and detrimental to the State; and to recommend Luxury, Avarice, Pride, and all kind of Vices, as being necessary to Public Welfare, and not tending to the Destruction of the Constitution: Nay, the very Stews themselves have had strained Apologies, and forced Encomiums, made in their Favour, and produced in Print, with design, we conceive, to debauch the Nation.

"These Principles having a direct Tendency to the Subversion of all Religion and Civil Government, our Duty to the Almighty, our Love to our Country, and Regard to our Oaths, oblige us to present,

"The Publishers of a Book, entituled, The Fable of the Bees, or, Private Vices, Publick Benefits, second Edition, 1723, And also,

"The Publishers of a Weekly Paper, call'd the British Journal, Numb. 26, 35, 36, and 39." (pp. 2, 3)

"The Doctrine of the ever-blessed Trinity has been exploded, the Authority of the Holy Scriptures deny'd, and a *Freedom of thinking* and acting *whatever Men please, (if done in Sincerity,* as it is called,) *is substituted instead of the Principles of the Gospel.* * * * (p. 4)

"We forbear to wound the Ears of this Honourable Court, by a particular mention of those many blasphemous Passages which have been published in Books of late. (p. 5)

"We the Grand-Jury do most humbly present the Author, Printers and Publishers of a Book entituled, The Fable of the Bees, or, Private Vices, Publick Benefits, with an Essay on Charity and Charity-Schools, and a Search

into the Nature of Society, the fifth Edition; to which is
added, a Vindication of the Book from the Aspersions
contained in a Presentment of the Grand-Jury of Middlesex. London, printed for J. Tonson, at Shakespear's-
Head, over-against Catherine-street, in the Strand, 1728.

"And we beg Leave humbly to observe, that this infamous and scandalous Book, entituled, The Fable of the
Bees, &c. was presented by the Grand-Jury of this County,
to this Honourable Court, in the Year 1723; yet notwithstanding the said Presentment, and in Contempt thereof,
an Edition of this Book has been published; together with
the Presentment of the said Grand-Jury, with scandalous
and infamous Reflections thereon, in the present Year
1728.

"We present also the Author, Printers and Publishers
of five blasphemous, impious, and scandalous Pamphlets,
entituled, A Discourse on the Miracles of our Saviour, in
view of the present Controversy, between Infidels and
Apostates, the fourth Edition, by Thomas Woolston, sometime Fellow of Sidney-College in Cambridge. London,
printed for the Author, sold by him next door to the Star
in Aldermanbury, and by the Booksellers of London and
Westminster, 1728.

"The second Discourse, with the like Title, the second
Edition, printed 1727.

"The third, the second Edition, printed 1728.

"The fourth, the second edition, printed 1728.

"The fifth, printed 1728.

"In the Title-Page of every of the said five blasphemous
"Pamphlets, it is inserted, that the same are printed for
"Thomas Woolston the Author thereof." (pp. 5, 6)

EDWARD ELWALL—1726.[60]

Edward Elwall (1676-1744) seems to have started in
life as a presbyterian, and as such was the victim of a

---

[60] The triumph of truth being an account of the trial of Mr. Elwall
before Judge Denton, for publishing a book in defense of the
unity of God; at the Stafford assizes in the year 1726. London,
printed for the Unitarian Society, 1816.
Dictionary of national biography, v. 17, pp. 340-342.
Aspland, L. M. Law of blasphemy, * * * London, 1884, p. 10.

high church mob. After this he became converted to the Baptists, still later John Hays converted him to Unitarianism, and entered upon some controversies in defence of his new faith, and also adopted some of the thought and literary eccentricities of the Quakers, probably because of sympathy with Penn. In this latter stage of development he became conspicuous as a sabatarian, closing his shop on Saturday and opening it on Sunday. He had much reputation for fair dealing and made quite a bit of money. He discarded his wig, raised a long beard, and wore a long blue mantle in the form of a Turkish habit out of respect for the unitarian faith of the Mahometans. There were also other pronounced eccentricities.

In 1724 he published his "True Testimony for God, and his sacred law, being a plain, honest defence of the first commandment of God against all Trinitarians under Heaven, 'Thou shalt have no other God before me'," which led to a local controversy and a prosecution for blasphemy. Elwall himself wrote an account of his trial, which had three editions in the author's lifetime. From the second edition of its publication the Unitarians made a reprint in 1816. This seems to be the only account accessible in America. For this edition, Priestley wrote a preface in which he expresses the opinion that Elwall "had certainly acted contrary to the express laws of this country, according to which this glorious man ought to have been sentenced to a severe punishment, as a convicted and avowed blasphemer." Some mention of the trial is made by Elwall in a treatise entitled "A declaration against all kings and temporal powers under heaven", printed in 1732. This I have not been able to consult.

Elwall tells us they quoted "many pages" of his book in the indictment which later was "near as big as half a door." This defendant pleaded his own cause which consisted of a dignified justification of his opinion made wholly from Bible texts, coupled with a denunciation of "that hell born principle of persecution and that it was hatched in hell", again making his justification from the Bible.

Judge Denton presided at the trial. After the close of
the defendant's argument, Robert Humpatch, a justice
of the peace, laid his hand on the shoulder of Judge Denton, and bore testimony to Elwall's honesty based upon
experience with him, as a next door neighbor for three
years. Also another justice spoke to the same effect. The
fact that Elwall seemed to have made honest effort by an
appeal to the archbishop of Canterbury for correction of
his views about the trinity seems also to have counted in
his favor. After this relation, he again pointed to the
difference between "things that are of a temporay nature
and concern civil society" and those "things that are of
a spiritual nature and concern my faith, my worship of
God and a future state". In the former he declared obedience, in the latter he repudiated their claim of jurisdiction. After a whispered conversation among the justices,
Elwall was asked to promise to write no more upon this
subject wherein he had given grave offence to his neighbors. Again he denied their right to exact the promise by
refusing to give it. Elwall says: "I perceived the Judge
was not in any wise displeased at my honest, plain, bold
answer; but rather in his heart seemed to be knit in love
to me, and he soon declared me acquitted."

Thus far it does not appear as though a jury had been
empanelled though a subsequent statement at least suggests a doubt. He mentions the judge's expression of
acquittal and the clerk's words discharging him, but
makes no mention of the empaneling or submission to a
jury or its verdict. The general precision of his account
suggests the great improbability of his silence upon that
subject, had a jury been empaneled. I conclude from this
somewhat uncertain narrative that the judges in effect
discharged the defendant upon the technical ground that
the facts stated did not constitute blasphemy and that
they were moved to this conclusion, not by applying the
law as they found it, but rather upon the purely personal
consideration that the defendant was known to them to
be a sincere man, who was quite harmless, because his
blasphemy was quite dissociated from those active sects
whose religious rebellion was but a part of their activities

toward promoting civil rebellion and political democracy. In other words unitarian blasphemy was politically harmless and not criminal, when unconnected with democratic desires.

WOOLSTON'S CASE—1729.[61]

Thomas Woolston was a fellow of Sidney College, Cambridge. He was indicted for this "blasphemous publication: 'A Discourse on the Miracles of our Savior, in view of the present controversy between Infidels and Apostates' ". Each of the five editions were presented, as appeared in our account of Mauderville's troubles. Woolston was convicted on four counts.

The report reads as follows: "The defendant having published several discourses on the miracles of Christ, in which he maintained that the same are not to be taken in a literal sense, but that the whole relation of the life and miracles of our Lord Christ in the New Testament is but an allegory, several informations were brought against him, in which it was laid that the defendant published those discourses, with an intent to vilify and subvert the Christian religion; and he being found guilty, Mr. Wooley moved in arrest of judgment, that those discourses did not amount to a libel upon Christianity, *since the Scriptures are not denied but construed* and taken in a different meaning from that they are usually understood in; *and by the same reason that making such a construction should be punishable by the common law,* so it would have been punishable by the common law before the Reformation to have taken the doctrine of transubstantiation allegorically; * * *. Raymond, Chief Justice: *Christianity in general is parcel of the common law of England and therefore to be protected by it.* Now whatever strikes at the very root of Christianity tends manifestly to a dissolution of

[a] Fitzgibbons report, p. 64.
2 Strangs, p. 834, cited 3 Merivale, p. 379.
1 Bernardiston's report, p. 162.
Holt on libels, p. 67, second edition.
Digest law concerning libels (1765), p. 58.
Folkard's Starkie. Law of slander & libel, 5th edition, p. 616.
Leland, John. A view of the principal deistical writers, vol. 1, p. 112, fifth edition, Lond. 1798.
Aspland, L. M. Law of blasphemy, 1884, p. 7.

the Civil government; and so was the opinion of my Lord Hale in Taylor's case. So that to say, an attempt to subvert the established religion is not punishable by those laws upon which it is established is an absurdity; if this were an entirely new case, I should not think it a proper question to be made; I would have it taken notice of, that we do not meddle with any differences of opinion, and that we interpose only where the very root of Christianity itself is struck at, *as it plainly is by this allegorical scheme,* the New Testament and the whole relation of the life and miracles of Christ, being denied; and who can find this allegory?"

Another report contains this: "Though there were professions in the book, that the design of it was to establish Christianity upon a true bottom, by considering these narratives in Scripture as emblematical and prophetical, the court said those professions could not be credited. * * *

"But the second of these points, the court said they would not suffer to be argued; for the Christian religion is established in this Kingdom; and therefore they would not allow any books to be writ, which would *tend to alter that establishment.*"

Woolston's "Discourse on the miracles of our savior" was translated into the French about 1780 by the celebrated Baron de Holbach.

THOMAS ASHLEY—1746.[62]

"The defendant being convicted of printing and publishing several printed Libels, intituled, 'Discourses on the Miracles of our Savior in view of the present Controversy between Infidels and Apostates,' was fined sixty Pounds, and to find two sufficient Sureties for his good Behavior for the Space of two Years, himself in 500£ and the Sureties in 250£ apiece."

---

[62] The King v. Thomas Ashley, Digest law concerning libels (1765) p. 125. Trinity Term, 19 Geo. 2. K. B. MSS.

JACOB ILIVE—1756.[63]

Jacob Ilive (1705-1763) was a type founder, printer, publisher of a magazine and a voluminous author, who wrote largely upon religious subjects. In June 1756 he was sentenced for writing and publishing such deistical literature as is now very common. His offending book was first published anonymously in 1754, under the title "Some Remarks on the excellent Discourses lately published by a very worthy Prelate [Thomas Sherlock] by a Searcher after Religious Truth". Then it was rewritten and enlarged.

"An information was filed * * * against the Defendant, for writing, printing and publishing a prophane and blasphemous Libel, entituled, 'Modest Remarks on the Bishop of London's several Discourses preached in the Temple Church, and lately published in two Volumes Octavo, in a Letter to his Lordship, with a Postscript; containing Dr. Sherlock's Creed, faithfully extracted from his own Writings, by Philostheos. (1 Thes. v. 21) *Prove all things hold fast that which is good;* tending to vilify and subvert the Christian Religion, and to blaspheme our most Blessed Lord and Savior Jesus Christ, and to cause his Divinity to be denied; and to represent him as an Imposter, and to scandalize, ridicule, and bring into Contempt, his most Holy Doctrine Life and Miracles, and also to cause the Truth of the Christian Religion, and the Matter contained in the Holy Scriptures to be disbelieved and totally rejected, by representing the same as spurious, fictitious, and chimerical, and as a gross Piece of Forgery and Priestcraft, and thereby to weaken, enervate, take away and destroy their Force, Influence, and Authority, and also to prejudice, poison, and infect the Minds and religious Principles of the People, by propagating and dispersing among them most impious and wicked Opinions concerning the Truth of all revealed Religion in general, to

---

[63] Dictionary of national biography, v. 28, p. 414.
Folkard's Starkie, Law of slander & libel, 5th edition, p. 617, marginal p. 596.
King v. Ilive, Digest of law concerning libels (1765), p. 83, 84, 126.

the endangering of the public Peace, State, and Government of this Kingdom.

"The Defendant * * * being convicted by his own Confession of writing, printing and publishing a most horrid, blasphemous ad wicked Libel, concerning the Truth of all revealed Religion in general, received the following Sentence to the Court, that he should be committed to Newgate, to be there kept in safe Custody for the Space of one Month; and that within the said Month he should be set in and upon the Pillory at Charing Cross, at the Royal Exchange, and at the End of Chancery-Lane, near Temple-Bar, and at the expiration of said Month he should be committed to the House of Correction of Clerkenwell, to be kept there to hard Labour for the Space of three Years, and at the expiration of the three Years, he should give Security for his good Behavior during Life, himself in the Sum of 100£ and two sufficient Securities in 50£ each and that he should pay a Fine of 6s. 8d. and at the End of the said three Years he should be remanded to Newgate, in execution of the said Judgment."

JAMES DIXWELL & EDWARD CABE—1763.[64]

"The like Information [as against Ilive] was exhibited the same Term against the Defendants [James Dixwell and Edward Cabe] for printing and publishing the [same] above Libel." Manifestly from this brief account the book involved was the same as that involved in the case of Jacob Ilivie already reported, namely: "Remarks on the two volumes of excellent Discourses lately published by the Bishop of London, 1755." [by Thomas Sherlock]

PETER ANNETT—1763.[65]

Peter Annett (1693-1769) was a deistical writer of considerable importance. In 1761 he published nine issues

---

[64] Digest of the law concerning libels, 1765, p. 84.
[65] Starkie, Law of libel, 1876, p. 596.
Folkard's Starkie, Law of slander and libel, 5th edition, (1891), p. 617.
1 Blackstone, William. [p. 395].
Digest of the law concerning libel [1765], pp. 83-84.
Burn's Ecclesiastical law, v. 2.
Dictionary of national biography, v. 2, p. 9.

of *The Free Enquirer,* attacking the Old Testament history. He was tried for blasphemy in 1763. How terrible these diestic opinions appear with the characterization of the indictment, is again illustrated in this case which charges "the defendant for writing, printing and publishing a certain malignant, prophane, and blasphemous libel intituled 'The Free Enquirer' tending to blaspheme Almighty God, and to ridicule, traduce and discredit His Holy Scriptures, and particularly the Pentateuch; to represent and cause it to be believed, that the Prophet Moses was an Imposter, and that the Sacred Truths and Miracles recorded and set forth in the Pentateuch aforesaid were Impostures and false Inventions, and thereby to diffuse and propagate irreligion and diabolical Opinions in the Minds of his Majesty's Subjects, and to shake the Foundations of the Christian Religion, and of the civil and ecclesiastical Government established in this Kingdom."

The defendant pleaded guilty. In consideration of poverty and age (70 yrs.) "and some symptoms of wildness that appeared on his inspection in court" he was let off with one month in Newgate, to stand twice in the pillory with a paper on his forehead inscribed "Blasphemy" and to the house of correction at hard labor for one year and fine of 6s. 6d. and to find security in 100£ for good behavior during life.

After his release he became a school teacher and had among his pupils James Stephen (1758-1832), afterwards Master in Chancery. As a founder of a Shorthand System he had a pupil in the distinguished Joseph Priestly. Annett's writings are of some interest as forming a connecting link between the deism of the early part of the eighteenth century and the more aggressive and outspoken deism of Paine and the revolutionary period.

JOHN WILKES—1764.[66]

An information charged the defendant with "printing and publishing a certain malignant obscene and impious libel entituled 'An Essay on Woman'; tending to vitiate and corrupt the Minds and Morals of his Majesties Sub-

---

[66] Digest of law concerning libels, [1765], p. 86.

jects; and to introduce and difuse amongst the people general Debauchery and Depravity of Manners and a total Contempt of Religion, Modesty and Virtue, and also to blaspheme Almighty God and to ridicule our Blessed Saviour and the Christian Religion." In this case the issues are seemingly confused.

It is believed that several forgeries of the "Essay on Woman" have been published as reprints of the original, which makes it uncertain just what was the basis of this prosecution. It seems probable from an investigation of several of these that the basis of the offence was a blasphemous use of the name of God in the poetic glorification of sexual intercourse and sexual ecstasy.

CHAMBERLAIN OF LONDON V. EVANS—1767.[67]

Reference to the following case is inserted here because it is the first case in which there is any suggestion of a relaxation from the old rule that any denial of any part of the Christian religion is intolerable. Of course, the House of Lords as a body did not approve the official opinion of Lord Mansfield. It is important however, that a man of his prominence should make the distinction between natural religion and revealed religion as to their relationship to the faith; and a distinction between essentials and non-essentials of the Christian religion as defining the limits of toleration. Inadequate as it now seems, that speech by Lord Mansfield was considered almost epoch making.

"In the year 1748 the Corporation of London made a bye-law imposing a fine of £400 upon every person who, being nominated as Sheriff by the Lord Mayor, declined standing the election of the Common Hall, and £600 upon everyone who, being elected, refused to serve the office, which fines were to be appropriated to the cost of building the Mansion House. The Corporation then proceeded to nominate and elect to office Dissenters, who were incapable

[67] Bonner, Hypatia Bradlaugh. Penalties upon opinion, pp. 23-24.
Parliamentary history, v. 26, p. 325.
Furneaux, Philip. Letters to the honorable Mr. Justice Blackstone, concerning his exposition of the Act of Tolerance, London, 1771. Appendix, no. 2, p. 264.

of serving by an Act of 13 Chas. II., which provided that no person should be elected into any Corporation offices who had not taken the sacrament in the Church of England within a year preceding the election. Several Dissenters, of whom one was blind and another bedridden, were elected as Sheriffs, and paid fines to the amount of upwards of £15,000. At length Evans and others refused to pay, urging that they could not be obliged by law to pay a fine for not serving an office to which by law they were ineligible. The City brought actions against them in the Sheriffs' Court—a court of their own—and in 1757 judgment was given in favour of the Corporation. Evans then took his case before the Court of Hustings, another City Court; and the previous judgment was there affirmed by the Recorder in 1759. Evans next, by writ of error, carried his cause before the Court of Judges delegate, called the Court of St. Martin's. The judges were Lord Chief Justice Willes (who died while the case was proceeding), Lord Chief Baron Parker, Mr. Justice Foster, Mr. Justice Bathurst, and Mr. Justice Wilmot. These, in 1762, unanimously reversed the judgment of the Sheriffs' Court and the Court of Hustings. The Corporation then, by writ of error, brought the case before the House of Lords; and in 1767, ten years after the first judgment given in the case, all the judges who had not sat as delegates gave their opinions on the question put to them, which, with one exception, were entirely in favour of Evans and against the Corporation. After the judges had spoken, Lord Mansfield, in his place as a peer, made his famous speech for toleration, which, however, did not seem to include 'Atheists and Infidels,' whom Lord Mansfield dismissed from consideration as not coming within the Toleration Act."

It was in this connection that Lord Mansfield made his famous speech for the toleration of all Christians. The date of it was Feb. 4th, 1767, and the place was the House of Lords. In this speech he gave the world a new view of the relationship of religion and the English Government. The following are his words upon this subject:

"The *eternal principles of Natural Religion* are part of the Common-law: The *essential principles of Revealed*

Religion are part of the Common-Law; so that any person
reviling, subverting, or ridiculing them, may be prosecuted
at Common-law. But it cannot be shown from the principles of Natural or Revealed Religion, that, independent
of positive law, temporal punishments ought to be inflicted
for mere opinions with respect to particular modes of
worship."

WILLIAMS' CASE—1797.[68]

The next case in order is that of: Rex v. Williams. This
prosecution was founded on the publication of Paine's
"Age of Reason," and conviction was had under the common law. In America, Paine's defense of Deism was circulated freely from the beginning of the last century.
Cheap editions have been circulated in England and
America, running, it is said, into millions of copies. So
far as I am informed this book has never been prosecuted
in America, and yet has been constantly on sale, as it is
now. This fact in itself indicates that in the early days
after our revolution, even those who opposed this book
must have taken quite generally for granted that the common law and statutes as to blasphemy had been annulled
by our Constitution. If these Connecticut statutes are in
force, according to the intention and interpretation of
those who passed them, in 1642, then doubtless Yale University is many, many times a criminal for circulating
this book.

But let us return to Lord Kenyon's discussion in that
last case, to discover the intensity of the official Trinitarian aversion to this Unitarian literature; and to redis-
cover the reason of these laws. Lord Kenyon in his instructions to the jury said: "The Christian religion is
part of the law of the land." After the verdict of guilty,
Lord Kenyon further expressed his abhorrence of this
deistical literature in the following remarks: "I have observed several persons, very likely from curiosity, taking
notes of what passed here. This publication is so shocking that I hope nobody will publish this. I mean that
a general denial of it will not make any part of that pub-

---

[68] Howell's state trials, v. 26, pp. 654-713.

lication. Nobody who has any regard to decency; nobody who has any regard to their own interest, will endeavor to disseminate this publication, by publishing what has passed today."

In this case Lord Erskine abandoned his famous rôle of defender of free speech (for all seditious utterances) to take up the prosecution of Williams. In calling for sentence he said: "There is no transaction of my humble life, my Lords, that I look back upon with such heartfelt satisfaction as the share I had in being instrumental in protecting the interests of religion and morals, which most unquestionably are the foundation, not only of all subordination to the government of a country, but to all the interests of civil society, in all parts of the world."

Mr. Justice Ashburst, in pointing out the enormity of William's offence, said: "the minute part of which he would forbear to particularize * * * Such wicked doctrines * * * were not only an offence against God, but against all law and government, from their direct *tendency* to dissolve all bonds and obligations of civil society. It was upon this ground that the *Christian religion constituted part of the law of the land.*"

In spite of the million of copies of Paine's "Age of Reason", that have been freely circulated, governments and Christian religion are jogging along much in the same old way. Beginning with the Williams Case there were many prosecutions on Paine's books. Among the common people of England, Paine's deism and his democracy were having a great effect in promoting the cause of those who disbelieved in the divine right of bishops claiming an apostolic succession, and the divine right of kings built upon a similar foundation.

DANIEL ISAAC EATON—1812.[69]

"No bishop no King". Thus did loyal orthodoxy accuse heretics of disloyalty. To repudiate all claims to apos-

---

[69] Prosecutions for political opinions. (political lectures, etc.) n. t. p. [London, 1790 (?)] 29 p.
The proceedings on the trial of D. I. Eaton, upon an indictment for selling a supposed libel, "the second part of the Rights of Man, combining principle and practice by Thomas Paine, before the

tolic succession in church authorities was psychologically identical with the repudiations of all heredity and divine rights in the political authorities. Thus it was that political and religious democracy were so often combined in the same person. Eaton illustrates this point.

First he appeared as the defender of the rights of the political heretic. Next we hear of his being prosecuted for selling the second part of Paine's "Rights of Man" after which he was again prosecuted for a seditious libel. A report of the trial reads thus: 'Trial of Daniel Isaac Eaton for publishing a supposed libel, comparing the King of England to a game cock, in a pamphlet entituled, Politics for the people; or Hog's wash; at Justice Hall in the Old Bailey, February twenty fourth, 1794. On this last accusation the jury however found him not guilty. The democracy and deism of Paine were but different aspects of the same attitude of mind just as the English Church and State only expressed different phases of the same state of mind.

Lord Ellenborough presided at this blasphemy trial founded upon parts of Paine's "Age of Reason". The sentence of that book upon which most emphasis was placed during the trial follows: "He that believes in the story of Christ is an infidel to God". It appeared during the trial that this book was then being published in Philadelphia.

Lord Ellenborough, in summing up to the jury, among other things said: "Lords Hale and Raymond have been quoted; and at more recent period, lord Kenyon, as expressly stating that *the Christian religion was the law of the land,* and must be protected as the law. * * * The whole object of the work is clearly summed up in the concluding sentence [quoted above] * * * which cannot leave a doubt on your minds as to the *pernicious tendency* of the publication.

"The defendant has told us, that the work was current

Recorder of London, June, 1793. D. I. Eaton, [1793] another edition. London, 1794, 48p.
31 Howell's state trials. pp. 927-958.
The Correspondent, v. 5, p. 223. N. Y. 1829.

in America, and had not been visited by any prosecution in that country. It is for them to administer the affairs of religion as a free state has a right to do; but their conduct is not to influence us. And in a free country, where religion is fenced round by the laws, and where that religion depends on the doctrines which are derived from the sacred writings, *to deny the truth of the book which is the foundation of our faith has never been permitted.*"

The defendant was found guilty. In an argument for leniency it was urged that the late Bishop of Carlisle, Lord Ellenborough's father, "had contended strongly for the necessity of tolerating all infidelity." Mr. Eaton was sentenced to eighteen months in jail and to stand in the pillory two hours at midday each month.

GEORGE HOUSTON—1813.[70]

In 1799 there appeared in Edinborough an anonymous book entitled, Ecce Homo etc., variously ascribed to Baron de Holbach and to Joseph Web (Webbe?.) A second edition was published in 1813. For this latter publication George Houston was convicted as the publisher of blasphemy, and sent for two years to Newgate and fined 200£. Later Houston went to America and there edited *Minerva* (1822, *et seq.*) and *The Correspondent* (1827-1830). Here he republished the blasphemous book in 1827.

Houston confessed himself the author of "Life of Jesus Christ," for such was its character. It is rather erudite for its time and very harmless indeed. The following is his account of the events.

"The first edition of the following work [Ecce Homo] was printed at Edinburgh in the year 1799; but it was not till 1813, when a second edition appeared in London, that it was publicly announced by the author. Two years imprisonment, and a fine of two hundred pounds sterling, was the consequence of this fearless act; and to justify so wanton an outrage the *pious* instigators of it sheltered

---

[70] Biographical dictionary of freethinkers, London, 1889, p. 177.
Ecce Homo! or a critical inquiry into the history of Jesus of Nazereth: being a rational analysis of the gospels. First American edition revised and corrected, New York. 1827.
The Correspondent, v. 1, pp. 109-128, also vol. 5, p. 223.

themselves under the fallacious plea, that the religion
which the writer attacked, was 'a part of the law of the
land, and therefore must be protected:' Thus tacitly
acknowledging, that they were incapable of maintaining
it without the assistance of the *civil* power."

JOHN WRIGHT—1817.[71]

The sworn information makes the blasphemy of Wright
to consist in this: "belief in the Doctrine of the Holy
Trinity was absurd and ridiculous;"—"that is was folly
to believe in what was called the atonement of the death
of Jesus Christ, as it was impious to suppose that a good
being would take an innocent victim to atone for the sins
of the wicked;"—"that as the idea of the soul surviving
the body was an absurd and ridiculous mental delusion,
that the idea of a future state was equally so."

Afterwards Wright published the sermon upon which
this charge was based, deeming it his best justification and
refutation. It appears therefrom that instead of the *atonement* of Jesus he had advocated the doctrine of *reconciliation* through Jesus; he did affirm the Divine Unity and
he denied a Separate State, which he affirms is not a
denial of a future State.

It has recently been asserted that a guess as to the
psychologic tendency of such metaphysical quibbles is the
determining factor in deciding whether or not a crime
has been committed. After the publication of the whole
sermon the case seems to have been dismissed without
trial. Evidently this court did not think to submit such
issues to a jury.

In the "Preliminary Remarks" for his published sermon Wright insists of Christianity that "its denunciation
are not against the errors of judgment, but the wickedness of action." This suggests the difference between a
constructive and actual breach of the peace so often insisted upon by the friends of tolerance.

---

[71] Note to Attorney General v. Pearson, 3 Merivale Report, p. 386.
A sermon delivered at the long room, Marble street, Liverpool, on
Tuesday, April 8, 1817, by John Wright, for which a prosecution is
commenced, on a charge of blasphemy, Liverpool, 1817.

IN CONCLUSION.

This is all that was found of prosecutions for religious offences. Effort has been made to relate *all* the essential factors that were discovered without regard to their support or contradiction of any theories that will be defended in the case at bar. So far we have pursued an arbitrary chronological arrangement.

It remains now to classify, rearrange and co-ordinate these decisions with the object of enabling us to see their social meaning as part of living moving human institutions, symbolizing slowly changing human impulses and corresponding changes in the human concept of interhuman relations and of religion. Thus it will be made to appear more clearly than now, that the fight for freedom of speech and of religion was but a part of the unconscious growth toward political and religious democracy, and that all blasphemy laws are in utter variance with the real social signficance as well as the verbal meaning of our constitutions.

The preceding abstracts stop with the adoption of the Connecticut constitution in 1818. This was an eventful period even in England. About this time began Richard Carlile's world-famous fight for liberty of the press in England. About one hundred and twenty of his friends went to jail with him. That fight helped to bring about a reversal of policy, lately registered by a decision in the House of Lords (1917) in the case of Bowman v. Secular Society. Of this more will be said later on.

XVIII.
A REVIEW OF BLASPHEMY
PROSECUTIONS.

Heretofore, we have reproduced in chronological order all that was found concerning prosecutions for religious offenses. How will we now treat this material? In legal literature I have never seen a discussion of intellectual method. Therefore it may help to formulate a brief statement which will make us more conscious of our methods and aims as we proceed. Let us then first proclaim these methods and aims and after that see what general meaning we can thus extract from the record.

A CASE-LAWYER'S METHOD.

If our dominant desires are functioning at the level of a mere case-lawyer who is more or less blind, we may act even from an unconscious compulsion, just as though we consciously wished to perpetuate former religious persecution, in whole or in part. Such persons will not seek nor will they consider the larger issues of intellectual freedom that were then in process of formulation and of being fought out. Therefore they will not discover the bearing of persecutory precedents upon constitutional constructions. From the necessity of their limitations these persons will study the precedents with a dominant impulse as if to discover in them meanings and justifications for the further infliction of pains for mere mental offenses. Such predisposition tends to the ignoring of the relation of these cases to the larger principles involved, or their potency as an exhibition of the evil sought to be remedied by our constitutional guarantees. By more or less crude analogy, the ancient tyrannous precedents will then be directly applied to present-day facts, without the intervention of principles as these might be understood at higher evolutionary levels. Thus the precedents and our constitutions can be made to satisfy any present judicial lust for power over opinions. If we recognize any distinction between a mere case-lawyer and an intellectually mature jurist, the test for this discrimination must be chiefly found in their differences as to intellectual processes. Let us then proceed with a statement of the more mature mental procedure in dealing with legal precedents.

THE JURIST'S METHOD.

To make the record of cases more useful to the problems of statutory and constitutional construction, those who use more mature intellectual methods will extract from those cases statements of truths, to be perfected if possible and then deductively applied to each present problem. For this purpose we need to analyze our cases, first, in order to abstract from each the essential factors which make it like unto other cases as to the possible general rules of law that may be discovered. Next we may reorganize this case-material in new classifications according to the similarity of the suppressed ideas with the hope of uncovering more completely the pernicious possibilities, and then arrange them all under general classifications. In making this rearrangement we will neglect the relatively immature mental processes which deal principally with concrete and obscure analogies between that past case and this present one. Thus we may arrive at the more mature intellectual methods which impel us to deal more intelligently and thoroughly with abstract relations, and with generalizations inductively derived. Then we may also formulate *the law,* as to blasphemy and as to the meaning of free speech, and formulate it in the sense of "law" as rules of conduct that are general in form and yet so precise as to furnish certainty and uniformity in the criteria of conduct. Without such certainty in the criteria of right and of crime, we inevitably preclude the important achievement of even approximate equality before the law.

Thus we can assimilate and integrate the concrete aspects of blasphemy, into larger generalizations which will present its true historic meaning in the form of general principles, or as general criteria of blasphemy. At the same time these principles carried to their logical conclusion should make even more plain the inherent evil factor which the dissenters opposed and which our constitutions sought to destroy forever. Thus we may come to understand more clearly the contrary principle, as a rule of action made obligatory by our constitutions. When thus we come to see the conflict of principle between blasphemy prosecutions and constitutional, religious and intellectual liberty we may achieve also some general criteria for determining the existence and meaning of the latter. With this done, we will have achieved a jurist's conception of constitutional law. The exactness and thoroughness with which we adhere to this more scientific method, that is to say: the emphasis which we place upon it, will depend upon the development and the temperament of each individual.

It is the choice and the use we make of precedents that will reveal our unconscious as well as conscious motives and our intellectual methods, and these in combination will determine the result. Thus do we automatically classify our intellectual status as we must, and justify ourselves as best we can. Those with an adequate evolutionary concept of desire and of mental processes will see in us and understand that which others fail to grasp. So do we quite unconsciously classify ourselves, as near to a most blind case-lawyer or to a real jurist. In the higher developmental stage of desire we function above the petty conflict /of unconscious and narrowly conditioned personal tendency. Then we will seek a relatively impersonal and more synthetic view of the historic and personal conflicts and through this we may be impelled to consciously promote the process of democratization, by means of a like promotion of its indispensible intellectual hospitality.

CRITERIA OF BLASPHEMY.

Let us now see if we can abstract from the blasphemy cases a few general truths about the motives which produced blasphemy laws, and the criteria of guilt under them. Then, perhaps, we can acquire a better view of such laws, and see them as the very evils which our constitutions were designed to destroy, and so bring ourselves to a better understanding of the *how* and *why* of that design.

A careful reading of the blasphemy cases makes it plain that at no time before our revolution did the blasphemous character of an idea depend upon the rhetorical form or the politeness of literary style. On its political side as "sedition" the objection to religious heresy was that it attacked the privileges and prerogatives that were claimed as a matter of divine right, founded on Christian "orthodoxy." Blasphemy as such was conditioned on the meaning of one's utterance, in comparison with and as a contradiction of orthodox doctrine. Neither did blasphemy then depend upon the judge's or the jury's opinion of the psychologic tendency to produce a disturbance of the civil peace. A hypothetical and imaginary tendency to "endanger the eternal soul" of others was the justification for such legislation, but even this was never made the criteria of guilt. Whether any utterance came within the scope of the blasphemy statute was a pure question of law determinable only by the judges. It was decided by them wholly with reference to its contradiction of essential orthodox doctrine. The judge was presumed to know what was orthodox just as he was presumed to know what was the law, for orthodoxy was the law.

Under our constitutional guarantees of a separation of church and state and for religious liberty, the reason for blasphemy laws utterly fail. Now our courts cannot determine what is orthodox religious doctrine, because its existence in the legal sense has been prohibited. Neither can it protect the legalized injustice or vested wrongs of the privileged classes, or those claiming to be such. A secular government can have no concern with the post mortem salvation of souls. For all those who have the desire and the capacity to see these truths the constitution will therefore be held to have repealed the common law as to blasphemy. Those whose desires and intellects function on a different evolutionary level may reach a contrary conclusion. So these latter will retard the growth of democracy and of liberty, as the German Kaiser and the Pope are doing. This is all the more evident when we further consider the nature and source of blasphemy laws, as being but the parliamentary ratification of the canon law.

It also appears from such a careful reading of the cases

based upon religious offenses that all of them were but special instances of a violation of the canon law against blasphemy. Again the reason for this is obviously found in the fact that all government was then supposed to derive its just powers from God and not as in America from the consent of the governed. Thus the parliamentary adoption of the canon-law was but a declaratory confirmation of what the then English theory of government already implied. The parliamentary approval wrought only the change of eliminating the papal authority, not the divine authority in politics.

CANON-LAW AND COMMON-LAW.

"Besides the papal institutions, there were many decrees of synods or ecclesiastical councils, especially in England, which may be ranked as parts of the canon law. At the dawn of the reformation (in the time of Henry VIII) an act passed, for the revision of the canon law, and providing that until that revision was made, all canons, constitutions, ordinances, and synodols provincial, then already made, and not repugnant to the law of the land or *the king's prerogative,* should still be used and executed. No such revision has been made. Clerical canons, made since that time, are no authority as to the laity, unless confirmed by act of parliament."[1]

Just here it may be useful to restate the three catagories of the canon-law definition of blasphemy, and to attempt some elucidating comment thereon. Blasphemy consisted in this: "First, when there is attributed to God that which is not proper to God, and second, when there is taken away from God that which is proper to God. To these two a third should be added, according to St. Thomas Aquinas that when there is attributed to the Creature, that which is proper to the Creator alone" (p. 166).

The first two categories obviously are distinguished mainly according to the form of the blasphemous statement. If one says that God is a purposeful divine imminence in the universe, he denies the ordinary conception

[1] Sullivan, William. Historical causes and effects, p. 424; citing, Blackstone's Commentaries. vol. 1, p. 74. [Blackstone, v. 1, pp. 82-83.]

of the divinity of Jesus, and therefore denies the trinity. At the same time such a statement attributes to God that which does not belong to the orthodox conception of him. Likewise, if I ascribe to any man the qualities or powers which orthodoxy credits God with monopolizing, then I am by necessary implication denying to God some quality of exclusive super-humanness which orthodoxy considers proper only to God. We must therefore conclude that all blasphemy is a mere denial expressed or implied, of anything which for the moment is deemed essential to orthodox religion, or to its political machinery, and that orthodoxy can have logical existence in the legal sense *only* when church and state are one.

When our constitutions disestablished all religion it was undoubtedly designed to include a repeal of the enactment which had made the canon-law a part of the common-law. If not this then the constitutional words have no meaning. Only through the union of church and state did the canon-law supply the reason and the essense of the laws against blasphemy. By destroying and prohibiting the union of church and state and by guaranteeing freedom of speech, in the clearest general terms that are possible, our constitutions prohibited blasphemy prosecutions.

From this point of view it can be said that our problem is to decide which will now prevail, canon-law or secular constitutions? Only by immature intellectual methods and their inadequate sophistries can the former be upheld or the two reconciled.

REVIEW OF ADJUDICATED CASES.

A careful reading of the cases reported as crimes against religion makes it clear that even though the judicial label was "sedition" every case presented a violation of the canon-law against blasphemy. To deny the divine right of the king was, of course, a denial of an orthodox essential. If we co-ordinate the judicial cases and the canon-law another fact becomes apparent, namely: All three classifications of the canon-law as to blasphemy and all the adjudicated cases of which any record is found, consist of the one essence, which is a denial, directly or by indirect necessary implication, of something which at the moment was considered essential to the fabric of orthodox theologic theory. Again, the essence of legalized orthodoxy varied according to the politico-religious fashion.

As we contemplate these facts we achieve a new under-standing of the essential content of the English judicial mind when it expressed the formula that: "Christianity is part of the law itself."[2] How else could a king or a bishop rule by divine right? Furthermore, the canon-law had been expressly enacted as part of statutory law.[3] The contemplation of these facts also give us a new valuation of the "intelligence" of those American judges who under our secular constitutions have approvingly repeated that statement about Christianity being part of the law itself.[4] Is it not merely that undemocratic desires impel some judges to an unintelligent parroting of a formula that gives emotional satisfaction to an immature lust for power? We can leave the answer to this psychologic problem for the psychologic specialist and for another time.

DIVINE-RIGHT-RULE AND BLASPHEMY.

Before the reformation the King ruled by divine right through the mediation of the Pope. After the reformation Henry VIII ruled by divine right without any interme-diary. Within their jurisdiction, the anglican bishops also ruled by divine right, and exercised even penal juris-diction, *not as the arm of the king or in the name of the king,* but in their own proper person as successors of the apostolic fathers of the church.[5] The logic of the cases is to the effect that Christianity was more than a part of the law. Christianity was the supreme and more fundamental part of the law. Blackstone formulates it thus: "Where the former determination is most evidently contrary to reason, [it is not law] much more if it be contrary to divine

---

[2] Taylor's Case, 1 Ventris 293; 3 Kebble 607; 2 Strange 789. See page 286 herein.

[3] Blackstone's Commentaries. v. 1, pp. 74-82-83.
[4] State v. Chandler, 2 Del. 553-556.
People v. Ruggles, 8 John (N. Y.), 290-294; 5 Am. Dec. 335.
Updegraph v. Com., 11 Serg. & Randle (Pa.), 394-401.
But for modern British attitude see: Bowman v. Secular Society, Ltd. Law Reports, Appeal Cases, Part IV Aug. 1, 1917, pp. 406-478.
[5] See. Richard Burton's Case, pp. 219-221 herein.

law."[6]   The orthodox conception of divine law was, therefore, supreme in a theocracy which came down from God, in much the same sense in which our democratic constitutions are held to be supreme because they came up from out of the people.   Under these circumstances, of course, "words against an archbishop are words against the government."[7]   Since the bishops also ruled by divine right it might equally have been said that words against an archbishop are words against God.   To deny anything orthodox in religion was to deny the very foundation upon which the government claimed to rest.   It was therefore optional whether one labeled certain utterances as blasphemy, sedition, or treason.   That is the inescapable meaning of those cases where prosecution followed a criticism of the doctrines of the bishops.[8]   However, the true human motive was always a mere matter of protecting the temporal advantages of the privileged, though the pretense was to protect God and the spiritual advantage for the soul.

Assuming Divine Attributes.

The same relation to the advantages of the privileged can be discovered also in those cases where the blasphemy consisted in attributing to a human "that which is proper to the Creator alone."

In the case of Abiezer Coppe (pp. 271-272) his book was burned as blasphemous because he assumed to himself the divine prerogative of issuing a final divine warning to prepare for the day of judgment.   Such pretensions obviously came in conflict with the monopoly of the bishops.

James Naylor (p. 282) allowed himself to be adored as God or Christ, claiming to be a spiritual king of Israel having power over the enemies of Christ, and therefore he was adjudged a blasphemer.   Again we see the supreme authority of the orthodox church being questioned.   This was in effect setting up a claim for a new sovereign of sovereigns.

Lodowicks Muggleton (p. 292) and John Reeve between

---

[6] Blackstone's Commentaries, v. 1, p. 70.
[7] Mence on Libel, p. 288-289.   edition of 1823; see also: Pocklington's Case, p. 248 herein.
[8] Legate, p. 182; Montagu. p. 192; Leighton, p. 197-199; Burton, p. 215-222, Pocklington, p. 238, etc.

them assumed to exercise the divine power to damn and to bless. Such persons also were obviously threatening to supercede both bishops and king.

An unnamed member of the Society of Love (p. 295) claimed familiar communion with God, assumed the "sacred attributes of God, sometimes gave out that she was the Virgin Mary and other times blasphemously taking upon herself other adorable names and titles." She presumed to pronounce damnation and salvation. Here again was the assertion of a nearness to God beyond that which the orthodox clergy were claiming. For these acts she was held to keep the peace, doubtless being a dangerous or audacious competitor of the existing aristocracy.

Sussannah Fowler (p. 314), another demented female, was also convicted of blasphemy for claiming to be a God and to possess the power to save and to damn. If this were tolerated it would necessarily endanger the bishops' pre-eminence and ultimately their "loaves and fishes."

John Asgill (pp. 319-322) published a book held blasphemous because of numerous erroneous and harmless theories by which he sought to prove, by the scriptures, that man may be translated from hence into eternal life without passing through death. Here again, through the medium of "misinterpreted" holy writ, a divine quality was ascribed to mere humans. When death loses its terrors the clergy will have lost the keys to "eternal life." Then their job becomes worthless and their prerogatives will vanish. In the House of Commons Asgill's book was declared "a crime higher than High Treason."

So then, on its human side as a matter of motive, blasphemy prosecutions always protected temporal privileges and prerogatives, such as are inconsistent with some present conceptions of democracy. On its religious side blasphemy dealt with "spiritual" pretenses and soul-protection. All these religio-moralistic pretenses of superhuman origin were mere masks, perhaps unconsciously but actually used, for the covert protection of privileges and prerogatives. By destroying the union of church and state it was sought by our constitutions to destroy this religio-political support for that which was undemocratic.

RULE ILLUSTRATED.

From the foregoing discussion some will doubtless achieve a new vision and it is hoped a clarified vision, for re-examining the prerevolutionary judicial attitude toward blasphemy as that was then formulated. We may profitably quote a few such authorities to confirm our foregoing speculations. Lord Holt, in his Law of Libels,[9] under the heading of "Offenses against religion," includes this: "All profane scoffing of the holy Scripture, or exposing *any part* to ridicule and contempt."[10]   Hawkins uses precisely the same language just quoted from Holt.

Having now clarified our mind to the point of seeing that a denial of *any part* of the official interpretation of Holy Scripture or of the Christian religion was blasphemy, let us view some specific doctrines that it was a crime to deny. Thus will we come to a concrete understanding of just how this blasphemy statute must have been interpreted in 1642 by those who enacted it, and how it must still be interpreted if it is to be enforced.   The court cannot amend the statute by new interpretations which alter the criteria of guilt.   If the statute as interpreted prior to 1818 is unconstitutional, then it cannot now be made to harmonize with the constitution by a judicial amendment of the statute.   All English and American statutes about blasphemy were but declaratory of the common law, and that in turn was merely declaratory of the canon-law.

"The statute law has likewise marked out certain offenses against Christianity in which it is merely declaratory of the common law.   *   *   *   Reviling the sacrament of the Lord's Supper with contemptuous words, etc., for which by 1 Edw. VI, c. 1 (which was repealed by 1 Mary, c. 2, and revived by 1 Eliz., c. 1 [1558-1603]) the offender shall be imprisoned, fined and ransomed."[11]

CRIME TO DENY TRINITY.

Lord Holt presents the following view of the law in relation to the doctrine of the Trinity. His word "profanely"

---

[9] P. 65, of second edition, 1816.

[10] Hawkin's Pleas of the Crown (seventh edition, 1795), v. 1, chap. 5, p. 12.   See also quotations in chap. 12, herein.

[11] Holt, on Libel, p. 65, of second edition, citing: 4 Black Com. p. 50.

must be interpreted in the light of what has preceded, namely: that a mere denial of the official concept of the Trinity is criminal blasphemy or profanity.

"By 3 Jac. 1. c. 21. Whoever shall use the name of the Holy Trinity profanely or jestingly, in any stage, play, interlude or show shall be liable to a penalty of ten pounds."

"By Will. III. c. 18, sec. 17 (1689-1703). Whoever shall deny in his preaching or writing the doctrine of the blessed Trinity shall lose all benefit of the act of toleration, etc. This act, in addition to depriving the offender of the privileges above mentioned, leaves the punishment of the offense, as a misdemeanor at common law."[12] This view that it is a crime to deny the Trinity is abundantly justified by cases of which an abstract has been hereinbefore published.[13]

Abraham Bishop in a Preface to the publication of an "Oration delivered at Wallingford on the 11th of March, 1801, before the Republicans of Connecticut at their general Thanksgiving for the election of Thomas Jefferson," protests against the blasphemy law of Connecticut, coupled with a demand for a constitutional form of government and religious liberty. He said: "Certainly the Trinitarian doctrine is established by law; and the denial of it is placed in the rank of felonies. Though we have ceased to transport from town to town, Quakers, Newlights and Baptists, yet the dissenters from our prevailing denomination are, even at this moment, praying for the repeal of those laws which abridge the rights of conscience."

If then this Connecticut statute against blasphemy is to be interpreted according to the Common law of England at the time, or according to the current colonial interpreta-

---

[12] Holt; Law of Libel, 1816, second edition, pp. 63-66.

[13] Legatt, 1612, p. 180; Wightman, 1612, p. 183; Best, 1643, p. 258; Biddle, 1648, pp. 265-268-269; Coppe, 1650, p. 272; Fry, 1650, p. 273; Racovian Catechism, 1652, p. 279-280; Muggleton, 1652-1676, pp. 288-289-292; Aikenhead, 1695, pp. 308; Kinnymount, 1697, p. 311; Toland, 1697, p. 312; Fowler, 1698, p. 313; Clendon, 1709, p. 323; Hall, 1709-1720, pp. 324, 331; (?) Manderville, 1728, p. 332; (?) Elwell, 1726, p. 335; (?) Ashley, 1746, p. 338; Ilive, 1756, p. 339. Dixwell and Cabe, 1763, p. 340; (?) Williams, 1797, p. 344.

tion, and has not been repealed by the Constitution, then all Universalists and Unitarians as well as Agnostics and Infidels are still penalized. Is there a court so bigoted as to enforce this statute as the judicial rules for its construction require?

Mr. Bishop and all those who favored the formation of a constitutional government in Connecticut frankly and earnestly demanded the repeal of all these laws, by means of a constitution guaranteeing religious liberty and free speech. They finally prevailed and their purpose was made effective and must be considered authoritative in interpreting the Connecticut Bill of Rights.

This purpose of the constitutionalists was perfectly understood by the upholders of the "established order," the State-church. Their understanding of the issue of the constitutionalists is made plain in "Count the Cost, an address to the People of Connecticut." There the case of the hated constitutionalists is thus stated: "They are obstinately determined to banish from the public mind all affection and veneration for the clergy, all respect for the institutions of religion and to reduce Connecticut to the condition which knows no distinction between 'him who serveth God and him who serveth Him not.'"[14] That purpose became dominant by the adoption of the Connecticut constitution. This then was the issue on which the constitution of Connecticut was adopted and supplies us with the key for its proper interpretation.

VARIOUS DENIALS OF ORTHODOXY.—1600-1642.

As illustrative of the rule that *any* repudiation of *any* doctrine deemed essential to religious orthodoxy is a blasphemy we may profitably recall the following cases already abstracted. Atwood (1605, p. 181) denied the antiquity of Christian doctrine, and discredited preaching and divine service. Bartholomew (1612, p. 182) repudiated the Nicene and Athanasian creeds, and other matters essential to the orthodox conception of the Trinity. Wightman (1612, p. 183) repudiated the Apostles Creed, as well as the Nicene and Athanasian creeds, denied the Trinity and disputed

---

[14] P. 6, Johnathan Steadfast [pseud.], Hartford, 1804.

362 BLASPHEMY.

much of orthodox interpretation of the Bible. Ogelvie
(1615, p. 185) asserted the temporal supremacy of the
Pope. This also was a denial of orthodox interpretation
of Holy Writ as to the apostolic succession. As to Dighton
and Holt (1616, p. 186) we know little more than that they
acted "to the great encouragement of schismatical and refractory persons." Mocket (1617, p. 187) probably committed no greater offence than to omit from his book the
first clause in the translation of the twentieth article of the
thirty-nine articles of faith. Thus he denied that the
Church had power to decree rites, and authority to settle
theologic controversies.

Traske (1618, p. 187) believed that Saturday should be
observed as the Sabbath. Scott (1603-1625, p. 188) questioned the Bible doctrine of witchcraft. Pare (1622, p.
190) disagreed with the established church as to the meaning of the Epistle to the Romans. Mountague (1626, p. 191)
excited a controversy as to whether the orthodoxy of the
King or of the Parliament should determine the guilt of
his book. Which of conflicting claims of orthodoxy will
the Connecticut Court apply in determining what is blasphemy? Leighton's great offence consisted largely in declaring the upholders of orthodoxy and persecution to be
"men of blood and enemies to God," thus repudiating the
established interpretation of Holy Writ. Political changes
resulted in declaring Leighton's opinions innocent and
orthodox. Which orthodoxy is legally orthodox under the
Connecticut statutes?

Pryn (1633, p. 208) was so puritanic as to oppose the
theatre. This false doctrine was officially repudiated by
the Queen taking part in her own royal person, and she
could do no wrong. Of course, Pryn's book must have been
"against all reverence and honor, which all Christians owe
to our Saviour Jesus" who was reigning through the royal
family. The long parliament declares Pryn's convictions
illegal. A new orthodoxy had come into political power.

Hayden (1634, p. 210) was punished for preaching
"against setting up images in churches." The Connecticut
puritans vehemently agreed with Hayden upon this subject. Will the court now assume that the Colonial puri-

tans adopted the common-law conception of blasphemy, and therefore penalized themselves? Burton (1637, p. 220) denied the divine right of the bishops, and accused them of introducing popish innovations. Thus he disputed the orthodox interpretation of the Bible. Pocklington (1640, p. 231 et seq.) was penalized for many minor manifestations of a leaning toward popery. Nathaniel Barnard (1640, p. 253) was penalized for his *opinion* over a controversy as to whether faith was more important toward securing salvation than works. This brings us to the date of the adoption of the Connecticut statute against blasphemy.

Various Denials of Orthodoxy.—1642—1818.

Paul Best (1643, p. 258) denied the Trinity. Knolles got into trouble for some anabaptist doctrine; exact information is not at hand. King James' Book of Sports (1644) was ordered burnt by the puritans because it repudiated the funerial characteristics of the puritan Sabbath. In the reign of James, puritans were punished for refusing to read the Book of Sports in their churches. Which view will be declared orthodox in Connecticut?

Archer (1645, p. 261) blasphemed by counselling sinners to be comforted because God was really the author of all that is, and sin, after all, a means of grace. Biddle (1647, p. 266) "the father of Unitarianism" was punished because he repudiated the orthodox conception of the Trinity by denying the divinity of the Holy Ghost. Clarkson's offense (1645, p. 269) probably consisted in denying the religious value of baptism by sprinkling. Erbery's offense (1646, p. 270) consisted in believing God too merciful to punish anyone. Coppe (1650, p. 272) appears to have suffered for believing in perfectionism, a denial of sin in the elect. Fry (1650, p. 273) denied the Trinity upon Scripture grounds.

Robert Norwood (1651, pp. 277-8-9) was imprisoned for asserting the blasphemous error that the soul of man is the essence of God; that there is no heaven or hell except what we experience here [hell and heaven are states of being, not places]; and that man has a trinity within himself; the soul that is God, the spirit that is the devil, and the body that is the beast. Also that Jesus did not die to pacify God's wrath.

The Racovian Catechism (1652, p. 280) was condemned for asserting that the essence of God was a unity, a single personality. This denied the orthodox meaning of the divinity of Jesus. Keach (1664, p. 282) was convicted of the terrible blasphemy of repudiating infant baptism and that God had not chosen the great but rather the poor and despised, and he scandalized the Liturgy.

John Morgan (1679, p. 297) was too orthodox because he received "Holy orders" from Rome. Delaune and Ralphson (1683, p. 301) offended because they did not accept the book of common prayer. Baxter in many ways denied the divine right and apostolic succession of the Anglican bishops and their conception of protestanism and therefore was "against the government." Blount (1693, p. 307) only reported fairly the religious views and arguments of Paganism "plausible in themselves, of the fallacy of which none but men of parts and learning can be proper judges." John Asgill (1707, p. 319) thought he proved by Holy Writ that "death is not obligatory on Christians, but that man may be translated hence into eternal life without passing through death." Terribly blasphemous of course!

Tindal (1710, p. 326) argued that a clergyman is God's ambassador, and therefore cannot be appointed by human authority. Dr. Mead (1723, p. 331) was prevented from publishing a book of Servetus, who himself had been burnt at the instigation of Calvin. Woolston (1729, p. 337) contended that the alleged miracles of Jesus were but allegorical expressions of truth. Ashley (1746, p. 338) was punished for the same book of Woolston. Annett (1763, p. 341) discredited the Pentateuch. Is there an intelligent judge who does not do so now? Williams (1797, p. 344) was convicted of blasphemy for publishing Paine's "Age of Reason." Many others were later punished for the same offense. Paine was a Deist and wrote his book to defend God against the calumnies of the orthodox church and of the Bible. Eaton's offense (1812, p. 346) was identical with Williams', while Houston's crime (1813, p. 347) was similar in nature.

In these early days men were seldom given much to the sacrilege of disputing whether the whale swallowed Jonah. Had they done so, it would clearly have been blasphemy. So it must now be blasphemy as a denial of part of Holy Writ. That is the inevitable consequence if the common law definition is to be enforced. Furthermore, the common-law conception of blasphemy as herein portrayed must be enforced unless the court usurpes the legislative function of altering the criteria of guilt, or else declares the blasphemy statute unconstitutional.

Delusions of Grandeur.

In those days of spiritual joy unbounded and prosecutions for blasphemy unrestrained, delusions of grandeur usually found religious expression and orthodox suppression. Thus Naylor, (1656, p. 280), Taylor, (1675, p. 285), Muggleton, (1653-1676, pp. 286-294), One of the Society of Love, (1678, p. 295) and Susannah Fowler, (1698, p. 313), all came to grief for their grandiose religious dementia. These unfortunates were blasphemers, vile blasphemers. When the religious egomania found expression in political ambition, they were of course punished as seditious persons. We have better ways now. When delusions of grandeur find religious expression we now put the victims in an asylum unless they succeed in starting a new religious society among those of nearly their own sort. If the delusions of grandeur express themselves in the conventional political manner we may send its victim to Congress, or maybe one occasionally gets upon the judicial bench to try his fellows for expressing opinions as blasphemers.

It requires delusions of grandeur to make one feel himself possessed of any absolute truth or absolute anything, and it is only upon our conscious or unconscious assumption of an absolute truth that we are inclined to punish another for expressing even an impolite disagreement.

Tolerance is Blasphemy.

In 1642, when the Connecticut legislation provided the

death penalty for worshipers of the wrong God and for blasphemers, Bible texts were cited in justification. In other words, the blasphemy statute was merely deemed to be declaratory of the divine law. This again points to the repeal of the blasphemy statute by the automatic operation of the Connecticut Constitution when it disestablished the State-church.

If expressed heresy must be punished as blasphemy because commanded by God through the Bible, and if to deny the accepted orthodox interpretation of the Bible is blasphemy, as the courts have often decided, then it follows that to advocate tolerance is a denial of a part of Christianity—and is blasphemy under the common-law. This very argument for tolerance is blasphemy because it repudiates those parts of the Bible which command prosecution.

This view also has judicial precedent to support it. One of the elements of Leighton's crime (1630, p. 196) was a complaint against the Bishops as "Men of blood" because they enforced the persecutory conception of "divine law." This was in effect a plea for tolerance. Likewise with Wilson. (1637, p. 227.) He had "scandalized the Governors and Government of the Church of England as persecutors of God's faithful ministers and people," the dissenters. Again, to complain of the persecution of those who are only enforcing the intolerance of God was a crime.

Among the many "blasphemies" of Muggleton (1653, pp. 289-290) was this, that he denied the courts "to be judges of blasphemy against the Holy Spirit." Again he was declared a blasphemer, because he said to the court: "We told you that you had no Commission from our God to be judge of spiritual things." Bury (1690, p. 305) seems to have been penalized for this fine statement of the meaning of tolerance: "No King is more independent in his own dominions from any foreign jurisdiction in matters civil, than every Christian is within his own mind in matters of faith." Obviously this was a denial of that essential of the Christian religion which asserted the rule by divine right. Treason and Blasphemy!

Daniel Defoe (1903, p. 316) argued for tolerance by an ironical justification of the extirpation of all dissenters.

For this he was imprisoned, and quite properly so from the viewpoint that to ridicule or heap contempt upon any part of Holy Writ is to be guilty of blasphemy. Mathew Tindall (1710, pp. 329-330) claimed that the people had the right to defend their rights against a person who had no authority to take them away. This intelligent declaration of freedom also was made a subject of criminal indictment.

The Connecticut colonists came from Massachusetts and brought their theocratic notions with them. The Massachusetts statute against blasphemy also cited Bible passages, to exhibit their subordination of the State to the Church. A Massachusetts precedent, therefore, becomes of great importance in Connecticut.

PUNISHED FOR TOLERANCE.

Roger Williams was banished from the Massachusetts colony probably in 1636. That is before the departure of the Connecticut Colonists. When in 1642 the latter adopted a statute against blasphemers and cited passages from the Bible in justification, it should be presumed that they incorporated into that statute the previous interpretation of the Massachusetts colony. It will appear that this interpretation was in perfect harmony with the English rule, that the denial of any part of the Bible was blasphemous. It will now be shown that to advocate tolerance when the Bible had commanded intolerance, was adjudicated a crime.

Roger Williams was banished from Massachusetts by a court which had already decided "that anyone was worthy of banishment who should obstinately assert that the civil magistrate might not intermeddle even to stop a church from apostacy and heresy."[15] Later it will be shown more fully just what was Roger Williams' conception of religious liberty and free speech. Then it will be claimed that his opinions are authoritative on the meaning of these parts of our Constitution.

Under the protection of the Rhode Island Colony, which Williams founded, he entered into a spirited controversy

---

[15] Bloody tenet of persecution, p. XV, edition of Lond., 1848.

in defense of his blasphemous attack upon intolerance. His various pamphlets upon this subject finally made a book which often has been reprinted. Williams' fundamental contention was that the civil power has no authority whatever over the human mind and conscience. The necessary corollary of this opinion, was that the churches of Connecticut and Massachusetts as well as that Church of England was anti-Christian in enforcing blasphemy laws. Of course, this implication was blasphemous because in conflict with an essential doctrine of orthodox Christianity. Prynne denounced the book as a "lycentious work," and the House of Commons ordered it burnt by the common hangman.[16] Thus again do we have precedent to the effect that the denial of that part of the Bible which commands persecution is a crime. Williams escaped England before he could be arrested.

The underlying logic of this is made plain by another good New England authority, Mr. Simon Backus. He wrote a pamphlet against those who were insisting on framing a Constitution that provided for a separation of Church and State. In this he said: "To say, therefore, that there is no occasion for the civil magistrate to interfere in matters of religion, is either to contradict plain and demonstrative fact; [as he had just before shown from Holy Writ] or else to charge the divine author of that dispensation with adding the sanction of his approbation and the seal of his authority to a useless and unnecessary institution."[17]

CONSTITUTION OVERRULES PRECEDENT.

If the court is not willing to hold that the mere advocacy of toleration is a crime, then this blasphemy statute will be declared unconstitutional. It is confidently believed that no court will usurp the legislative function of changing the well-established criteria of guilt in this penal statute, in order to make it less offensive to the Constitution. No such mere amendment can wholly eliminate

---

[16] Jour. of House of Commons, v. 3, 20 Car. I, p. 585.
[17] A dissertation upon the Right and Obligation of the Civil Magistrate to take care of the interests of religion and provide for its support, p. 15

the conflict between blasphemy prosecutions and constitutional religious and intellectual liberty. The correctness of this last statement will be made more obvious by
a thorough study of the precise issue which had been contended for and which were decided by our constitutional
guarantees.

WITCHCRAFT AND COMMON LAW.

A most important part of the Christian religion and of
Holy Scripture, according to the dominant conception in
Connecticut and England of 1642 and after, was a belief in Witchcraft. It would seem to follow, as a logical
necessity from the juridical meaning of "blasphemy," in
1642, that it included a denial of those parts of Holy
Scripture which declare or assume the truth of witchcraft. This is in harmony with both the legal and ecclesiastical thought of the time, both in England and in Connecticut.

I have just read a book entitled: "A Tryal of Witches
at the Assizes held at Bury St. Edmonds for the county
of Suffolk on the tenth day of March, 1664, before Sir
Mathew Hale, K.T., then Lord Chief Baron of His Majesties' Court of Exchequer," published in 1682. Therein is
a record of instructions given to jurors, which reads as
follows: "That there were such creatures as witches he
(Lord Hale) made no doubt at all; For first, the scriptures had affirmed so much. Secondly, the wisdom of all
nations had provided laws against such persons, which is
an argument of their confidence of such a crime. And
such hath been the judgment of this kingdom as appears
by that act of parliament which had provided punishments
proportionable to the quality of the offense. And desired
them strictly to observe their evidence; and desired the
great God of Heaven to direct their hearts in this weighty
matter they had in hand; for to condemn the innocent,
and to let the guilty go free, were both an abomination to
the Lord" (p. 50).

"In conclusion the judges and all the court were fully
satisfied with the verdict, and thereupon gave judgment
against the [13] witches that they should be hanged. . . .

And they were executed on Monday, the seventeenth of March following, but they confessed nothing."[18]

A century later the learned Sir William Blackstone said: "To deny the possibility, nay, actual existence of witchcraft and sorcery, is at once flatly *to contradict the revealed will of God in various passages of both the Old and New Testament,* and the thing itself is a truth to which every nation in the world hath in its turn born testimony, either by example seemingly well tested, or by prohibitory laws which at least suppose the possibility of commerce with evil spirits."[19]   But to flatly contradict *"any part"* of the holy scriptures was blasphemy, according to the common law authorities.   Therefore, to deny witchcraft is a crime today under the Connecticut statute against blasphemy, which was passed in 1642, and which is now sought to be enforced.

In New England the following "authorities" were used in support of Witchcraft:

Keeble, Common Law, Chapter on Conjuration, pp. 217-220.

Sir Matthew Hale's Tryals of Witches, 1682.

Glanville's Collection of Sundry Trials of Witches in England and Ireland in the years 1658-61-64-81.

Bernard's Guide to Jurymen.

Baxter and Burton, Histories about Witches.

Cotton Mather, Memorable Providences relating to Witchcraft.

Of course these authorities in turn rested upon "Holy Writ" itself.

THE BIBLE AND WITCHCRAFT.

To make it still more plain that a denial of witchcraft is the denial of an important doctrine of the Bible, and, therefore, of Christianity, as that still is understood by many and as that was generally understood during the eighteenth century and before, we will now quote a few of the many Bible passages which expressly or impliedly affirm the belief in Witchcraft:

---

[18] See also Annals of Witchcraft, by Drake, preface, p. 81.
[19] Blackstone Commentaries, p. 59, edition of 1850.

1. "Thou shalt not suffer a witch to live." Exodus xxii, 18.

2. "There shall not be found among you anyone that maketh his son or his daughter to pass through fire, or that useth divination, or an enchanter, or a witch, or a charmer, or a consulter with familiar spirits, or a wizard, or necromancer." Deut. xviii, 10-11.

3. "A man also, or woman, that hath a familiar spirit, or that is a wizard, shall surely be put to death: they shall stone them with stones." Lev. xx, 27.

4. "He observed times, and used enchantments, and used witchcraft, and dealt with a familiar spirit, and with wizards: he wrought much evil in the sight of the Lord, to provoke him to anger." 2 Chronicles xxxiii, 6.

5. "Now the works of the flesh are manifest, which are these: adultery, fornication, uncleaness, lasciviousness, idolatry, witchcraft, * * * seditions, heresies." Gal. vi, 19-20.

6. "And it came to pass, when Joram saw Jehu, that he said, is it peace Jehu? And he answered, what peace, so long as the whoredoms of your mother Jezebel and her witchcrafts are so many?" 2 Kings ix, 22.

7. "Because of the multitude of the whoredoms of the well-favored harlot, the mistress of witchcrafts, that selleth nations through her whoredoms, and families through her witchcrafts." Nahum iii, 4.

8. "And the soul that turneth after such as have familiar spirits and after wizzards that go a whoring after them, I will even set my face against that soul and will cut him off from among his people." Lev. xxii, 6.

9. "Saul had put away those that had familiar spirits and the wizards out of the land." Samuel xxxviii, 3.

10. "For rebellion is as the sin of witchcraft." Samuel xv, 23.

11. "And I will cut off witchcraft out of the land." Micah v, 12.

12. "Many of them also which used curious arts brought their books together and burned them." Acts xix, 19.

13. "But there was a certain man called Simon, which

before-time in the same city used sorcery and bewitched
the people of Samaria." Acts viii, 9.

14. "If a man abide not in me, he is cast forth as
a branch, and is withered, and men gather them and cast
them into the fire, and they are burned." John xv, 6.

"In the opinion of the eminent Italian Jurist, Bartolo,
witches were burned alive in early times on this [last]
authority."[20]

BLASPHEMY TO DENY WITCHCRAFT IN CONNECTICUT.

The New England indictments against witchcraft read:
"entertaining familiarity with Satan, the enemy of mankind, and by his help doing works above the course of
nature." (Ibid.)

In Connecticut (1642) we find this law against witchery:
"If any man or woman be a witch—that is, hath or consulted with a familiar spirit—they shall be put to death.
Exodus xxii, 18; Leviticus xx, 27; Deuteronomy xviii, 10,
11."[21]

In the New Haven Colony, 1655, it was provided: "If
any person be a witch, he or she shall be put to death,
according to Exodus xxii, 18; Leviticus xx, 27; Deuteronomy xviii, 10, 11."[22]

Fairly complete accounts of the enforcement of these
laws are contained in "The Witchcraft Delusion in Colonial Conn., 1647-1697, by John M. Taylor." There can be
no doubt whatever that a belief in Witchcraft was an
essential part of the belief in the "Holy Scriptures," according to the official religion of the Connecticut Colonies
till long after 1642. This is so, whether we view the official
religion as local and particular, or view it as identical
with the official religion established in England .

We have also seen that according to the Common-law
the denial of "any part" of the Christian religion or the
"Holy Scriptures" constituted blasphemy. It inevitably
follows that the Connecticut statute against blasphemy,
whether interpreted according to the obvious convictions

---

[20] The Witchcraft Delusion in Colonial Connecticut, 1647-1697, by John
M. Taylor, p. 17.
[21] Colonial Records of Connecticut, vol. 1, p. 77.
[22] New Haven Colonial Records, vol. 11, p. 576, Code 1655.

of those who passed the law, or according to the principles of the Common-law, it penalizes the denial of Witchcraft. This finds a precedent, when James I of England ordered the burning of Scots' most scholarly "Discovery of Witchcraft." (pp. 188-190 herein.)

It is believed that there is not a court in this country that has the courage or the disposition to enforce this blasphemy statute according to the letter and purpose of those who passed it. Neither has the court any constitutional authority to alter that established interpretation or that purpose, because this would be tantamount to the judicial amendment of the statute. The very essence of a legislative amendment consists in an alteration of the criteria of guilt. Neither can the Common-law import of "blasphemy," nor the evident legislative intent, be reconciled either with the fair import of the words of our constitutional guarantees, with their historical interpretation, or with the purpose of those who demanded and caused the constitutional guarantees to be adopted into our organic law.

From these considerations it would seem to follow quite conclusively that this statute must be declared unconstitutional.

XIX.

PSYCHOLOGY OF FEAR, DEMOCRACY AND FREE SPEECH.

Mr. H. N. Brailsford has recently reminded us once again that, "the human factor in politics is vastly more important than paper constitutions." It is very plain to me that our present numerous censorships cannot be justified out of our constitutions but are read into them. Manifestly here we are not dealing with an objective consideration of a legal problem but with the psychologic status and imperatives of judges. Therefore, it is of importance that we endeavor to understand this psychic aspect of the problem perhaps as a means of ultimately aiding in the enlargement of our liberty.

To achieve the most intelligent constitutional construction we must possess an understanding of the behavior of the emotional forces which have supplied even unconscious impulses toward censorship and which may supply the unconscious predeterminants with which we approach the construction of the free speech guarantees of our organic law. By becoming more conscious of the genesis and behavior of the impulses that make for tyranny we tend to become more efficient at checking our lust for power according to the requirements of democratic development. But we never will understand the larger meaning of democratic development unless we understand the state of mind which it implies just as well as we understand its outward manifestations. We can be deceived by seeming democratic forms and institutions, unless we also have a thorough understanding of the various mental states which these may symbolize.

In legal arguments there is a uniform absence of the psychologic viewpoint. The cause for this is not properly to be ascribed to its unimportance. The condition is better explained by the fact that the lawyer's usual university education has never yet afforded him an opportunity to study genetic and evolutionary psychology. It

374

is this viewpoint which is being emphasized in this discussion.

THE STATIC CONCEPT OF LAW.

For the want of a conscious genetic and evolutionary concept of law, the lawyer is almost compelled to act and think as if the law were a static thing, even as to that part of the law which finds its only formulation in judicial opinions. Hence we blindly follow the words of Blackstone, Kenyon, Mansfield and the rest, when we define liberty of the press under our constitutions. Even when we lawyers do think of the law as a growing thing, it will usually be thought of as a growth of something outside ourselves just as we think of a tree growing. We seldom think of the law as a mere symbolism for a growth in the desire and the understanding of human beings.

From the relatively static concept of law there follows the extravagant over-valuation and misuse of the verbalism of precedents. In consequence of this, legal arguments resolve themselves largely into disputes about the acquired meaning of words rather than painstaking effort to understand the behavior of the conscious and subconscious forces which determine the choice of the words and verbal forms, and control the changing concepts which these legal formulas symbolize.

EVOLUTIONARY CONCEPT OF LAW.

A more enlightened view would induce lawyers to concern themselves less with the backward look in search of tyrannous precedents to be parroted, and more with a forward look in an earnest effort to promote intellectual evolution in relation to law. From this viewpoint the formal statements of the law are reduced to mere symbols of a vital human growth.

The more important thing then is to understand the changing and growing concept symbolized, rather than to quarrel about the word symbols in which it may be expressed. Quite as often does the "law" change by injecting new meanings into the old word-symbols as by changing the formulas themselves. It is this that gives the use of precedent its sinister possibilities, whenever

more emphasis is placed upon using the old formula than
is placed upon understanding the varying mental contents
which it may express. Again, this changing mental content cannot be adequately understood except in relation
with a concept of intellectual evolution. Only thus can
we understand the reason of the law in its best sense.
Thus far I know of no court that has exhibited any such
understanding of the psycho-genetic and evolutionary aspects of the free speech problem. as that is presented under
our American constitutions. The time therefore should be
ripe.

From the psychologic viewpoint the growth of the
law expresses an evolution in our desires, accompanying
a similar evolution in our understanding of the relations
and behavior of humans. The formal statement we call
law is but the outward symbolization of the feelings and
thoughts of men. Often the words remain the same, while
a revolution goes on as to the mental content which the
words symbolize. From this viewpoint we cannot approach
a full understanding of the law without understanding the
impulses and desires of the men who frame or declare the
law. These desires must be understood in their psycho-
genetic sense rather than in their verbal expression.

TOWARD DEMOCRACY AND FREE SPEECH.

A retrospect on the evolution of society and the state
shows a general growth toward the more thorough democratization of human institutions. It behooves us therefore to study our problem also in its relation to the psychology of democracy and its opposite.

When our personal interests are seen *or felt* to be in conflict with the interests of that whole of which we are but
a small part, then we tend to resent the "dangerous tendency" of democratizing protests or education. Under such
circumstances we tend to distrust the people as a whole to
deal intelligently *with us,* who are, or wish to be, the beneficiaries of legalized graft, of pious privileges, or economic
and political advantage. Therefore, under varous names
and pretences sedition and blasphemy are punished to the
same extent, that those who enjoy political power more

than public service, do also fear democracy. When the dominant motive is service and more democracy, we do not fear the loss of political or other power and so we no longer desire censorship. For the same reason officially approved education is usually united to that which tends to perpetuate special privileges according to the contemporary fashion. Therefore, the disadvantaged and disinherited must not be allowed to formulate their own grievances in their own way, nor to acquire that kind of education which will make them more efficient at understanding the shortcomings of the privileged, or at superceding existing institutions and superstitions, by something more democratic and more intelligently just.

FREEDOM, MATHEMATICS AND ANTI-PRIVILEGE.

We penalize only those opinions for which we cannot supply a mathematical demonstration and by means of which an efficient privileged minority secure relative prosperity and ease at the expense of others. So kings, priests and other privileged classes, always impede the progress of democratization. Legally protected "spiritual" pretenses always give support to temporal privileges and prerogatives. Sceptre and mitre, luxury and want, are but different symbols for anti-republican institutions and mental attitudes.

Mathematics has always been open to ridicule and contemptuous aspersion with the consent of mathematicians. Religion and divine right mastery has never been equally open to attack with the consent of kings or priests. Therein is the essence of an aristocracy. The "truths" of religion and the divine justice of our economic systems, are undemonstrable and peculiarly profitable for some specially privileged ones. Mathematical truths are open to demonstration, and democratically serviceable to all alike. Hence the difference in the human factor.

Equality of education and experience would give us much more of the substance as well as the forms of democracy. Those whose interests are equally centered on both will never be tempted toward censorship, even without a written constitution that prohibits censorship.

Those whose interest in democracy is limited to its outward forms will be tempted to explain away our guarantees of free speech so that the privileged few may not have
their peace of mind disturbed. Is it not time that the
theologian and other beneficiaries of legalized injustice
be disprivileged, and their theology and economics be as
much subject to ridicule and contempt as the multiplication table? It is not so now.

ARISTOCRATS BY FEELING.

All those who *feel* like unto the beneficiaries of privileges and prerogatives, even though unconscious that their
feelings are of that class, will automatically contend for
the protection and perpetuation of undemocratic inequalities, perhaps without any understanding of the genesis of
their thought upon the subject. Even the victims of
slavery are thus impelled to fight for the enslaving system.
All such tend to react automatically against intellectual
freedom when it is used to criticise that which gives them
a feeling of grandeur. It is these deluding feelings that
prolong the popularity of priestcraft, kingship and bu-
reaucracy and of Blackstone's conception of mental freedom. Whether conscious or unconscious the motive and
conduct of the adherents of privilege is as if to protect
themselves against the disturbance of their peace of
mind in the enjoyment of imaginary or real parasitic
privileges, such as are the usual product of legalized injustices and vested wrongs. That is probably the chief
disturbance of the peace which they justly fear from ideas,
and that fear is the only true psycho-genetics of censorship,
even when it is not acknowledged or not known to be that.
It is these aristocratic impulses, often not understood or
only half understood, that have brought into existence the
dogmatic and blind following of Blackstone, as to free
speech. It is these immature impulses and intellectual
methods that produce special pleas and question-begging
epithets, in the effort to uphold the words of our constitutional guarantees, while ignoring their historic import,
the evil to be remedied and the corresponding significance
attached to the words by the framers of these guarantees.

Aristocratic feeling and fears induce the reversion to Blackstone and intellectual tyranny.

I said that this was true of all those who *feel like unto* the beneficiaries of legalized injustice and vested wrong. In fact they may be the victims of the system which they uphold. This is the greatest of the slave-virtues. The victims of witchcraft and of religious persecution often believed in the laws under which they suffered, though in a particular case they may have thought them misapplied or misinterpreted, or capable of some advantageous or insignificant amendment. So also the feudal, chattle and wage slaves fought for slavery. It was always a crime to teach them the injustice of the enslaving system. Such education "tended" to disturb the peace. The road of progress is littered with the shattered remains of childish dreams of peace. Intellectual progress and democratic liberty are deemed more important than the dead calm of ignorance and bliss wherever the democratic spirit prevails. Then we will insist upon keeping open the road to progress in democracy even at the risk of disturbing the peace.

UNITY OF SLAVE AND MASTER.

There is in the feeling of humans an element of unity between the conscious, willing, parasitic aristocrats and the satisfied slave, who defends the system that really wrongs him. Both fear to assume the independent responsibility which greater democracy would impose. So kings, priests, economic despots and slaves lean upon each other and jointly array themselves in war against the critics of the system upon which, through long habit, they both *feel* themselves to depend. The relatively intelligent leaders and beneficiaries of religious, political and economic superstition and its most benighted victims, all tend to combine in their persecuting desires. The intelligent ones resent the endangerment of the "right" to be parasitic and privileged. The most ignorant resent the imputation that their "sacred wisdom" is the evidence of their worldly ignorance. Nothing justifies the inference that our constitutions were meant to afford these passions a special protection against criticism which is always conducive to their being outgrown. Those who do protect them do not act like democrats.

In undemocratic conditions the beneficiaries of things as they are always claim something like a property right in the servile devotion of the "inferior" who is the source of revenue and the upholder of privilege.

From such a viewpoint every efficient criticism of the prevailing system of church, state or prevalent system of exploitation was of "dangerous tendency," that is, it endangered the privileges of the privileged. In a democracy no one can be protected as in a claim of property in the political, economic or religious beliefs of another. In such matters our constitutions promise a fair field and no favors. Hence there can be no such crime as blasphemy, verbal sedition, or a constructive disorderly conduct, committed by words alone. Those who can enforce such laws either know not the genesis or nature of their own impulses or else they are possessed by very crude notions of democracy. These then are read into our constitutions and not read out of them. It is these childlike motives and intellectual methods that produce our Blackstonian constitutional interpretations.

IMMATURITY OF ARISTOCRACY

In the face of actual (as distinguished from theoretic) democratic equality in welfare both masters and slaves are the unconscious victims of that fear of responsible independence, which characterizes the emotional attitude of the child toward its parent. What we fear, even though foolishly, we also hate. Therefore even the victims of tyranny so often hate the emancipating freedom and its attendant responsibility, which is of the very essence of a true democracy. Neither the privileged nor the willing slaves feel that they can exist without each other. Both unite to oppose mental freedom that compels the reconsideration and revaluation of their most cherished mutuality of dependence, and the revolution of the theories and superstitions by which it is upheld. That is why the aggressive friends of free speech are so few. The framers of our constitutions thought the time had come to wean the infants from their emotional and intellectual dependence and make them democratically free. Has the time come for our courts to enforce that view?

We tend to hate those who fundamentally or passionately challenge habitual conditions and forms, political, economic, institutional or religious, because all such criticism tends to disturb our peaceful repose in a delusional grandeur as masters or beneficaries of things as they are, beneficiaries in fact, in fancy or only in subconscious feeling association. So the slave and the master fight together, to perpetuate the system which in different ways enslaves them both. They are alike the victims of childish modes of feeling, and of dependence. Our judges imitate this mode of feeling and thinking if they define intellectual freedom to consist in the absence of only one or two *means* of abridgment and ignore the other modes, as well as the historic issues of freedom. They do this because of a childish feeling of dependence upon things as they are, a fear of innovation and of being weaned to the solid food of more democratic institutions. This I conceive to be the psychologic explanation for the fact that *courts,* lawyers and the penalizable critics of things as they are, have so long quietly acquiesced in Blackstone, Mansfield, Kenyon, Ellenborough, and the other defenders of intellect with a limited liberty by permission. Our courts still seem to desire to perpetuate that undemocratic system, although clothing it in a meaningless verbiage of freedom.

STANDARD OF DANGEROUS TENDENCY

Every one with enough ignorant passion to be offended must of necessity deem everything to be of evil tendency which questions the omniscience of this passionate ignorance. Passion and fear of unconventional thoughts or words are symptoms of immaturity and conflict, that is, of ignorance, and all these conduce to the desire for censorship. Our censorial longings therefore become the measure of our immature passions, and of our aristocratic leanings. The inertia of respectable mediocrity, in the complacency of its good natured and pretentious culturine, renders a solemn acqiuescence to the demands of bigotry and mum-

bles plausable excuses in the cumbersome verbiage of pon-
derous "moral" decrees. Of course those who merely
acquiesce in censorship also lack the understanding to see
that it is the *conduct* based upon passionate and orthodox
ignorance *that needs to be suppressed,* rather than the
idea which opposes it. Such opposition tends to stimulate
development though itself conceived on an equally immature level. Which will we now punish or suppress? The
actual disturbance and material injury inflicted by the
passionately ignorant hearer or reader, or the speech which
only *tends* to provoke them? Where do our constitutions
indicate that free speech means that the mere speech may
be punished as a preventative of the former? Can any
one find it in the free speech guarantees? Only if he fears
to assume the responsibility of more democracy in himself.

But how can we know that it is only the passion of our
ignorance that tempts to the exercise of censorial powers?
In the case of judicial action I conceive the tests to be
clear and convincing. The judge's utterances will always
show whether his judgments are merely theoretic inventions based upon undemocratic desire, or are founded
upon the facts of experience, inductively used to check the
less mature impulses.

TEST OF EXPERIENCE

If a man has delivered a lecture denouncing religion,
the wage system, courts or anything else, and there is no
actual disturbance of the peace nor any material resultant
injury to any one, that is an experimental fact as to the
psychologic tendency of his utterance, and is far more
conclusive than any contrary phantasy or speculation of
judge, jury or legislature. If in spite of this test a judge
submits to the jury the question of the criminality of that
speech, and either for himself or in his instruction to the
jury, justifies a verdict of guilty on the theory that such
a speech has an unrealized tendency to disturb the peace,
then he is inventing a theory to explain and justify a personal emotional urge. The same is true if such a constructive psychologic "tendency" is made an excuse for
circumventing our constitutional guarantees. In the

hypothetical case the tendency and its constructive breach of the peace contradict the only concrete evidence on the subject which is, that *this speech under the particular circumstances of its delivery did not produce the feared disturbance.* The evil tendency therefore, exists more in the fearful feelings and phantasies of the judge than in the observed facts. Manifestly it is the *judicial fear and desire* which then controls the finding and not the evidence, nor a previously enacted law.

Such is the case in every prosecution for intellectual offense, no matter what may be the official or judicial pretence. *If actual disturbance or actual and material* injury had resulted that could easily be proven and would then be made the essence of the offense, instead of having the prosecution proceed against the words as such. In the former case the "crime" would no longer be one of the intellect only.

POPULAR IDEAS SHALL NOT BE PRIVILEGED

Men cannot be prevented from bringing to religion, politics or economics all the weakness, folly, disorderly fancies, disturbed emotions and defective intellectual processes with which they approach every other problem. No valid reason can be given why any of these, more than mathematics, should be shielded from the criticism of such ignorance or immaturity. *Our constitutions make no exception.* If intelligent criticism is to be endured, surely the ill tempered criticism of the uncultured must be stlil less harmful either to morality or the state. To fear either is to distrust the people, is to fear democracy.

If we ourselves have attained an intellectual status above that of one who coarsely rails at our pet conviction, we can with calm amusement listen to the verbal expression of his childish passion and fancies. If we have not attained to the superior intellectual level, the state should not protect us from the discomfiture of our unsettled immaturity. The other fellow's ignorance is entitled to equal play, even though it is less popular. The state should rather compel us to listen in outward calm, that our inward hurt may urge us to greater efforts toward the more mature attitude

of feeling and toward greater understanding. It is by
our mistakes and pains that we are tempted to learn. Our
constitutional guarantees of unabridged intellectual opportunity are not limited to the passionless formulas of
the mathematician, but are guaranteed to all *humans as
such*, regardless of their beliefs, their vocabulary, their
aesthetic feeling or their education. If we read into our
constitutions any such distinctions or limitatons then we
are ourselves but intellectualizing some immature feeling
which compels us to ignore facts and the historical issues
of theory, upon which a judgment was recorded in our
constitutions. This judgment reversed the former practice
and its supporting theories. Under that constitutional
mandate our morbid sensitiveness, about religion, politics
or economics, can receive no protection and can furnish
no pretext for penalizing those who express contempt for
our pet doctrine any more than for mathematics.

The Undemocratic Predisposition

Those judges who are satisfied to adopt Blackstone's
definition of liberty of the press must share, even though
unconsciously, some of the undemocratic fears and desires
which made Blackstone satisfied with the prevailing
English method of curtailing intellectual intercourse. The
makers of our constitutions were not satisfied therewith.
All censorship creates and protects inequalities, that is,
privileges. In other words, all censorships are undemocratic.

Those judges who thus approve Blackstone's anti-
democratic methods may not be conscious that their impulses can be characterized as undemocratic. They may
even be so unconscious of them as to be deceived into the
belief that they are *wholly* moved by external circumstances. The psychologist knows better. He knows that
the dynamics come from within, and from the past, and
that these determine the use that we make of Blackstone's
definition. For the psychologist that use is conclusive
as to the character of our dominant impulse. Already it
has been pointed out that undemocratic censorial desires
are the evidence and product of relative immaturity, that
is parasitism. Yet some lawyers act as though they desire

to canonize Blackstone. Thomas Jefferson consciously desired to "uncanonize" Blackstone. That marks the difference between aristocratic and democratic predisposition.

IMMATURE INTELLECTUAL METHOD

The immaturity of parasitic desire is accompanied by a like immaturity of intellectual method. This exhibits itself in the narrowness of vision, which excludes from conscousness and from consideration most, or all but one, of the past modes of abridging intellectual liberty. It likewise ignores the justifications once offered for censorship, and fails to ask if these can have any validity under our different theory and form of government. And lastly such intellectual methods always ignore the issue of the great confiict waged through the centuries, and which finally culminated in our "bills of rights" effecting a reversal of the policy which Blackstone described and upheld. The judge who ignores all these factors, blindly to follow Blackstone, is very clearly evading the realities of his problem and thereby is exhibiting not only a leaning toward immature and undemocratic desire but also immature intellectual processes. When will we reach a mature stage in our juridical development? The manner of meeting these issues of free speech will supply the answer.

The beneficiaries of legalized injustice and of vested wrongs, of "established" error or sanctified ignorance, always have feared too much critical education of the masses. Everything which puts the beneficiaries of privilege to the bother of defending their "rights," that is to say their habitual way of lookng at things and feeling about things, disturbs their peace of mind and is of "dangerous tendency." Thus are all censorships begotten and defended. Our constitutions give no evidence of sympathy with this or that method of restraining this or that kind of intellectual intercourse. Our constitutions declared for the whole of mental freedom and for all people. Many there are who still believe the priest and his theologies, or the millionaire and his millions, more sacred and useful than the chemist and his formulae. Our constitutions however, guaranteed equality in freedom and so no special pro-

tection can be given to the teaching of theologians or em-
ployers which are not accorded to the teachings of the
chemist and mathematician, or the revolutionary.

Those who framed our 'bills of rights" were not omniscient and therefore did not assume to possess any absolute truths. Where all truths are relative, and all humans
equal before the law, there no opinion whatever can be
either too true or too sacred to be laughed to scorn. The
right of free speech includes the right to make others
laugh, even at the gods.

Whether we approach the problem from the viewpoint of
the historic methods of abridging free speech and with
the view of framing a synthetic definition of free speech, or
from the psychologic or democratic viewpoint we always
arrive at the very antithesis of Blackstone's conception of
intellectual freedom.

The aversion or fear of liberty induces a confusion of
thought as between unabridged free speech and the absence
of only one or two modes of achieving the curtailment
of intellectual activity. We have seen that the immature
desires for censorship and the accompanying immature
methods by which the desire is intellectualized, when
psychologically understood are but part of a general attitude toward life which is comparable to the parasitism
of the infant. This means that censorship is produced at
the other end of the development from that at which we
find self-reliant independence, which makes us willing to
take chances on the whole of democratic intellectual freedom and equality, and equally willing and able to abide
the outcome with complacency.

In short all inclination toward censorship is part of the
psychology of fear; is a symptom of that relative emotional and intellectual immaturity, which fears the larger
democracy, and justifies the fear by phantasies and metaphysical speculation, instead of seeking to look all the
realities of the problem squarely in the face and making
use of a synthetic view to check our relatively infantile
fear. When our courts achieve that freedom and scientific attitude and methods, full freedom of speech will ob-

tain and a maximum of character development will result to all from enforcing that concept of free speech.

Those whose desires have reached approximate maturity will thus be enabled to co-ordinate the largest possible related facts, to the end of checking their immature fears and the resultant impulse for legalized violence for the suppression of unpopular ideas. Instead they will promote an intellectual dominance by means of the absolute free competition of all minds, not only for the perpetuation and promotion of inequalities, but also for competition toward a maximum of service to the process of democratizing welfare.

THE FEELING OF INFERIORITY.

It is believed that a thorough analytic study of the psychology of those favoring censorships would show that all censorship is essentially a manifestation of the psychology of fear. Generally speaking it is a fear to face the realities of their personal, political, social, economic, industrial or intellectual status, as seen by hostile critics. From another approach censorship may be the expression of a desire to live in a world of phantasy wherein we feel or act as though this is the best possible world, at least for those who are dominated by a fear of innovation. From still another viewpoint this censorial attitude of mind may be expressed as the product of a subconscious fear, that further democratization (or its friends) somehow challenge or threaten our subconscious urge for the feeling of personal worth, or our desire for relative importance, or superiority. This vanity is often but a *feeling*, rather than an objectively derived or consciously entertained opinion which we can or do justify by standards of social worth or service. With this comes the dread that these upstart reformers, whom we *feel* to be so inferior, will establish some new social order which we dread to cope with. In proportion to the intensity (not the consciousness) of our fear of being made aware of some inferiority, just so strenuously will we demand a censorship to avoid facing that issue. Censorship is one of the means which can be efficiently employed to exclude the arrogant challenge of things as they are, or of those persons who desire something different. This challenge is always an unwelcome reminder that the messenger of unpleasant reality impliedly claims a superiority over us, and we resent that. When psychologically considered, our response of legalized violence toward the critic is always the unconscious confession, not that necessarily we really are inferior, but that at least in our subconscious impulses there lurks a dominating fear of becoming conscious of some inferiority. If we are not now conscious of any factor of our own inferiority perhaps that only means that we have crowded the unpleasant facts out of memory.

Here I am suggesting psychologic processes and mechanisms which are not yet generally understood. Those who may wish to achieve a better understanding should have themselves psycho-analysed. If this is too burdensome the reader may acquire some understanding of my meaning by reading: A. Adler, "The Neurotic Constitution." If any wish to see how these unconscious fears dominate judicial action, even to the choice of words in which decisions are expressed, such may read "The Psychologic Study of Judicial Opinion" in the *California Law Review*, Jan. 1918 This last article is written by myself. The intelligent reading of these two items will furnish much toward illuminating my meaning in the above paragraphs, and in what follows.

DELUSIONS OF GRANDEUR.

A feeling of inferiority always tends to induce compensatory delusions of grandeur. Because of this fact of psychologic behavior all religious zeal necessarily approaches more or less toward megalomania, which is felt desirable as an escape from present, or unconscious past depressed states. Such persons tend to claim, with more or less vehemence, super-morality and special sanctity. From this hysterical moral sentimentalism to relative perfectism or the doctrine of personal sinlessness is but a small step, and marks the growth toward feeling and conduct like unto that of an omnipotent and omniscient person. Only a little beyond is the claim of special prophetic powers or divine authority. Every asylum has its reincarnated

Jesus, its holy-virgin, its mouthpiece of God, or a living God. Many of those who came in conflict with the blasphemy laws were the victims of such delusions of grandeur, and collided with similar but more systematized delusions, "established" by law. Just to the degree of intensity that we dread the feeling of inferiority, with the same intensity will we crave that satisfaction which comes from compensating delusions of grandeur. With equally great force will come a corresponding urge toward censorship, approaching irresistibility if accompanied by the power to impose it.

The unorthodox megalomaniacs are friends of toleration till they achieve the power to persecute. In the meantime the orthodox consider them as blasphemers, because the heretics ascribe to humans qualities which orthodoxy says belong only to God, and to itself. This same situation from another point of view means that the heretics deny the jurisdiction or authority of the specially recognized or legalized priesthood to play the role of relative omniscience in matters of religion. Therefore, religious zeal in unorthodox channels or zeal for the irreligious, is always blasphemous. This is true because heretical zealots must necessarily deny some essential of orthodoxy and so impairs its moral sentimentalism and irritates ecclesiast, and therefore tend to a disturbance of the civil peace. That is to say, it 'tends" to the destruction of spiritual aristocracy and priestly privileges, and therefore is resented. Partial tolerance, when considered psychologically, means only an imperfect or mild tendency toward megalomania. All blasphemy laws and all censorships manifest only varying degrees of intensity and varying degrees of consciousness in a protest against democracy. Every form of censorship is a denial of equality of intellectual opportunity, and of the indulgence of an equality of zeal, and therefore every blasphemy law is a denial or limitation upon democracy. When there is a union of church and state, heresy also tends to impair the political prerogatives by divine right, and is frankly suppressed for its democracy.

The framers of our constitutions thought the time had come for the establishment of a complete democracy, as to religion. The time is now, the place is here, and the immediate opportunity is in this case for the enforcement of that democratic ideal. By declaring this blasphemy law unconstitutional, notice should be served upon the religious megalomaniacs that they are expected to keep the peace even though that involves the termination of all their remaining legalized privileges and prerogatives, and upholds the zealous propagation of all that is unorthodox. The Trinity and the multiplication table must equally submit to criticism, denial, ridicule, or contempt, if we are to uphold democracy in relation to religion. The decision in a case of this kind will show just how much of constitutional democracy some judges believe in.

CHAPTER XX.
OVERT ACT AND ACTUAL INJURY
versus
EVIL PSYCHOLOGIC TENDENCY.

Now it is intended to repeat some fragment of the libertarian contentions upon which a final judgment of approval was passed by our constitutional conventions. This will show conclusively that free speech in relation with religious liberty meant that no man should be punished simply because those of contrary opinion, or lovers of a different literary or oratorical style, professed to believe that the disapproved utterance contained an evil psychologic tendency.

In some quarters, notwithstanding our constitutional guarantees for intellectual freedom and equality, it has been thought that the legislature may still penalize as blasphemy any irreligious utterance which, for any reason or for no reason at all, some court and jury may profess to believe possessed of a tendency toward a breach of the peace. Such views as to the meaning of our constitution seem plausible, just so long as we ignore the antecedent history of these provisions, and therefore read into the constitutional language some of our own emotional attitudes or feeling-desires.

In or after the seventeenth century no jury at common-law was ever expressly empowered to create its own *ex post facto* criteria of crime. Fixing standards of guilt was theoretically a matter of parliamentary legislative discretion, though the power has been frequently usurped by judges. It was never the conceded province of a common-law jury to indulge its own fancy or legislative discretion, for judging guilt by its own whims about a psychological tendency. Only tyrannous legislators and like minded judges and theologians, justified the enactment of blasphemy laws by such speculations about the psychologic tendency. But even then no such speculation was allowed to enter into the deliberations of a jury.

It will now be shown that in considering the limits of legislative jurisdiction, quite uniformly the intelligent friends of liberty made the distinction, between a mere psychologic tendency on the one hand and an actual and material injury on the other. More precisely expressed in modern phraseology, the contention which found approval in our constitutional guarantees may be thus generalized: *Before an expressed idea can be penalized there must have resulted an actual and material injury, or another resultant overt act designed to produce and capable of inflicting such injury, which possibility must be determined according to the known laws of the physical universe.*

Let us enter with an open mind upon the following review of the historic contention for mental freedom, with the fixed determination of deriving therefrom the true historic meaning of free speech as that was conceived by its friends, and by their successors written into our organic law.

THE BEGINNINGS OF THE CONTROVERSY.

Upon the authority of Tacitus, the learned Peter Bayle tells us that it was the Emperor Augustus who first made all defamatory libels to be high treason. He quotes the historian as follows: "Augustus had revived the law concerning violated majesty; a law which in the days of our ancestors, had indeed the same name, but implied different arraignments, and crimes; namely, those against the state, as when an army was betrayed abroad, when seditions were raised at home; in short when the public was faithlessly administered, and the majesty of the Roman *people* was debased: *these were actions, and actions were punished, but words were free.* Augustus was the first who brought libels under the penalties of this wrested law, being provoked by the insolence of Cassius Serverus, who had in his writings wantonly defamed men and ladies of illustrious quality.' For which reason another historian [Suetonius] observes, that it was a novelty to see a lady of the family of Claudii accused before the people, as guilty of high treason, for having said in the hearing of a prodigious multitude, that stopped her coach, would to God my brother would return into the world and lose another fleet, that there might be fewer people at Rome. The commentators observe here a two-fold novelty; one in the sex of the accused, and the other *in entitling a simple wish a treason.* * * * I find in Suetonius that this Emperor did not punish satirical discourses nor writings that concerned him." [1]

Two things are noteworthy in the foregoing statement: *"Actions were punished but words were free."* It is this distinction between overt acts capable of direct actual and material injury, and mere words, with a speculation about their psychologic tendency, that marks the difference between intellectual liberty and the state's jurisdiction to penalize conduct. The other important thing is that in Rome a woman was punished for wishing the return of tyrannous rule over the people. For this no one could now be punished.

This distinction is further emphasized by the statement of Suetonius that the "Emperor did not punish satirical discourses nor writings that concerned him." The Star Chamber reversed this by penalizing the defamation of the upper classes but not giving equal protection to mere humans as such. Tiberius continued the innovation of Augustus but later so extended the laws as to punish those who attacked his person. "Cremutius Cordus in vain pleaded that he had written nothing offensive against Tiberius, or the Empress. * * * This was not sufficient to clear him of his pretended crime of having praised Brutus and Cassius." Cordus insisted upon the contrast between criminal overt acts and mere words. He said: *"I am so guiltless, conscript father, that my words only are accused."*

Under the reign of Augustus there were no false pretences, of a concern for the defamer, or a desire to protect him against assault. Then the claim was that "a subject who defames his neighbor, usurps one of the rights of the sovereign, and that it belongs solely to the sovereign to inflict the pain of infamy."[2] Here also have we submitted to a reversal of theory. Under the common law all sorts

[1] Historical and critical dictionary, second edition, vol. 5, pp. 743-746.
[2] Peter Bayle: Historical and critical dictionary, 2nd edition, v. 5, pp. 745.

of libels were punished frankly to perpetuate the existing regime, political and religious. In other words the British punished libels as a means of protecting the beneficiaries of vested wrongs and legalized injustices. In America we no longer punish such conduct under the name of *libels*, or verbal sedition. We call it "disorderly conduct" which is disorderly or injurious only by construction. We justify this under the false pretence of protecting heretics against being assaulted. Thus to change the name of an offense, and to add a false pretence, often passes for free speech, mental liberty and equality of intellectual opportunity. How much longer will this continue to be so? Can it survive direct attack by the method of historic interpretation of our constitutions? We will see.

This brief recital and critical comment has been made to enable us to see our problem in larger perspective and in its wider scope. In doing so we do not forget that thus we are going a little beyond the narrow range of religious liberty, in recognition of the fact that there is a unity in all intellectual freedom.

SAINT HILARY, about A. D. 335.

Let me emphasize a little further the antiquity of the distinction which is now being urged. We will quote two more early statements and then pass on to the seventeenth and eighteenth centuries. We now begin with Saint Hilary.

"Much they suffered in the days of Constantine, unto whom the words of Hilary in this case are worthy consideration: Let (saith he) your clemency take care and order, that the Presidents of the provinces look to Public Civil Affairs, which alone are committed to them, but not meddle in things of religion, and again: Let your gentleness suffer the people to hear them teaching whom they desire, whom they think well of, whom they choose."[3] As we approach nearer to our own time the statement of the distinction between "religious" and "civil" affairs, as effecting the jurisdiction of the state, will grow in clarity.

---

[3] A peace-offering in an apology and humble plea for indulgence and liberty of conscience [John Owen] London, 1667, p. 26.

THEODOSIAN CODE, A. D. 438.

Says the learned Peter Bayle, in 1738: "But upon this head can anything be nobler than this edict [A. D. 438] of the Emperor Theodosius? * * * 'If any person, void of modesty and shame, shall by wicked and slanderous detraction, go about to blast our reputation, and wantonly traduce and defame our government, it is our pleasure that he be not subjected to punishment nor suffer any hardship or severity on that account, because, if this proceeded from levity, it ought to be despised, if from madness, it deserves pity and compassion, if from a design to do an injury, it ought to be forgiven. We therefore will that no man be punished, or prosecuted for such slanderous speeches, and that they be referred to our cognizance that we may weigh and consider the saying of men by their characters, and may judge whether they ought to be passed by or inquired into.' "[4] Why is not that a perfect statement of the import of free speech in relation to religion?

In this Theodosian Code we see the same distinction implied namely, between a mere expressed and inefficient desire to do harm and an overt act capable of inflicting actual and material injury. Now let this matter stand as a background against which we will silhouette the more modern controversy for intellectual freedom. In order to put emphasis upon the historic issues which culminated in our constitutional guarantees, let us skip the intervening development of this conflict, down to Martin Luther and then skip to the seventeenth century. From here onward we will confine that material more closely to the subject of religious liberty.

MARTIN LUTHER (ABOUT) 1535.

The real fight for religious liberty found its first efficient exponent through the reformation inaugurated by Martin Luther (1484-1546). It is said that, "In the early part of his career he was one of the most intolerant champions of the papal authority." Perhaps he was one who could live and grow, and so felt no fear of inconsistency.

[4] Peter Bayle: Historical and critical dictionary, 2nd edition, v. 5, p. 760.

As a chief factor in the movement his words are of very great importance.

In his book on the civil magistrate he says this: "The laws of the civil government extend no further than over the body or goods, and to that which is external: for, over the soul God will not suffer any man to rule, only he himself will rule there: therefore, wheresoever the civil magistrate doth undertake to give laws unto the soul and consciences of men, he usurpeth that government to himself, which appertaineth to God."*

M———— S———————— —1644.

This next quotation is from an anonymous author. Its importance lies only in the suggestion that there is a duel psychologic tendency to be considered. There is a tendency to a disturbance of the peace always resulting from a suppression of utterance which is more dangerous than the speech itself.

"External compulsion in matters of Religion, is of a proper and direct tendencies, to make men twofold more the children of sin (and so of wrath) than they were before, or would be otherwise."[5]

Modern psychologists who specialize on the behavior of the emotions have confirmed this view of the psychologic tendency of forcible repression, almost to a demonstration. If any desire is suppressed by force rather than the desire itself being developed to change, the immediate effect is to intensify that desire. If in this condition its natural expression is effectively suppressed, then the result is that the repressed energies find some compensatory outlet. Usually this is more indirect and more anti-social than a mere speech could be. Thus come all those hysterical manifestations which in their further development produce so large a share of criminals and of the insane. Yet there are

---

*Tracts on liberty of conscience and persecution, 1614-1661. Edited by the Hanserd Knollys Society with an historical introduction by Edward Bean Underhill. London, 1846. p. 220, citing: Luther's, Sammtliche Schriften, 10r, Th. ss. 438, 452. Halle, 1742. For similar sentiments see also: pp. 23, 93, 121, 300, 360, and elsewhere in, Tracts on liberty of conscience, etc.

[5] M. S. to A. S. with a Plea for libertie of conscience. Lond. 1644. p. 55.

many so ignorant of psychology as to believe that a jury of farmers and shop-keepers are able to weigh up and balance the psychologic tendencies involved in such matters.

JOHN MILTON—1644.

John Milton (1608-1674), of immortal fame, published his "Areopagitica" in 1644. On the establishment of the Protectorate he became Secretary under Cromwell, and later quite naturally perhaps was imprisoned by order of the Commons. In 1683 some extracts of his book were burned at Oxford. Those judges who wish to believe that the fight for intellectual freedom was only a demand for the repeal of laws creating previous restraint and leaving punishment after publication for disapproved opinions, need to read the whole of Milton's famous tract. One looks in vain for such distinction as our courts sometimes assert, although Milton wrote when the previous restraint was in force. Unfortunately he felt too intensely about Catholics to make it possible to apply his general principles to them. In this respect his friend Roger Williams was more consistant. All of Milton might well be reproduced here, but space limits give room for only a few paragraphs (from the Grolier edition, 1890) showing how unafraid he is of the spooks of dangerous psychologic tendency.

"Till then, books were ever as freely admitted into the world as any other birth; The issue of the brain was no more stifled than the issue of the womb (p. 38). * * * 'To the pure all things are pure,' not only meat and drinks, but all kind of knowledge, whether of good or evil; the knowledge cannot defile, nor consequently the books, if the will and conscience be not defiled. For books are as meats and viands are; some of good, some of evil substance; and yet God in that unapocryphal vision, said without exception, 'Rise, Peter, kill and eat,' leaving the choice to man's discretion. Wholesome meats to a vitiated stomach differ little or nothing from unwholesome; and best books to a naughty mind are not unapplicable to occasions of evil. Bad meats will scarce breed good nourishment in the healthiest concoction; but herein the difference is of *bad books, that they to a discreet and judicious reader serve in many respects to discover, to confute, to forewarn, and to ILLUSTRATE.* * * * All opinions, yea, errors, known, read and collated, are of main service and assistance toward the speedy attainment of what is truest. * * * For those actions, *which enter into a man rather than issue out of him,* and therefore defile not, God uses not to captivate under a perpetual childhood of prescription, but trusts him with the gift of reason to be his own chooser. * * *

"I cannot praise a fugitive and cloistered virtue, unexercised and unbreathed, that never sallies out and sees her adversary, but slinks out of the race, where that immortal garland is to be run for, not without dust and heat. Assuredly we bring not innocence into the world, we bring impurity much rather; that which purifies us is trial, and trial is by what is contrary. *That virtue therefore which is but a youngling in the contemplation of evil, and knows not the utmost that vice promises to her followers, and rejects it, is but a blank virtue, not a pure; her whiteness is but an excremental whiteness.* * * *

"Since, therefore, the knowledge and survey of vice is in this world so necessary to the constituting of human virtue, and the scanning of error to the confirmation of truth, how can we more safely, and with less danger, scout into the regions of sin and falsity, than by reading all manner of tractates, and hearing all manner of reason? * * * Truth and understanding are not such wares as to be monopolized and traded in by tickets and statutes and standards. * * * Give me the liberty to know, to utter, and to argue freely according to conscience, above all [other] liberties. * * *

"Though ye take from a covetous man all his treasure, he has yet one jewel left; ye cannot bereave him of his covetousness. Banish all objects of lust, shut up all youth into the severest discipline that can be exercised in any hermitage, ye cannot make them chaste that came not thither so."[6]

---

[6] Grolier edition, 1890, pp. 38, 49, 50, 51, 52, 53, 56, 57, 58, 107, 163.

Not a word here of abolishing previous restraint for sub-sequent punishment. Not the slightest fear of evil psychologic tendency!

JEREMY TAYLOR—1647.

Jeremy Taylor (1613-1667) was one of the most distinguished men of his stormy time. He was several times in jail for intellectual offences, and was "Chaplaine in Ordinarie to His Majestie" Charles I. After the Restoration he was promoted to the Episcopate. "Among the ranks of the deprived clergymen there was no more illustrious name." His "Discourse on Liberty of Prophesying" is his best known work. It displeased Charles I, and it is said that Taylor had as many copies as possible bought up and destroyed.[7]

For us it is enough to know that he drew the same line between liberty and its opposite that we have found in others. "The mere doctrines and opinions of men are things spiritual," says he, "and therefore not Cogniscible by a temporall Authority; and the Ecclesiastical Authority, which is to take Cognisance is it selfe so Spirituall that it cannot inflict any punishment corporall. And it is not enough to say that when the Magistrate restraines the preaching such opinions, if any man preaches them he may be punished (and then it is not for his opinion, but his disobedience that he is punished) for the temporall power ought not to restraine Prophesyings, when the public peace and interest is not certainly concerned."[8]

EDWARD BAGSHAW—1660.

Edward Bagshaw the younger (1629-1671) was the son of a distinguished royalist, politician and author. He was eratic, and well educated at Oxford and Cambridge. In 1659 he was ordained by the eminent Bishop Brownrigg. While vicar of Ambrosden he elected to be one of 2000 clergymen to be ejected in 1662. Having criticised the king, government, church and state he was imprisoned during 1663-1664. "He exceeded most if not all of them [nonconformists] in natural and acquired parts." Soon he

---

[7] Dictionary of national biography, v. 55, pp. 422-429.
[8] Discourses on the liberty of prophesying, p. 255, ed. of 1647.

again became "involved in 'conventicling' and the inevitable 'sedition,'" and once more imprisoned.*

"Nor is there any Hope, that the world should be freed from cruelty, disguised under the name of zeal, till it please God to inform all Magistrates, how far their Commission reaches, that their Province is *only over the Body*, to repress and correct those morall vices, to which *our outward man* is subject."[9]

In a later pamphlet he says this: "A Christian Liberty consists not in Freedom of Practice, but in freedom of judgment." This is criticised as a foundation for conformity in Non-essentials and he concludes thus:

"Liberty of Judgment without Liberty of Practice suitable to that Judgment, is not only a vain and ludicrous, but a burdensome and vexatious thing, and especially *in the service of God*, while we always outwardly do that, which inwardly we do not approve, is nothing else but direct Hypocracie."[10]

THE DECLARATION OF BREDA—1660.

Even Royalty once gave temporary verbal approval to the line we are trying to draw between actual and constructive disturbance of the peace:

"His present majesty [1683] in his Declaration from Breda, April 4 [1660], speaks thus: "'We do declare a liberty to tender consciences, and that no man shall be disquieted, or called into question, for differences in opinion, which do not disturb the peace of the Kingdom.' Which was also the declared sense of most of the nobility and gentry at that time, to which they subscribed their names."[11]

From October, 1660 to November 1680, this Declaration of Breda was nine times more or less definitely affirmed either by King or Parliament.

* Dictionary of National Biography, v. 2, p. 402-3.
⁹ The great question concerning things indifferent in religious worship, by Edward Bagshaw. Third Edit. Lond. 1660, p. 16
¹⁰ The second part of the great question concerning indifferent things in religious worship by the same author [Edward Bagshaw] Lond. 1661, pp. 13-14.
¹¹ Plea for nonconformists, pp. 117-119, ed. of 1800.

While, of course, this liberty was not yet extended to all, it does show that in those to whom it applied, liberty of utterance meant anything short of an actual breach of 'e peace. Of course, Charles II forgot the Declaration of Breda when expediency demanded and power made repudiation possible. So too, Courts sometimes explain away the free speech guarantees when the constitution interferes with their lust for power.

JOHN OWEN—1667.

"But all these considerations [for toleration] are quickly, in the thoughts of some, removed out of the way, by pretences that the indulgeance and liberty desired, will certainly produce all sorts of evils both in Religion itself, and in the Civil state. * * * The arguments in this case insisted on, consist merely in conjectures, jealousies and suppositions of what may come to pass, no one knows when, or where; it is easie for any to dilate upon them at their pleasure, nor is it possible for any to give satisfaction to all that men may conjecture, or pretend to fear. * * * It is sufficiently evident that they are all false or mistaken suppositions, that can give countenance to these pretences." Then this author goes on at length to give his reasons for this assertion, by reference to historical facts.

"But it is yet further objected, that the indulgeance desired hath an inconsistency with public peace and tranquility, the other head of the general accusation before mentioned. Many fears and suspicions are mustered up, to contribute assistance unto this objection also. For we are in the field of surmise which is endless and boundless. * * *

"We find it indeed still pretended, that the allowance of meetings for the worship of God, however ordered and bounded, will be a means to procure and further sedition in the Commonwealth, and to advantage men in the pursuit of designs to the disturbance of the Kingdom."[12]

---

[12] A peace-offering in an apology and humble plea for indulgeance and liberty of conscience [John Owen, D.D] London. 1667. pp. 30, 31, 32.

Thus Owen denies the validity of all of those fears or deems them outweighed by resultant good. In other words, intellectual liberty is demanded in spite of fears and theories about the imaginary consequent dangerous psychologic tendencies thereby let loose.

JOHN LOCKE—1667.

John Locke (1632-1704), Oxford lecturer, physician and philosopher, needs no introduction. His "Essay Upon Toleration" was a lengthy treatise written in 1667. A part of his thesis was that religious liberty consisted in limiting the power of the magistrate to functions clearly necessary for the preservation of the peace. So far then he is an authority on the meaning of intellectual liberty, though he found reasons for deviation from consistency when his anti-Catholic feelings were involved. He wrote while laws requiring licensing were still in force, but nowhere even remotely suggests that the mere abolition of previous restraint is the essence of intellectual liberty.[13]

"It [religion] is not instituted in order to the erecting an *external pomp,* nor to the obtaining of ecclesiastical domination, *nor to the exercising of compulsive force;* but to the regulating of men's lives according to the rules of virtue and piety. * * *

"I esteem it above all things necessary to distinguish exactly the business of civil government from that of religion, and to settle the just bounds that lie between the one and the other. * * * *Civil interests I call life, liberty, health, and indolency of body; and the possession of outward things,* such as money, lands, houses, furniture, and the like. * * * All the power of civil government relates only to men's civil interests, is confined to *the care of the things of this world,* and hath nothing to do with the world to come. * * *

"A church then I take to be a voluntary society of men, joining themselves together of their own accord, in order to the public worshipping of God, in such a manner as they

---

[13] Quotations and references given in text are from the edition of 1689, pp. 2, 4, 11, 12, 19, 20, 26, 27, 28, 29, 30, 31, 37, 38, 42, 58, 70, 71, 73, 74, 75, 77, 86, 87.

judge acceptable to Him, and effectual to the salvation of their souls. * * * No man by nature is bound unto any particular church or sect. * * * The end of a religious society is the public worship of God. * * * All discipline ought therefore to tend to that end, and all ecclesiastical laws to be thereunto confined. Nothing ought nor can be transacted in this society, relating to the possession of civil or worldly goods. *No force is here to be made use of, upon any occasion whatsoever;* for force belongs wholly to the civil magistrate. * * * The arms by which the members of this society are to be kept within their duty are exhortations, admonitions, and advices. If by these means the offenders will not be reclaimed, [they] should be cast out and separated from the society. This is the last and utmost force of ecclesiastical authority. * * * The person so condemned ceases to be a part of that church. Care is to be taken that the sentence of excommunication, and the execution thereof, carry with it no rough usage, of word, or action, whereby the ejected person may anyways be damnified in body or estate. * * *

"No private person has any right, in any manner, to prejudice another person in his civil enjoyments, because he is of another church or religion. * * * If any man err from the right way, it is his own misfortune, no injury to thee. * * *

"When they [churches] are not strengthened with the civil power, then they can bear most patiently and unmovedly the contagion of idolatry, superstition and heresy, in their neighborhood; of which, in other occasions, the interest of religion makes them to be extremely apprehensive. * * *

"Nobody * * * neither single persons nor churches, may, nor even commonwealths, have any just title to invade the civil rights and wordly goods of each other, upon pretense of religion. * * * If Christians are to be admonished that they abstain from all manner of revenge, even after repeated provocations and multiplied injuries, how much more ought they who suffer nothing, who have had no harm done them, forbear violence, and abstain from all manner of ill-usage toward those from whom they have received none? * * *

"Whatsoever may be doubtful in religion, yet this at least is certain, that no religion which I believe not to be true, can be either true or profitable unto me. * * * Men cannot be forced to be saved whether they will or no. And therefore, when all is done, *they must be left to their own consciences.* * * *

"As the magistrate has no right to impose by his laws the use of any rites and ceremonies in any church, so neither has he any power to *forbid* the use of such rites and ceremonies as are already received, approved, and practiced by any church. You will say, by this rule, if some congregations should have a mind *to sacrifice infants, or, as the primitive Christians were falsely accused, lustfully pollute themselves in promiscuous uncleanness, or practice any other such heinous enormities, is the magistrate obliged to tolerate them, because they are committed in a religious assembly? I answer, no.* These things are not lawful in the ordinary course of life, nor in any private house; and therefore, neither are they so in the worship of God, or in any religious meeting. But indeed if any people congregated on account of religion, should be desirous to sacrifice a calf, I deny that that ought to be prohibited by a law. * * * *For no injury is thereby done to any one, no prejudice to another man's goods.* And for the same reason he may kill his calf also in a religious meeting. * * * *The part of the magistrate is only to take care that the commonwealth receive no prejudice, and that there be no injury done to any man, either in life or estate.* * * *

"It may be said, what if a church be idolatrous, is that also to be tolerated by the magistrate? In answer, I ask, what power can be given to the magistrate for the suppression of an idolatrous church, which may not, in time and place, be made use of to the ruin of an orthodox one? * * * The civil power can either change everything in religion, according to the prince's pleasure, or it can change nothing. If it be once permitted to introduce anything into religion, by the means of laws and penalties, there can be no bounds put to it. * * * No man whatever ought therefore, to be deprived of his terrestrial enjoyments upon account of his religion. *Not even Americans, [Indians], subjected unto a Christian prince are to be punished, either in body or goods, for not embracing our faith and worship.* * * *

"But idolatry, may come, is a sin, and therefore not to be tolerated. If they said it were therefore to be avoided, the inference were good. But it does not follow that because it is a sin it ought therefore to be punished by the magistrate. *The reason is because [it is] not prejudicial to other men's rights nor does it break the public peace of societies.* * * * Nay, even the sins of lying and prejury are no more punishable by laws; unless in certain cases, in which the real turpitude of the thing and the offense against God are not considered, but only the *prejury done unto men's neighbors, and to the commonwealth.* * * *

"The magistrate ought not to forbid the preaching or proffering of *any speculative opinions in any church because they have no manner of relation to the civil rights of the subjects.* If a Roman Catholic believe [in transubstantiation]; if a Jew do not believe the New Testament. * * * If a heathen doubt of both Testaments, *he is not therefore to be punished as a pernicious citizen.* * * * I readily grant that these opinions are false and absurd. *But the business of laws is not to provide for the truth of opinions, but for the safety and security of the commonwealth, and of every particular man's goods and person.* And so it ought to be. For truth certainly would do well enough, if she were once left to shift for herself."

Almost every page insists that the limit of jurisdiction for State interference is to be made at the line of actual and material injury.

THOMAS DELAUNE—1683.

Thomas Delaune (d. 1685) was a Baptist laymen, devoted to translations and other literary work. In response to a challenge contained in a book by Dr. Benjamin Calamy, "A Scrupulous Conscience," Delaune wrote his "Plea for the Non-conformists." This book resulted in

his conviction for seditious libel.   He was imprisoned and
his book publicly burned.   This book "was for many years
a standard Baptist apology, and was printed seven
times between 1683 and 1706, when DeFoe wrote his
preface for it."   An American edition was published at
"Ballston, Saratoga County," in 1800.   Its circulation in
America makes it a more immediate factor in the interpretation of our constitutional guarantees of intellectual
freedom.

Delaune draws the line where it had been drawn by all
those who wished to substitute mental liberty for mere
tolerance.   He says: "All I desire is that scrupulous consciences *who trouble not the peace of the nation,* should
be dealt withal, [at least] as weak brethren, according to
Rom. XIV, 1 and not ruined by penalties for not swallow-
ing what is imposed under the notion of decency and order."[14]

HUBERT LANGUET—1579 (1689).

Hubert Languet (1518-1581) was born in France, studied
civil law in Italy, and then went to Melanchthon at Wit-
temberg.   Thus he became a protestant.   He spent several years in travel during which king Gustavus of Sweden
commissioned him to entice Frenchmen skilled in the
sciences to come to Sweden.   In 1559 he accompanied the
prince of Orange into Italy.   Augustus, elector of Saxony
invited him to the court in 1565, and nominated him his
envoy to the court of France.   He held other important
posts.   He published a number of Latin essays.   Among
these appears to have been "Vindiciæ contra tyranus,"
published in 1579.   An English translation was issued in
1689, from which the following is quoted.[15]

"Those which confess that they hold their Soul and lives
of God, as they ought to acknowledge, they have then no
right to impose any tribute upon Souls.   The King takes
tribute and custom of the Body, and of such things as are
acquired or gained by the industry and Travel of the Body,

---

[14] Plea for non-conformists, p. 189.   See also: Dictionary of national
biography. v. 4, p. 315.
[15] Rose, Rev. Hugh James.   New general biographical dictionary,
Lond. 1853, v. 9, p. 190.

God doth principally exact his right from the Soul, which also in part executes her functions by the Body. * * * The Princes exceed their bounds not contenting themselves with that Authority which the Almighty, and all good God hath given them, but seek to usurp that sovereignty, which he hath reserved to himself over all men, being not content to command the Bodies, and goods of their Subjects at their pleasure, but assume licence to themselves to inforce the Consciences, which appertains chiefly to Jesus Christ, holding the earth not great enough for their ambition, they will climb and conquer Heaven itself. * * * *If their assaults be verbal, their defence must be likewise verbal*, if the Sword be drawn against them, they may also take Arms, and fight either with tongue or hand, as occasion is."[16]

[EDWARD?] HITCHIN—1710 (?), AND JOSHUA TOULMIN.

The following data was not examined at its original source for the want of time. Joshua Toulmin (1740-1815) who is credited with endorsing the sentiment as a dissenter, historian and biographer, published 49 separate items not including magazine articles or posthumous volumes. His sentiments may be gathered from the fact that Thomas Paine was burnt in effigy before his house. In 1794, on the recommendation of Priestly he received a degree of D. D. from Harvard. This was partly in recognition of his services in editing Neal's, History of Puritans.[17] The Hitchin referred to hereafter is assumed to be the author of Infant Baptism, who later became a Unitarian.

"Mr. [Edward?] Hitchins hath said: 'I would not have a Socinian persecuted for denying the Deity and Atonement of Christ any more than I would a Jew for blaspheming my Messiah, or denying that the true Messiah is yet to come; nor would I dare to use one Mean to prevent

---

[16] Vindiciae contra tyrannos: A defence of liberty against tyrants, or of the lawful power of the prince over the people, and of the people over the prince. Being a treatise written in Latin and French by Junius Brutus, and translated out of both into English. * * * London, 1689, pp. 2, 14, 34.
[17] Dictionary of national biography v. 57, p. 82.

their obtaining Liberty to worship their own God in their own way.' " This declaration is quoted with approval in his "Genuine Protestanism,"[18] and again approved by Joshua Toulmin.[19]

It will be observed that there is no qualification to the effect that denial of essentials will be permitted if done in proper literary style and in ladylike manner. Neither of these eminent dissenters nor any single person who favored the free speech clauses of our American Constitutions ever dreamed of demanding intellectual liberty only according to literary style or education. They demanded it as a *human* right, which implies that every man might express himself according to his own accustomed mode of speech, dependent upon temperament and education. Neither did any one of these libertarians ever utter the falsehood that liberty of the press consists only in the absence of previous restraints. That was the definition of English Tories such as Mansfield, Kenyon, Ellenborough and Blackstone.

REV. JOHN HOADLEY—1718.

Archbishop John Hoadley (1678-1746) a very celebrated man of his time, although an orthodox clergyman yet seems to have taken substantially the same view of religious freedom as the dissenters. I find this expressed in "A Sermon Preached before the Honorable House of Commons." I quote from the second edition.

"There is nothing, I think, plainer in the Rules of Civil Society than that no Man is to be abridged of his rights in it, but for those things which *immediately* effect its security. * * * So that to compel Men to this outward conformity either by using them as Schismatics from the body of Christ, or as unfit and dangerous Members of the Civil Society, is not just either to Politics or Christianity."[20]

---

[18] Page 45.
[19] Two Letters on the Application to Parliament, by the Protestant Dissenting Ministers, pp. 82-83.
[20] A sermon preached before the honorable house of commons, January 30th, 1717, second edition 1718, pp. 12, 13. See also: Dictionary of national biography, v. 27, p. 21.

By the word "immediately" in the phrase "immediately effect its security" I take it he means to negative the indirect problematic injury achieved through an intermediate person who might be induced to a breach of the peace. This is borne out by his consenting, as a primate, to the abolition of restrictions on Roman Catholics, whose doctrines in his time were deemed to be of very dangerous tendency.

In another place Bishop Hoadley makes still more clear his adherence to the distinction between jurisdiction in civil affairs and in psychological or spiritual affairs. His words are these: "In civil affairs they [dissenters] can give up the exercise of their rights by chusing, appointing or consenting to an arbitrator, judge or governor, finally to determine their civil controversies between man and man, but in the case of religion, supposing them once vested with the right before mentioned, it is not in their power to give it up because resulting from the nature of true religion, which requires choice and will, in every particular man's own conduct; no one can give it up without destroying the foundation of all that can be called religion in man. But if every private Christian has not this right in him, by what method came the superiors to have it? * * * I shall leave to others the glory of putting the ecclesiastical constitution of this realm and the religion delivered by Christ for synonymous terms."[21]

JOHN WICKLIFFE—1729.

"I too have observed with Sorrow and Concern the many books and pamphlets that have been published against our Holy Religion, that is, I am sorry that any Men should be so much mistaken as to conceive of that Religion as false, which to me appears to be most true. And I must agree with these Gentlemen, that all Books and Pamphlets published against our most Holy Religion, have a direct Tendency to propagate Infidelity: Methinks the Consequence is pretty natural, if they mean by Infidelity, as I suppose they do, a disbelief of the Christian Religion. But *I can by no means agree with them when*

---

[21] Here requoted from p. 112, Appendix of two letters addressed to the Right Rev. prelates.

they add, and consequently to the Corruption of all Morals:
And for this plain reason, because, tho' a Man should dis-
believe the Christian Religion, it would not follow
that he would commit Murder, or have any desire to do
it. * * *

"Therefore, if by the Blasphemy and Profaneness in this
Paragraph, these Gentlemen mean the Infidelity before-
mentioned, or Disbelief of the Christian Religion, and the
Publication of such Disbelief; and if by Suppression in
this Paragraph, they mean a Suppression by force; then
I do say, that the Suppression of Blasphemy and Profaneness (meaning by Suppression and Profaneness as
aforesaid) is so far from being of Service to his Majesty,
and the Protestant Succession, that I think nothing can
be more contradictory to the Design of it.

"The Protestant Succession was established among us
by the good Providence of God, for the Protection of our
Religions and Civil Rights and Liberties. *Religious Liberty, or Liberty with regard to Religion, seems to consist
in nothing else but thinking about Religion in what way
we judge proper, and the openly avowing and expressing
such Thoughts,* and worshipping God, as we judge proper.
And it is a Right which every Man ought to enjoy, (and
which therefore the Protestant Succession was design'd
to protect) to exercise this Liberty in all Instances *not
hurtful* to anybody else. Civil Liberty is a Liberty to do
what we judge proper: This therefore is likewise our Right,
with the same Restriction as before, that we *don't hurt* any
body else by it. * * *

"How absurd then is it, thus to blend the Interests of
Religion and the State, *i. e.* the Interests of this World,
and the next, which have really nothing to do with one
another, (farther than as I shall observe hereafter) the
one resting in the Minds and Consciences of Men, the
other in the outward Peace and Affluence of the Publick.

"Indeed, if Infidels attack your Religion *by force,* you
must defend it by force. Presentments, Dragoons, or
anything that comes next to hand: But *so long as they
keep themselves to Writing, 'tis quite inconsistent with*

the Spirit of the Gospel to use force, tho' in the Defence of it. * * *

"We chuse such a Religion, because we think it will carry us to Heaven; and such a Form of Government, because we think that most conductive to the Safety and Happiness of the Publick: Which are very different Considerations, and quite independent of each other. * * *

"If Infidels endeavour to propagate their Infidelity *by force*, those Endeavours must, to be sure, affect the State; and in such case, I should thank a Grand-Jury who would take care, ne quid detrimenti Respublica capiat. But so long as *Infidels keep themselves to Writing only, and Argument*, if the State suffers anything in the Dispute, it must be by the Folly and Wickedness of those who make the State a Party, by using force. *They who first use force on either side the Question, are the Enemies of the State; and as such the State ought to have a watchful Eye over them.*"[22]

CHARLES MONTESQUIEU—1748.

Charles de Secondat Montesquieu (1689-1775) is characterized by Bourke as "a genius, not born in every country or in every time, with a Herculean robustness of mind." Although in a benighted century he was the President of the Parliament of Bordeaux and a baron, he did much for progress toward democracy. He "commanded the future from his study more than Napoleon from his throne." His book, "The Spirit of the Laws" was published in 1748, and, according to the opinion of Mr. Justice Holmes, "probably has done as much to remodel the world as any product of the eighteenth century." The references to this book, all show, as well as the Constitution itself, how the thought provoked by the book helped to shape our institutions. This fact makes his views upon the relations of religion and the penal code a matter of direct bearing upon the historical interpretation of freedom of speech and religious liberty.

---

[22] Remarks upon two late presentments of the grand-jury of the county of Middlesex. * * * by John Wickliffe, London, 1729. pp. 8, 9, 10, 17, 20, 21.

On the subject of religion, he emphasizes the essential difference between human and divine laws, and argues reservedly for general toleration of all religion, and concludes:

"When the legislator had believed it a duty to permit the exercise of many religions, it is necessary that he should enforce also a toleration among these religions themselves. * * * *Penal laws ought to be avoided in respect to religion.*"

In the matter of verbal treason, Montesquieu seems very exact in his statements and comprehensive in his thought. In the English law religious offences were at times treated as a special form of treason, and indictable under the latter designation. Only a few lines will need quoting from Montesquieu on this aspect. He says:

"Nothing renders the crime of high treason more arbitrary than declaring people guilty of it for indiscreet speeches. * * * *Words do not constitute an overt act;* they remain only an idea. When considered by themselves, they have generally no determinate signification, for this depends on the tone in which they are uttered. * * * Since there can be nothing so equivocal and ambiguous as all this, how is it possible to convert it into a crime of high treason? Wherever this law is established, there is an end not only of liberty, but even of its very shadow. * * *

"Overt acts do not happen every day; they are exposed to the naked eye of the public, and a false charge with regard to matters of fact may be easily detected. Words carried into action assume the nature of that action. Thus a man who goes into a public market-place to incite the subject to revolt incurs the guilt of high treason, *because the words are joined to the action, and partake of its nature. It is not the words that are punished, but an action in which words are employed. They do not become criminal but when they are annexed to a criminal action; everything is confounded if words are construed into capital crime; instead of considering them only as a mark* [evidence?] *of that crime.*"[23]

---

[23] The spirit of the laws, v. 1, p. 232, 233. Aldine ed.

REV. JOHN JONES, *et al*—1749.

The Rev. John Jones, (1693-1752) appears to have been an exceedingly modest editor, author, and clergyman. His writings were mostly published anonymously or after his death. In 1749 he published a collection of short extracts from the writings of Anglican divines advocating the necessity and expediency of a trenchant revision of the liturgy. The following is quoted from that book.

" 'The Church of Christ, as a society separate from the State, hath (what all societies must have) proper bands of union; upon a breach of which, she may declare any person breaking them, as no longer in her fellowship. Were the civil Magistrate in this case *neuter,* and did he no otherwise interpose, than by his protection of the Church in her regular exercise of this authority; no grievance, I should think, could be here complained of. And the supposed Neutrality of the Magistrate, as to *civil* penalties, would then leave the persons excluded from this society, easy and secure from such penalties.' Dr. Marshall's Letter to Dr. Rogers, annexed to Roger's Vindicat, p. 310-311. This declaration of Dr. Marshall's (wherein he says he agrees with his friend Dr. Rogers) carries in it a great and momentous truth, and that of greater consequence to the real interest of Christianity, than the bulk of mankind seems to be aware. To which we shall only add, for the present, those just remarks of the learned Mr. John Needham, in his Visitation-sermon before the Clergy at Warnford, 1710. 'We no where find our blessed Savior to have given any other authority to his Church, for punishing offenders, or for reclaiming the erroneous, but what is expressed by exhortation, reproof, or exclusion from the communion and privileges of the faithful. Which is a demonstration to me, that no other were intended by Him, or are lawful to us. He would have religion, which is a reasonable service, served only in humane and reasonable ways, such as at once may make the world believe and love his institutions. And if, in some extraordinary cases, the Apostles, endowed with extraordinary powers, *thought fit to inflict extraordinary punishments on men's bodies, I think this no sufficient*

warrant and authority to us, till the same powers and
emergencies return again into the Church.' Our Reformers were of the same judgment, as appears by many
instances in history, and in their writings: See Particularly the *Institution of a Christian Man, tit. The sacrament of orders*, p. 46a. See also, Bishop Stillingfleet's
discourse concerning the power of excommunication in a
Christian Church; and his Life, 8vo. 1710, p. 15, 16, refer-
ring to that discourse."[24]

ANTHONY ELLYS—1763.

Anthony Ellys (1690-1761) was the Bishop of St. Davids.
He was a distinguished member of the orthodox church,
and had written a book in defense of the sacramental tests
as a protection for the established church. Yet he was
perhaps rather liberal-minded for a Bishop. After his
death, his friends, in 1763, published his manuscript
"Tracts on Liberty Spiritual and Temporal of the Protestants of England." The defense of sacramental tests was
included. A new edition was published in 1767, from
which these quotations are made. Much of the book is
directed against Popery, and parts evince considerable
erudition and astute reasoning. In spite of his aversion
to complete mental freedom, he recognized the nature of
the issue between himself and the friends of unabridged
intellectual liberty, and, after stating how far, in his
opinion, penalties may be imposed for erroneous opinion,
he states also the opinion of his more liberal opponents
thus:

"But here most of the friends of liberty stop: They do
not allow that the same course may be justly taken in
the case of errors which, without being in themselves, or
by plain consequence, *anyway hurtful to the civil state*,
are only repugnant to sacred truth made known by reason
or by divine revelation. They think that by persons by
whom errors of this latter kind only are held, no force

---

[24] Free and candid disquisitions relating to the Church of England and
the means of advancing religion therein addressed to the govern-
ing powers in church and state and more immediately directed to
the house of convocation [by Rev. John Jones] London, 1749.
Footnote, p. 177. See also: Dictionary of national biography, vol.
30, p. 127.

or civil punishment can, merely on that account, be justly employed, either in the way of punishment, or even of restraint of them from public worship, with an intention to make them embrace the truth in religion.

"Not but these friends of liberty admit, in the first place, that divers errors of such a nature may be very blameable in the sight of God, when they have proceeded from a great corruption in the understanding, and that corruption derived from their *ill-affections and passions* not resisted and governed as they ought to have been. If any particular writer in our country has too crudely and generally asserted the innocency of error, this never hath been the doctrine of Protestants in general."

Here then is a frank confession of the nature of the issue being urged by the friends of unabridged intellectual liberty, as their contention is seen by one who opposed their claims. There can then be little excuse for our courts failing to understand what the friends of liberty meant by that which they had written into our constitutions.[25]

"LETTERS CONCERNING LIBELS"—1764.

As further exhibiting the contentions of friends of liberty of the press, to be an insistence upon the distinction between an actual and a constructive breach of the peace, there will now be quoted an anonymous phamphlet entitled: "A Letter Concerning Libels, Warrants, etc." The quotations are from the second edition, London, 1764.

"Members [of Parliament] are clearly entitled to Privilege in all misdemeanours, for which sureties of the peace cannot be demanded. But sureties of the peace cannot be demanded but in actual breaches of the peace. The writings of anything quietly in one's study, and publishing it by the press, can certainly be no actual breach of the peace. Therefore a member who is only charged with this, cannot thereby forfeit his Privilege.

"I thought that no common man would allow any writing or publishing, especially where extremely clandestine,

---

[25] Tracts on liberty spiritual and temporal of the protestants of England. 1767, pp. 55-56.

to be any breach of the peace at all; and that none but lawyers, on account of the evil tendency sometimes of such writings, had first got them, *by construction,* to be deemed so.   I had no idea that it was possible for any lawyer, however subtle and metaphysical, to proceed so far as to decide mere authorship, and publication by the press, to be an actual breach of the peace, as this last seems to express, *ex vi termini,* some positive bodily injury, or some immediate dread thereof at least; and that, whatever a challenge, in writing, to any particular might be, *a general libel upon public measures could never be construed to be so.*   And I knew it was not required of any one in matters of law, to come up to the faith of an orthodox divine, who, in incredible points, is ready to say *Credo quia impossibile est.*   (I believe it because it is impossible). * * *

"No case is so common as that of women exhibiting articles of peace against their husbands; now I do not believe that if any wife was to allege as a foundation for such articles, her husband's having wrote a libel against her; let the libel be ever so false, scandalous and malicious; that Lord Mansfield would make the husband find surities for the peace, or for his future good behaviour on that account."

In this present case Mockus was sentenced by the police court to furnish such a bond upon the most absurd theory that his alleged blasphemy made such a bond necessary. After considerable argument making clear the same distinction between actual and constructive injury, by reference to the remedy, as in personal libel where an action will lie for trespass on the case, a remedy applicable only for a wrong without force, whereas for an actual breach of the peace the remedy is by action for trespass, *vi et armis,* our author continues thus:

"I never heard till very lately that Attorney Generals, upon the caption of a man supposed a libeller, could insist upon his giving securities for his good behaviour.   It is a doctrine injurious to the freedom of every subject, derogatory from the old constitution, and a violent attack, if not an absolute breach of the liberty of the press.   It is not law and I will not submit to it."[26]

ROBERT MORRIS—1770.

Robert Morris, Barrister at Law, and Secretary to the supporters of the Bill of Rights, in London, 1770, published "A Letter to Sir Richard Aston Knt. one of the judges of his Majesties Court of King's Bench, and later Chief Justice of the Common Pleas in Ireland." This was the outgrowth of the prosecution for seditious libel, of Woodfall for publishing the "Letters of Junius." Morris also makes the objection to determining the guilt in seditious libel according to psychologic tendency. He says: "It is impossible for *ley gens* * * * to know what is safe to publish and it is equally impossible for a lawyer to give advice. He cannot from any musty reading of books know the effect, which a publication may produce in the minds of men; and therefore cannot divine whether it be a libel. I should doubt, whether a panegyric upon Mr. Justice Aston might not be deemed so. The lawyers cannot define a libel without reference to other terms, which are uncertain' till determined by a Jury."[27]

REV. PHILIP FURNEAUX—1770.

Observing the chronological order would induce us to insert quotations from Dr. Furneaux's most valuable treatise at this point. So much has already been quoted from him (pp. 105 to 112 herein), that more space will not be given. A re-reading is recommended. On page 106 attention was called to the similarity of views and language existing between Fourneaux, and Jefferson's, Virginia, Resolution on Toleration. Since that page went to the printer it was discovered that among the several editions of Furneaux's, Letters on Toleration, one was published in Philadelphia in 1773. This makes his views of increasing importance in the interpretation of our con-

---

[26] A letter concerning libels, warrants, etc., second edition, Lond. 1764, pp. 17-18-19.

[27] A letter to Sir Richard Aston Knt. One of the judges of his majesties court of King's Bench, and later Chief Justice of the Common Pleas in Ireland, p. 55.

stitutional guarantees, because his book is now more gene-
tically related to that public sentiment upon which those
guarantees came into being.

REV. ANDREW KIPPIS—1772.

Andrew Kippis (1725-1795) was a non-conformist minister and a noted biographer, and held numerous positions
of trust and honor in the Presbyterian Church and outside
of it.   His principal literary work is the "Biographia
Britannica."   Besides this, he wrote a number of books
and magazine articles.*   In 1772 he first published "A
Vindication of the Protestant Dissenting Ministers."   A
second edition was published in 1773, from which the following quotations are selected as representative of numerous similar sentiments.   In replying to the suggestion
"Preaching is an *overt act* of some importance to the state,"
he says, among much other matter :

"Upon whatever religious principles any man may pretend to act, or whatever pleas of conscience may be urged
by him, if he hurts his neighbor in person or property,
if he disturbs his fellow creatures in the exercise of their
rights and privileges, he ought to be restrained and
punished.   This is the precise point at which it becomes
the duty of the State to interfere, and if the State should
interfere sooner, and extend its jurisdiction to opinions,
under the pretext of their eveil tendency, it will be impossible to know where to stop.   Speculations and fancies
about the tendencies of opinions may be carried on to the
entire destruction of liberty, and the vindication of every
species of tyranny and persecution.   An over-zealous
Armenian will be ready to contend that several doctrines
are contained even in the Thirty Nine Articles of the
Church of England, which are calculated to have a bad
effect on the morals and happiness of mankind.   An over-
zealous Calvinist will as warmly plead, that the power
ascribed to man by some divines, and other tenets held by
them, are extremely prejudicial to the interests of holiness.
* * * Accusations of a similar nature might be produced
against a variety of religious sentiments, till, at length,

* See: Dictionary of national biography, v. 31, pp. 195-197.

not liberty only, but piety and charity, would be lost in the contest."[28]

Kippis refers to Furneaux and Fownes for further justification of this position.

"TWO LETTERS," ANONYMOUS—1773.

I have before me an anonymous pamphlet issued in the interests of English Dissenters. It is entitled "Two Letters addressed to the Right Rev. Prelates." Here the demand for intellectual freedom is thus stated: "If the profession of Christianity give no protection to the civil power, let it be dispensed with, and let toleration be granted without any reserve or limitation whatever, according to the rights of mankind. * * * I hope if they solicit parliament any more, it will be for an absolute and unconditional repeal of religious penalties. * * * Our thoughts and principles are supremely independent of any civil power. When we injure our fellow citizens we fall under its cognizance; till then we ought to range free and unconfined wherever truth leads, otherwise every persecution in the world may be defended. * * * *I am never safe but whilst his authority is confined to actual offences against the peace of society.* This distinction is plain, obvious, and sufficient, and will forever keep religion and government from being confounded together, or invading each other. God forbid I should contend for a toleration that would exclude one honest man on the face of the earth, *whatever he believes,* and I will venture to say, however this latitude may startle some ignorant or bigoted minds, the more it is considered, the more it will be approved till the reasonableness of it is as universally admitted as the clearest axiom in nature."[29]

REV. JOSEPH FOWNES—1773.

This author (1750-1789) was one of the more distinguished of dissenting ministers. He has been quoted already (pp. 113-116). What is there said needs to be re-

---

[28] A vindication of the protestant dissenting ministers, 1773, pp. 99-100.

[29] Two letters addressed to the Right Rev. prelates who a second time rejected the dissenters' bill, London, 1773, pp. 24-26.

read here for its clear cut statement of the difference between a speculatively ascertained psychologic tendency and an overt act of physical aggression.

Here I take occasion to correct a surmise hereinbefore made, that Fownes had come to America. The correction is based upon a biographical introduction to the third edition of Fownes' "Inquiry," which was formerly overlooked.[30]

JEREMY BENTHAM—1776.

This distinguished author also· drew the line between free speech and the rightful jurisdiction of government at the point of actual physical resistance to government and so repudiated the idea that a mere speculative and imaginative psychologic tendency could properly be punished. His words have already been quoted on page 113, and will not be repeated.

RICHARD PRICE—1777.

Richard Price (1723-1791) was a non-conformist minister and writer on moral, political and economic questions. One of his books that probably attracted more attention than others was "Observations of Civil Liberty and the Justice and Policy of the War with America," 1776. In recognition of his services in the cause of liberty, Dr. Price was presented with Freedom of the City of London, and it is said that the encouragement derived from this book had no inconsiderable share in determining the Americans to declare their independence. * * * He was the intimate of Franklin. * * * In the winter of 1776 he was actually invited by Congress to transfer himself to America. * * * In 1783 he was honored by being created L.L.D. by Yale College at the same time with George Washington. * * * In 1791 Price became an original member of the Unitarian Society.[31]

---

[30] An enquiry into the principles of toleration; the degree in which they are admitted by our laws; and the reasonableness of the late application made by the dissenters to parliament for an enlargement of their religious liberties. By Joseph Fownes. The third edition. To which is prefixed an introductory preface, containing some account of the author. By Andrew Kippis, D.D., F.R.S. & S.A. Shrewsbury, 1790.

[31] Dictionary of national biography, v. 46, pp. 334-337.

Dr. Price wrote: "Religious liberty likewise is a power of acting as we like in religion, *or* of professing and practising that mode of religious worship which we think most acceptable to the Deity. * * * All have the same unalienable right to this liberty; and consequently, no one has a right to such a use of it as shall take it from others. Within this limit, or as far as he does not encroach on the equal liberty of others, every one has a right to do as he pleases in religion. That the right to religious liberty goes as far as this every one must allow, who is not a friend of persecution; and that it cannot go further is self-evident, for if it did there would be contradiction in the nature of things; and it would be true, that everyone had a right to enjoy what every one had a right to destroy. If, therefore, the religious faith of any person leads him to hurt another, because he professes a different faith; or if it carries him in any instance to intolerance, [in action, not idea], liberty itself requires he should be restrained, and that, in such instances, he should lose his liberty."[32]

JAMES ADAIR—1785.

James Adair, sargeant at law, recorder of London, whig member of parliament, and king's sargeant, was one of the distinguished liberalizing forces of England. With Erskine and others he appeared in some of the great historic trials of his time. He also left a number of controversial pamphlets.

In "Discussions of the Law of Libels" in the form of dialogue Lond. 1785 (anonymous, but ascribed to James Adair) I find this: "The character of the offense as you describe it,[33] has rather an anomalous appearance; your definition does not necessarily require it to have been attended with actual injury to the public: the injurious public consequences of it are not positive, but merely presumptive. It is, in this respect, I think, distinguishable from offences in general which consist rather in the injury itself than in the bare tendency of it. Other offences

---

[32] Additional observations on the nature and value of civil liberty and the war with America. Lond. 1777, pp. 11-12.
[33] Hawkin's Pleas of the Crown. b i, c. 73, sec. i. 3.

require realities to their composition, this is wholly composed of presumptions and probabilities. * * *

"The public tranquility, as it is the only security of an arbitrary government, is the object to which it sacrifices every other. *The apprehension of a disturbance of the public peace from the resentment of the individual is, I think, rather imputable to the suspicious vigilance and timidity of a bad government than to the firmness of a good one.*"

If "tendency to a breach of the peace" is the test of criminal jurisdiction, thên our author argues that "all those affronts, which in the sense of modern honor, are considered as signals for an appeal to the 'trial by battle' become criminally cognisable."

"For even where intended violence to any one is manifested by direct and positive menaces, the law does not punish such intention, but merely takes security that it shall not be committed, *not from the party against whom,* but from whom it is apprehended. In this case the party is punished who is presumed to have excited a resentment of which himself is to be the object" (p. 47). Our author suggests that he might reach a different conclusion if a libel was designed to produce an assault upon some one other than the libellant himself.

"This character of this offence [Libel] as you describe it (Hawkins' Pleas of the Crown, b. 1 c., 73 sec. i, 3), has rather an anomalous appearance; your definition does not necessarily require it to have been attended with actual injury to the public; the injurious public consequences of it are not positive, but merely presumptive. It is, in this respect I think distinguishable from offences in general which consist rather in an injury itself, than in the bare tendency to it. Other offences require realities to their composition, this is wholly composed of presumption and probabilities. * * *

"The public tranquility as it is the only security of an arbitrary government, is the object to which it sacrifices every other. * * * I think I perfectly understand the spirit of Lord Coke's eulogium on the Court of Star Chamber, 'this court, the right institution and antient orders

thereof being observed, doth keep all England in quiet.'
(4 Inst. c. 5.) * * * In the darkest pages of our history,
I collect the purposes of this institution from the purposes
to which it has actually been employed."[34]

AN ANONYMOUS CRITIC—1791.

This critic of Blackstone's conception of free speech has
already been quoted (see p. 116 herein). He also repudiated the test of psychologic tendency as the basis for
criminal jurisdiction. At this time, attention is again
called to the statement already quoted, to make the present
record more complete.

REV. ROBERT HALL—1793.

Rev. Robert Hall (1764-1831) was an English Baptist
minister of great reputation.[35] Among other matters he
published "Christianity Consistent with the love of Freedom" 1791; "Apology for Freedom of the Press," 1793,
which was separately republished. There has been also
published his collected works in six volumes.

He expresses the limits of liberty in these words: "The
most capital advantage an enlightened people can enjoy
is the liberty of discussing every subject which can fall
within the compass of the human mind; while this remains, freedom will flourish; but should it be lost or impaired, its principles will neither be well understood or
long retained. To render the magistrate a judge of truth,
and engage his authority in the suppression of opinions,
shews an inattention to the nature and design of political
society. * * *

"To comprehend the reasons on which the right of public
discussion is founded, it is requisite to remark the difference between *sentiment* and *conduct*. * * *

"Nor is there any way of separating the precious from
the vile but tolerating the whole. * * *

"The doctrine of tendencies is extremely subtle and com-
plicated. * * *

---

[34] Discussions of the law of libel by [James Adair]. Lond. 1785,
p. 27, 33, 35, 44, 47. See also: Dictionary of national biography, vol.
1, p. 69.
[35] Dictionary of national biography, v. 24, pp. 85-87.

"This dread of certain opinions, on account of their tendency, has been the copious spring of all those religious wars and persecutions, which are the disgrace and calamity of modern times. * * *

"The law hath amply provided against *overt acts of sedition and disorder*, and to suppress *mere opinions* by any other method than reasoning and argument is the height of tyranny. Freedom of thought being intimately connected with the happiness and dignity of man in every stage of his being, is of so much more importance than the preservation of any constitution, that to infringe the former under pretence of supporting the latter, is to sacrifice the means to the end. * * *

"When public discontents are allowed to vent themselves in reasoning and discourse, they subside into a calm; but their confinement in the bosom is apt to give them a fierce and deadly tincture. The reason of this is obvious. As men are seldom disposed to complain till they at least imagine themselves injured, so there is no injury which they will remember so long, or resent so deeply, as that of being threatened into silence. This seems like adding triumph to oppression, and insult to injury. The apparent tranquility which may ensue, is delusive and ominous; it is that awful stillness which nature feels, while she is awaiting the discharge of the gathered tempest. * * *

"If the Government wishes to become more vigorous, let it first become more pure, lest an addition to its strength should only increase its capacity for mischief. * * *

"The free use of our faculties in distinguishing truth from falsehood, the exertion of corporeal powers *without injury to others*, the choice of a religion and worship, are branches of natural freedom which no government can justly alter or diminish, because their restraint cannot conduce to that security which is its proper object."[36]

CHRISTOPHER MARTIN WIELAND—1795.

Christopher Martin Wieland (1733-1813) was a voluminous writer sometimes called the Voltaire of Germany.

---

[36] An apology for the freedom of the press, and for general liberty. London, 1793, pp. 2, 3, 4, 13, 18, 21, 53, 54.

He was also professor of philosophy and polite literature. Here is part of a discussion of his, which appeared in England and which deals with the imaginary excesses in the use of intellectual freedom. These statements by Mr. Wieland have an obvious application to the penalizing of a mere offensive literary style. It should be said however, that Mr. Wieland was not insistent upon complete intellectual liberty.

"I know not what cause many nice people may have for being so quarrelsome with the liberty of the press: but of this I am well assured, that Augustus or Titus would have taken it very ill of any one who should have suggested to either of them only the thought of wanting to suppress the freedom of speaking and writing (printing was not in being in their times) on account of the too bold use a Laberius, for example, had made of it. What opinion should we have entertained of the wisdom of a Solon, if he had caused daily to be weighed out to his Athenians, by ounces and scruples, how much it were proper for them to eat, because sad experience teaches, that one or other at times eats more than is fit? And do you think, that even Solon himself, supposing he had providently ventured so far, would have bought himself off *by the distinction between freedom of eating and freedom of gormandizing*, with the grandfathers of Socrates and Aristophanes? I hope then that I have perfectly set your mind at rest by this little effusion of my thoughts. He that has abused the freedom of eating into gluttony, must be contented to swallow a digestive powder or an emetic. He that has abused the freedom of the press into licentiousness, merits, for the first offence—a reprehension for his future caution: but the freedom of the press remains, notwithstanding, like the freedom of eating, as unlimited as before—or—so much the worse."[37]

TUNIS WORTMAN—1800.

This American author and staunch friend of Jefferson also repudiated the "tendency" test of criminality. He

---

[37] Varieties of literature, from foreign literary journals and original manuscripts now first published, volume the second. London, 1795. pp. 255-6.

has been quoted among Blackstone's critics (page 121 herein). Re-reading is recommended. This book was circulated as propaganda material for years before the adoption of the Connecticut Bill of Rights.

PHILAGATHARCHES—1810.

This author is another of the few who have successfully concealed their identity. His book of 1810, was issued in the second edition, in 1811. Coming eight years before the adoption of the Connecticut constition it was thought material here.

"One gross abuse of liberty, in freely publishing our sentiments to the world, is, the profanation of the Divine character, by denying some of the perfections of the Godhead; by attributing to him other properties, which his revealed will denies that he possesses; and, by the sacrilegious application of his 'Holy and Reverend' name, to vicious, or even ordinary subjects.

"In close connection with this description of the abuse of liberty is the inculcation of infidel principles, which teach us to renounce the doctrines and precepts of scripture; to reject, as spurious, that revelation which God has given of his will; and to trust the light of human reason to guide us to eternal happiness. But, while these are crimes of enormous magnitude in the estimation of God, for which he will bring these impious transgressors into judgment, they are not proper subjects of the magistrate's coersion; *they do not disturb the peace of the state; and, therefore, the publication of them cannot fall within his jurisdiction, as conservator of the publick peace.*" *

The American development of this same concept of free speech, through Roger Williams, James Madison and Thomas Jefferson, will be told later. So far we have traced much of the demand and meaning of religious liberty with special emphasis on England. The reading of this record makes it plain almost to a demonstration, that for some, centuries before the adoption of our constitu-

---

* Hints on toleration: in five essays: * * * suggested from the consideration of The R't. Hon. Lord Viscount Sidmouth, and the Dissenters, by Philagatharches. London, 1811, pp. 274-275. First edition published at Broxbourn, 1810.

tional guarantees, the friends of intellectual limitation always justified their censorship by the claim that blasphemous opinions had a tendency to disturb the peace. The friends of mental freedom asserted that such speculations about a psychologic tendency were not sufficient to give the state jurisdiction to punish the expression of disapproved ideas. Their contention was that the expression of human thought *as such* must be absolutely free up to the point where actual and material injury results. It was this latter view which was approved and written into our constitutions for the very purpose of destroying the former practice and repudiating the theory by which it was sought to be justified.

If some American courts seem to have acted as if this was not the case, one can only excuse them by understanding that the judges were merely expressing their personal desires or bigotry and were not considering nor passing upon the historical facts or issues involved. These have never been even considered or mentioned in such a case as this. Thus the judges also make it plain to us that they had not reached that stage of maturity in their intellectual processes where men are tempted to submit their whims, caprices, and prejudices to the check and justification of the widest scope of the objective realities of their problem. An effort is here being made to present much of the available material for such objective check and justification. It remains for each person to whom it may come to reveal their own intellectual status by making such use of this material as their respective desires prompt and their mental capacities permit.

When enough persons come to feel in accord with the thought of the foregoing leaders in the movement for intellectual freedom, paper guarantees become possible. When our courts think in accord with this pre-revolutionary growth toward mental liberty, paper constitutions will be made efficient, not mere meaningless "scraps of paper." What will the verdict be?

CHAPTER XXI.
ROGER WILLIAMS, JAMES MADISON, AND THOMAS JEFFERSON.

This contest for intellectual freedom and its meaning, which has been set forth with much precision as it worked out in England, will now be traced to American soil. Here we may again remind ourselves that the correct interpretation of our constitutional guarantees of freedom is nowhere more appropriately sought than in the historic issues which were decided, the former policies that were overruled, and in the evil sought to be remedied, by our constitutions.[1] It is also important to remember that none of the pre-revolutionary historical data either from England, or from Roger Williams in America, has ever been considered by any American court, as an aid to ascertaining the meaning of intellectual liberty in relation to religion.

ROGER WILLIAMS AND SECULARISM.

In England the slowly changing attitude toward tolerance may be said to date from Milton's immortal "Areopagitica," published in 1644. The Star Chamber court was abolished in 1641. During its existence a youth named Roger Williams took shorthand notes of the speeches and proceedings. Thus, doubtless, he learned something of what does *not* constitute liberty. He probably studied law with Sir Edward Coke, but abandoned that calling for the ministry. He left for America December, 1630, and settled in Massachusetts. .

The founders of the Connecticut colonies came from Massachusetts and brought with them all the theocratic notions of the dominant Puritan faction. Roger Williams had been under their suspicion for some time for his too great liberality, and the circumstance of his expulsion has been briefly related.

---

[1] Reynolds v. U. S., 98 U. S. 145-162.
Gibbons v. Ogden, 9 Wheaton 1; 6 Law. Ed. 1.
Scott v. Sanford, 19 Howard 393; 15 Law. Ed. 691.
Boyd v. U. S., 116 U. S. 616-622-625.
So. Carolina v. U. S., 199 U. S. 437.

The colony of Rhode Island which Williams founded was built upon an entirely different theory of government from any that had previously obtained in America or Europe. Here we find the first declaration of a democracy, and the beginnings of a secular state devoted to toleration in a new sense. We must understand Roger Williams' conception of tolerance if we would understand the meaning of constitutional freedom of speech and press, especially on the subject of religion.

The colony at Providence undertook to define and defend human liberty in matters of religion, instead of that "liberty of the gospel" by which others sought to dominate in temporal affairs. Roger Williams and his followers were for the protection of complete intellectual freedom, and in 1637 went so far as to disfranchise a man for refusing liberty of conscience to his wife[2] in not permitting her to go to meeting as often as she desired.

During the following years there raged a considerable American controversy over the subject of free speech in matters of religion. In this controversy Williams published a number of tracts in criticism of the intolerance of his Massachusetts and Connecticut neighbors and in defense of his own position against the attacks of the Puritan divines. The collection of Williams' tracts has been republished under the title of "The Bloody Tenet of Persecution." I quote from the London edition of 1848. Here we find the beginning of the free speech controversy in Rhode Island, in Connecticut and in the United States. For over a century this controversy raged between theocracy and democracy, and between free speech and blasphemy laws. By the time the American constitutions were formed, these ideas of Roger Williams had secured the ascendency over the idea of the majority among the earlier Massachusetts and Connecticut colonists. Under the leadership of Jefferson and the Virginia Act of Toleration, our American constitutions recorded the people's verdict in favor of the contentions of Roger Williams for a separation of church and state, and in favor of free speech for

---

[2] Bloody Tenet of Persecution, p. 28; also: Records of the Colony of Rhode Island, p. 16.

all controversies over religion. To understand the significance of that new constitutional policy of freedom of discussion, we must compare the idea of the earlier colonists with those later and contrary ideas which found expression in the constitutions of Connecticut and of the United States.

TRUTH VS. PEACE.

In his discourses Williams personified the two sets of ideas under the form of a dialogue between *Peace* and *Truth..* These words really symbolized the conflict quite perfectly. The friends of censorship and repression always make their justification to depend upon the importance of immediate and transient peace-requirements. In the interests of this immediate peace they are willing to suppress irritating claims of truth, and to ignore the more remote and less apparent advantages of intellectual freedom.

The friends of free speech always place the emphasis upon the relatively greater importance to be attached to claims of truth. In consequence of this different valuation, the friends of truth say that for its sake we must take some chances on disturbing the immediate peace, but we believe that in the long run peace will be more lasting, because more intelligently conditioned, where all claims of truth are given full freedom to be heard.

The early Connecticut settlers had the *absolute* and only divine truth, and wanted only "the liberty of the gospel." Therefore, in a conflict between mere heretical claims of truth and their own absolute truth and peace of mind, they always decided in favor of the latter. The Rhode Island colonies were perhaps equally certain that they possessed the absolute truth, but disagreed with their neighbors as to methods of propagating truth. They placed emphasis on free speech for all, as the very best means of establishing truth more perfectly in the minds of men. The Connecticut and Massachusetts colonists placed their confidence in the efficacy of forceful suppression of "error." A more modern conception is that all claims of truth should be tolerated because none of us can have the absolute truth; because all "truth" is but a partial and incomplete aspect of the absolute truth and is a relative and a purely personal concept.

In order to make clear the conflict between the ideas of tolerance entertained by Roger Williams, and embodied in the Federal and the Connecticut constitutions, and those views entertained by earlier colonists as embodied in the blasphemy statute of 1642, it becomes necessary to give a more thorough portrayal of Williams' contention, even at the risk of becoming tiresome.

THE PROSECUTION IS BREACH OF THE PEACE.

When Williams was told that he erred in defending the rights of those who expressed themselves with such "arrogance and impetuousness as of itself tended to the disturbance of the peace," he drew the line between spiritual peace and civil peace. He pointed out how a company of men might "hold disputations, and in matters concerning their society may dissect, divide, break into schism and factions, sue and implead each other at the law, wholly break up and dissolve into pieces and nothing, and yet the peace of the city not be in the least measure impaired or disturbed." Citing other illustrations, he concludes: "And notwithstanding those spiritual oppositions in point of worship and religion, yet hear we not of the least noise, nor heed we, if men keep but the bond of civility, of any civil breach, or breach of civil peace among them, and to persecute God's people then for religion, *that only was a breach of civilty itself.*"

He classifies his opponents with satanic accusers in these words: "Which charge [that dissenters are arrogant and impetuous], together with that of obstinacy, pertinacity, pride, troublers of the City, etc., Satan commonly loads the meekest of the saints and witnesses of Jesus with" (p. 49). This he justifies by reference to the Bible. Thus he makes plain that he does not intend to heed the cry of fear of disturbing the peace, which is too easy a pretense in the hands of persecutors.

I will now quote some of this dialogue between *Peace* and *Truth* which will show that Roger Williams believed in tolerance even for irritating disputation. Instead of encouraging the intolerant spirit by suppressing the irritating speech, his theory encouraged tolerance by punishing those whose intolerance induced them to disturb the civil peace by using force to suppress irritating utterances.

"Truth" continues thus: "God's people, in delivering the mind and will of God concerning the kingdoms and civil states where they have lived, have seemed in all show of common sense and rational policy, if men look not higher with the eye of faith, to endanger and overthrow the very civil state, as appeareth by all Jeremiah's preaching and counsel to King Zedekiah, his princes and people, insomuch that the charge of the princes against Jeremiah was that he discouraged the army from fighting against the Babylonians, and weakened the land from its own defense; and this charge, in the eye of reason, seemed not to be unreasonable or unrighteous, and yet in Jeremiah no arrogance, nor impetuousness."

ACTUAL VS. CONSTRUCTIVE DISTURBANCE.

"Lastly [says Truth] God's people, by their preaching, disputing, etc., have been, though not the cause, yet accidentally the occasion of great contentions and divisions, yea, tumults and uproars in towns and cities where they have lived and come; and yet neither their doctrine nor themselves arrogant nor impetuous, however so charged: for thus the Lord Jesus discovereth men's false and secure suppositions, Luke xii, 51; *'Suppose ye that I am come to give peace on earth? I tell you, nay; but rather division; for from henceforth shall there be five in one house divided, three against two, and two against three, the father shall be divided against the son and the son against the father, etc.* And thus upon the occasion of the apostles' preaching the kingdom and worship of God in Christ, were most commonly uproars and tumults wherever they came. For instance, those strange and monstrous uproars at Iconium, at Ephesus, at Jerusalem, Acts xiv, 4; Acts xix, 29, 40; Acts xxi, 30, 31." * * *

"I acknowledge that such may be the way and manner of holding forth, either with railing or reviling, daring or challenging speeches, or with force of arms, swords, guns, prisons, etc., that it may not only tend to break, but may actually break the civil peace or peace of the city.

"Yet these instances propounded are cases of great opposition and spiritual hostility and occasions of breach of civil peace; and yet as the borders, or matter, were of gold, so the specks, or manner (Cantic. i. [II]) were of silver: both matter and manner pure, holy, peaceable, and inoffensive.

"Moreover, I answer, that it is possible and common for persons of soft and gentle nature and spirits to hold out falsehood with more seeming meekness and peaceableness, than the Lord Jesus or his servant did or do hold forth the true and everlasting gospel. So that the answerer would be requested to explain what he means by this arrogant and impetuous holding forth of any doctrine, which very manner of holding forth tends to break civil peace, and comes under the cognizance and correction of the civil magistrate, lest he build the sepulchre of the prophets, and say, *If we had been in the Pharisee's days,* the Roman emperor's days, or the bloody Marian days, *we would not have been partakers with them in the blood of the prophets,* Matt. xxiii, 30, *who were charged with arrogance and impetuousness."* * * *

"*Truth* [continuing]. I answer: When a kingdom or state, town or family, lies and lives in the guilt of a false god, false Christ, false worship, no wonder if sore eyes be troubled at the appearance of the light, be it never so sweet. No wonder if a body full of corrupt humors be troubled at strong, though wholesome, physic—if persons sleepy and loving to sleep be troubled at the noise of shrill, though silver, alarums. No wonder if Adonijah and all his company be amazed and troubled at the sound of the right heir, King Solomon, 1 Kings i [41, 49]—if the husbandmen were troubled when the Lord of the vineyard sent servant after servant, and at last his only son, and they beat, and wounded, and killed even the son himself, because they meant themselves to seize upon the inheritance, unto which they had no right, Matt. xxi, 38. Hence all those tumults about the apostle in the Acts, etc. Whereas, good eyes are not so troubled at light; vigilant and watchful persons, loyal and faithful, are not so troubled at the true, no, nor at a false religion of Jew or Gentile.

"Secondly. Breach of civil peace may arise when false and idolatrous practices are held forth, and yet no breach of civil peace *from* the doctrine or practice, or the manner of holding forth, *but from that wrong and preposterous way of suppressing,* preventing, and extinguishing such doctrine or practices by weapons of wrath and blood, whips, stocks, imprisonments, banishment, death, etc.; by which men commonly are persuaded to convert heretics, and to cast out unclean spirits, which only the finger of God can do, that is, the mighty power of the Spirit in the word."[3]

It is believed that this makes it plain that Roger Williams repudiated the idea that punishment should be inflicted upon a speaker for a speculative opinion about the ill tendency of his utterance, and that the only ill tendency which should come within the cognizance of the criminal courts was the actually demonstrated tendency of intolerance in the listener, but only if he should allow it to express itself in actual overt acts of disorder against the civil peace. Williams' view was thus in harmony with those of the English Dissenters already quoted. This view finally prevailed in our constitutions and becomes authoritative as to the meaning free speech upon religious subjects.

MADISON AND VIRGINIA LIBERTY.

Virginia is another state in which we may see the controversy for religious liberty developing in such a manner as to shed light upon the meaning that should be given to our constitutional guarantees. The leaders of the movement in Virginia were James Madison and Thomas Jefferson. The opponents were mainly those of the Episcopalian faith, that being originally the established church of Virginia.

Madison as a boy had been shocked by the sight of persecution, and so became a libertarian in spite of his wholly orthodox environment and education. In the Virginia Convention of 1776 he was among its youngest members. George Mason drew the declaration of rights which included the following on the subject of toleration:

"That religion or the duty which we owe to our Creator, and the manner of discharging it, can be directed only by

---
[3] The Bloody Tenet of Persecution. pp. 48-53.

reason and conviction, not by force or violence; and therefore, that all men should enjoy the fullest toleration in the exercise of religion, according to the dictates of conscience, unpunished and unrestrained by the magistrate, *unless under the color of religion any man disturb the peace, the happines or safety of society,* and that it is the mutual duty of all to practice Christian forbearance, love, and charity toward each other."

To those who do not make intelligent discriminations between mere tolerance and a guaranteed liberty; or between actual and constructive breaches of the peace; or the uncertainties of disturbing "happiness" and the certainties in the criteria of guilt essential to "law," might readily have been content to accept the foregoing declaration and smooth sounding phrases as quite adequate. Not so with Madison.

Let me tell the story in the words of Gaillard Hunt, the editor of "The Writings of Madison." He says: "Almost alone in this assemblage of wise men Madison saw the fundamental error contained in these words. According to his belief there could properly be no recognition of religious *rights of tolerance;* no man could properly be granted *permission* to worship God according to the dictates of his conscience, for this was every man's right. Moreover, the clause might easily be so twisted as to oppress religious sects, under the excuse that they disturbed 'the peace, the happiness, or safety of society.' Therefore, he offered as an amendment this substitute:

"That religion, or the duty we owe our Creator, and the manner of discharging it, being under the direction of reason and conviction only, not of violence or compulsion, all men are equally entitled to the full and free exercise of it, according to the dictates of conscience; and therefore that no man or class of men ought on account of religion to be invested with peculiar emoluments or privileges, nor subjected to any penalties or disabilities, unless under color of religion the preservation of equal liberty and the existence of the State be *manifestly* endangered."

If this clause had been adopted the struggle for religious liberty in Virginia would have been ended. Mason, however, adopted part of the amendment, so as to eliminate the word tolerance, but did not adopt that part which insisted upon equality, such as an established church always destroys, especially in the matter of financial support, even though bare toleration be granted to others. As the clause came forth and was adopted it read as follows:

"That religion, or the duty we owe to our Creator, and the manner of discharging it, can be directed only by reason and conviction, not by force or violence, and therefore all men are equally entitled to the free exercise of religion, according to the dictates of conscience; and that it is the mutual duty of all to practice Christian forbearance, love, and charity toward each other."

Madison's amendment was too far a variation from the former practices of the colony, to be then adopted. The last declaration did not prohibit state support of the clergy, nor did it provide any means of compelling forbearance. However, the seed had been sown and bore fruit later. Eight years had elapsed when Madison found himself a member of the House of Delegates in 1784. Following the Revolution, a great decline as to religious observances came into existence. This furnished a seeming "moral" justification for the desire of the clergy to be supported by the state. Patrick Henry introduced a bill for levying a tax to support teachers of Christian religion. The influential members mostly supported the bill. All that Madison and his friends could do was to secure a postponement so as to get time to make public opinion.[4]

At the request of others Madison drew up a "Memorial and Remonstrance to the Honorable General Assembly of the Commonwealth of Virginia" against the bill. The remonstrance found so many signatures that in the session of 1785, the bill introduced by Patrick Henry was overwhelmingly defeated. It is well for our purpose that we reproduce a part of this remonstrance which deals with equality before the law as bearing upon the construction of our constitutional guarantees. In this Memorial the remonstrants object: "Because the bill violates that equal-

---

[4] So far I have followed Hunt. See: James Madison and Religious Liberty. Ann. Rep. of Amer. Hist. Ass. v. 1, pp. 165 to 171, 1901.

ity which ought to be the basis of every law; and which is more indispensable, in proportion as the validity or expediency of any law is more liable to be impeached. 'If all men are, by nature, equally free and independent' all men are to be considered as entering into society on equal conditions, as relinquishing no more, and therefore retaining no less, one than another, of their natural rights; above all are they to be considered as retaining an 'equal title to the free exercise of religion according to the dictates of conscience.' Whilst we assert for ourselves a freedom to embrace, to profess, and to observe the religion which we believe to be of divine origin, we cannot deny an *equal freedom to those whose minds have not yet yielded to the evidence which has convinced us.* If this freedom be abused, it is *an offense against God, not against man.* To God, therefore, and not to man, must an account of it be rendered."[5]

JEFFERSON AND TOLERATION.

This agitation against a state supported clergy prepared the way for that true religious liberty which Madison had sought in vain to have incorporated in the Bill of Rights in 1776. Taking advantage of this changed and liberalized sentiment, Madison completed his victory by introducing the famous bill for religious liberty which was prepared by Jefferson. Of course there were, and are now, throughout the United States many who disapprove of religious liberty. However, it is written into our constitutions and should be maintained by our courts until the constitutions are amended. Since the opinions of men like Rogers Williams, James Madison and Thomas Jefferson were written into our constitutional guarantees, their opinions become authoritative on matters of interpretation, even though individual judges may disagree as to the expediency of this policy. On this account it becomes worth while to reproduce their opinions in such an argument as this. Accordingly, the present essential part of the Virginia Resolution follows:

"To suffer the civil magistrate to intrude his power in

---

[5] Memorial and Remonstrance, p. 7.

the field of Opinion, or to restrain the profession or propagation of principles *on supposition of their ill tendency,* is a dangerous fallacy, which at once destroys all liberty, because he, being of course judge of that tendency, will make his opinions the rule of judgment, and approve or condemn the sentiments of others only as they shall square with or differ from his own. It is time enough for the rightful purpose of Civil Government for its officers to interfere *when principles break out into overt acts* against peace and good order."[6]

It is important to acquire a clear view of the difference in the concept of mere religious toleration, as expressed in the first declaration of George Mason, and the concept of Jefferson, as expressed in the final resolution. The former manifestly expressed only revocable tolerance, limited by the whim or caprice of any Court which might declare the "peace, the happiness, or safety of society" to be in danger. By using the disjunctive "or" and especially by including the word "happiness," it was evidently designed that mere unpleasant and undefined psychologic tendencies should be a sufficient justification for abridging intellectual freedom. Jefferson demanded that only overt acts of disorder resulting from speech should be punishable.

Thomas Jefferson in his "Notes on the State of Virginia" devotes a chapter to the subject of religion. He reviews the past laws for persecution and indicates the changes that have been wrought. As further indicating his insistence upon actual and material injury as criteria of the jurisdiction of the magistrate, he says: "The legitimate powers of government extend to *such acts only as are injurious to others. But it does me no injury for my neighbor to say there are twenty gods or no God. It neither picks my pocket nor breaks my leg.*"[7]

Jefferson's concept, as expressed in the Virginia Act of Toleration, and amplified in the quoted portion of his Notes on Virginia, expresses a very different concept from that of Blackstone and the prior English courts. Jefferson's is the concept of an unabridgable mental liberty. Here

---

[6] Watson on The Constitution, v. 2, p. 1379.
[7] P. 231—second edition.

no one may be punished for the expression of any idea whatever, merely as a disapproved idea, nor on the basis of any theoretic evil psychologic tendency imagined to arise therefrom. Here we have a positive and specific denial of the right to punish any opinion whatever, on the mere basis of a supposed ill tendency. No discretion is allowed to interfere according to whether the opinion is disapproved theology, or concerns the politeness of style in which a theologic opinion is expressed. The magistrate cannot interfere until opinions "break out into overt acts against peace and good order." This, of course, is the essence of making actual and mateial injury the basis of criminality. This declaration of the meaning of religious liberty was adopted in Virginia in 1785, and was the forerunner, and so measurably interpretive, of the subsequent constitutional provisions for a separation of church and state, for religious liberty and for unabridged freedom of speech and press. (See: Reynolds v. U. S., 98 U. S. 162.)

CHAPTER XXII.
CHRISTIANITY AND THE LAW.

Thus far we have seen that the real motive for blasphemy laws was the protection of the privileges and prerogatives of the privileged class. The moralistic justification for such persecution was that to question the established religion was a denial of the claimed source of authority in the prevailing theocracy, and so tended to disturb the peaceable enjoyment of privileges and prerogatives of those who governed, and also tended to destroy the government itself. The better to sustain their undemocratic advantage, it was suported by a claim of divine right, first through the mediation of the Pope, and later directly and without any intermediary. Thus blasphemy became necessarily viewed as a sort of lesser treason, and official Christianity was the supreme part of the law. Canon law was deemed the foundation stone of the common law.

It has been shown that the divine right dogma, for the protection of privileges and prerogatives are wholly inconsistent with our more democratic conceptions. It is our theory that laws and governments come up from out of the people, and not down from above the populace. This is wholly inconsistent with blasphemy prosecutions. However, against this contention there are some American decisions which follow the early British precedents in holding that Christianity is a parcel of the law of the land.[1] It now remains to destroy the value of such American precedents by the more thorough examination of the reasoning, the facts and a modern British precedent which supports the contrary view. The questions then are, first: from the more enlightened and democratic viewpoint can it be admitted that Christianity was ever properly a part of our law? Second: if so, then we still ask if that concept was not prohibited by the general intellectual development as expressed by our constitutional guarantees of religions liberty, equality and free speech?

---

[1] Mahoney v. Cook, 26 Pa. St. 347.
Sparhawk v. Union Pass. R. Co., 54 Pa. St. 406.
Charleston v. Benjamin, 2 Strobh. L. So. Car. 521, 49 Amer. Dec. 608.

CHURCH AND STATE.

It appears[2] that centuries ago the ecclesiastical courts probably attended to the greater part of the offences that were penalized in that relatively simple social order under their jurisdiction. The reason for this is plain from the theologic viewpoint. The Rev. J. Dodd[3] expresses the old conception thus: "All law in the abstract, emanated from, and is based upon, the originating will of God. 'By me Kings reign,' saith Wisdom[4] 'and Princes decree justice.' And St. Paul, too, puts forward the principle very prominently to the law-giving people to whom he addressed his epistle. 'There is no power but of God.' 'The powers that be,' i.e. whether of legislation or administration 'are ordained of God.'"

For centuries the effort was to apply this literally. So came the legal maxim that "The best rule is that which advances religion." Thus also do Noy, Blackstone and others tell us that statutes contravening the divine law are void.[5]

THREE STAGES OF EVOLUTION.

Roughly speaking the controversy over the relation of the Church and State may be divided into three stages. In the first stage there is almost a universal acquiescence in the supremacy of the ecclesiastical and theologic authority. Here the theory is that the State is but the secular arm of the Church for establishing the government and will of God upon earth, and all authority comes from on high, from above the people. The King is practically the creature of the Pope or priests and a "God upon the earth." Canon law is authoritative in the determination of common-law. The chief function of the King is to aid and serve the clergy, or as they would say to serve the religion of the only true God.

In the second stage of this development the union of Church and State is theoretically just as thorough and complete as before, but the emphasis is reversed. Now

[2] From Stephen's Hist. Crim. Law of England, v. 2, p. 400 to end.
[3] Hist. of Canon Law, p. 6.
[4] Prov. VIII, 15.
[5] Broom's Legal Maxims. Eighth Edit. p. 13 and authorities cited.

the secular authority is of recognized dominance, and the Church becomes a mere tool of the secular power. Instead of the throne being subordinated to the priesthood, we now find the priesthood subject to the government, though still recognized as part of it. Here the authority and the influence of the spiritual aristocrats has become more or less subordinated to the power of the temporal aristocrats, or at worst it is equal and co-ordinate. The transition is one away from the power of God, and the authority of his "mouthpieces" toward the supremacy of those possessing the greater economic power and the authority of the secular phases of their political institutions. Now the more important function of the clergy is to give support to privileges and prerogatives of secular aristocrats.

The third stage finds all authority of God and of the special power of the ecclesiasts in the affairs of government as such, to be theoretically repudiated as also is the special authority and political right of a secular aristocracy. Now the process of change has gone to its logical conclusion. Those who are unprepared for this complete transformation verbally console themselves that they are still only the new intermediaries between God and those who exercise political authority. Such affirm that the voice of the people is the voice of God, because for them it is so difficult to give up our human weaknesses for aristocratic distinctions founded upon the claim of super-human affiliations. Such persons still prove their own aristocracy by insisting that their religion is even now part of the law. With those who are completely emancipated from the medieval mode of thinking, political authority and power from above the people has been supplanted by a political power and authority arising wholly and purely from out of the people, merely as human beings, not as agents of Omnipotence. This is the road from theocracy through secular aristocracy to a political democracy. This evolution will now be traced in our juridical history, that it may receive proper recognition in the interpretation of our constitutional guarantees of intellectual and religious liberty.

REASON VS. AUTHORITY.

We have already exhibited the opposition of the "dissenters" to the concept that the more orthodox Christianity is a part of the law. Parallel with this was a gradual increase in the judicial curtailment of this doctrine. As early as 1649, Chief Justice Kebble expressed such a limitation in these words: "You say well: The law of God is the law of England, and you have heard no law else, but what is consonant to *the law of reason which is the best law of God,* and here is none else urged against you."[6] Thus to insist upon determining the law of God by reliance upon reason instead of relying upon ecclesiastical authority, is a contradiction of the predominant judicial attitude voiced by Blackstone, and it is the entering wedge of the process of secularization and of democratization.

Among the writers of legal treatises there were at least two conspicuous critics of the theory that Christianity is part of the law. The first of these was Major John Cartright, a staunch friend of the American Revolution and of freedom of speech.[7] It was his book which inspired Jefferson's letter upon the same subject, which is hereinafter quoted. In the same year (1823) appeared Richard Mence's vigorous criticism of this doctrine.[8]

The next definite limitation that I find imposed upon the concept of Christianity as part of British law, is made in Sixth Report of the Commissioners on Criminal Law. They say:

To remove all possibility of further doubt the Commissioners on Criminal Law have thus clearly explained their sense of this celebrated passage. "The meaning of the expression used by Lord Hale that 'Christianity was parcel of the laws of England,' though often cited in subsequent cases, has, we think, been much misunderstood. It appears to us that the expression can only mean, either that as a great part of the securities of our legal system consist of judicial and official oaths, sworn upon the Gospels, Chris-

---

[6] Lilburne's Case, 4 Howell's State Trials, 1307.
[7] The English constitution produced and illustrated, Lond. 1823, pp. 388-398.
[8] Mence, The Law of Libel, p. 321; Edition of 1824.

tianity is closely interwoven with our municipal law; or that the laws of England, like all municipal laws of a Christian country, must upon principles of general jurisprudence, be subservient to the positive rules of Christianity."[9]

The next instance of a new modification was made by Lord Coleridge first in the case of R. v. Pooley, 1857. This was reaffirmed by him in the celebrated prosecution for blasphemy, against Charles Bradlaugh in 1882. There it is said:

"I am aware that a more severe and strict view of the law has been put forth by persons entitled to respect. That any attacks upon the fundamental principles of the Christian religion, and any discussion hostile to the inspiration or perfect purity of the Hebrew Scripture is, however, respectfully conducted, against the law of the land, and is a subject matter for prosecution. As at present advised, I do not assent to that view of the law. It is founded, as it seems to me, upon misunderstood expressions in the judgment of great judges of former times, who have said, no doubt, that inasmuch as Christianity is *in a sense* part of the law of the land, and as Christianity adopts and assumes the truth *in some sense or other,* of inspiration, and *in some sense or other* assumes the purity of the Hebrew Scriptures, anything which assails the truth of Christianity, or asperses the purity of the Hebrew Scriptures, however respectful, is a breach of the law. *I fail to see the consequences from the premises* because you may attack anything that is part of the law of the land, in respectful terms, without committing a crime or a misdemeanor, otherwise no alteration in any part of the law could ever be advocated by anybody. Monarchy is part of the law of the land; Primogeniture is part of the law of the land. and deliberate and respectful discussion upon the first principles of government, upon the principles of the law of inheritance, upon the principles which should govern the union of the sexes, on that principle so far as I can see, would be an indictable libel. *The consequences seem to*

---

[9] Moxon's Case, 2 Townsend's Modern Reports 390; A. D. 1840.

me so extreme and untenable as to show that the premises must be wrong.[10]

In 1863 there came on another branch of this case against the co-defendants Ramsey and Foote. There was discussed the rule that anything is a blasphemous libel simply and without more because they question the truth of Christianity. The court said: "I repeat, these dicta cannot be taken to be true in the sense in which it was true when these dicta were uttered, that Christianity is part of the law of the land. In the times when these dicta were uttered, Jews Roman Catholics, Non-conformists of all sorts were under heavy disabilities for religion and were regarded as merely having civil rights."[11] It might also have been mentioned tha' while the Church was still legally established, England had become in a large measure democratized. The King and the courts now held their authority from the people, and not from God either directly or through the priesthood.

Next in order comes a case in the House of Lords in 1917. Here the doctrine that Christianity is a part of the law of the land, or ever was properly so, is repudiated.[12] This will be referred to again after we have reviewed the parallel evolution in America.

JEFFERSON VS. HALE

It has now been shown that Lord Hale's statement that Christianity is parcel of the laws of England has been much discredited in recent English decisions. It remains to trace this same growth in America. Thus it is hoped to destroy the last vestige of reason which can be assigned in support of blasphemy laws.

Jefferson and some others went farther than the English courts in attacking Hale's doctrine. We will exhibit these attacks, made upon the original sources antecedent to

---

[10] R. v. Bradlaugh, 15 Cox Crim. C. 217-225. See also: Whorton, Criminal Law, v. 3, pp. 2116-2118.

[11] R. v. Ramsey & Foote, 1 Cababe and Ellis Reports (Nisi Prius), p. 126.

[12] Bowman v. Secular Society, Limited; Law Reports, Appeal Cases, Part IV, pp. 406-478.

Hale's decision. I will precede Jefferson's criticism by
that of an anonymous writer.

He says: "I have examined the Year Book cited. The
passage is to be found in the case of Humphrey Bohun
against John Broughton, Bishop of Lincoln, and others—
a suit for disturbance in refusing to induct Thomas Young,
presented by Bohun to the living of Holborne, in the county of Middlesex. The bishop pleads that on the same day
another claimant, to wit, John Brown, had presented *his*
clerk, Richard Ewenson; that the law of the Holy Church
in such case is that until the contest be decided by judgment on inquisition in a suit *de jure patronatus* (on the
right of presentation), the ordinary is not bound to admit,
and that it is the duty of the two contending patrons to
institute such a suit, and not the duty of the ordinary.
This not having been done within six months, it becomes
the duty of the ordinary to *present* that there may be no
vacancy. The sentence quoted is Prisot's opinion, in page
40b of the Year Book. The translation of the passage is
as follows: *'To such law as the Holy Church hath under
ancient record* (that is preserved in old books; the French
of holy scripture, is not ancient scripture, but *sainte*
ecriture), *it becometh us to give credence; for this is common law* (that is, this constitutes the common law of the
church) *upon which common law all other laws are founded; and so, sir, we are bound to acknowledge the law of
the holy church; and in like manner they are bound to
acknowledge our law. And, sir, if it appear to us that the
bishop has acted as an ordinary would have acted in like
case, we ought to acknowledge it as good, otherwise
not.'* "[13]

"I was glad to find in your book [so wrote Jefferson to
Major John Cartwright] a formal contradiction, at length,
of the judiciary usurpation of legislative powers; for such
the judges have usurped in their repeated decisions that
Christianity is a part of the common law. The proof of
the contrary, which you have adduced, is incontrovertible;
to wit, that the common law existed while the Anglo-Saxons
were yet Pagans, at a time when they had never yet heard

---

[13] Cooper's Law of Libel, pp. 175-176.

the name of Christ pronounced, or knew that such a character had existed. But it may amuse you to show when and by what means they stole this law upon us. In a case of *quare impedit*, in the Year Book, 34 Henry VI, folio 38 (1458), a question was made how far the ecclesiastical law was to be respected in a common law court? And Prisot, chief justice, (c. 5) gives his opinion in these words: '*A tiel leis qu'ils de seint eglise ont en ancien scripture, covient à nous a donner credence; car ceo common ley sur quels touts manners leis sont fondés. Et auxy, sir, nous sumus oblègés de conustre lour ley de saint eglise, et semblablement ils sont obligés de consustre nostre Ley. Et, sir, si poit apperer or à nous que l'evesque ad fait come un ordinary fera en tiel cas, adong nous devons ceo adjuger bon, ou auterment nemy,'* &c. See s. c., Fitzhugh's Abridgement qu. imp. 89; Brooke's Abridgement, qu. imp. 12. Finch, in his first book, c. 3. is the first, afterwards, who quotes this case, and misstates it thus: 'To such laws of the the church as have warrant in *holy scripture,* our law giveth credence;' and cites Prisot, mistranslating 'ancien scripture' into 'holy scripture'; whereas Prisot palpably says, 'to such laws as those of holy church have in *ancient writing,* it is proper for us to give credence;' to wit, to their ancient written laws. This was in 1613, a century and a half after the dictum of Prisot. Wingate, in 1658, erects this false translation into a maxim of the common law, copying the words of Finch, but citing Prisot. Wingate, max. 3, and Shepard, tit. 'religion,' in 1675, copies the same mistranslation, quoting the Year Book, Finch and Wingate. Hale expresses it in these words: 'Christianity is parcel of the laws of England,' 1 Ventris 293; 3 Kebble 607; but quotes no authority. By these echoings and re-echoings, from one to another, it had become so established in 1728, that in the case of the King v. Woolston, 2 Strange, 834, the court would not suffer it to be debated whether to write against Christianity was punishable in the temporal courts at common law. Wood, therefore, 409, ventures still to vary the phrase, and say 'that all blasphemy and profaneness are offenses by the common law,' and cites 2 Strange; then Blackstone, in 1763, IV. 59, repeats

the words of Hale, that 'Christianity is part of the common law of England,' citing Ventris and Strange; and
finally Lord Mansfield, with a little qualification, in
Evans' case, in 1767, says that 'the essential principles
of revealed religion are parts of the common law,' thus
engulphing Bible, testament and all into the common law,
without citing any authority. And thus we find this chain
of authorities hanging, link by link, one upon another, and
all ultimately upon one and the same hook, and that a
mistranslation of the words 'ancien scripture,' used by
Prisot. Finch quotes Prisot; Wingate does the same; Shep-
pard quotes Prisot, Finch, and Wingate; Hale cites nobody. The court, in Woolston's case, cites Hale. Wood
cites Woolston's case; Blackstone quotes Woolston's case
and Hale; and Lord Mansfield, like Hale, ventures it on
his own authority. Here I might defy the best read lawyer
to produce another scrip of authority for this *judiciary
forgery;* and I might go on further to show how some of
the Anglo-Saxon priests interpolated into the text of Al-
fred's laws, the 20th, 21st, 22d, and 23d chapters of Exodus,
and the 15th of the Acts of the Apostles, from the 23d to
the 29th verses. But this would lead my pen and your
patience too far. What a conspiracy this, between church
and state!! Sing tantararara, rogues all; rogues all;
sing tantararara, rogues all!"[14]

More potent as a binding authority than all of these is
the official declaration of the United States under the
treaty-making power.

This is shown by a "Treaty of Peace and Friendship,
between the United States of America and the Bey and
subjects of Tripoli of Barbary," communicated to the Senate May 26, 1797.[15]

"Article 2 [of this Treaty]: *As the government of the
United States of America is not in any sense founded on
the Christian Religion,* as it has in itself no character of en-
mity against the laws, religions, or tranquillity of Mussul-

---

[14] See Appendix to Cooper's Law Libel, p. 82; Jefferson's Works, v. 4,
pp. 397-398; Remsberg's Six Historic Americans, p. 83. In sending
a copy of the Cartwright letter to Cooper, some revisions were made.
[15] American State Papers, Class I, Foreign Relations, vol. 2, p. 18;
United States Statutes at Large, vol. 8, Foreign Treaties, p. 154.

mans; and as the said states never entered into any war, or act of hostility against any Mahometan nation, it is declared by the parties, that no pretext, arising from religious opinions, shall ever produce an interruption of the harmony existing between the two countries." Dr. Philip Schaff of Union Theological Seminary, N. Y., says that he learned "from Dr. Francis Wharton that the treaty was framed by an ex-Congregational clergyman"[16] and not by irreligious men.

Article 6 of the U. S. Constitution provides: "All treaties made, or which shall be made, under the authority of the United States, shall be the supreme law of the land; and the judges of every state shall be bound thereby, anything in the constitution or laws of any state to the contrary notwithstanding."

President Jefferson refused to issue a thanksgiving proclamation because he regarded "the government of the United States as interdicted by the Constitution from intermeddling with religious institutions. their doctrines, discipline or exercises."

In Ohio the Supreme Court had before it a question as to the validity of a deed executed and delivered on Sunday. The court accepted as good English law the rule that the Christian religion is part of the common law. After quoting the constitutional guarantee for religious liberty, the court said: "It follows that neither Christianity or any other system of religion is a part of the law of this state. We sometimes hear it said that all religions are tolerated in Ohio; but the expression is not strictly accurate; much less accurate is it to say that one religion is a part of our law and that all others are only tolerated. It is not by mere toleration that every individual is protected in his belief or disbelief. He reposes not upon the leniency of government or liberality of any class or sect of men, but upon his natural indefeasible rights of conscience."[17]

"Those who make this assertion [that Christianity is part of the law] can hardly be serious, and intend the real import of their language. If Christianity is a law of the

---

[16] Church and State in the United States, p. 41, note 2.
[17] Bloom v. Richards, 2 Ohio St. 390.

State like every other law, it must have a sanction. Adequate penalties must be provided to enforce obedience to all its requirements and precepts. No one seriously contends for any such doctrine in this country, or, I might almost say, in this age of the world. The only foundation—rather, the only excuse—for the proposition that Christianity is part of the law of this country is the fact that it is a Christian country, and that its constitutions and laws are made by a Christian people."[18]

It is interesting to note that a recent decision of the House of Lords goes very far in this same direction, but under very great difficulty. In the face of the admission that a mere denial of any part of Christianity has been very often declared to be blasphemy, it is now held that this was not a correct conception of the law "at any time." Likewise the oft repeated formula that Christianity is part of the law has been deprived of about all practical meaning. Those interested in this latest English development will wish to read a keen review of the situation by Dean R. W. Lee, entitled "The Law of Blasphemy."[19] *After* reading that very penetrating analysis one should read the decision of the House of Lords, which provoked it.[20] Our American courts can easily avoid a similar embarrassment. To this end we need only to rely upon the common sense meaning and the historical interpretation of our constitutional guarantees of religious and intellectual liberty Thus we must come more directly and more conclusively to the result that Christianity can bear no legal relationship to our laws and that therefore no prosecution can be here maintained to punish blasphemy in any of its aspects.

---

[18] Board of Education v. Minor 23 Ohio St. 211; 13 Amer. Rep. 233. State v. Bott, 31 La. Ann. 663; 33 Amer. Rep. 224.

[19] *Michigan Law Review*, v. 16, pp. 149-157, Jan. 1918.

[20] Bowman v. Secular Society, Ltd., Law Reports, Appeal Cases, Part IV, pp. 406-478. 1917.

STATE OF ILLINOIS.

COUNTY COURT FOR LAKE COUNTY.

PEOPLE OF ILLINOIS
vs.
MICHAEL X. MOCKUS.

(The defendant was arrested on a charge of blasphemy, alleged to have been committed early in 1917, at Waukegan, Ill. The information charged that in a public lecture the defendant had defamed Jesus, his Mother and the Bible. The defendant, by his attorney, made a motion to quash the information upon the ground that various American constitutional guarantees had annulled the common-law crime of blasphemy. Judge Perry L. Persons sustained the motion in a written opinion filed March 3, 1917. The following is Judge Persons opinion from Waukegan *Daily Gazette,* March 3, 1917.)

(Not satisfied with this termination of the case the prosecuting attorney secured an indictment on the same facts. The same motion was made before Judge Edwards presiding in the Circuit Court for Lake County. Judge Claire C. Edwards again sustained the motion. He filed no written opinion. In both cases the argument covered a much wider scope than that presented in Judge Persons' opinion.—THEODORE SCHROEDER.)

"This motion, while admitting for the purpose of the argument the allegations stated in the information, questions the sufficiency in law of the information in this case as now amended, by which the Defendant Mockus, is charged with the offense of blasphemy, so called. It is

451

conceded that no legislative inhibition against blasphemy exists in this state; that this information is based on the common-law of England in force in so far as not abrogated by constitutional limitation or statute; that in this state no governmental or state religion exists as such; that the separation of church and state is absolute; and that this case both in the charge made and as to the facts alleged, is without a precedent in our Appellate Courts and Supreme Court.

"The court has carefully considered the exhaustive argument of the defense and the able reply of the assistant state's attorney, and the very nature of the offense charged involves the consideration by a court of the question of religion in its relation, if any, to the commonwealth, and I have been aided in arriving at my conclusion as to the merits of this motion by certain expressions of our Supreme Court in its opinion, in the case of the People vs. Board of Education, 245 Illinois; the court says on page 340, concerning the religious freedom enjoyed by all citizens of the commonwealth: 'The free enjoyment of religious worship includes freedom not to worship.' And again on page 341, reference is made to an act at one time pending in the Virginia legislature. In the very nature of things religion or the duty we owe the Creator is not within the cognizance of civil magistrate 'To intrude his powers into the field of opinion and to restrain the profession or propagation of principles on the supposition of their ill tendency is a dangerous fallacy which at once destroys all religious liberty.' And again: 'it is time enough for the rightful purpose of civil government for its officers to interfere when principals break out into overt acts against peace and good order.'

" 'In these two sentences,' says the Supreme Court of the United States, 'is found the true distinction between what properly belongs to the church and what to the state.' Again on page 349, the same opinion of our Supreme Court continues: 'It is true that this is a Christian state; the great majority of its people adhere to the Christian religion * * * But the law knows no distinction between the

Pagan, the Protestant and the Catholic. All are citizens. Their civil rights are precisely equal. The law cannot see the religious differences because the constitution has definitely and completely excluded religion from the law's contemplation in considering men's rights. In considering men's rights there can be no distinction based on religion. * * * All sects, religious or even anti-religious, stand on an equal footing;' again on page 346 the court says: 'the importance of men's religious opinion and differences is for their own and not for a court's determination; with such differences whether important or unimportant the courts or governments have no right to interfere. It is not a question to be determined by a court * * * what religion or what sect is right. That is not a judicial question. All stand equal before the law, the Protestant, Catholic, Mormon, Mohammedan, the Jew, the Free Thinker, the Atheist. Whatever may be the view of the majority of the people the court has no right and the majority has no right to force that view upon the minority, however small.' If our Supreme Court is correct, would not the Jew, lawfully, honestly and freely expressing his opinion that Christ was an Imposter, in the language of this opinion subject him to the same charge of blasphemy now against this defendant? The exact offense with which the defendant is charged in this case is that he spoke certain blasphemous words, which I do not care to repeat, maligning Jesus Christ, and notwithstanding his conduct in so doing, reprehensible as it may seem to many of us in the use of the scurrilous language attributed to him, under the law, in our judgment, the defendant cannot be held for trial on the charge of blasphemy standing alone, unaccompanied by acts of violence or other breach of the peace. From my earliest recollection, my environment has been such that I cannot refrain from saying that I regret that this is true, but the common law offense of blasphemy under the law in this state is not an offense subject to punishment or prosecution, and the judgment of the court is that the motion to quash is sustained, the defendant discharged, and the sureties on his bond released."

MOCKUS ONCE MORE.

From: *The Truth Seeker,* Oct. 12, 1918.

There seems no immediate danger that the Mockus case
will become ancient history, and yet it is dragging along
over so much time that it becomes almost necessary to
recapitulate past events to make the new ones intelligible.

Mockus was convicted of blasphemy in the police court
of Waterbury, Conn., in the summer of 1916. An appeal
was taken to the District Court. At the first trial the jury
disagreed. At that time it was offered that if the defend-
an would enter a plea of guilty he might go at liberty on
a suspended sentence. He declined this offer wishing to
try out the question of his right to continue his Free-
thought lectures unmolested. At the next trial Theodore
Schroeder appeared as associate counsel, for the defence
and as representing the Free Speech League and the Freethinkers of America. Constitutional questions were presented during the whole day's session of court. Then the
case was continued that the lengthy argument might be
submitted in writing. Numerous continuances followed.
In the meantime Mr. Schroeder has been writing a 450-
page book on the constitutional rights of Freethinkers to
speak their minds.

In the course of time, the Hon. F. M. Peasley succeeded
Judge Reeves, who had heard the constitutional argument. Judge Peasley overruled the demurrer by which
the constitutional questions were raised. He overruled
Mr. Schroeder's argument, frankly admitting that he had
not read it, and explicitly stating that he would not read
it, although he considered the case of great importance,
and in spite of the fact that he was sure the argument
would be interesting. To many this will seem a rather
extraordinary position for a judge to assume.

During the excitement created by Mr. Schroeder's long
constitutional argument, made back in 1916, the defendant seems to have been quite forgotten, and so he was
allowed to leave without being required to give a new

454

bail-bond for his subsequent appearance in court. Notwithstanding this, he was anxious to have a test case made and was so far willing to take chances on the results. For about two years, while going about his lecture work, he has at regular intervals reported his whereabouts to his attorneys, so that he could be notified if wanted for the trial. In this manner he was last heard from in the early part of this summer (1918).

His case was to be called for trial Sept. 24, but the defendant did not appear. His attorneys reported that letters sent to his last known address had been returned undelivered. Whether he is sick, dead or over in France is not known. The prosecutor agreed to an extension of time for Mockus to report.

What will happen next? Mr. Mockus may in due time report to his attorneys and have a new date fixed for his surrender and trial. If not then a requisition may be issued and the defendant if found in another state may be arrested and with the approval of the governor may be returned to Connecticut. Here an interesting fight may occur. First to induce the governor not to give the defendant up to the Connecticut authorities. This might be based upon constitutional grounds and the seeming difficulty of getting a fair trial before Judge Peasley.

Again: The argument before Judge Peasley raised several questions of law under the constitution of the United States. This may furnish ground for going into the Federal Court and making a test case there on these Federal questions. In this event an appeal will lie to the U. S. Supreme Court. After that, if all fails, Mockus can be brought back to Connecticut for trial, leaving only the state constitution and statutes to be interpreted. Evidently if Mockus is alive and allows his attorneys to go through all these devious pathways, then the gaiety of the nation will be occasionally refreshed for some years to come. If Mockus is alive it is hoped he will inform his attorneys, if any effort is made to compel his return to Connecticut.

In the meantime Mr. Schroeder is going steadily on with his preparation. Four hundred and fifty pages of the argument is in type and a contract for printing this first volume has just been signed. The second volume will deal more especially with questions arising under the Federal constitution. The numerous installments of the argument in THE TRUTH SEEKER and other journals, and conversations had with Mr. Schroeder, gives reason to believe that this discussion of blasphemy laws will be without precedent both as to its length and its extraordinary character and contents.